THE WORLD BANK
INSPECTION
PANEL

THE WORLD BANK
INSPECTION
PANEL: *In Practice*

IBRAHIM F. I. SHIHATA

SECOND EDITION

Oxford University Press

Oxford New York
Athens Auckland Bangkok Bogata Buenos Aires Calcutta
Capetown Chennai Dar es Salaam Delhi Florence Hong Kong Istanbul
Karachi Kuala Lumpur Madrid Melbourne Mexico City Mumbai
Nairobi Paris Sao Paulo Singapore Taipei Tokyo Toronto Warsaw

and associated companies in

Berlin Ibadan

Copyright © 2000 The International Bank for Reconstruction and Development/
THE WORLD BANK
1818 H Street, N.W.
Washington, DC 20433, U.S.A.

Published by Oxford University Press, Inc.
198 Madison Avenue, New York, New York, 10016

Manufactured in the United States of America
First printing January 2000

The findings, interpretations, and conclusions expressed in this study are entirely those
of the author and should not be attributed in any manner to the World Bank, to its affiliated organizations, or to members of its Board of Executive Directors or the countries
they represent. The boundaries, colors, and other information shown on any map in this
volume do not imply on the part of the World Bank any judgement on the legal status
of any territory or the endorsement or acceptance of such boundaries.

Library of Congress Cataloging-in-Publication Data has been applied for.

Contents

Foreword to the Second Edition

Ibrahim Shihata is uniquely qualified to write on matters pertaining to the World Bank Inspection Panel. He was deeply involved in the discussions that led to the creation of the Panel and was responsible for writing the first draft of the Resolution establishing it. He also published the first book ever written on the Panel (the first edition of this book) and has since been involved in all discussions by the Bank's Management and Board of issues relating to the Inspection Panel. When practice departed from the text of the Resolution, he was the first one to call attention to that phenomenon and to propose solutions.

In this second edition of his book, Shihata adds many clarifications in light of the Panel's actual experience, summarizes all the requests submitted to the Panel, explains how they were dealt with by the Panel, Management, and Board, assesses that record, and describes in detail the two review processes of the Panel's experience that took place in the Bank's Board in 1996 and 1998/99, respectively. He also elaborates on the relevant issues of accountability and liability.

Equally important, this second edition lists in its annexes all major documents related to the Panel's work as well as the Bank's updated statements on policies and procedures most relevant to that work.

As the first edition of this book proved to be the main source of information on the Resolution Establishing the Inspection Panel, this edition, I believe, provides the information, analysis, and documents required to gain a full appreciation of the Panel's role and experience.

May I add that I am most grateful to Ibrahim Shihata for completing this work so comprehensively, effectively, and so promptly. He has played a unique role in the World Bank, and we are privileged to have his scholarly works to record the history and background to our contribution to the global development process.

James D. Wolfensohn
President
The World Bank Group

Foreword to the First Edition

Fifty years of development experience indicate that the vast majority of World Bank operations meet the Bank's own high standards and objectives: to promote sustainable development and reduce poverty.

However, any group of individuals directly and adversely affected by a Bank-supported project can now ask an independent Inspection Panel to investigate complaints that the Bank has failed to abide by its policies and procedures. Thus, the Panel provides a safety net in the exceptional cases where the Bank's own high standards might not be met. In that sense, the Panel is a positive step toward strengthening the links between the Bank and the people affected by the operations it finances.

The Bank was the first among multilateral, global organizations to establish such an Inspection Panel. This book analyzes its origins, functions, and objectives. Since Ibrahim Shihata was one of the Panel's main architects, the book offers a uniquely insightful perspective.

As the world is changing rapidly, international institutions also must change. Efficiency, results-orientation, and participation have become more important in today's world than ever before. The Inspection Panel is part of the Bank's evolving policy of improving its effectiveness, strengthening accountability, and increasing openness—all of which augment the Bank's capacity to fulfill its goal of helping to improve people's living standards throughout the world.

Lewis T. Preston
President
The World Bank Group

Introduction to the
Second Edition

This is a revised and much expanded version of my book, *The World Bank Inspection Panel* (1994), the first study published on this important mechanism and its possible effects on the operations of the World Bank,[1] which also included the texts of all the then relevant documents. Providing information and documents not otherwise available at the time of its publication, the first edition of this book has served as a major reference book on the Panel, and it has been used both in the Bank's deliberations and in various academic circles.

The first edition was written shortly after the Resolution establishing the Panel (referred to throughout this book as "the Resolution") was adopted by the Bank's Executive Directors in September 1993.[2] It recorded as accurately as possible the developments that led to the establishment of the Panel and the deliberations of the Bank's Board that concluded with the adoption of the Resolution. So detailed were the Executive Directors' discussions reflected in the book that approval of its publication was sought and received beforehand from the Board.[3]

---

1. As used in this book, the term "World Bank" or "Bank" means both the International Bank for Reconstruction and Development (IBRD) and the International Development Association (IDA), unless it is clear from the context that only the first of these institutions is meant. Otherwise, each institution will be identified by its acronym.

2. The terms "Executive Directors," the "Board of Executive Directors," and the "Board" are interchangeably used in this book to refer to the Board of Executive Directors of the Bank, which consists of twenty-four members representing all member countries. Of these, five are appointed individually by the largest five shareholders, and the rest are elected by the Board of Governors through constituencies of Governors. At present, three such constituencies consist each of one country only (China, Russian Federation, and Saudi Arabia).

3. Under the Board's Rules of Procedures, Board proceedings are confidential, unless the Board decides otherwise.

The book was first written as an analytical study for the benefit of the Bank's Board. Executive Directors serve only for a two-year period, unless re-appointed or re-elected. As time passes, personal recollections of the intended meaning and the underlying purposes of past Board decisions may fade away. The book served as a ready source of information on the Resolution and was often quoted by Executive Directors in subsequent discussions. It has also been used by Panel members as an introduction to their work and the detailed requirements for the exercise of their mandate. Bank operational managers who have seen their earlier activities subject to several complaints submitted to the Panel since early 1995 may have found in the book a ready description of the mechanism they came to deal with on a regular basis. However, while the first edition had the advantage of analyzing the Resolution and recording how its provisions were formulated and for what purpose, it had the shortcoming of not reflecting and commenting on the Panel's experience (which simply was not there at the time). This second edition makes up for this and explains at length how the Resolution has been applied (or not applied) in practice. It also elaborates on questions that were previously mere hypotheses (such as the possibility of legal action against the Bank for violation of its policies). In addition, it includes a new set of annexes providing Bank documents related to the Panel and updating the Bank's Operational Policies as reformulated in recent years.

In my introduction to the first edition of this book, I described the provisions of the Resolution as "living phenomena, the meaning of which will no doubt be further influenced by the manner in which they will be applied in practice." This observation, applicable generally to any legislative text, proved to be particularly relevant to the constituent instrument of the Inspection Panel. Due to a variety of factors described in this new edition, the Panel's practice actually departed from the original Resolution in important ways, mainly because of choices agreed upon by the Executive Directors in specific cases or what seemed to the Panel to be the choices of Executive Directors. There are also indications that the Panel may have invited or inspired some of these choices. The "additional review" asked for by the Board whenever it was unable to reach a decision authorizing inspection may not be that different from the "preliminary review" that the Panel had introduced from the beginning (in August 1994) in its Operating Procedures when, "after receiving management response, the Panel is satisfied that Management has failed to demonstrate that it has followed or is taking adequate steps to follow the Bank's policies and procedures."[4] Both amount to some form of an early investigation not envisaged under the Resolution, as this book explains. The Bank staff, with their usual zeal, also hurried to produce "remedial action plans" agreed with, and to be executed by, the borrower within the short period in which, under the Resolution, they are required only to prepare Management's response to the request. This latter, unintentionally "pre-emptive," act clearly differed from the reports expected from Management at that stage, according to the Resolution. However, it was found by many Board members to provide a convenient alternative to the investigation process. Such remedial plans did not cover corrective measures for failure in the Bank's actions and omissions, which are the subject of inspection under the Resolution. The matter reached the point where the Panel felt that the Board, through its practice, had practically modified the Resolution, and that the Panel's focus should be on the harm suffered or to be suffered by affected parties, rather than on the Bank's compliance or non-compliance with its policies and the causal relationship, if any, between the Bank's actions or omissions and the alleged harm.

A second review of the Panel's experience was thus needed. It addressed these issues candidly and resulted in a Board approach that realized the advantages of returning to the Resolution's requirements. This edition provides, *inter alia*, the first detailed description and analysis of the Board reviews of the Panel's experience.

---

4. The *Inspection Panel Operating Procedures*, para. 34 (August 19, 1994), reproduced as Annex I-1-2 to this book.

Both in its first edition and in this expanded version, the only purpose has been to state the facts as this author has witnessed them and to provide analysis and express views based on these facts. Other commentators on the Panel's work (especially those observing it from outside the Bank) may have different perceptions of the facts, and they certainly have expressed different views reflecting their own convictions and special concerns. These other views, to the extent they are known to this author, have also been mentioned in this book whenever they seemed to be relevant.

Each chapter of this book is written in a manner meant to reduce the need for reading the book as a whole in order to fully comprehend a particular chapter. Cross references are provided, however, to help the reader identify in more detail the relevant parts in other chapters. Some intended repetition has resulted from this approach.

Acknowledgments

I am most grateful to James D. Wolfensohn, President of the World Bank Group, for writing the foreword to this book. Mr. Wolfensohn has been a great supporter of the Panel's mission and has taken a keen interest in its work.

I am also grateful to the members of the Inspection Panel for the excellent relationship they have maintained with me through the years, which contributed to my understanding of their work and the difficult choices they face at times.

I am very thankful to Sabine Schlemmer-Schulte for her extensive assistance in the preparation of this second edition, especially Chapter Three and the section on lender's liability in Chapter Five. Anna Chytla has provided valuable research on the section on privileges and immunities in Chapter Five and, with Daoud Khairallah and David Rivero, reviewed that section. Bank lawyers, David Mead (East Asia), Elizabeth Adu and Mpoy Kamulayi (Africa), Ferenc Molnar and Alberto Ninio (Latin America), who worked on Panel cases, respectively, reviewed the cases in Chapter Three for accuracy. W. Paatii Ofosu-Amaah and Rudy van Puymbroeck read and commented on the entire Chapter which was then also reviewed by Eduardo Abbott, the Panel's Executive Secretary.

Michelle Lemaire patiently typed and proofread the whole manuscript, and Don Reisman and Nicola Marrian arranged for its publication.

Needless to say, all the above share in any credit, and the author alone is responsible for the shortcomings.

Ibrahim F. I. Shihata
Washington, D.C.
June 1999

The views expressed in this book are those of the author and should not be attributed to any other source unless otherwise indicated in the book.

Introduction to the First Edition

"Almost all nations observe almost all principles of international law and almost all of their obligations almost all of the time."[1] A stronger statement may be safely made about the observance by international organizations, especially international financial institutions, of their rules and procedures. However, no standing mechanisms independent from the governing organs of such organizations have hitherto existed to hear and investigate complaints by private entities and groups affected by their activities regarding deviation from their established policies and procedures—not, that is, until the World Bank[2] established its independent Inspection Panel in late 1993.[3] The importance of this step is not only due to the fact that it opened for the first time a venue through which such alleged deviation may become subject to independent inspection at the request of private entities and groups, thus giving them the opportunity to invoke the Bank's system of accountability.[4] It is also due to the probability that it has set in motion a process whereby similar fora would be established in other international organizations in response to the

---

1. Louis Henkin, *How Nations Behave—Law and Foreign Policy* 47 (1979).

2. The terms *World Bank* and *Bank* are used in this book to cover both the International Bank for Reconstruction and Development (IBRD) and the International Development Association (IDA), unless the context indicates that reference is to the first institution only.

3. *See Resolution of the Executive Directors establishing the Inspection Panel* (No. 93-10 for the IBRD and 93-6 for IDA), approved on September 22, 1993, and circulated as document No. SecM93-988 (IBRD) and SecM93-313 (IDA), September 23, 1993 (hereinafter *Resolution*) (Annex I-1-1 to this book). The first three members of the Panel were appointed by the Executive Directors on April 15, 1994.

4. *Compare* Daniel D. Bradlow, The World Bank Votes to Establish an Inspection Panel, 6 *Third World Debt in the 1990s* 2, 3 (Brussels, November 1993). For further details on the effect of the Inspection Panel on the Bank's accountability, *see* Chapter Five, *infra*, at 237 *seq.*

drive towards greater transparency and accountability in the work of multilateral institutions.

Whether confined to the World Bank or emulated in other international organizations, the creation of an independent inspection panel to investigate the extent to which an international organization complies with its rules will have a bearing on more general issues of international law and policy. These pertain in particular to the access by private persons or entities to international remedies against the actions or omissions of international organizations, especially when these otherwise enjoy general or special immunity from legal action. Such access is not only relevant to the rights of these private persons or entities but also to the interests they represent, including environmental and other interests where international organizations have or may be given a mandate. From a broader perspective, such issues could potentially influence the evolution of the international law of human rights, especially the international procedural safeguards necessary for the protection of such rights.

The World Bank's Inspection Panel initiative is the subject of this first-hand account of the developments which led to the establishment of this Panel, the principles expected to govern its work, and the details that will define its activities. While no evaluation can be made at this stage of the work of the Panel, as it is yet to be initiated, the analysis will highlight the relevance and importance of the Panel, both in itself and as a precedent on the international scene.[5] Some thoughts will also be offered in the concluding chapter with respect to the expected costs and benefits of this initiative to the Bank and its members, which will no doubt be influenced by the degree of success or failure the Panel will have in meeting the expectations and anxieties it has generated both within and outside the institution.

The purpose of this study is simply to ensure a better understanding of the inspection function as envisaged in the Resolution establishing the Panel. It will attempt to serve this

---

5. On August 19, 1994, the Inspection Panel adopted a set of *Operating Procedures.* These procedures are reprinted in Annex I-1-2 to this book.

purpose by shedding light in the first chapter on the circumstances that led to the establishment of the Panel and the factors that influenced its final shape. By placing the provisions of the Resolution establishing the Panel in their historical context and recalling in the second chapter the discussions that preceded their adoption, and that explain their particular features, the reader will be able to develop an understanding of these provisions as living phenomena, the meaning of which will no doubt be further influenced by the manner in which they will be applied in practice. Such understanding is perhaps the best safeguard against possibilities of abuse, under-utilization, or excessive use of the inspection function.

1

Evolution of an Independent Inspection Function in World Bank Operations

I. Motives for the Establishment of an Inspection Function

The creation of an operations inspection function in the World Bank came as a response to a new Bank Management's concerns with the efficiency of the Bank's work. These concerns coincided with, and were influenced by the emphasis by sources inside and outside the Bank on what they perceived as the Bank's inadequate attention to the standards reflected in its rules.[1] The Bank President's proposal to establish this function thus mentioned explicitly two distinct but interwoven concerns. The first was the President's concern—which turned out to be widely shared by Executive Directors, government officials, Bank staff, and some external parties—that the Management of the Bank's portfolio of loans required improvement. The second concern—prevalent among external parties, and reflected in the views of some Executive Directors—was that the Bank was perceived to be less

---

1. For a different account of the history of the establishment of the World Bank Inspection Panel, *see* Lori Udall, *The World Bank Inspection Panel: A Three Year Review*, Chapter One (October 1997, edited and published by the "Bank Information Center," a private non-governmental organization [NGO]). According to that account, the establishment of the Panel resulted from pressure by NGOs, especially Washington-based ones, and through them, from threats by an influential member of the U.S. House of Representatives to block the U.S. contribution to the 10th replenishment of IDA resources if the Panel was not established.

accountable for its performance and less transparent in its decision-making than it should be.[2]

A.   Internal Factors: The New Management's Concern with Performance

It is significant that the initial concern was a managerial one. Upon taking office in September 1991, Lewis T. Preston, the then new President of the World Bank, made it clear that he wanted to review the overall efficiency of the Bank's operations. Mr. Preston was aware, through his long experience in international finance and the extensive consultations he undertook before and immediately after taking charge, that the Bank's performance had been questioned in spite of its generally recognized high standards. A Task Force headed by an experienced senior manager, Willi A. Wapenhans,[3] was convened in February 1992 to examine the quality of the Bank's loan portfolio. One of the findings of the Task Force's report (known in the Bank as the "Wapenhans Report"), submitted to the Bank's Board of Executive Directors in November 1992,[4] was that the Bank staff

---

2. Memorandum from the President, *Operations Inspection Function: Objectives, Mandate and Operating Procedures for an Independent Inspection Panel* (R93-122/2, para. 2), September 10, 1993 (limited circulation).

3. At the time Mr. Wapenhans started this assignment, he was Senior Adviser to the President after having been reassigned from his office as Vice President for Europe and Central Asia. Prior to that, Mr. Wapenhans was Senior Vice President, External Relations, Personnel and Administration. In the seventies and eighties, he was Vice President, East Africa, and Vice President, Middle East and North Africa.

4. The findings of the Wapenhans Report were submitted to the Executive Directors as *Effective Implementation: Key to Development Impact* (R92–125), November 3, 1992. They are summarized in *Getting Results: The World Bank's Agenda for Improving Development Effectiveness,* 1–7 (July 1993). In this book, the terms *Board* and *Executive Directors* are used interchangeably to refer to the Bank's Board of Executive Directors which is responsible for the conduct of the general operations of the Bank and is delegated by the Bank's Board of Governors to exercise the latter's powers except those reserved in the Bank's Articles of Agreement to the Board of Governors. *See* the Articles of Agreement of IBRD (Article V, Section 2(b) and 4) and the Articles of Agreement of IDA (Article VI, Sections 2(c) and 4).

were often concerned about getting as many projects as possible approved under the Bank's lending program. In such an "approval culture," less attention had been given to the commitment of borrowers and their implementing agencies, or to the degree of "ownership" assumed by borrowers of the projects financed by the Bank and the policies underlying them. At the project level, the leading design problem identified was that projects had become too complex. The Task Force concluded, *inter alia*, that the Bank should improve the performance of its portfolio through changes in its own policies and practices.

An action plan to respond fully to the recommendations of the Task Force was submitted to the Bank's Board on July 22, 1993.[5] It outlined the specific measures to be undertaken within the areas of concern mentioned in the "Wapenhans Report." A number of staff working parties and special studies were consequently launched to address some of the Task Force's recommendations, and Management was asked to present a progress report to the Board by June 1994.

The plan, which built on "best practices" already in use in the Bank, introduced more efficient and client-oriented business practices and processes. The plan further insisted on the need to address effectively issues that had come to the forefront of the development debate in recent years. These issues included participation in the design and implementation of a project by the people to be affected by it, project "ownership" (in the sense of the borrower's commitment to the project's objectives, conviction of its priority, responsibility for its preparation, and attention to its execution), the involvement of relevant non-governmental organizations in the Bank's work, and better ways of monitoring the performance of the Bank and its operations. In this respect, the plan referred to a review to be "commissioned to take account of experience with inspection functions in selected member countries,"[6] which would consider whether a new inspection function was needed to augment the Bank's existing supervision, audit,

---

5. *Portfolio Management: Next Steps, A Program of Action*, July 22, 1993.
6. *Id.*, para. 60.

and evaluation functions. Knowing that the preparatory work for the launching of such a function was in an advanced stage, the plan's authors highlighted the Bank's need for access, when necessary, "to a reliable source of independent judgment about specific operations that may be facing severe implementation problems" and concluded that "the interests of the Bank would be best served by the establishment of an independent Inspection Panel."[7]

B.   *External Factors: Mounting Demands*

The second major force driving the establishment of the Inspection Panel was a new concern with the transparency of World Bank operations and the Bank's accountability for its role regarding them. This concern was prompted by mounting criticism from non-governmental organizations[8] and echoed by influential circles in certain member countries with large subscriptions in the Bank's capital and large subscriptions/contributions to the Bank's affiliate, the International Development Association (IDA). This external criticism had been driven by a broader concern that international organizations were not adequately accountable for their activities and by the perception that the Bank, as an important instrument of public policy in areas of international concern, needed to be more open and responsive. The criticism escalated in 1993, in the course of the finalization by donor countries of the Tenth Replenishment of the resources of the IDA. At a time when some U.N. member states threatened to withhold part of their assessed contributions to the United Nations until that organization set up an independent Inspector General's office,[9] the inspection function became one of the key

---

7. *Id.*

8. *See* Ibrahim F.I. Shihata, The World Bank and Non-Governmental Organizations, 25 *Cornell International Law Journal* 623 (1992), also reproduced and updated in Ibrahim F.I. Shihata, *The World Bank in a Changing World, Volume Two* (1995), Chapter Six.

9. *See* the U.S. proposal for an Office of Inspector General, submitted to the 48th session of the U.N. General Assembly on November 24, 1993; U.N.

tests of the Bank's public credibility. Another related and equally sensitive issue, in terms of the institution's public image, was the Bank's policy of information disclosure, which will be discussed below.[10]

II.   The Narmada Lesson

The most important case to draw public attention to the account-ability issue involved two major projects supported by the World Bank on the Narmada River in India: the *Narmada River Development (Gujarat) Sardar Sarovar Dam and Power Project, and the Narmada River Development (Gujarat) Water Delivery and Drainage Project*. Agreements with the World Bank to par-tially finance both projects were signed in 1985 and became effective on January 6, 1986.[11] Although the IDA credit for the canal project was fully disbursed and closed on July 1, 1992, the International Bank for Reconstruction and Development (IBRD) loan and the IDA credit for the dam project were still under dis-bursement when issues related to the project's implementation attracted world-wide attention.

Under construction since 1987, the projects include a large concrete dam, a 1,200–megawatt powerhouse, transmission lines, a water conveyance system that includes the Narmada main canal (460 kilometers) to the Rajasthan border, branch and distributo-ry canals, and a drainage network to serve an irrigation area of about 2 million hectares in Gujarat. In addition to causing major environmental impacts, the dam project was originally expected to require the resettlement of 70,000 persons (an estimate that subsequently had to be increased to 120,000) from a submersion

---

Document A/C.5/48/35 (1993). On the role of the inspectorate proposal in the U.S. congressional debate over U.N. appropriations for fiscal year 1994 (H.R. 2519, October 14, 1993), *see* Dick Thornburgh, Today's United Nations in a Changing World, 9 *American University Journal of International Law and Policy* 215, 220 n. 17 and 222 (1993).

10. *See infra,* Section V of this chapter.

11. Development Credit Agreement No. 1553–IN, and Loan Agreement No. 2497–IN.

area of approximately 370 square kilometers. Resettlement of a similar magnitude was later anticipated as a result of the canal project, but this had not been foreseen at the time of project appraisal. World Bank funding represented only about 10 percent of overall costs, and the undisbursed balance of the IBRD loan was eventually cancelled at the request of the Indian government.[12]

From the beginning of project implementation, local and international non-governmental organizations had criticized both the environmental assessment and the resettlement and rehabilitation component of the Narmada projects. As the criticism intensified, Barber Conable, the then President of the World Bank, decided in March 1991, at the request of some Executive Directors, to commission an independent review chaired by Bradford Morse, retired Administrator of the United Nations Development Programme and former U.S. Congressman. The objective of the review was "to conduct an assessment of the implementation of the ongoing Sardar Sarovar projects as regards (a) the resettlement and rehabilitation of the population displaced/affected . . . and (b) the amelioration of the environmental impact of all aspects of the project," with reference to "existing Bank operational directives and guidelines."[13] According to the agreement with Mr. Morse, the review was not to be presented or perceived as a commission of inquiry, and the processes of consultation with various interested groups were not to have any mediation or adjudication function.

The independent review team visited the project sites and focussed on the resettlement and rehabilitation of the affected population, as well as on the amelioration of environmental impacts, taking into account the views of those directly affected

---

12. *Compare* Udall, *supra* note 1, at 11, where she erroneously states that the Bank cancelled the undisbursed portion of the loan.

13. Terms of Reference dated March 14, 1991 issued by the President of the World Bank following his appointment of Mr. Morse to address this issue on August 30, 1991. It may be noted that the *establishment* of the "Morse Commission" was not formally discussed by the Bank's Board, even though some Executive Directors took an active role in this matter.

by the project, local NGOs, and concerned governments and institutions. The final Morse Report was delivered to the Bank, and discussed by its Board, in June 1992.[14] Among its findings, the report noted "a failure to incorporate Bank policies into the 1985 credit and loan agreements and subsequent failure to require adherence to enforceable provisions of these agreements;" and its recommendations included "a review of Bank procedures to ensure that the full reach of the Bank's policies is implemented."[15] The first remark was not quite accurate. Both the credit agreement and the project agreement for the dam project included extensive provisions and important technical details for environmental and resettlement measures. Moreover, the Bank's staff disagreed with some of the other findings in the report. A Management Response issued on June 23, 1992, however, acknowledged several flaws and proposed, among remedial actions, that a review of resettlement performance be undertaken throughout the Bank's portfolio, together with strengthening Bank staffing, skills mix, and review procedures.[16] Neither the Morse Commission nor the Washington-based NGOs that took great interest in the matter were satisfied with the Bank's proposals. The latter publicly threatened that "NGOs and other activists would put their weight behind a campaign to cut off funding to the Bank."[17]

---

14. The report was published by its authors, (without the prior Bank permission required in the agreement with Mr. Morse), as Bradford Morse & Thomas R. Berger, *Sardar Sarovar: The Report of the Independent Review* (Ottawa: Resource Futures International 1992) (hereinafter Morse Report); *see also* Thomas R. Berger, The World Bank's Independent Review of India's Sardar Sarovar Projects, 9 *American University Journal of International Law and Policy* 33 (1993). Mr. Berger, a Canadian human rights lawyer, co-chaired the Morse Commission and was active in writing its report.

15. Morse Report, *supra* note 14, at 353–54; but *see also* T.R. Berger, *supra* note 14, at 28–32.

16. *India: The Sardar Sarovar (Narmada) Projects: Management Response* (SecM92–849), June 23, 1992. The Bank-wide resettlement review, initiated in 1993, was completed in April 1994; *see The Bankwide Review of Involuntary Resettlement 1968–1993*, Report prepared by the Task Force for the Bankwide Resettlement Review, Environment Department (April 1994).

17. *Financial Times*, 21 September 1992, at 6. A similar ad was placed in the New York Times and the Washington Post newspapers.

After a further Board discussion of follow-up steps in October 1992, an internal review was undertaken of the "Bank-wide lessons" from the experience of the Narmada projects.[18] Submitted to the Executive Directors in May 1993, it reiterated some of the main findings and criticism of the Morse Report on the implementation aspects of both the resettlement and rehabilitation and the environment action plan.

Although the *Narmada* case thus undoubtedly fueled the debate on the World Bank's accountability and on potential new remedies, none of the recommendations and proposals made in its context mentioned the creation of a standing inspection body. Attention at this stage was limited to existing internal mechanisms to monitor and control the quality of the Bank's operations, which included, as shown in the *Narmada* case itself, the possibility of establishing an *ad hoc* independent commission for this purpose.

III. Preexisting Control Mechanisms

Under its Articles of Agreement, the Bank is required to make arrangements to "ensure that the proceeds of any loan are used only for the purposes for which the loan was granted."[19] As a development institution, the Bank is also expected to exert its best efforts to ensure that projects achieve their development objectives and, in particular, to work with the borrowers in identifying and dealing with problems that arise during implementation. Hardly a project can be completed without facing implementation problems. Some of these problems cannot be foreseen, such as abrupt changes in the economic or political situation of the country where the project is located, in project management, or even in the weather. No matter how well a project has been

---

18. Hans Wyss, *Bankwide Lessons Learned from the Experience with the India Sardar Sarovar (Narmada) Project*, annexed to SecM93–516, May 24, 1993 (limited circulation).

19. IBRD Articles of Agreement, Article III, Section 5. *See also* IDA Articles of Agreement, Article V, Section 1(g).

prepared and appraised, its development benefits cannot be fully realized if it is not properly executed. Over the years, the Bank has accumulated unique experience in helping borrowers to resolve project implementation problems, which it uses to "feed back" into the design and preparation of future projects and into the improvement of its policies and procedures. More recently, and following the "Wapenhans Report,"[20] the Bank has been taking additional measures to improve the management of the development projects and programs it finances. These measures are designed to make the Bank more effective in pursuing its basic goal of reducing poverty in its borrowing countries. The newly established Inspection Panel is meant to "complement the responsibilities and functions of the existing systems for quality control in project preparation and implementation," as the Bank's President emphasized in presenting this function for the first time to the staff.[21]

In effect, the existing mechanisms for ensuring quality control and compliance with the requirements of the Bank's Articles of Agreement operate at three stages of the project cycle: preparation, supervision, and evaluation.

A.   *Project Preparation*

Although formal responsibility for project preparation rests with the borrower, the Bank often assists in the borrower's preparatory activities in a number of ways.[22] Existing procedures for project design and appraisal include a number of safeguards not only for the economic soundness of Bank-financed projects but also for advance consideration of environmental and social impacts, and for prior public consultations on these impacts. In particular, Operational Policy (OP) 4.01 on Environmental Assessment,

---

20. *Supra* note 4.

21. The World Bank Inspection Panel, Letter from Lewis T. Preston to all Staff, September 24, 1993.

22. *See* Warren C. Baum, *The Project Cycle*, at 8–10 (World Bank publication, 1982). The processes involved have been simplified and shortened under an electronically operated Project Documentation System without affecting the substance of the work required.

which replaced the earlier Directive on the subject,[23] aims at ensuring that the environmental effects of projects are discerned as early as possible in the project cycle and measures are incorporated to avoid, minimize, or mitigate adverse impacts of the project or to enhance environmental benefits. Part of this assessment process consists of mandatory consultations with affected groups and local NGOs for major, highly risky, or contentious projects. For these projects, the Policy also provides for the borrowing government's establishment of independent environmental advisory panels. Similar borrower's advance assessments of social impacts, including consultation with affected groups, are required under the OP concerning involuntary resettlement[24] and indigenous peoples[25] and are routinely carried out in conjunction with environmental assessments. The Bank's Environment Department carries out annual reviews to monitor the effectiveness of these assessments.[26]

For projects on international waterways, the World Bank's Operational Policy provides for optional recourse to the technical advice of independent experts, to be selected from a roster of ten "independent and highly qualified experts."[27] Their technical opinion "will be for the purposes of the Bank only, and shall not in any way determine the rights and obligations of riparians."[28]

---

23. *See* OP 4.01 on *Environmental Assessment* (January 1999), replacing Operational Directive (OD) 4.00 on E*nvironmental Assessment* (October 1989); *see The World Bank and the Environment: A Legal Perspective,* Chapter Five in Ibrahim F.I. Shihata, *The World Bank in a Changing World, Volume Two,* 183–236 (1995). Procedures for consultation have been further enhanced in this and other respects by the more open information disclosure policy adopted by the Bank in 1993, as explained in Section V of this chapter, *infra.*

24. OP 4.12 (September 1998), replacing OD 4.30 on *Involuntary Resettlement* (June 1990).

25. OD 4.20 on *Indigenous Peoples* (September 1991), currently being converted to OP 4.10.

26. The Bank has so far carried out two reviews of its experience with environmental assessment, the first covering the period of 1989 to 1992, the second covering the period of 1993 to 1997. *See Annual Review of Environmental Assessment 1992* (SecM93–212), February 25, 1993, and *The Impact of Environmental Assessment—A Review of World Bank Experience* (World Bank 1997).

27. OP 7.50 on *Projects on International Waterways,* Annex A.

28. *Id.,* para. 6.

Dam and reservoir projects would also be covered by the provisions in OP 4.01 referred to earlier,[29] for the borrower's establishment of an advisory panel composed of independent, internationally recognized environmental specialists to advise the borrower periodically on environmental aspects of the project, starting in the preparatory phase and continuing throughout the life of the project. Establishment of this panel is not mandatory, however, and the reconnaissance study may advise that a panel is not needed. For example, in the controversial case of the *Thailand Third Power System Development Project (Pak Mun)*,[30] the borrowing government, with the concurrence of the Bank staff, decided after the initial assessments and consultations not to establish an environmental panel.[31] At the request of the Bank's Board, however, the *Pak Mun* project—which will result in the submersion of 60 square kilometers of land and require the resettlement of an estimated 5,000 persons—underwent a mid-term review by an expert panel composed of a World Bank task manager and three external consultants. In addition, OP 4.37 (Safety of Dams) requires the establishment of a dam safety board for major dams.

B.   Project Supervision

The purpose of the Bank's supervision of the implementation of the projects it finances is to help ensure effective project execution by identifying and dealing with problems and issues as or before they arise. As a *lending* institution, the Bank must monitor progress in implementation and compliance with loan conditions, always ensuring that loan proceeds are appropriately used only for the purposes of the project, as required by its Articles of

---

29. OD 4.00, para. 4 and Annex B on *Environmental Policy for Dam and Reservoir Projects* (April 1989).

30. Loan Agreement No. 3423–TH. *See Thailand: Pak Mun—The Facts, The Background: Questions and Answers* (SecM94–138), February 10, 1994.

31. Decision confirmed by the Board of Executive Directors on December 10, 1991 with the objection or abstention of some Directors.

Agreement. As a *development* institution, the Bank must also help the borrower obtain the greatest benefits from its loans, in particular by identifying and assisting in the resolution of operational and managerial problems.

During the negotiation of Bank loan agreements, the staff of the Bank and the borrower normally agree on a schedule of borrower progress reports to be submitted by the borrower. Once a loan has been approved by the Bank's Executive Directors, supervision concentrates on familiarizing new borrowers and implementing agencies with the Bank's requirements on the procurement of goods and services financed by the loan, disbursement of the proceeds, reports on the progress of work, and audits of the project's accounts and those of the project agency.

The Bank reviews the borrower's progress reports, and Bank staff visit project sites and facilities to review progress, provide advice, and obtain information. They do not, however, make decisions on behalf of the borrower. An important element of project supervision concerns procurement, which must be carried out in accordance with the Bank's "Guidelines" on procurement. These "Guidelines" become binding on the borrower through their incorporation, with appropriate amendments, if needed, in every loan agreement. Although the borrower—not the Bank—is responsible for preparing the specifications and tender documents, evaluating bids, and awarding the contracts, the Bank's role is to make sure that these "Guidelines" are observed so that loan proceeds may be disbursed for the contract. If the Bank declines to issue its "no objection" when required before the award of large contracts, it is still for the borrower to decide whether to follow the Bank's advice or to proceed as it intended. The Bank can only declare a misprocurement that results in withdrawing Bank financing for the contract; it cannot force a decision on the borrower. (It may be noted in this respect that one of the actions resulting from the "Wapenhans Report"[32] was the new requirement that borrowers use standard procurement documents prepared by the Bank.)

---

32. *See Getting Results, supra* note 4, at 14.

The Bank, in accordance with the Action Plan prepared in response to the recommendations of the "Wapenhans Report,"[33] and, more intensively, under the 1997 Strategic Compact proposed by the current Bank President, James D. Wolfensohn, and approved by the Executive Directors, continues to increase the resources used for supervision in order to reinforce borrowers' project and program implementation. Every new operation now has a clear implementation plan, developed with the implementing agencies concerned, which allows the project's progress to be tracked and provides an early warning of problems that may arise.

Further actions taken by the Bank include the issuance of new guidelines to focus performance assessments more clearly on the progress being made toward the operation's goals. The Bank has introduced a more systematic method of dealing with "problem projects." For projects in problem status for more than twelve months, departmental managers are now required to agree with the borrower on a specific action plan for the following year, which may include the possible restructuring or cancellation of the loans. Other guidelines require that completion reports further review and make recommendations about the sustainability of what has been achieved. Finally, the Bank has expanded the use of project implementation "mid-term reviews" (which in the past were carried out mainly for sector investment loans), and has shifted more of the responsibility for its lending operations away from its Washington headquarters to its field offices.[34] Seventy-four such offices were operating at the end of 1998.

The increasingly intensified role of the Bank in the supervision of implementation does not mean that the Bank replaces the borrower, as the owner of the project, who is solely responsible for any harmful effect it may inflict on private groups or individuals as a result of such implementation. In fact, while the Bank's policies aim at the avoidance of such harmful effects, the Bank does not take any action with direct effect on parties other than the borrower, and any effect of its actions vis-à-vis the borrower

---

33. *Id.*
34. *Id.* at 16.

cannot have any effect on third parties unless the borrower reflects them in its implementation of the project.[35]

C. *Project Evaluation*

In contrast with *supervision*, which is understood in the Bank to apply during the project execution period, *ex post evaluation* looks more broadly at the probable impact in the borrowing member country of the completed project compared to original expectations. The latter process takes place after the project is completed and the loan is disbursed in order to provide an account for the use of the Bank's loan resources, draw lessons from the experience, and, more generally, to enhance the Bank's internal and external accountability and transparency. The Bank's evaluation system has two stages: First, six months after the closing date of the loan, staff responsible for supervision during implementation prepare a project implementation report on the execution and initial operation of the project, and the costs and benefits derived and to be derived from it. Also, the borrower's and the Bank's performance of their respective obligations under the loan agreement and the accomplishment of the purposes of the project are evaluated. Second, a representative sample of completed operations is independently evaluated. To ensure its independence and objectivity, this *ex post* audit is carried out by the Operations Evaluation Department (OED), which is functionally separate from the operating staff of the Bank and reports directly to the Board. In addition to "the performance audit on selected completed projects," the OED's mandate includes "evaluation studies focusing on selected issues and sectors." Although it reviews ongoing operations in the context of such studies in order to update and test findings from completed projects, it does not review such individual ongoing projects in the same way it reviews completed projects. OED also comments informally and selectively on executive project briefs (project information documents) to ensure that lessons

---

35. *See* Chapter Five, Section II, for details.

learned from past experience are taken into account in the design of new projects.[36]

To assess the performance of completed operations, OED looks at their technical, financial, economic, social, and environmental aspects and provides ratings of overall performance and sustainability. The results and recommendations, after they have been reported to the Executive Directors, are meant to be fed back into the design and implementation of policies and lending operations. OED's annual review of evaluation results, after discussion by the Executive Directors, is then issued to the public.

This evaluation function should enable the Bank to draw lessons from past experience and to disseminate them to improve the management of development assistance and to support member countries in the development of their own evaluation capacities. The Action Plan measures prepared in response to the "Wapenhans Report" also included strengthening of the OED's role. For example, OED is now expected to build up its program of impact evaluations that take a second look at a project five to ten years after the completion of loan disbursements. OED is also expected to focus on country portfolios in selecting the operations to be evaluated and in planning evaluation studies programs. Finally, OED has diversified the scope of its evaluation studies to include, for example, evaluations of the Bank's operational policies and processes and quick studies of topical issues.[37]

D.   *Other Audits and* ad hoc *Evaluations*

The Internal Auditing Department (IAD) of the Bank undertakes periodic and independent audits of operational, financial, administrative, personnel, and information resource management systems and other activities, to assess their efficiency, compliance

---

36. *See* Joint Audit Committee, *Report on Portfolio Management and the Evaluation Function* (R93–7), April 13, 1993.

37. These measures were originally elaborated in *Getting Results, supra* note 4, at 16–17.

with policies, and effectiveness, and it identifies opportunities for improvement.

Special evaluations have also been undertaken *ad hoc* for a specific project (Narmada) or for particular categories of projects, such as the Bank-wide staff review of resettlement issues, initiated in the wake of the *Narmada* case.[38] A comprehensive evaluation of the pilot phase of the Global Environment Facility (GEF) was carried out in 1993 by an independent panel of experts with the assistance of internal evaluators.[39] The latter procedure, needed as a prelude to the restructuring and replenishment of the GEF, differed from standard OED practice concerning Bank-financed projects. Covering projects where the Bank was only a trustee and an implementing agency, it involved an evaluation of the implementation of ongoing projects (none of the GEF projects having been fully implemented at the time) as well as the quality of preparatory work on projects not yet approved. It also differed from the standard "supervision" of Bank-financed projects in that it was directed by outside experts (rather than by Bank staff).

IV. Internal and External Initiatives for Change

Both the "Wapenhans Report" and the *Narmada* case received wide attention inside and outside the Bank, with a new focus on the debate over the adequacy of existing control mechanisms. The debate triggered a number of proposals in the course of 1993, some originating within the Bank and others from member governments and external critics. All contributed, no doubt, to the process culminating in the establishment of the Inspection Panel.

---

38. *Supra* note 16.

39. See *Report of the Independent Evaluation of the Global Environment Facility Pilot Phase*, November 23, 1993. The evaluation was carried out in response to a request by the governments participating in the GEF, formulated at their Abidjan meeting in December 1992.

A.   *The Four Executive Directors' Proposal*

On February 10, 1993, a group of four Executive Directors, representing borrowing and non-borrowing countries, submitted a
memorandum to the President (hereinafter referred to as the
"Four Executive Directors' Proposal") calling for the establishment of an independent in-house capacity through an evaluation
unit for *ongoing* projects. The proposal, to which a fifth Executive
Director later associated himself, envisaged a small permanent
unit, with one to three inspectors selected from among experienced *Bank officers* "of the highest caliber with the necessary
independence," presumably appointed by or with the concurrence of the Board. The unit would be located within the Bank,
possibly under the Director-General, Operations Evaluation, but
otherwise independent from the Bank's OED, and would operate in the following way: first, it would receive requests for
inspection—from borrowers or Executive Directors. After deciding on the eligibility for inspection of the requests filed, it would
undertake the relevant inspection. In addition, random evaluation initiated by the unit would focus on a sample of projects in
the loan portfolio. The Board would "normally take note" of the
findings of evaluations and the unit's recommendations but
would "ask for an increased role in cases of special importance."
A selective mechanism to reasonably limit the number of evaluated projects was also suggested.

The President requested a review of the proposal by senior
staff in consultation with its authors and with other Executive
Directors, also taking into account relevant national experience
with comparable inspection offices. A staff report analyzing this
proposal, co-authored by a staff member and a former Director-
General, Operations Evaluation, concluded that there was no
apparent need for a permanent inspection unit. It suggested
instead that an inspection function be established in the form of
an *ad hoc* inspection capacity. Inspection would be commissioned
by the President on his initiative, or on the request of Executive
Directors, staff, or third parties. The President would also designate an "operational ombudsman" through whom "staff and

others" could raise issues for review. Following a positive assessment that inspection was warranted, the President would appoint one or two inspectors to investigate the case and would forward their report to the Board together with Management's response. This suggestion was not considered further and the matter was overtaken by subsequent events.

Meanwhile, the issue had generated public discussion in several member countries as well as specific proposals from concerned governments, academic observers, and non-governmental organizations.

B.   The Ombudsman Proposal

Testifying before a Canadian Parliamentary Committee in February 1993 and before a U.S. Congressional Committee in May 1993, Professor Daniel D. Bradlow, of the American University's Washington College of Law, advocated the appointment of a World Bank ombudsman for complaints about Bank operations and policies.[40] The ombudsman would be an independent Bank official appointed by and directly responsible to the Bank's Board, with a mandate to investigate and respond to conflicts "relating to the staff's implementation of the Bank's operating rules and procedures and administrative practices." His competence would be limited to issuing non-binding recommendations to the Executive Directors, while the final decision-making power would lie with the latter. "The ombudsman authority would end once loan disbursements were complete *and* the project/program was being reviewed by the Bank's OED."[41] Complaints could be filed "by any party with a direct

---

40. Daniel D. Bradlow, Opening Statement to the Sub-Committee on International Financial Institutions, Canadian House of Commons Standing Committee on Finance, February 18, 1993; and Statement to the Subcommittee on International Development, Finance, and Urban Affairs Committee, U.S. House of Representatives (May 1993). *See also* Daniel D. Bradlow, Why World Bank Needs an Ombudsman, *Financial Times,* July 14, 1993, at 13.

41. *Financial Times, supra* note 40. (Emphasis in original.)

interest in the substance of the complaint," directly with the ombudsman or through the Bank's Resident Representatives. Such complaints, to be eligible for investigation, however, should comply with minimum standards, such as the submission of supporting evidence about the complainant's direct interest in the matter; the relationship of the complaint to ongoing Bank operations and to the implementation of Bank rules, practices, and procedures; the exhaustion of alternative channels of relief; and the submission of the complaint within a reasonable period after the alleged injury.

The ombudsman would also be able to "recommend changes in the applicable rule, procedure, or administrative practice," while the Board would "always retain [the] final decision-making power." The ombudsman would thus act as an instrument for the Board to detect deficiencies in the Bank's rules and procedures. Through an annual report made available to the public at large, the ombudsman would "provide the international community with independent information on the developmental and human impact of Bank operations and thus contribute to the debate which would take place about the role of the Bank in providing sustainable development."[42]

Professor Bradlow's proposal was studied in the Bank, and the author of this study had the occasion to discuss it with him at length. The idea, which at one point seemed to be gaining ground, was dropped when it became clear that an inspection *panel*, rather than an individual ombudsman, was more likely to meet rising expectations.

---

42. *See also* the earlier proposal for a "private attorney general" by Professor David Wirth, Legitimacy, Accountability and Partnership: A Model for Advocacy on Third World Environmental Issues, 100 *Yale Law Journal* 2645, 2664 (1991), which went even further in the direction of an adjudicatory mechanism. *See also* the more extensive proposal of establishing a "watchdog agency" independent from the Bank, which "would have the capacity to monitor, report on, and intervene in the World Bank lending process." in Jonathan Cahn, Challenging the New Imperial Authority: The World Bank and the Democratization of Development, 6 *Harvard Human Rights Journal* 159 (1993).

C.   The Proposal for an "Independent Appeals Commission"

Testifying before the same U.S. Congressional Committee in May 1993, several U.S. NGOs advocated withholding U.S. funding for the 10th IDA Replenishment (IDA–10) unless several conditions were met by the World Bank.[43] These conditions included the establishment of an "Independent Appeals Commission" that would have jurisdiction to investigate complaints from any member country or from individuals and NGOs in developing countries. The commission would have access to Bank information, and all its decisions would be made available to the public.

With the authority to "recommend modification, suspension, or cancellation of a World Bank-financed project," the proposed Commission would "investigate and pass judgment on complaints regarding violations of all World Bank policies, procedures, and loan and credit agreements, the World Bank's Articles of Agreement and By-Laws, and international human rights and environmental law." The Commission's "judgments" would be final and binding unless reversed by a two-thirds majority of the Bank's Board of Executive Directors. Such a comprehensive mandate would cover violations alleged to have occurred "during the course of the design, appraisal, monitoring, or

---

43. *See* statements on behalf of the Environmental Defense Fund, National Wildlife Federation, and Natural Resources Defense Council before the Sub-Committee on International Development, Finance, Trade and Monetary Policy of the Banking, Finance and Urban Affairs Committee, U.S. House of Representatives, May 5, 1993. *See also* David Hunter and Lori Udall, *Proposal for an Independent Appeals Commission* (Environmental Defense Fund and Center for International Environmental Law, 1993). Earlier proposals included an appeals mechanism proposed in 1990 by the Natural Resources Defence Council, *see* E. Christenson, *Green Appeal, A Proposal for an Independent Commission of Inquiry at the World Bank* (NRDC, 1990), and a 1992 proposed model by the Center for International Environmental Law (CIEL) for an appeals function at the EBRD. *See* Chris A. Wald and Durwood Zaelke, Establishing an Independent Review Board at the European Bank for Reconstruction and Development: A Model for Improving MDB Decision Making 2 *Duke Environmental Law and Policy Forum* 59 (1992).

implementation of an ongoing World Bank-financed project or program."

Composed of nine members (none of them nationals of the same country or of the nationality of the claimant or from the country where the project is located) appointed by the Bank's Board (with two nominated by NGOs), and acting separately from the Bank's OED, the Independent Appeals Commission would operate in panels of three persons. All decisions, though previously termed "recommendations" or "judgments," would be "final and binding." The budget would be borne by the World Bank, and the Commission would be "housed separately from the World Bank" in Washington, D.C. The proposal also suggested that, pending the creation of such a commission, the World Bank should be required to establish an ombudsman office by December 1993 to fulfill the same functions.

The formulation of these conditions for IDA–10 did not at the time progress beyond a U.S. House of Representatives committee draft,[44] and they eventually entered the U.S. appropriations legislation in October 1993 in a substantially modified form.[45] However, the discussion gave a clear indication of an emerging trend in the U.S. Congress to favor strongly the establishment of a commission or panel of inspectors in the World Bank and in other international financial institutions. This obviously influenced the position of the U.S. Administration in the Bank's Board discussions before the adoption of the Panel Resolution in September 1993.

----

44. Sub-Committee on International Development, Finance, Trade and Monetary Policy of the Banking, Finance and Urban Affairs Committee, U.S. House of Representatives, Draft International Development and Debt Relief Act of 1993, May 26, 1993 (calling for the establishment of an independent appeals commission in the World Bank).

45. *See* Report of the House/Senate Committee of Conference on H.R. 2295 (103rd Congress, 1st Session, Report 103–267 of September 28, 1993) (instructing the Treasury Department to urge establishment of independent inspection entities in each international financial institution, and of an "independent commission to review the operations and management structure" of these institutions).

V. The Related Issue of Information Disclosure

In the context of the 1993 U.S. congressional approval process of World Bank Group appropriations—especially IDA–10 and allocations for the Global Environment Facility (GEF) the issue of "accountability" (in particular, through the inspection function) was always closely linked to the issue of "transparency" (that is, disclosure of information), particularly in the environmental field.

Under the U.S. International Financial Institutions Act, as amended by the 1989 International Development and Finance Act (the *Pelosi Amendment*),[46] the U.S. Executive Director in the World Bank has been required since December 1991 "not to vote in favor of any action proposed to be taken . . . which would have a significant effect on the human environment" unless an environmental impact assessment had been made available to the Bank and to affected groups and local NGOs "at least 120 days before the date of the vote."[47] Subsequent U.S. appropriations legislation in October 1992[48] expanded the requirements for timely availability of draft and final environmental assessment reports "to the public in borrowing and donor countries" and made GEF funding subject to the establishment of "clear procedures ensuring public availability of documentary information" on all GEF and GEF-associated projects, as well as consultation with affected peoples in recipient countries and with NGOs.

Partly in response to these new concerns about the timely availability and publicity of environmental assessment reports,[49]

---

46. 22 U.S.C. § 262 n–7, Section 1307(d), as inserted by Section 521 of Public Law 101–240 on December 19, 1989, to become effective after two years.

47. This requirement would be held inapplicable if the Secretary of the Treasury found compelling reason to believe that disclosure would jeopardize the confidential relationship between the borrower country and the Bank.

48. Section 5323 of the *Foreign Operations, Export Financing, and Related Programs Appropriations Act 1993* (Public Law 102–391) of October 6, 1992.

49. *E.g.,* a temporary rule issued on June 10, 1992 by the U.S. Department of the Treasury, 31 CFR Part 26, 57 Federal Register No. 112, at 24544 (subsequently suspended) called for making all World Bank environmental assessments publicly available in Washington, DC.

which were also reflected in the IDA–10 Deputies Report,[50] and taking into account similar—though less far-reaching—developments in other member countries[51] and related recommendations by the *Rio Earth Summit* (the United Nations Conference on Environment and Development) in June 1992,[52] the Bank's Executive Directors had already held informal discussions on the information disclosure issue in July and August 1992.[53] As a result, a revision of the then applicable Bank Directive and Operational Procedures on disclosure policy[54] had been initiated, including the preparation of specific procedures for GEF projects. The process culminated in an intensive Board discussion of a new document on the Bank's disclosure of information policy on August 26, 1993,[55] followed by the finalization of new procedures in September 1993.[56] Under the revised Bank policy and procedures, more Bank documents became publicly available and a new Public Information Center (PIC) was established to respond to requests for documents and information from any interested party. In particular, all environmental assessments for projects to be financed by the World Bank are made available in

---

50. International Development Association, *Additions to IDA Resources: Tenth Replenishment,* approved by the Executive Directors on January 12, 1993, paras. 21–22.

51. *E.g.*, the European Community's Council Directive 90/313/EEC on the Freedom of Access to Information on the Environment of June 7, 1990, which required EC member states to enact implementing legislation by December 31, 1992. While this Directive has no bearing on World Bank operations, it reflects the shared concern of European countries with the issue of public access to information in matters affecting the environment.

52. *E.g.*, *Agenda 21, see* sections 23.3–3, 27.9(g) and 38.43–44 of UNCED report, A/CONF.151/26/Rev.1, vol. I (1992).

53. On July 7 and August 6, 1992. The discussion was based on a legal memorandum by the author; *see Some Legal Aspects of the Bank's Policy on Disclosure of Information*, Memorandum of the Vice President and General Counsel (R92–145), July 24, 1992.

54. Administrative Manual Statement 1.10, originally issued in 1985, amended in 1989.

55. Summarized in *Expanding Access to Bank Information* (SecM93–927), August 31, 1993, as approved by the Executive Directors.

56. Bank Procedures (BP) 17.50 on *Disclosure of Operational Information* (September 1993); *see also The World Bank Policy on Disclosure of Information* (World Bank, March 1994).

borrowing countries to affected groups and local NGOs, and subsequently through the PIC.[57] It must be kept in mind that this work proceeded in parallel, and in continuous interchange, with the ongoing discussions on the inspection function.

VI. Preparatory Work by the Bank's Management and Board

All of the above-mentioned elements and developments had a bearing on the preparatory work undertaken within the Bank during the first half of 1993. As requested by the President, a staff paper was prepared for Board discussion, in light of the Four Executive Directors' Proposal of February 10. The paper, dated June 10, 1993, analyzed existing governmental inspection practices in three member countries (Canada, Germany, and the United States)[58] and concluded that these were functionally comparable to existing World Bank evaluation mechanisms. It went on to present and assess the Four Executive Directors' proposal of February 10, 1993, together with a second alternative proposal.[59]

Under this second scenario, an independent in-house "Inspection Panel" consisting of three inspectors would be

---

57. For the projects financed by the IBRD only, the PIC would not make the assessment reports publicly available, if the borrower objects, in deference to the ownership rights of the borrower. The situation is different for IDA projects as was agreed in the context of the IDA–10 replenishment.

58. In *Canada*, development assistance operations are subject to review by the audit and evaluation staff of the Canadian International Development Agency (CIDA); CIDA does not have an independent inspection function. In *Germany*, the Federal Ministry for Economic Cooperation and Development evaluates ongoing projects with a focus on identified problem cases, and occasionally conducts *ex post* evaluations of completed projects. In addition to these evaluations by the Ministry, the two implementing agencies (GTZ and KfW) routinely produce project completion reports (after two to three years of the operation of the project). In the *United States*, independent inspectors carry out financial audits, investigations of alleged fraud or misuse, and evaluations of departmental programs (including ongoing ones).

59. *Operations Inspection in the Bank: Issues and Options,* Draft Report submitted to the Executive Directors (R93–122), June 10, 1993.

appointed by the Board on the recommendation of the President. As proposed in other models, it was understood that the Panel members would be of the highest professional and personal caliber and reputation, and recruited from outside the Bank, although former staff members could also be eligible. As in the Four Executive Directors' Proposal, the Panel proposed in the Management paper would receive complaints from individual Executive Directors and affected parties. The eligibility criteria for complaints would also be similar, although the party lodging the complaint would be required to first seek explanation from Bank Management before approaching the Panel. While the paper insisted that "responsibility for the concerns raised would rest with the borrower," any concern about the Bank's adherence to its own operating rules and procedures would justify the Panel's intervention. Following an inspection, the Panel would submit recommendations to the President (on projects under preparation) and to the Board (on projects under implementation). It would also provide them with an annual report discussing the final disposition of the complaints received.[60]

The recommendations in the paper of June 10, 1993, attempted to reconcile many goals. These included accommodation of the various views expressed and options suggested, both inside and outside the Bank, the paramount objectives of improving "accountability" and "transparency" and fostering borrowers' ownership of projects and public participation in their design and implementation, in the context of poverty reduction and environmental protection efforts. The paper concluded that "in light of a review of the advantages and disadvantages of alternative approaches, the most effective arrangement would be the establishment of an independent in-house Inspection Panel."

---

60. An earlier draft of this paper had also considered possible recourse to an *ombudsman* procedure for operational concerns voiced by working level staff, analogous to the existing ombudsman function for personnel matters, but had discarded this option mainly in view of the confidentiality requirements in staff relations.

Although these recommendations did not go unchallenged,[61] they provided a basis for discussion by the Bank's Executive Directors in an informal seminar held on July 9, 1993. The seminar discussion showed broad agreement on the need for an inspection function, although there was no consensus on any of the two options proposed (the Four Executive Directors' Proposal and the alternative suggested in the paper). Concerns were expressed, in particular, about the potential risks of the Panel's interference with the role of the Board or Management and about triggering a large volume of complaints at considerable cost.[62]

A revised paper was prepared by Bank Management in light of these discussions and of further written suggestions by an Executive Director who attempted to reconcile the two options. The revised paper was submitted to the Executive Directors' Committee of the Whole on August 6, 1993, together with a draft resolution.[63] The paper defined the inspection function and mandate as well as the complaints' screening mechanism and specified the role of the Board in appointing inspectors, approving inspections, and receiving recommendations. Although the paper continued to refer to an inspection unit, the appended draft resolution[64] explicitly envisaged an independent three-member

---

61. The Four Executive Directors, who authored the February 10, 1993, proposal, submitted, on June 22, 1993, a critique of the June 10, 1993, paper indicating their preference for their original proposal, as restated to also authorize evaluation of projects at the request of affected parties and NGOs after the concurrence of a majority of the Executive Directors.

62. In the course of these discussions, I had the occasion to note that the risks inherent in either option could be substantially reduced through precise procedural requirements. I also noted, however, that although final decisions in the proposed alternative remained in the hands of Management (in cases concerning project preparation), or of the Board and Management (for projects under implementation), both would be hard pressed not to depart from recommendations by the inspectors.

63. *Functions and Operations of an Inspection Function* (Draft R93–122/1), August 6, 1993.

64. Draft IBRD/IDA Resolution on *The World Bank Independent Inspection Panel*, August 5, 1993. The text was based on an earlier draft originally submitted by the General Counsel to the President's Office on June 23, subsequently revised on July 20, and reviewed by the President and Vice Presidents on July 26.

Inspection Panel, with powers to hear complaints presented either by a group of four or more Executive Directors, or by one or more persons directly affected by a failure of the Bank to follow its operating policies, rules, and procedures.

The revised paper was considered by the Executive Directors in a meeting of the Committee of the Whole on August 26 and 27, 1993. While there was still some support for an in-house inspection unit under the Director-General, Operations Evaluation, a majority of participants favored the establishment of an independent panel. Discussions focused on the mandate of the panel; the need for a two-year review of the panel's operation; the issue of access to the panel, or the standing of complainants, for affected parties and Executive Directors; the role of the Board in approving inspections; participation by borrowing governments; membership and cost of the panel; the possibility of suspension of projects under investigation; coverage of projects under preparation and projects under implementation; follow-up action; and reports.

In light of the discussion, a further revised text was submitted as Memorandum of the President to the Executive Directors on September 10, 1993, together with a revised draft resolution.[65] The Memorandum described details of the composition, jurisdiction, and operational procedures of the proposed panel, as specified in the draft resolution; and gave a budget estimate based on the assumption that the workload of the panel would justify full-time employment of three panel members, supported by an executive secretary and special consultants.

The decisive executive session of the Board took place on September 21, 1993, and was extended to the following day. The session began with a presentation of the above-mentioned President's Memorandum, but the meeting focused exclusively on the text of the revised draft resolution (dated September 9, 1993). In the process, it was further amended and adopted, as amended, on September 22.

---

65. *See* R93–122/2, *supra* note 2.

2

The Resolution Establishing the Panel: A Study of the Resolution as Issued— Its Drafting History and Interpretation

Introduction

This chapter explains the main features of the Inspection Panel, established by the Bank's Board of Executive Directors in September 1993[1] (its first members were appointed in April 1994).[2] The analysis is based on the text of the Resolution establishing the Panel (the Resolution), the several drafts of the paper prepared by the Bank's Management for the Board discussion of the subject,[3] the successive draft resolutions prepared by the

---

1. *Resolution of the Executive Directors (the Board) establishing the Inspection Panel* (No. 93–10 for the IBRD and 93–6 for IDA), circulated as document No. SecM93–988 (IBRD) and SecM93–313 (IDA) (September 23, 1993) (hereinafter *Resolution*) (Annex I–1–1 to this book).

2. R94–56; IDA/R94–60, April 5, 1994, approved on April 21, 1994. The first three members of the Panel were Mr. Ernst-Günther Bröder, a German national (Chairman), Mr. Alvaro Umaña Quesada, a Costa Rican national, and Mr. Richard E. Bissell, a U.S. national. Since that time, Mr. Bissell has been replaced by Mr. James MacNeill, a Canadian national, in August 1997, and Mr. Umaña by Mr. Edward S. Ayensu, a national of Ghana, in August 1998. Mr. Bröder chaired the Panel in its first two years, was succeeded by Mr. Bissel and Mr. Umaña, each for one year, before becoming the chairman again in his last year of service. Mr. MacNeill was elected chairman of the Panel after Mr. Bröder stepped down from that post, effective March 1, 1999.

3. *See* draft reports dated June 10 and August 6, 1993, and the President's Memorandum of September 10, 1993, referred to, *supra*, in Chapter One, Section VI (limited circulation).

office of the Bank's General Counsel to formulate concepts as they evolved in the discussions of the Bank's Management and Board,[4] and the discussions that led to the adoption of the Resolution. In other words, the analysis in this chapter describes the Panel as it was meant to be, according to the intended meaning of the text of its constituent resolution and the features considered at the time of the adoption of that text. These features include the objectives of the Panel's inspection function; the scope of its mandate; the eligibility criteria for accessing the Panel and thus invoking the inspection function; the role the Panel is expected to play, including the procedural aspects of its work and the relevant reporting requirements; the Panel's composition; and, finally, the administrative and financial arrangements pertinent to the Panel. The discussion will also cover issues that arose during the application of the Resolution, some of which are discussed further in the following chapters.

I.   Objectives of the Inspection Function

Although the Resolution does not include a statement on the objectives of inspection and the reasons that led to the creation of this function in the Bank, the operating paragraphs of the Resolution, Management papers submitted to the Bank's Board, and the discussion of these papers and of the draft resolution by Board members provide rich details about these matters. According to paragraph 12 of the Resolution, the affected party's standing before the Panel is not based on just any kind or degree of harm it may have suffered in connection with a Bank-financed project. Rather, it is limited to cases when "its rights or interests have been or are likely to be directly affected by an action or omission of the Bank as a result of a failure of the Bank to follow its operational policies and procedures with respect to the design, appraisal, and/or implementation of a project financed by the Bank, (including situations where the Bank is alleged to have

---

4. *See* draft resolutions dated June 23, July 20, August 5, and September 9, 1993, referred to, *supra*, in Chapter One, Section VI (limited circulation).

failed in its follow-up on the borrower's obligations under loan agreements with respect to such policies and procedures)." Thus, the President's memorandum submitted to the Board on September 10, 1993, to which the last draft resolution was attached, explained, "[t]he objective of an inspection function in the Bank should be to provide independent judgment that would help resolve major differences in cases where it is asserted that rights and interests of parties are adversely affected because the Bank has failed to follow its operating policies and procedures in the design, appraisal and/or implementation of Bank lending operations."[5] Such function would, according to the same report, "complement the existing system for quality control in project preparation and supervision during implementation."[6] As a result, the President's memorandum made clear that the inspection function "would not diminish the role of the Board in the governance of the Bank," a point stressed as well by many Executive Directors during discussions, or "reduce, or otherwise modify, the accountability of the President for the management of Bank operation."[7] Nor would the function "disrupt the efficient conduct of Bank business," "duplicate the functions of OED or IAD"[8] (the Operations Evaluation Department and the Internal Auditing Department) or "provide an over-all assessment of the status of the Bank's portfolio."[9] Rather, the Panel is established as a facility within the Bank "designed to be consistent with and to complement the responsibilities and functions of the existing structure of the Bank."[10] Its function is limited to

---

5. *Operations Inspection Function: Objectives, Mandate and Operating Procedures for an Independent Inspection Panel,* Memorandum from the President, R93–122/2, September 10, 1993, at para. 7. The Board, which concentrated its discussion on September 21–22, 1993, on the draft resolution, did not specifically approve this report that reflected the ideas codified in the draft resolution before the changes were introduced in the Board discussion. Earlier papers were submitted as "draft reports" for discussion purposes in the preparatory stage.

6. *Id.,* para. 8.

7. *Id.,* para. 9.

8. *Id.,* para. 12.

9. *Id.,* para. 9.

10. *Id.*

issues that are the Bank's responsibility within the limits defined in the Resolution, and not those that may be the responsibility of other parties. Its function is not, therefore, to rule on complaints against the government of a borrowing country or "to adjudicate differences of views between a government and its citizens."[11] Rather, its concern was intended to be with the Bank's non-compliance with its own operating policies and procedures—a non-compliance that causes harm, present or future, to affected parties.

With this purpose clear in the minds of the drafters of the Resolution, the early discussion in the Executive Directors' seminar of July 9, 1993, revealed other related reasons or justifications for the establishment of the inspection function that were summarized in the September 10, 1993, Management report to the Board as follows:

- "Citizens of developing and developed countries increasingly ask for transparency and accountability of development institutions. The World Bank, as the leading development agency, should respond positively and constructively to this demand.
- The Bank is responding effectively to the challenges of the developing countries and the countries in transition. The existence of an independent body will increase the credibility of the Bank.
- The cases where major conflicts arise with affected parties will be dealt with more efficiently and consistently by a permanent and independent structure than by *ad hoc* bodies.
- The borrowers involved, if they wish, will have a better opportunity to present and defend their position and get the attention of the public and the media in the developing and industrialized countries.
- The professional competence and integrity of Management and staff will be protected if an independent

---

11. *Id.,* para. 24.

investigation assesses the facts and actions taken.

- Members of the Board, and directly affected parties, will have an additional, independent instrument to ensure that projects under preparation or implementation are fully compatible with the policies and procedures of the Bank."[12]

Although the interest during the preparation of the Resolution thus focused on an institutional issue (ensuring the Bank's compliance with its own policies and procedures in project lending), the Panel itself seems to have developed, over time, important nuances in understanding its mission. In the words of its former chairman, Alvaro Umaña Quesada, the Panel understood this mission to include two main functions: "to monitor Management's compliance with the Bank's operational policies and to assess 'material harm' on affected or potentially affected populations."[13] Reflecting the views of the Panel as a whole,[14] he concluded, however, that the first function, which he described as a "policing function," was "less useful to the Board since the Panel's 'verdict' does not lead—nor should it lead to any action beyond correcting failures in project design or execution."[15] In a number of earlier Panel reports to the Bank's Board and its Committee on Development Effectiveness (CODE), and also in the writings of its former chairman, Mr. Umaña, the focus has shifted from the Bank's compliance with its policies to assessing and redressing the harm suffered by affected people. The Panel, in fact, concluded that this important shift, traces of which could be found in its own reports on specific cases, had been adopted by the Bank's Board.[16] The Board's position on this matter was

---

12. *Id.*, para. 6.

13. Alvaro Umaña Quesada (ed.), *The World Bank Inspection Panel: The First Four Years (1994–1998)*, 326 (1998). Mr. Umaña was a member of the Panel from its inception until the end of July 1998. He was the Chairman of the Panel in the last year of his tenure.

14. *See* Chapter Four, *infra*, at 174–175 and 191–193, and Chapter Five, *infra*, at 219–222.

15. Umaña, *supra* note 13, at 326.

16. *Id.* where he states that "[a] review of past Board decisions reveals that the Panel's role in checking compliance with operational policies has been

clarified beyond doubt in the second review of the Panel's experience, as will be discussed in Chapter Four.

II.   Scope of the Panel's Mandate

A.   *Institutional Coverage*

The Resolution establishing the Panel explicitly indicates in its last paragraph that its work covers both the International Bank for Reconstruction and Development (IBRD) and the International Development Association (IDA). Indeed, the Resolution was adopted in a joint session of the Boards of these two institutions (which consists of the same Executive Directors) and was formally adopted as a resolution of the IBRD and IDA.[17]

During the Board discussion of the draft Resolution, some Executive Directors suggested that the International Finance Corporation (IFC) should also be included in the Panel's work. No similar question was raised with respect to the Multilateral Investment Guarantee Agency (MIGA). This matter, however, could only be considered by the respective Boards of these organizations. (IFC's Board has the same membership as the Bank's Board, but it was not included in the joint session of the Boards of the IBRD and IDA where the Resolution was adopted; MIGA's Board may have a different membership, even though, in practice, most of its members are members of the Bank's Board).[18] Whether the Resolution's application may be extended to cover the operations of IFC and MIGA, with appropriate procedural modifications as may be needed, and

---

downplayed, while its role in addressing actual or potential harm to local populations and assessing remedial actions has been emphasized." For an analysis of the Board practices, *see* Chapters Three and Four, *infra*.

17. *See Resolution, supra* note 1.

18. The IFC provides financing for private enterprises without government guarantee; MIGA encourages the flow of foreign private investment mainly through offering guarantees against non-commercial risks. *See* Chapters Three and Four, *infra,* for developments related to the possibility of establishing an inspection function for IFC and MIGA operations.

whether under such modified procedures the Panel may cover the World Bank Group's private sector operations in general are issues presently under consideration, as discussed in Chapter Four.

The Resolution does not specifically mention whether the inspection function applies to the Bank's activities as the trustee and main "implementing agency" of the Global Environment Facility (GEF), where a large number of projects are being implemented, first under GEF's pilot phase and now under the restructured GEF.[19] Projects financed through GEF resources, but administered by the Bank, could give rise to environmental controversies similar to those that would typically engage the Inspection Panel under Bank-financed projects.

The issue of the inclusion of the activities of trust funds administered by the Bank, and in particular of Bank-implemented GEF projects in the Panel's work was not raised during the lengthy discussion of the proposal to establish the Panel. It seems, however, that the exclusion of GEF activities would run counter to the purpose of its establishment and would unduly restrict the scope of its coverage. The Bank, as trustee of the GEF and a major implementing agency of its projects, undertakes to administer GEF funds with the same care it administers its own funds.[20] Several Bank operational policies and procedures specify

---

19. The Global Environment Trust Fund was established under the GEF by Resolution of the Bank's Board No. 91–5 of March 14, 1991, circulated as document SecM91–15 (IBRD and IDA), April 12, 1991, which established the GEF as a pilot facility. *See also* 30 *International Legal Materials* 1735 (1991). The Ozone Projects Trust Fund was included under the umbrella of the GEF in this pilot phase. Agreement on the restructuring of the GEF as a "permanent" facility (not including the Ozone Projects Trust Fund) was completed in March 1994, and new resolutions by the Bank's Board (Res. 1994–2, IBRD, and 1994–3, IDA, dated May 24, 1994) established the restructured GEF, subject to approval by the Board of Governors of the arrangements with the other implementing agencies. Agreement on the first and second replenishment of GEF's resources was reached in May 1994 and July 1998, respectively.

20. *See* para. 3 of Annex B of the "Instrument" establishing the restructured GEF, adopted by the Resolutions of the Bank's Board mentioned in note 19. A similar provision appeared in the 1991 Resolution establishing the GEF.

that they apply equally to projects financed from GEF trust funds.[21] There is no reason to shield the Bank's activities as trustee and implementing agency of the GEF from the scrutiny offered through the inspection function to other Bank activities regarding the design, appraisal, and implementation of projects, to the extent that Bank policies are applicable. The benefits of such scrutiny to the institution and its members seem to apply equally whether the project involved is financed directly by Bank resources or through the GEF. In all such cases, however, inspection will be limited to the Bank's compliance with its own policies and procedures that apply to GEF projects. It will not extend to issues of compliance with other policies and procedures to be adopted separately by the GEF Council unless the Bank agrees otherwise or adopts the same as its own policies and procedures. Although the extension of the inspection function to Bank-implemented GEF projects, when limited to compliance with applicable Bank policies and procedures, seems justified, it may well need to be confirmed by the Bank's Board and, as a matter of GEF policy, by its Council. The issue became relevant in practice, in the case of the *Ecodevelopment Project* in India,[22] where the Panel commented briefly on the Bank's departure from GEF guidelines under the GEF's grant that co-financed the project, without indicating that it needed a specific authorization to investigate this matter.

B.   *Subject-Matter of Requests for Inspection*

1.   *Bank's Actions or Omissions*

As envisaged in the Resolution, the Panel can only be seized of requests related to actions or omissions of *the Bank* (the

---

21. *See, e.g.*, OD 4.01, *Environmental Assessment* (October 1991), replaced recently by OP 4.01, Environmental Assessment (January 1999), and BP 17.50, *Disclosure of Operational Information* (September 1993). *See also* OD 9.01, *Procedures for Investment Operations under the Global Environment Facility* (May 1992).

22. *See* Chapter Three, *infra*, at 133 *seq.*

International Bank for Reconstruction and Development [IBRD] and the International Development Association [ ]) that demonstrate a failure *by the Bank* to follow *its own* operational policies and procedures with respect to the design, appraisal, or implementation of a Bank-supported project.[23] Unlike project "appraisal," which is a function carried out by Bank staff, project preparation and implementation are basically the borrower's responsibility. The Bank often plays a role, however, in assisting the borrower in project preparation[24] and always supervises the borrower's implementation of the project it finances. The Panel will be concerned only with the failure of the Bank to carry out its expected duties under its own policies and procedures throughout these stages of the project cycle. Such a failure, with respect to the "design and appraisal" of projects, refers to the Bank's actions or omissions in the project preparation, pre-appraisal, and appraisal stages. The failure with respect to project "implementation" specifically includes the Bank's failure to follow-up on the borrowers' contractual obligations under the Bank's loan agreements, which reflect the Bank's policies and procedures.[25]

2.   *Projects Financed or to Be Financed by the Bank*

Although the language of the Resolution speaks of "a project financed by the Bank," it was also meant to cover projects under consideration for Bank financing where violation of Bank policies and procedures in design or appraisal may occur. As will be shown in the following chapter, the first request submitted to the Panel related to a project of this type, and the "Clarifications" of the Resolution made by the Board in 1996 made that point clear.[26]

---

23. Resolution, para. 12.
24. *See supra* Chapter One, Section III(A) and Warren C. Baum, *The Project Cycle,* at 8–10 (World Bank publication, 1982). "There are even exceptional circumstances in which the Bank itself does preparatory work." *Id.* at 9.
25. *Resolution,* para. 12.
26. *See* Chapter Three, *infra,* at 102 *seq.* and Chapter Four, *infra,* at 169. The text of the 1996 *Clarifications* appears in Annex I–2 of this book.

A complaint that is not related to a specific Bank operation—where no issues of project design, appraisal, or implementation are raised—cannot be eligible for Panel inspection even if Bank policies are alleged to have been violated in a broader context. This matter, though clear under the Resolution, has been subject to some controversy in practice before it was clarified beyond doubt, as will be discussed in the following chapters.[27]

3.   Project and Adjustment Operations

The Resolution was drafted with the inspection of Bank-financed projects in mind. No mention was made of adjustment operations during its discussion. The concern was primarily focused on the Bank's serious violation of its policies that might cause harm to the environment or to people in the countries where projects financed or to be financed by the Bank are located.

The term *project*, however, is not limited to the typical physical projects for construction, industry, agriculture, and the like. In a detailed legal memorandum issued early in 1984, more than ten years before the Panel started its operations, the requirement in the Bank's Articles of Agreement (the Articles) that its financing be "for specific projects" except "in special circumstances" was elaborated on in some detail.[28] Based on the Articles' drafting history, the ordinary meaning of the word *project*, and the Bank's practice, the memorandum concluded that the term *specific projects* used in the Articles may be read in that context simply to mean "the allocation of resources for specific productive purposes (including such ancillary components as may be required for such purposes)."[29] In this sense, the financing of a list of items under a so-called "program loan" or "sectoral loan"

---

27. *See* Chapter Three, *infra*, at 105 *seq.* and Chapter Four, *infra*, at 169.

28. *See* Article III, Section 4 (vii) of the IBRD Articles of Agreement and Article V, Section 1 (b) of the IDA Articles.

29. *Project and Non-Project Financing under the IBRD Articles*, Memorandum of the Vice President and General Counsel, dated March 1, 1984 (SecM84–1053), December 21, 1984 (limited circulation).

would be covered by the term *specific project* as long as it would serve a specific, predetermined productive purpose or purposes (for example, to finance imports needed for an economic or social sector according to a specific plan meant to benefit that sector).

The meaning of the term *project* as used in the Resolution arose in discussions between the Panel and Bank Management in relation to a specific request submitted to the Panel in 1995, which was not registered. It was agreed then that "the term *project* as used in the Resolution has the same meaning as used in the Bank practice."[30] This statement, which received the concurrence of the Bank's Board, both on that occasion and in the first review of the inspection function, was understood from the beginning by the chairman of the Panel to mean that adjustment operations fall under the scope of the Panel's mandate if other eligibility requirements have been met. Management, however, had always dealt with adjustment lending as a non-project form of lending permitted under the "special circumstances" exception, not under the general rule of specific project financing.

When the question arose later under another Panel case regarding alleged Bank failures in the implementation of an adjustment operation, Management's position, with which the Panel disagreed, was that implementation of policy measures in the context of an adjustment operation supported by the Bank was the responsibility of the borrower. According to that response, there was no place for inspection of Bank failures when harm would result from the action or omissions of the borrower. The Panel's recommendation, based on other grounds—that no investigation was needed in the case at hand—and the Board's approval of that recommendation, left no opportunity for a discussion of the underlying issue and the difficult questions it could raise.

---

30. The case at hand did not relate to a project loan or an adjustment loan but generally alleged that Bank policies dictated that the Bank should not lend to a specific country under certain circumstances. Management was in agreement with the Panel's decision not to register the request, but for a reason different from that mentioned by the Panel. *See* Chapter Three, *infra*, at 105–107.

One such question relates to the extent of the Bank's accountability for adjustment operations. The assumption is that adjustment, both in its design and implementation, is basically a government responsibility. (The development policy letter, which details the adjustment program, is always signed by a government representative, usually the Minister of Finance, and addressed to the Bank.) From a legal standpoint, the borrowing government does not undertake in the loan agreement to carry out the adjustment program outlined in the unilateral letter of development policy. However, the loan is made in reliance on that letter and is either disbursed fully after this program is implemented (in a one-tranche loan) or in tranches following the execution of the set of measures to which each tranche is tied (in the loans of two or more tranches). It may be validly argued that the Bank has some accountability for the design and appraisal of an adjustment program, given the usual deep involvement by Bank staff in the finalization of the letter of development policy, and the requirements of Bank policies regarding adjustment operations.[31] The same argument does not automatically apply, however, to the *implementation* of adjustment measures. The Bank cannot deem the failure of a borrowing government to take these measures as a violation of the government's legal obligations under the loan agreement, as the latter does not obligate the borrowing country to carry out those measures. The Bank can only withhold disbursement of the loan tranche that was conditioned on the carrying out of the measures related to such disbursement. This fine legal point is not always clear to those who study the matter without reading the legal documents.

The Resolution also requires the affected party that requests inspection by the Panel to prove that it has suffered or is likely to suffer a material harm resulting from a serious violation by the Bank of its own policies and procedures. Adjustment operations involve broad policy measures to be taken by the government of the borrowing country that may have profound effects on large segments of the population. There are always winners and losers

---

31. *See* OD 8.60 on *Adjustment Lending* to be converted into OP 8.60.

under any reform. The Bank cannot simply be held accountable for the inevitable harm inflicted on losers in the reform process. Only the harm directly resulting from the Bank's serious violation of its operational policies is relevant to the Panel. For instance, if the borrower, under an adjustment program supported by a Bank loan, decided to downsize its civil service by 100,000 employees, those who obviously suffer the harm of job loss cannot have a case before the Panel unless they can prove that that harm was the direct result of a serious violation by the Bank of its policies.

If a failure is established on the part of the Bank regarding an adjustment program it has supported, the question of defining *affected parties* in this case remains. Can it be so broad and vague as to include "the high income groups" or "the low income groups" in the country, for instance? Or should it be specifically defined to include, for example, the workers in a specific factory who lose their jobs under a privatization program?[32]

As a practical matter, it may be difficult at this stage to exclude from the Panel's mandate complaints related to adjustment loans. Although the Board did not comment on the eligibility question in the one case involving an adjustment operation (because of the Panel's recommendation not to investigate), the Panel did consider a request related to such an operation as eligible, and the Board's silence was seen by the Panel as a tacit concurrence. There is a clear need, however, for the Board to discuss the scope of inspection in adjustment operations and, in particular, to define in generic terms those groups who may submit requests for inspection under them. Short of this, the Panel may be faced with *actiones populares* claiming that the whole population or broad segments of it have been directly and adversely

---

32. For the possible effect of adjustment programs on the rights and interests of individuals in connection with requests before the Inspection Panel, *see* Enrique R. Carrasco and M. Ayhan Kose, Income Distribution and the Bretton Woods Institutions: Promoting an Enabling Environment for Social Development, 6 *Transnational Law and Contemporary Problems* 1, 45 (1996); and Sabine Schlemmer-Schulte, The World Bank's Experience with Its Inspection Panel, 58 *Zeitschrift für ausländisches öffentliches Recht und Völkerrecht (ZaöRV)—Heidelberg Journal of International Law* 354, 370 (1998).

affected. This outcome certainly was not the intention of the drafters of the Resolution, nor could it be based on an objective reading of its text.

4.   Operational Policies and Procedures

Operational policies and procedures are defined in the Resolution to include the policies and procedures described in the Bank's documents, such as Operational Policies (OPs), Bank Procedures (BPs), Operational Directives, (ODs) and earlier similar documents. The practice of the Bank has seen several series of operational statements as well as *ad hoc* circulars embodying its policies and procedures. These documents constitute instructions from the Bank Management to its staff and are separate from the policy papers submitted to the Board for approval. Approval of the latter papers is normally reflected in the Board's Minutes and does not take the form of resolutions, a form normally used when there is a need to present the Board's decisions to other parties.

Before the Bank's reorganization in 1987, its operational policies were contained mainly in Operational Manual Statements (OMSs) and Operations Policy Notes (OPNs). These were both issued, under the authority of the President, by the then existing office of the Senior Vice President, Operations, in the form of general instructions, supplemented occasionally by Operational Circulars or less formal notes from the Senior Vice President, Operations. Following the 1987 reorganization, OMSs were gradually reflected in new documents called "Operational Directives" or "ODs," some of which included changes from earlier OMSs and some of which were completely new. Unlike the OMSs and OPNs, which were not discussed in the Board,[33] a small number of ODs, because of the sensitivity or complexity of

---

33. An exception is Operational Manual Statement 2.32 (1985) (hereinafter "OMS") on *Projects on International Waterways,* which was drafted as the conclusion of a detailed paper approved by the Board. (This OMS was reissued later as OD 7.50 (1990) and now as OP/BP 7.50 (1994)). Most, but not all, OMSs reiterated policies previously approved by the Board.

their subject matter, were discussed in draft in Board seminars before their issuance by Management. These included the ODs on environmental assessment,[34] poverty,[35] and procedures for investment operations under the GEF.[36] Subsequent developments resulted in the Board's increased interest in discussing ODs before they were issued by Management.[37]

Problems in implementation led a number of Executive Directors to question whether the ODs were binding instruments. This writer, then General Counsel of the Bank, maintained that the ODs were Management's general instructions issued for staff guidance.[38] They should be consistent with the Bank's Articles of Agreement, as interpreted by the Board, and with Board-approved policies. They should be followed by staff within the limits of flexibility provided in the ODs themselves. Management is accountable to the Executive Directors for the consistency of the ODs with Board-approved policies, and the staff are accountable to Management for the observance of the ODs, with such latitude as their text might explicitly indicate. Management, as the issuer of these instructions, could amend them or, when necessary, allow deviation from them to the extent that such amendment or deviation did not violate the Bank's Articles of Agreement or any Board-approved policy.

Because the office of the Senior Vice President, Operations, no longer exists, the Bank's current procedure requires that deviation from the policy statements in force (OPs and the remaining

---

34. OD 4.00, Annex A (1989), replaced by OD 4.01 (1991), and ultimately replaced by OP 4.01 (1999).

35. OD 4.15 (1992).

36. OD 9.01 (1992). This draft OD was circulated to the Executive Directors and was later issued in the absence of a request for discussion.

37. In mid-1992, the Board agreed that, for papers with policy proposals that are considered difficult or controversial, "[i]n cases where the Board-approved policy covered sectors where Bank involvement was new or significantly altered, a follow-up Board seminar would be arranged at an appropriate time to discuss how Management had translated the policy into a new Operational Directive." *Report of the Ad-Hoc Committee on Board Procedures* (the Naim Report) (R92–103), May 28, 1992, approved June 23, 1992.

38. Each OD has a statement on its front page indicating that it was issued "for the guidance of the staff."

ODs) can only occur with the approval of the Office of the President, unless the statement itself allows exceptions to be made by the Regional Vice President, the Country Director, or another designated Bank official. When approval by the Office of the President is required, it is normally obtained from the Managing Director concerned, after consultation with the Vice President and General Counsel. Naturally, statements that reiterate Board-approved policies cannot be changed with respect to these policies before the Board approves such changes. The ODs and OPs discussed in draft by the Executive Directors before they were issued by Management have also acquired a certain status that suggests that deviation from them, when it does not violate a formally Board-approved policy, would still need prior consultation with, or subsequent approval by the Board. Such changes, if introduced without the Board's knowledge, can create tensions in the Board-Management relationship that ought to be avoided. Deviation from the ODs and OPs would, in any event, be brought to the attention of the Board at the time the Board considers a specific operation. Exceptions that are not authorized by the text of the OD or OP, however, must be kept to a minimum if these documents are to serve their purpose and if the Bank is to avoid undue differentiation among its borrowers. It is recognized that the ODs and OPs are not meant to be "marching orders" for a specific operation but general operational codes that are written to apply in different situations. They, therefore, allow for the differentiations and exceptions deemed acceptable at the time of their issuance, but they do not totally exclude other changes if procedures are properly followed.

Although not all the standards provided for in the OPs and their predecessor documents have been binding on the staff (it depends on the wording of each standard), the staff must exert their best efforts to achieve those stated in binding terms. Actual achievement of these standards may depend on the action of other parties, notably the potential borrower or borrower. In the latter case, the staff must make sure that the borrower's contractual obligations towards the Bank would require the borrower to achieve these binding standards, and the Bank should maintain serious follow-up to ensure the observance of such obligations. This important point and its implications will be dealt with in further detail in Chapters Four and Five.

Some ODs were seen to be at times too detailed or reflecting what should be sought and not necessarily what could be done in practice. The limits of flexibility in the application of the ODs were not always clear either, especially those written before their drafters were aware of the controversy regarding the nature of these documents. Differences on this issue and the desire of the Bank's Management to streamline and simplify the Bank's business practices led, after an informal discussion by the Executive Directors, to the Management's decision in late 1992 to gradually replace the ODs by OPs and BPs, which would be binding on the staff, as well as by Good Practices (GPs), which would disseminate knowledge and indicate successful examples without being binding. This is the process that came to be known in the Bank practice as *conversion*.

Under current procedures, policy papers submitted to the Board for approval that address difficult or controversial issues normally have the draft OP attached to them. The OP, issued after Board approval of the policy, would reflect the policy as agreed by the Board.

Although not all OMSs and OPNs have been converted to ODs, and not all ODs have been converted to OPs and BPs, the conversion process, at mid-1999, is near completion.[39] Because some earlier statements are yet to be converted and the earlier version of converted statements will apply, in any event, to the loans that were negotiated when these statements were in force (as explicitly stated in them), controversies may arise before the Panel on whether certain details in a specific OMS, OPN, or OD are provided as technical advice to the staff or are meant to be strictly complied with. This issue will require a careful reading of these documents in the context in which they were issued and in the light of their objective in guiding the staff's work. Obviously,

---

39. *See* Annexes II–1–1 to II–14 to this book, including OPs in force and listing ODs, OMSs and OPNs remaining in force.

it is to the benefit of all that this issue be settled for future projects by the conversion of the remaining OMSs, OPNs, and ODs to the new operational documents, the nature and role of which are much clearer to the Bank staff.

The Resolution establishing the Panel indicates that policy statements, Bank Procedures, and still-applicable ODs and similar documents (for example, the OMSs and OPNs) are operational policies and procedures. If they are violated, the Panel may receive complaints. It explicitly excludes, however, non-binding "Guidelines and Best Practices and similar documents or statements."[40] The current Good Practice series falls under these excluded documents.

A question may be raised with regard to Bank rules that are not reflected in the specific instruments mentioned in the textual definition of *operational policies and procedures*.[41] Practically all operational rules are reiterated in these instruments, however. If an operational rule incorporated in the Bank's Articles of Agreement or in the decisions of its Board is not mentioned in this list of documents, its violation would still be subject to the Panel's review, if the other applicable eligibility conditions are met.

---

40. *Resolution,* para. 12. The term *guidelines* may lead to some confusion, especially as certain Bank guidelines are meant to be binding, as is the case for the "Procurement Guidelines," which were in fact discussed on several occasions by the Bank's Board and are incorporated, by reference, in each loan agreement. (Procurement issues are excluded, however, from the scope of the Panel's work as will be explained in the text, *infra.*) To avoid this confusion, Management decided in late 1993 not to use the term *guidelines* in the operational circulars to be issued to staff. The term is still used, however, in the environment guidelines issued by the GEF Secretariat.

41. The first draft resolution on the Inspection Panel dated June 23, 1993, referred in its para. 12, to "operating *rules* and procedures." (Emphasis added.) A draft dated August 5, 1993, which was the first draft resolution discussed by the Executive Directors (in their Committee of the Whole meeting of August 26, 1993), referred in its para. 12 to "operating policies, rules, and procedures" and included the definition of that phrase as it now appears in the final text. The word *rules* was dropped, however, from the text formally presented to the Board, dated September 9, 1993, because it was suggested in internal Management discussion that it could lead to confusion and was not needed in view of the textual definition.

A recent attempt has been made by Management to present the Bank's operational policies in five categories: "Operational Strategies" (six OPs or ODs and three GPs); "Environmental, Social, and International Law Safeguards" (nine OPs and ODs and one OPN); "Fiduciary Requirements" (ten OPs and one OD); "Project Analysis and Review Requirements" (six OPs and one BP); and "Internal Processing Requirements" (fourteen OPs and six BPs).[42] In addition, the "business products" of the Bank are listed to include: "specific investment" loans, "sector investment and maintenance" loans, "financial intermediary" loans, "emergency recovery" loans, "technical assistance" loans, "structural adjustment" loans, "sector adjustment" loans, "rehabilitation" loans, "hybrid" loans (part adjustment, part investment), "debt and debt service reduction" loans, "learning and innovation" loans (small loans to finance pilot projects), "adaptable program" loans (a series of similar loans covering a sector or a subsector), "guarantees," and "country economic and sector work."[43]

None of the above categorizations has an impact on the work of the Inspection Panel. Whatever the Bank staff is *required* to follow under OPs, ODs, and the like falls within the purview of the Panel, with the exception of procurement matters. All the "business products" listed above, excepting adjustment loans and debt and debt service reduction loans, qualify as project loans according to current practice in the Bank.

It may be reasonable that guarantee operations (which involve Bank guarantee of private sector loans) be made subject to the same inspection function that would apply to the IFC and MIGA, the different procedures of which would be justified by the special needs of private sector operations.[44]

---

42. *World Bank Operational Policy Reform: Progress Report* (CODE98–13, March 5, 1998), Annex 2. The OPs/BPs/ODs most relevant to the work of the Panel appear in Annex II to this book.

43. *Id.*

44. Efforts to develop an inspection function suitable for private sector operations are discussed *infra* in Chapter Four, at 157 *seq.*

5.   Scope of the Bank's Failure—Extent of Staff Obligations under Bank Policies

Some of the Bank's policies, and especially its procedures, are addressed only to the Bank staff. Most Bank operational policies, however, describe the manner in which Bank-financed projects are to be prepared and implemented and thus pertain mainly to actions the Bank should seek from its borrowers. Some of these actions may be required before negotiation of the legal documents or before their presentation to the Board. Policies related to project *implementation* are normally reflected in covenants that appear in the loan agreement or in a project agreement attached to it. In some cases, detailed action plans are attached to these agreements detailing the borrower's obligations. Since the borrower, and not the Bank, implements the project, the Bank's failure would occur in such cases when it fails to reflect its operational policies in the actions required from the borrower or when, after reflecting them as required, it fails to properly supervise project implementation to ensure that the borrower abides by its contractual obligations. The harm to affected parties resulting from project implementation would, in the first instance, be attributed to those who implemented the project, even though there could be instances where the Bank had contributed to the harm by not strictly following its policies in the design or appraisal of the project, in the actions it requires from the borrower, or in the supervision of their implementation.

In all of these respects, if the Bank's binding policies or procedures relate exclusively to measures to be taken by Bank staff, a failure would take place if the staff fail to take such measures as envisaged, unless, of course, there were exceptions allowed under the policies and procedures that were properly followed. If, on the other hand, the policies related to potential measures to be taken by the borrower, as is often the case under Bank operational policies (for example, the preparation and implementation of environmental assessment reports or resettlement plans), the staff responsibility would be limited to seeing to it that the borrower's obligations were clearly provided for, the plans expected from the borrower were drawn up in time (as defined in Bank policies), and such obligations and plans were then carried out by the borrower as agreed. Clearly, the obligation of the staff with respect to actions to be taken by the borrower is not to guarantee that the intended outcome will materialize in each case, but to make their best effort, with the due diligence required under the Staff Rules, to ensure that the borrower will indeed carry out its obligations. To quote a French legal expression, this is an *"obligation de moyens"* and not an *"obligation de résultat."*

An illustration may further clarify this point. The Bank's OD 4.30 on involuntary resettlement[45] requires that such resettlement should be avoided or minimized. Where displacement of people is inevitable in the context of a specific project, however, displaced people will be (i) compensated for their losses at full replacement cost; (ii) assisted with the move and supported during the transition period; and (iii) assisted in their efforts to improve their former living standards, income earning capacity, and production levels—or at least helped to restore these levels. These requirements do not mean that the Bank is under the obligation to directly provide compensation to displaced persons, assist in their move, or assist in their efforts to improve or at least restore their living standards. They mean that the Bank must ensure that the *borrowers* meet these requirements in Bank-financed projects *through covenants in the loan agreement* and an *adequate resettlement plan.* Bank failure can not in such cases be judged by whether some displaced persons have not been properly compensated (that is, by harm in the abstract). It should be judged by whether the Bank has provided for these requirements in the loan agreement and has exercised adequate supervision of their implementation, including, if the Bank deems it appropriate under the circumstances, suspension and cancellation of the loan in case of serious violations. The latter sanctions are discretionary, however, and the Bank's preference not to resort to them for objective reasons cannot by itself be considered a failure to

---

45. OD 4.30, issued June 1990, at para. 3(a) and (b), recently "converted" to OP/BP 4.12.

observe Bank policy. Concern with the harm regardless of Bank compliance blurs the distinction between the Bank's actions and omissions, the subject-matter of the Panel's mandate, and the actions and omissions of other parties (such as the borrower) that the Resolution explicitly excludes from that mandate.

In order, therefore, to attribute to the Bank an existing or potential harm associated with a project, it is not enough to prove that the project is being or will be financed by the Bank. The harm must result, in whole or in part, from the Bank's own failure—either in accepting the project design, in appraising the project, or in the supervision of its implementation. Without this clear distinction and the causality related to it, a confusion between the Bank's failure and the borrower's failure would always lead to divisive and possibly counterproductive discussions on the inspection function as perceived in the Resolution.

In the conclusions of the second review of the inspection function, adopted by the Board on April 20, 1999, and discussed later in Chapter Four, it was further explained that the material adverse effect of the Bank's violation would not be assessed in the abstract or in relation to the project goals but in comparison with the situation before the project existed.

6.   Preliminary Requirements Regarding the Subject-Matter

Not every departure by the Bank from the binding statements on its policies and procedures is subject to the Panel's jurisdiction. In fact, three conditions must be *prima facie* evident for such failure to be considered by the Panel:

> 1. The subject matter of the request for inspection must have been submitted earlier to the Bank's Management, and Management must have failed to demonstrate that it had either followed the Bank's policies and procedures or at least taken adequate steps to that end.[46]

---

46. *Resolution,* para. 12.

2. The alleged failure on the part of the Bank should have had, or should threaten to have, a material adverse effect.[47]
3. The alleged violation of the Bank's policies and procedures must, if established, be, in the judgment of the Panel, of serious character.[48]

Clearly, the Panel is not required in the first stage of ascertaining eligibility to see to it that the last two conditions are *definitely* met. If it did, there would hardly be a need for further investigation.

At this early stage, the Panel is not expected to investigate Management's actions in depth. It will only ascertain, (i) whether the requesting party had first sought remedies from Management and, if that was the case, whether the latter's reply had convincingly disposed of the matter, (ii) whether there is *prima facie* evidence that the party submitting the request *has suffered,* or is threatened to suffer a material harm resulting from Bank failures, and (iii) whether the seemingly material harm could reasonably be related to what seems to be a serious violation of Bank policies and procedures applicable to the design, appraisal, or implementation of the project involved. Assuming other conditions are met, the Panel's recommendation that an inspection is warranted will depend on the answers it reaches to these preliminary questions.

Except for the reference to the "harm suffered by or threatened to" the affected party, no criteria are provided in the Resolution for the materiality of the adverse effect or the seriousness of the violation, which means that the Panel will have to exert its judgment on these matters (when it decides on whether to recommend an investigation), subject to possible Board review (when it considers the Panel's recommendation).

A mere admission by Management that the Bank's policies or procedures were not followed in the design, appraisal, or implementation of a project is not likely to obviate the need for

---

47. *Id.*
48. *Id.,* para. 13.

inspection, because the Panel may still find it appropriate to explore the dimensions of such a failure and the extent of the harm resulting from it, if any. If such an admission is made, it has to be accompanied by a statement of the remedial steps Management will take to correct its own failures. Under these circumstances, the Panel, if satisfied with Management's answers, may find no need for inspection. However, if the Panel considers proposed Management actions to be inadequate, or, when new complaints arise with respect to the manner in which such actions are being implemented, the Panel may still recommend investigation.

7.   Barred Complaints

In addition to these requirements, four types of requests for inspection are specifically barred by the Resolution.

The first is only a logical exclusion. Since the main purpose of inspection is to allow for an objective evaluation that would open the way for corrective action by the Bank if such action proves necessary or desirable, *the scope of the Panel's coverage is limited to matters that involve actions or omissions by the Bank, not those that are the responsibility of other parties, such as the borrower or potential borrower.*[49]

Another logical exclusion relates to *matters over which the Panel has already made recommendations on the occasion of earlier requests,* unless, of course, new evidence or circumstances not known at the time of consideration of the earlier request by the Panel justify a new review.[50] (This would not be unlike the revision procedure in judicial proceedings that is allowed only if new evidence not known by the court at the time it issued its decision is presented.)

A third exclusion concerns *time-barred complaints (that is, those filed after the closing date of the loan that finances the project*

---

49. *Resolution,* para. 14(a). For elaboration on this point, *see* Chapter Four, *infra,* at 176 *seq.*

50. *Id.,* para. 14(d).

involved).[51] Such a closing date is specified in each loan agreement but is extendable by the Bank. In fact, this exclusion also covers the situation where the loan has been substantially disbursed. To avoid disputes over the meaning of such substantial disbursement, the Resolution provides, in a note to paragraph 14(c), that a loan will be deemed to have reached that stage "when at least 95 percent of the loan proceeds have been disbursed."[52] This means that the Panel's jurisdiction extends to projects where the Bank's involvement predates the Resolution so long as disbursement of the Bank's loan has not exceeded 95 percent of the loan proceeds. (Technically, this does not mean that the Resolution has a retroactive effect; it only emphasizes its immediate effect, up to a certain point in the future of each loan.) As will be shown in Chapter Three, this precise requirement has nevertheless invoked a controversy in the context of a specific case submitted to the Panel.[53]

The fourth and last exclusion relates to complaints against Bank borrowers *with respect to the procurement of goods and*

---

51. *Id.,* para. 14(c). The *closing date* is defined as "the date specified in the loan agreement on which the Bank may terminate, by notice to the borrower, the right of the borrower to withdraw funds from the loan account." *See* OD 13.30 *Closing Dates* (April 1989).

52. Interestingly, the August 5 draft of the Resolution introduced the time exclusion in a much more liberal fashion to include "complaints filed two years or more after the Closing Date of the loan financing the project with respect to which the complaint is filed." Objections to this language were voiced by Executive Directors during the meeting of the Board's Committee of the Whole on August 26 on the ground that it extends the Panel's review over matters falling within the purview of the Bank's Operations Evaluation Department (OED); *see* Chapter One, *supra,* at Sections III(c) and VI. The September 9 draft resolution simply excluded "requests filed after the Closing Date of the loan financing the project with respect to which the request is filed." The addition "or after the loan financing the project has been substantially disbursed" was inserted during the Board discussion on September 21, 1993. It was originally suggested that a loan would be substantially disbursed if 75 percent of its proceeds were paid by the Bank. Other proposals were made by Executive Directors for higher percentages on the wrong assumption that this would further limit the scope of projects under inspection. The controversy over the definition resulted in agreement to provide for the 95 percent requirement, but in an explanatory note to the relevant provision in the Resolution.

53. *See infra,* at 127–129.

services financed by Bank loans, including those from losing ten-
ders (paragraph 14(b)). The reference in the text is to actions of
the Bank *borrowers*. However, loan agreements require the Bank's
consent before the award by the borrower of large contracts (as
these are defined in the loan documents), and the Bank has definite policies in the procurement of goods and services funded by
its loans (which, *inter alia*, mandate international competitive bidding as a general rule, subject to a number of exceptions). The
intention was to exclude procurement matters whether the complaint is against action by a borrower or by the Bank. As explained
during the Board discussion of September 21, 1993, where the
matter became the subject of a lengthy debate, procurement disputes are different in nature from the typical issues that justified
the establishment of the Panel. They also often involve suppliers
from countries other than the borrowing country. More important, the number and frequency of such complaints could cause a
major disorientation of the Panel's work. Mechanisms to deal with
procurement-related disputes are in place and have worked rather
well. For these reasons, the Resolution should be read to exclude
not only "complaints against procurement decisions by Bank borrowers," but also "complaints from losing tenderers," even if
those were addressed against the Bank. This point was explained
in detail during the discussion of the draft Resolution by the
Executive Directors, who accepted this broad exclusion on practical grounds. A literal reading of the text of paragraph 14(b) of the
Resolution could suggest, however, that the exclusion is limited in
all cases to complaints against procurement decisions of Bank borrowers and does not apply to any decision by the Bank or its staff
with respect to procurement. Such a literal reading would render
the text of paragraph 14(b) of the Resolution superfluous, as it
would be a mere repetition of the exclusion in paragraph 14(a).[54]

---

54. The reason the text of paragraph 14(b) of the *Resolution* refers only to
"decisions by Bank borrowers" is that the Bank maintains that all procurement
decisions are taken by borrowers, even if the Bank's consent is required before
such decisions are made. *See* para. 12 of the Management report referred to in
supra note 5: "Since procurement decisions are the responsibility of the borrower, procurement related disputes, which are subject to separate review procedures in the Bank, are excluded."

The broader meaning expressed in the above terms in the first edition of this book was confirmed by the Bank's Board during its first review of the Resolution in 1996, as will be shown in the following chapter.[55]

Finally, the scope of the Panel's mandate is generally delimited by its nature and purpose. Although this is not specifically mentioned in the Resolution, it is inherent in any institutional function. It was also clear in the discussion which preceded the Resolution[56] and found expression in the following paragraph of the Management report that introduced the final text of the draft resolution to the Board:

> The purpose of the Inspection Panel is to carry out independent administrative reviews, not to conduct judicial proceedings. It would collect information on matters complained of, provide an independent assessment and make recommendations to the President and the Executive Directors. It would not have power of decision. . . . [n]or would it be within the purview of the Panel to make recommendations on the adequacy or suitability of existing policies and procedures.[57]

---

55. *See infra,* at 172.

56. Other exclusions appeared in earlier drafts of the *Resolution,* but were dropped in the final text. These included, in the first draft of June 23, 1993, "complaints from staff members and former staff members of the Bank with respect to which the Bank's Appeals Committee or Administrative Tribunal has jurisdiction" and "complaints with respect to projects for which the Bank under its normal procedure has no responsibility because the loan has been fully repaid." Another exclusion also appeared in the internal draft of July 20, 1993, with respect to "issues concerning compliance by Bank staff with the Bank's financial policies, which will continue to be addressed by the Internal Auditing Department." It was pointed out in internal Management discussions that such exclusions were too obvious to require explicit provisions. It may be argued, however, that while a project for which the loan is fully repaid does not invoke obligations on the part of the borrower, it may still invoke Bank's accountability for its failure. It should be noted, nonetheless, that full repayment by definition takes place after the loan is entirely disbursed, a fact that bars inspection under the *Resolution.*

57. *See supra* note 5, para. 8. Panel recommendations according to the final text of the *Resolution* are to be made only to the Board. *See also* Chapter Five, Section I(B), *infra.*

The fact-finding, evaluative nature of the Panel's work was re-emphasized in the conclusions of the Board's second review of the inspection function, as detailed in Chapter Four.

III. Eligibility of the Party Requesting Inspection

In addition to the requirements elaborated in the previous section related both to the type of requests to be submitted to the Panel, which constitute its jurisdiction *ratione materiae,* and the time limit on the projects to which such requests may be related, which constitutes the Panel's jurisdiction *ratione temporis,* the Resolution specifies also in detail the eligibility requirements of the persons authorized to submit such requests (that is, the Panel's jurisdiction *ratione personae*).[58] The latter requirements were, in fact, subject to a number of changes in the successive drafts of the Resolution as well as to considerable discussion in the meetings of the Board's Committee of the Whole on August 26–27, 1993, and in the Board's meetings of September 21–22, 1993. The main issue underlying these discussions was limiting the scope of inspection to serious cases in order to avoid too much disruption in the Bank's work.

The Resolution makes it clear that a request for inspection has to be submitted by "an affected party in the territory of the borrower which is not a single individual," or the representative of such party, or by an Executive Director of the Bank. (It can of course always be made by the Board of Executive Directors itself.) Although eligibility of requests by an Executive Director was subject to a lengthy debate in the discussion leading to the adoption of the Resolution (as will be discussed in detail), the requirement of "affected party" appeared in all earlier drafts, with differences in details regarding whether such party should be in the territory of the borrower, could be an individual, or could have representation from outside its country.

---

58. *See Resolution,* para. 12.

A.   Meaning of "Affected Party"

The term *affected party* is defined in the Resolution in two respects: First, "the affected party must demonstrate that its *rights or interests* have been or are likely to be *directly affected* by an action or omission of the Bank."[59] However, not any effect will qualify for this purpose. Whether actually suffered or merely threatened, such an effect, as already mentioned, must, according to the Resolution, be a "material adverse effect."[60] Second, the action or omission by the Bank which gave, or will give, rise to such material adverse effect must represent a failure of the Bank to follow its operational policies and procedures,[61] a failure deemed to be of a "serious character."[62] To put it in simpler words, an affected party for the purpose of the Resolution is *a party whose rights or interests have been or are likely to be directly and adversely affected in a material way as a result of a serious violation by the Bank of its operational policies and procedures with respect to the preparation, appraisal, or implementation of projects.*

1.   Rights and Interests

The terms *rights* and *interests* should be given their usual legal meanings. Limiting requests to these submitted by parties whose

---

59. *Id.* (emphasis added). This requirement was introduced in the September 9, 1993, draft Resolution in response to queries by Executive Directors in the Committee of the Whole discussion of August 26, 1993, regarding the meaning of the expression *affected party*.

60. *Resolution*, para. 12.

61. *Id.*

62. *Id.*, para. 13. *Compare* Article 173, para. 4 of the EEC Treaty and the "settled case law" of the European Court of Justice where *locus standi* in the judicial review of financing decisions by EC organs is limited to a person affected in a manner that differentiates him/it from all other persons and that the existence of harm suffered or to be suffered is not in itself sufficient to confer *locus standi* because such harm may affect, in a general abstract way, a large number of persons who could not be determined in advance in such a way as to distinguish them from individually concerned persons. *See Greenpeace and Others v. Commission*, Case T-585/93, Court of First Instance, [1995] ECR II–2205, upheld in appeal by the European Court of Justice, Case C–321/95 P, 1988 WL 171598 (CEA 1998).

rights or interests have been actually violated or threatened is clearly meant to exclude requests based on an alleged public interest in which the requester has no personal stake. The combination of rights and interests is meant to broaden the scope of coverage, however, so as to include not only titles, powers, and privileges protected by law but also substantiated claims to such titles, powers, and privileges and the avoidance of harm (in the sense of bodily injury or financial loss) that otherwise may affect the requester. Alleged rights by an affected party have to be based on the law applicable in the territory where the alleged harm has taken place, including treaties incorporated in that law to the extent that they directly extend rights to private parties. Affected rights could be rights *in rem*, such as property rights of persons who have to be resettled as a result of a Bank-financed project, or rights *in personam* that impose obligations on a specific person or persons that could be interrupted by measures taken in the implementation of a project. Although loan agreements between the Bank and its borrowers do not create rights in the legal sense to third parties (such as persons affected by the project) *vis-à-vis* the Bank,[63] they may create interests (in the ordinary meaning of the word and not necessarily as a basis of legal claims) that they may invoke against the borrower. This is illustrated, for instance, in possible third parties' interest in the proper application by the borrower of the protective measures agreed upon in the loan documents, whose violation could create harm to such parties. Violation of those interests would normally be invoked *vis-à-vis* a Bank borrower, not the Bank. They would, however, justify a request for inspection by the Panel only if they have allegedly resulted from a serious non-compliance by the Bank with its policies, provided of course that other eligibility conditions are met.

2.   *Conditions to Be Ascertained on a* prima facie *Basis*

As eligibility has to be established before investigation takes place, these requirements suggest that the Panel should assure

---

63. For details, *see* Chapter Five, Section II, *infra*.

itself at this early stage: (i) that the affected party must be a party that *claims, with reasonable evidence,* that it has suffered or may suffer material damage, and (ii) that such alleged damage *could reasonably have resulted* from the alleged policy violation by the Bank. The materiality of the alleged damage is left for the Panel to determine when it recommends whether an investigation should be carried out. It is noteworthy that the Resolution used in this respect the term *affected party,* not the term *interested party,* which was used in a separate document on information disclosure policy prepared for the Board at the same time.[64] In that document, *interested party* was meant to cover more broadly any party that expressed interest. This is clearly not the meaning of *affected party* in the Resolution establishing the Inspection Panel. The Resolution further provides that the affected party must state in its request "the harm suffered by or threatened to such party."[65] Clearly, such party cannot simply be an entity claiming it acts on behalf of the public, without any specific harm being suffered or threatened to be suffered by it. The burden of proof that a material damage has been, or is likely to be suffered, falls initially on the affected party. So is the proof that a causal link exists between the Bank's alleged failure to follow its policies and procedures and such material damage. The Panel need not, however, examine such point in depth at this stage; it must only be assured of its seriousness. In other words, the Panel, in making its recommendation on whether to investigate, is not supposed to act as a court of law determining with judicial finality the existence of the damage, its extent, and the causality between it and the Bank's actions or omissions. It must only be reasonably satisfied that such elements are met on a *prima facie* basis before it recommends an investigation. The Panel is supposed to find out at this first stage whether an investigation is warranted, not to carry out the investigation. Failing to see that distinction could result in collapsing the two stages

---

64. (SecM93–927), August 31, 1993; *see also* BP 17.50 on *Disclosure of Operational Information* (1993), issued after the adoption of the Bank's new policy on this matter.

65. *Resolution,* para. 16.

envisaged in the Resolution into one and negating the Board's role to authorize investigation.[66]

3.   *Requester to Be a Community of Persons*

The Resolution further provides that the affected party *must not be a single individual.* Such a requirement was absent in the drafts preceding the Board's Committee of the Whole meeting of August 26, 1993. In fact, such earlier drafts consistently referred to complaints by a "person or persons directly affected." The change resulted from a comment by an Executive Director during the August discussion. Referring to the experience of the national aid agency of his country, he indicated that allowing individuals to make complaints could open the door to frequent, frivolous requests causing unwarranted disruption. The point was met with general support for limiting requests to those made by a "community of persons." The expectation was that if adverse effects were to take place, they would not likely be confined to one person. The resolution provides as examples

---

66. *Compare* paras. 34–35 on *"Preliminary Review"* and para. 36 on *"Initial Study"* of the *"Operating Procedures"* adopted by the Inspection Panel on August 19, 1994. Under the assumption that the Panel must, before it is authorized to investigate, firmly establish that (i) Bank failure exists and has had or threatens to have a material adverse effect, (ii) that failure represents a serious violation of Bank policies or procedures, and (iii) Management's response does not appear adequate to meet the requester's concerns, the "Operating Procedures" provide for the Panel's undertaking a *preliminary review* complemented if need be by an *initial study*, in order to determine whether these three conditions are met even though they provide that the Panel "may not investigate Management's actions in depth at this stage." This provision, which is to apply if the Panel is satisfied that "Management has failed to demonstrate that it has followed, or is taking adequate steps to follow the Bank's policies and procedures," may not leave room for new findings if the actual investigation is authorized by the Board. It has nonetheless been encouraged by the Board's request in a number of cases for an *additional review* by the Panel when the decision to authorize investigation was difficult to reach. *See* Chapter Three, *infra.* The practice was later confirmed in the 1996 Clarifications issued by the Board, as explained in Chapter Four, *infra,* but it was seriously questioned and reversed during the second review of the Panel's experience, as will be explained in that chapter.

requests by "an organization, association, society, or other grouping of individuals."[67]

The "Operating Procedures" issued by the Panel in August 1994[68] suggested, however, that "any group of two or more people . . . who believe that as a result of the Bank's violation their rights or interests have been or are likely to be adversely affected in a direct and material way" may submit a request for inspection.[69] This was also the view of some commentators.[70] It was not, however, the intended meaning, nor is it the objective meaning of the words. A *community of persons* in the ordinary sense is a group of people whose members are connected to each other by means of personal or professional ties, "a discursive network" to use the description of an acclaimed sociologist.[71] In the context of the Resolution, it clearly assumes the sharing of some common interests or concerns that prompts its members to act as a community. Such a sense of community need not precede the events that led to the request for inspection; it may result from the sharing in the alleged harm that causes affected parties to act together as a community of persons.[72]

This matter was addressed in the legal opinion issued by this author to the Bank's Board on the occasion of the first request for inspection received by the Panel.[73] That opinion made it clear

---

67. *Id.*, para. 12.

68. *See Operating Procedures,* Annex I–1–2 of this book at para. A4.(a).

69. *See* Inspection Panel, *Operating Procedures* dated August 19, 1994, and reprinted as Annex I–1–2 to this book.

70. *See* Kathigamar Nathan, The World Bank Inspection Panel—Court or Quango, 12 *J. Int'l. Arb.* 135, 141 (1995); Daniel D. Bradlow, A Test Case for the World Bank, 11 *American University Journal of International Law and Public Policy* 247, 261 (1996).

71. Günther Tuebner (ed.), *Global Law Without a State,* 7 (1997).

72. *Compare* the case law of European Community courts, where it had consistently been held that "an association formed for the protection of the collective interests of a category of persons could not be considered to be directly and individually concerned for the purposes of the fourth paragraph of Article 173 of the [EEC] Treaty, by a measure affecting the general interests of that category." *Greenpeace and Others v. the Community, supra* note 62, at para. 14.

73. *See Role of the Inspection Panel in the Preliminary Assessment of Whether to Recommend Inspection,* Legal Opinion of the Senior Vice President and General Counsel, January 3, 1995 (SecM95–11, January 3, 1995). Also published as Annex I–4 of this book.

that the intention of the Resolution, as well as its explicit language, requires eligible complaints to be submitted by a "community of persons," not just any two or more individuals. Requests submitted individually by two or more persons, each acting in his own single capacity, without any common link between them, will not meet that requirement. Although a group of individuals need *not* have a juridical personality in order to qualify as a "community of persons," it has to be a group that shares a commonality of interests that prompt them to act together in submitting the request. The Board endorsed the meaning of the language of the Resolution articulated in the legal opinion, including the point on the affected party.[74] As will be explained in the following chapters, the Board's understanding of this term was further confirmed on the occasion of the first review of the Resolution and reiterated in the conclusions of the second review.[75]

4.   Requester to Be in the Territory of the Borrower

The Resolution describes the affected party as a party "*in the territory of the borrower.*" This requirement was intentionally introduced in the Board discussion of September 21, 1993, to exclude requests by advocacy groups and other interested parties outside the borrowing country. Attempts to lift that requirement and allow foreign NGOs to present claims to the Panel were made during the first review of the Resolution, but without success.[76] Although it is not explicitly mentioned, it is implied that the affected party cannot be the borrower itself. Bank loan agreements (the General Conditions) provide that disputes arising under them between the Bank and the borrower are to be settled by negotiation and, failing this, by arbitration. If the borrower is not the government, the latter is required, in the case of IBRD

---

74. Minutes of the Meeting of the Executive Directors of the Bank and IDA held on February 2, 1995 (XM95-1), February 10, 1995, at para. 5.

75. *See Clarifications,* para. 4 (a) Annex 1–2, and *Conclusions,* para. 9 (a) Annex I–3, of this book.

76. *See* Chapter Four, *infra,* at 166–169.

loans, to act as the guarantor. Disputes arising under guarantee agreements are also to be settled by negotiation and arbitration. (In practice, disputes between the Bank, on the one hand, and borrowers and guarantors, on the other hand, have always been resolved through negotiation.) Reference to affected parties in the Resolution should therefore be read as a reference to groups of people with common interests and concerns (whether or not they act as a corporate body or otherwise have a juridical personality as a group) whose rights or interests are specifically affected in a negative way by the alleged violation. Such groups must have a real presence in the territory of the borrower, which, in the case of associations and other incorporated entities, would normally mean that they should have substantive activities in such a territory. Typically, though not necessarily, they would be in the specific area of the project financed or to be financed by the Bank loan. If the corporation does not have real activities in the country where the alleged harm has taken place, other criteria such as incorporation in that country or registering an office there just for the purpose of submitting a request should not be relevant. The idea is to limit the process to requesters who are genuinely in the territory of the borrower. To argue otherwise would deprive this requirement of any practical value.

5.   *Anonymous Requests*

The many eligibility issues the Panel has to examine in the initial stage, especially the issue of the material harm, require that those who request inspection be known to the Panel. If Management is to give a complete response to the request it may also need to know who is alleging to have been affected and it certainly should know in which way the alleged effect has resulted from the Bank's serious violation of its operational policies or procedures. In other words, under the circumstances of a specific case, the requesters' identity should be known to Management. This simple proposition was contested in practice, however, with some apparent confusion between the concepts of anonymity and confidentiality.

In the *Arun III* case, Nepal, the request was submitted by an NGO on behalf of the affected group, including two persons who asked that their names remain anonymous. The Panel's recommendation to investigate refers to this inaccurately in terms of "two requesters [asking] for anonymity." The request by the NGO was valid, however, as it would have been even if the authorization to the NGO had been signed only by those using their names. Management did not raise the issue in its response. In the *Yacyretá* case, Argentina/Paraguay, the request was submitted by an NGO and a number of individuals. It included letters from the allegedly affected individuals authorizing the NGO to act on their behalf, but asking that their names be kept strictly confidential. The Panel's report to the Board suggested that the Panel obtained first-hand knowledge on the harm suffered by the anonymous requesters during the field visit. Earlier on, Management's response to the request indicated that "such an anonymity imposes serious constraints on Management's ability to respond fully to the request." Clearly, the requesters' concern was that their names remain undisclosed to their government. This is a question of confidentiality. Whether the requesters' names could have been given by the Panel to Management on the basis of confidentiality is a different matter that will be discussed further. In the *NTPC* case, India, the Panel correctly used the term *confidentiality* for the requesters' demand that "their names be made available only to the Panel members, but otherwise remain confidential." Neither Management nor the Board took issue with that particular demand. In the *Highland Water Project*, Lesotho/South Africa, the request was submitted in the name of residents of a township in South Africa with the statement that the "community resolved to file the claim anonymously." Although this may sound as if it were the first truly anonymous request, the Panel's report to the Board, which recommended on other grounds that no inspection be carried out, stated, that "[t]he requesters asked that their names be made available only to the Panel members but otherwise remain confidential." Management questioned if they were acting on behalf of the community or in their individual capacities. In both this case and in the *Yacyretá* case, however, requests for confidentiality were somehow deemed to make the requests anonymous (that is, nameless, which does not seem accurate to this writer).

It is clear that eligibility of a request for inspection cannot be established if the requester is truly anonymous (that is, if the Panel knows nothing about its name and identity).[77] Whether the Panel discloses the names of requesters against their wishes is another matter. The circumstances of the request should determine if it is necessary to disclose such names to Bank Management for preparation of an adequate response. If this is the case, the requesters should be informed by the Panel and, with their agreement, their names will be kept confidential by both the Panel and Management. If the requesters refuse to allow disclosure within these limits and circumstances, Management would not be in a position to give a useful response or otherwise address the alleged harm. The Panel should decide under the circumstances whether there is a basis for it to take any further action.[78]

B.   *Representation of the Affected Party*

No reference was made in the drafts preceding the Board's Committee of the Whole discussion of August 26, 1993, to representation of the affected party in the submission of requests to the Panel. The debate in the Committee of the Whole on whether an affected party may have a foreign representative (for example, a Washington-based law firm or NGO) revealed a difference of views between some Executive Directors representing

---

77. This is confirmed in para. 22(e) of the *Operating Procedures* issued by the Panel, which excludes, among other types, "requests that are manifestly frivolous, absent, or anonymous." *See* Annex I–1–2.

78. *Compare* para. 18(b) of the Panel's *Operating Procedures, id.,* which requires that the notice of registration "will include the name of the project, the country where the project is located, the name of the requester unless anonymity is requested, and a brief description of the request." Clearly, the word *anonymity* here means *confidentiality,* otherwise there would be clear contradiction with para. 22 cited in the previous note.

developed countries who favored such foreign representation and borrowing countries' Directors who opposed it. The September 9, 1993, draft resolution provided for the principle of representation but left open whether such representation would be local or foreign.[79] The issue was obviously of great importance to the concerned NGOs in developed countries that wanted to be in a position to represent affected parties in borrowing countries who, in the judgment of these NGOs, may not always be able to present their case against the Bank. It was also an important issue for some of the governments of borrowing countries, which feared intervention of foreign parties in the relationship between these governments and their citizens and the increased politicization and internationalization of their domestic issues. Board discussion led to agreement on a compromise solution whereby a foreign representative may be allowed to act on behalf of an affected party "in the exceptional cases where the party submitting the request contends that appropriate representation is not locally available and the Executive Directors agree with this contention at the time they consider the request for inspection."[80] The requirement of Board approval of such foreign representation was meant to assure those who feared abuse of this arrangement that the Board remained the final arbiter on whether the situation justified it. The text clearly excludes complaints by external NGOs acting on their own, and the Board discussions that preceded its adoption confirm this point beyond doubt. Eligible complaints would have to originate with the affected party, which, as the concerned principal, could act on its own or through an agent

---

79. The September 9, 1993, draft provided for requests by "a party other than a single individual . . . or its representative [in the territory of the borrower]." The bracketed words, which appeared as such in that draft, were meant to introduce the concept of foreign representation for further discussion in the Board meeting of September 21, 1993. They indicated that the Bank's Management was not averse to such representation.

80. *Resolution*, para. 12. The occasion of non-local representation of a requester has arisen recently for the first time. The sixteenth request before the Panel was submitted by a U.S. NGO on behalf of allegedly affected people living in the area where a project to be financed by IBRD and IDA is to be implemented.

appointed by it. Such a representative, according to the Resolution, "shall present to the Panel written evidence that he is acting as agent of the party on behalf of which the request is made."[81]

C.   Requests by Individual Executive Directors

The earliest draft resolution, dated June 23, 1993, included two alternative possibilities: Under the first option, complaints could be presented "by an Executive Director [of the Bank] or by a person or persons directly affected by an action or omission of the Bank." Under the second, complaints could be presented "by a person or persons directly affected by a Bank action or omission or by an Executive Director on behalf of such a person or group."[82] The difference between the two alternatives was clear—under the second option the Executive Director who submits the request would be acting only as the agent or representative of the affected party. These two formula were replaced by the following language in the internal draft of July 20, 1994: "The Panel shall hear complaints presented to it by an Executive Director or a group of Executive Directors or by a person or persons directly affected [. . .]."[83] Following discussion within the Bank's Management and with individual Executive Directors, the draft dated August 5, 1993, which was later discussed in the Board's Committee of the Whole, spoke, instead, of requests "by a group of four or more Executive Directors or by a person or persons directly affected" provided that the requests by an affected party would, from the beginning, be "subject to approval by the Executive Directors."[84] The Panel was authorized to investigate a request made by four or more Executive Directors without having to go back to the Board for approval of the investigation. If in the opinion of the Panel the complaint failed to meet the eligibility criteria *ratione materiae* or *ratione*

---

81. *Id.*
82. Para. 12 of draft resolution dated June 23, 1993 (limited circulation).
83. July 20, 1993, draft, para. 12 (limited circulation).
84. August 5, 1993, draft, para. 11 (limited circulation).

temporis, however, the Panel would decline to investigate unless the Board, as such, decided that the complaint ought to be investigated.[85] These provisions were questioned by many Executive Directors during the meeting of the Board's Committee of the Whole of August 26, 1993, who pointed out that the requirement of four Directors was excessive. As a result, the revised text submitted to the Board meeting (draft dated September 9, 1993) mentioned that, "[s]ubject to approval by the Executive Directors, the Panel shall hear requests for inspection presented by *any* Executive Director or by a party other than a single individual or its representative [in the territory of the borrower]."[86] Although this provision reflected earlier discussion by the Executive Directors in August 1993, it aroused the greatest controversy in the Board meetings of September 21–22, 1993.

Some Directors objected strongly to allowing any Executive Director to present requests to the Panel, fearing that the Directors' offices would become conduits for frequent submissions of complaints by their respective national NGOs, which would not otherwise be eligible to submit requests. Opponents against the lodging of requests by individual Executive Directors gave several reasons. Executive Directors, it was argued, should go through Management if they felt there was cause for an investigation; direct access to the Panel by individual Directors could only lead to politicization of the inspection process; this avenue would open wide the door for outside pressure on the Directors' offices; it would put the Executive Directors on the same level as outsiders although they are part of the institution and have other means for ascertaining facts relevant to their work; if the requests were to be made on behalf of affected parties, the Executive Director could help affected parties in his constituency make such a request directly in their names; getting an Executive Director involved in complaints against the Bank could create a conflict of interest for Executive Directors and could cause problems with

---

85. *Id.*, para. 18.
86. Draft dated September 9, 1993, para. 12 (emphasis added).

their authorities; and, finally, such access would unreasonably increase the Directors' workload.

To counter these arguments, a case was also made for allowing individual Executive Directors direct access to the Panel. Some Directors argued that this was an inherent power of each Director, that it would be inconsistent with Bank and Board policies and practice to deprive an Executive Director of this power, and that such a deprivation would result in the inability of Directors to meet their responsibilities under the Articles of Agreement. It was also noted that if requests were limited to affected parties in the borrowing countries, access to the Panel might become unduly limited because most of the requests were expected to originate with NGOs in developed countries!

Further arguments arose as to whether Executive Directors, as officials of the Bank, could act as agents or representatives of the complainants before the Panel and whether the right of an Executive Director to access Bank facilities, including the projected Panel, could be hindered by the simple fact that it was not mentioned in the Resolution.[87] By the end of the first day of discussion in the Board (September 21, 1993), no agreement could be reached on the right of individual Executive Directors to submit requests to the Panel. A large number of Directors seemed to have been against allowing for such a right, however. (The requirement that such access was subject, in the draft text, to Board approval seemed to have been lost in the debate; when it was mentioned, it was strongly objected to by those who favored the Directors' unhindered access to the Panel.)

When the Board met on the following day, it had before it a revised draft of the Resolution, with three different options for the relevant paragraph (paragraph 12), prepared by the

---

87. This author, then General Counsel of the Bank, took the position before the Board that Executive Directors are expected to act as principals, not as agents to complainants, and that if it was agreed to give them individually the right to present complaints, this should be provided for in the Resolution to avoid future differences over that matter.

General Counsel in an attempt to assist the Board in resolving the controversy.[88] Option A provided access to the affected party, his local representative, or another representative in exceptional cases, but added that: "[i]n view of the institutional interest of Executive Directors in the observance by the Bank of its operational policies and procedures, any Executive Director also may ask the Panel for an investigation of an alleged violation of such policies and procedures, subject to the requirements of paragraphs 13 and 14." Option B was identical to Option A, except for the sentence quoted above on requests by any Executive Director, which did not appear in Option B. Option C allowed an individual Executive Director to submit *to the Board* a request that a certain alleged violation of the Bank's operational policies and procedures be investigated by the Panel, with the addition that, if the Board agreed to this request, the Panel could proceed with the investigation without having to seek another Board approval of the investigation.

Option C attracted some of the Executive Directors who had previously opposed access to the Panel by individual Directors. Other opponents expressed again their concern that the Directors' offices of major developed countries would serve as a "mail box" for the NGOs of these countries, who would tend to submit complaints to these offices even when no serious violation or material harm was involved. During the Board discussion, this writer had the occasion to explain that (i) the Executive Directors as officials of the Bank were to follow their own convictions about what was in the best interest of the institution, and (ii) if an Executive Director had access to the Panel, (a) he/she would have to be satisfied in each case that the alleged violation was serious enough to warrant his/her intervention and (b) he/she would first have to exhaust resort to Management and would be expected to submit the request to the Panel only if he/she remained unsatisfied with

---

88. The introduction of a third option was intended to break the deadlock. Some of the adherents of each of the other two positions could find a basis in it for modifying their positions, thus enabling a compromise to emerge.

Management's reply. This writer also explained that the main difference between Options A and C was that in the latter option the Board would decide on whether to let the Panel proceed with the investigation without the benefit of the Panel's advice on whether an investigation was warranted, such advice being required in all cases under paragraph 19 of the draft Resolution, in the absence of a provision to dispense with it (as was envisaged in the situation addressed by Option C). On the basis of a suggestion by an Executive Director, this writer further indicated that Option A might explicitly specify that requests submitted by individual Directors to the Panel would be made only in "special cases of serious alleged violations" of the Bank's operational policies and procedures, to allay fears regarding possible abuses. Paragraph 13 of the draft Resolution would thus state that the Panel would have to satisfy itself that the violation was of a serious character in such cases. (This addition to paragraph 13 was extended at the end to apply to all cases, not only to the case of requests by an Executive Director. The reference to this requirement in paragraph 12, where requests for inspection are made by an Executive Director, was maintained, however, for the purpose of emphasizing that such requests would not constitute a normal practice but would be confined to "special cases of serious alleged violations.") The text of paragraph 12 would also distinguish between requests by individual Executive Directors and requests by the Board as a whole. In the latter case, the Panel would proceed directly with the investigation without having to ascertain the eligibility of the request or the seriousness of the alleged violations. In the case of requests by individual Executive Directors, under Option A as revised, the Panel would still be required to submit to the Board its recommendation on whether to proceed with the investigation, and the Board would be the arbiter on the decision to proceed, thus exercising control over any possible abuse.

With these clarifications, the Board reached a consensus on Option A as revised, which was seen in the light of these clarifications as a partial merger of Options A and C.

IV. A Checklist of Eligibility Requirements— A Summary

Concern with eligibility issues was central to the Board discussion of the Resolution and covered a good part of its text.[89] It was also the subject of the first legal opinion requested by Executive Directors from the General Counsel with regard to the Inspection Panel (on the occasion of the Panel's report to the Board recommending investigation of the first case submitted to it).[90] This concern was based mainly on the conviction of Management and many Executive Directors at the time that, without eligibility criteria known in advance to potential requesters, the Panel would be flooded by unchecked and possibly irresponsible requests that would unduly disrupt the Bank's work. It was also based on the emphasis most Board members placed on the two-stage approach to ensure Board responsibility for the scope of this new and untested process. As we shall see in the following chapter, eligibility issues were also raised by Management in relation to almost every registered request for inspection submitted to the Panel and were dealt with extensively by the Panel and the Board, whenever the Panel recommended investigation. This is not unusual; the intended purpose of the first stage of the process was to establish to the satisfaction of the Board whether the request meets all eligibility requirements.

In ascertaining whether such eligibility criteria have been met, it is important for the Panel and the Board alike to realize that it would not be possible to establish some of these criteria (especially the seriousness of the violation and the materiality of the damage resulting from it) in a definitive way before a full investigation takes place. Because, by definition, a recommendation to investigate precedes the investigation, such a recommendation can therefore be based only on preliminary conclusions to be confirmed or rejected after the investigation. Any attempt to

---

89. *Resolution,* paras. 12–14.
90. Note 73, *supra.*

reverse this order by expecting the Panel to establish these criteria beyond doubt before it recommends investigation (through a
process carrying a different name) could, in fact, render superfluous the investigation envisaged by the Resolution. As mentioned
earlier, it would practically do away with the prior Board approval
of such investigation. (From the beginning, however, neither the
Panel nor the Board seems to have acted on this understanding,
as shown in other parts of this book,[91] although the situation
now has been clarified as a result of the Board's second review of
the Panel's experience.)[92]

A common sense understanding of what the Resolution
requires from the Panel in ascertaining eligibility of the requests
submitted to it before recommending to the Board whether
investigation is warranted is presented in the following check-list.
As someone who was deeply involved in the drafting of the
Resolution and who has followed all the Board discussions related to it, including those related to actual requests for inspection
(up to June 1998), this writer finds it useful to restate the eligibility requirements in simple language. Although this may seem
repetitious, it is necessary, given the confusion and divisiveness
that have characterized debate of this matter so far.

1. Before hearing the request, the Panel will, as a first step,
    ascertain that "the subject matter of the request has been
    dealt with by the Management of the Bank and Management
    has failed to demonstrate that it has followed, or is taking
    steps to follow, the Bank's policies and procedures."[93] This

---

91. For the Panel's provision for a "Preliminary Review" and "Initial
Study" to establish the violation and the harm, *see* note 66, *supra*, of this chapter. For the Board's repeated requests for "additional reviews" from the Panel
after the latter had recommended investigation, *see* Chapter Three, *infra*, at
113–114, 120–121, and 129. And for the Board's adoption of the "Preliminary
Assessment" procedure in 1996 (until its repeal after the second review), *see*
Chapter Four, at 162 *seq*.

92. Reference is to the Board decision to revoke the preliminary assessment
procedure and to accept, as a matter of course, the Panel's recommendation to
investigate unless objective technical issues are raised. *See* Chapter Four, *infra*,
at 186–187.

93. Para. 13 of the *Resolution*.

clearly means that a request will not be admitted by the Panel if it finds that (i) the subject-matter of the request had not been submitted at all to Management beforehand; or (ii) after it had been submitted, Management had responded to the requester in a manner that the Panel finds satisfactory (either because that earlier response had shown, to the Panel's satisfaction, that Management had from the beginning complied fully with Bank operational policies and procedures or had already, to the Panel's satisfaction, taken steps to ensure that these policies and procedures would be fully respected). Clearly, if the Panel finds that Management had not responded adequately to the requester's prior complaints or if the Panel was not in a position to make a judgment on the adequacy of that early Management's response to the requester (which is not to be confused with its subsequent response to the Panel), it would then register the request and judge the matter in light of Management response to the Panel and any other information it may acquire.

2.   The Panel will ascertain that the complaint has been submitted by two or more persons who have common interests or concerns among them and who are in the territory of the borrower.[94] If the claim is submitted by a foreign representative, the Panel will ascertain that no local representation was available and advise the Board on this point when it submits its recommendation to it.[95] Board approval is required for such foreign representation.

3.   The request has to be related to a matter on which the Panel has not previously made a recommendation (on whether to investigate) unless new evidence or circumstances not known at the time of the request have emerged.[96]

4.   The request has to assert a serious violation by the Bank of its operational policies and procedures (that is, those related to the design, appraisal, and/or implementation of a

---

94. Para. 12 of the *Resolution,* as interpreted by the Board.

95. Only the Board may authorize foreign representation in exceptional cases. *See* para. 12 of the *Resolution.*

96. Para. 14(d).

project the Bank has financed or is considering financing).[97] Such assertion must be based on evidence that seems to be credible.

5. The request has to assert that the alleged violation resulted or is likely to result in a material harm to the requester because its own rights or interests have been or are likely to be directly affected in a negative way. *Prima facie* credible evidence to this effect should be included in the request. Harm resulting from actions or omissions of parties other than the Bank (such as harm caused by the borrower alone) can not be the subject of the Panel's investigation.[98]

6. The request has to be submitted before the loan to which it is related has been "closed" or at least 95 percent disbursed.[99]

7. The request has to relate to a matter that is not a procurement matter.[100]

Only when the requirements listed above are met to the Panel's satisfaction, would the Panel's recommendation to the Board to investigate the matter be fully consistent with the Resolution, as interpreted by the Board.

A period of 21 days has been set by the Resolution for the Panel to ascertain the above requirements. This period was deemed reasonable because of the understanding that the Panel would not be carrying out any investigation at this stage but would only assess the situation on the basis of the *prima facie* evidence backing the requester's allegations, Management's response to the Panel, and the other information the Panel may obtain from the requesters, Bank staff, and files.[101]

---

97. Para. 12.
98. Para. 14(a).
99. Para. 14(c).
100. Para. 14(b), as interpreted by the Board.
101. Clearly, the practice of the Panel and the Board was different from the description of the Resolution's requirements stated above. A return to the original framework is expected as a result of the second review of the Panel's experience, as explained in Chapter Four *infra*, at 187–188 and 199.

V.   The Inspection Process—Procedural Aspects and Safeguards

With the precise delineation of the terms of reference of Panel members and of the qualifications of the parties who can properly activate the Panel's function, it is clearly important that the Panel acts within the boundaries and according to the procedures stated in the Resolution. During the preparatory stages, fears were expressed, as shown earlier, that some Executive Directors might be pressured by NGOs in their countries to invoke the Panel's role beyond its defined mandate. Risks were also highlighted regarding possible adverse effects on the respective roles of the Bank's Board and Management, on the Bank staff's attitude and their work on future projects, and on the Bank's liability to third parties.[102]

The temptation to expand the role of the Panel beyond the limits stated in the Resolution could be fed by the high expectations of those who see in it an instrument to drastically change the World Bank to their liking and by the disappointment of those who fail to see it moving in that direction. To avoid the risk of such expansion and to ensure that the Panel would properly play the role envisaged for it, the Resolution specifies in precise terms the steps to be followed in invoking the inspection function and in the conduct of such function by the Panel.

A.   Activating the Panel's Role: The Request for Inspection

Although the steps specified in the Resolution mainly address the situation when inspection is requested by an affected party, this is only one of three ways of activating the work of the Panel. A request by one or more Executive Directors and a request by the Board are the others. Neither of the latter types of request has been made to the Panel so far, however.

---

102. For a treatment of the risk factors, *see* Chapter Five, at 229–235 and 241 *seq.*

In the case of a request by the Board, the Panel will proceed directly with the investigation and present its findings to the Board for decision after the Board receives Management's recommendations. In the other two cases, the Panel must first ascertain whether its investigative function can be exercised according to the Resolution and report on this preliminary question to the Board. Any further action by the Panel will depend on the Board's decision. In ascertaining that question, the Panel will naturally analyze whether the request was submitted by an eligible party (jurisdiction *ratione personae*), was not time-barred (jurisdiction *ratione temporis*), and relates to a matter falling within the Panel's mandate (jurisdiction *ratione materiae*), all according to the details specified in the Resolution and elaborated above.[103] Only when the Panel is satisfied on these three counts, including the seriousness of the alleged violation and the exhaustion of the recourse to Management, would the Panel recommend that an investigation be carried out. It was agreed from the beginning that the Board will consider this recommendation according to its normal procedures. This could be on a "no-objection" basis, if the matter seems to be a straightforward, non-controversial, routine matter, or in a Board meeting. Earlier drafts of the Resolution provided for the "no-objection" procedure in all cases (unless an Executive Director requests consideration of the question in a Board meeting), but this was opposed in the Board discussion of September 21–22, 1993. The Resolution simply states that "[t]he recommendation of the Panel shall be circulated to the Executive Directors for decision within the normal distribution period."[104] If this recommendation is against investigation, the Secretary's Department of the Bank is expected to circulate it for approval on a "no-objection"

---

103. *See* Sections II to IV of this chapter.

104. *Resolution*, para. 19. According to the Rules of Procedure of the Executive Directors of the Bank, the President prepares the agenda for Board meetings. In practice, routine matters which are deemed to be non-controversial are circulated to Board members for approval on a "no-objection" basis. The normal distribution period (*i.e.*, the period between circulation and Board consideration [or approval on a no-objection basis], is three weeks).

basis. There is nothing to prevent a Board member in this case from requesting discussion, and there is nothing to prevent the Board from asking the Panel to investigate the matter, notwithstanding the Panel's earlier recommendation. If, on the other hand, the Panel's recommendation is for the conduct of an investigation, the Board's approval is normally expected to be sought also on a "no-objection" basis unless the Panel or Management see that the question warrants Board discussion or any Executive Director requests such discussion. This was the understanding of the Board when the text of paragraph 19 of the Resolution was approved as stated. In all instances, the decision to proceed with the investigation is that of the Board; otherwise the two-stage approach that seemed at the time so essential to Board members would be forsaken. As we shall see in Chapter Four, although the principle remains intact, the Board has agreed as a result of its second review of the Panel's experience (completed in April 1999) to allow the Panel to proceed with investigation whenever it so recommends, unless one or more Executive Directors request discussion of certain "technical" objective criteria, but not the merits of the alleged violation or harm.[105]

If the Board's decision, whether in a meeting or not, is for the carrying out of the investigation, the Board will allow, in case the request was submitted by an affected party, for the representation of such party by a representative from outside its country, should the affected party have so requested on the basis that no appropriate representation was available locally.[106] The new procedure resulting from the second review does not negate the requirement that the Panel receives Board clearance of such foreign representation before it proceeds with the inspection process.

The procedure to be followed in the submission of the request and in the preliminary handling of it by the Panel is spelled out in detail in the Resolution. The request for inspection,

---

105. *See* Chapter Four, *infra*, at 187–188 and 199–200.
106. *Resolution*, para. 12, and the elaboration in Section III of this chapter.

which is required in all cases to be in writing, must state "all relevant facts."[107] It must explain, in all cases, (i) the nature of the alleged action or omission by the Bank in violation of its operational policies and procedures; (ii) the actions taken to bring such violation to the attention of Management; (iii) Management's response to such action; and (iv) all "the steps already taken to deal with the issue."[108] In case of a request by an affected party, the facts stated in the request must include "the harm suffered by or threatened to such party" by the Bank's action or omission.[109]

Once a request is received from an Executive Director or an affected party (or its representative), the Chairperson of the Panel must promptly inform the Board and the President. No distinction is made in this respect in the Resolution between requests related to projects under consideration and to projects under implementation. In all the drafts preceding the Board's discussion and approval of the Resolution in September 1993, such a distinction was maintained in deference to project appraisal being a Management function. The Board's role with respect to specific projects normally begins at the time the proposed loan is submitted to the Board for approval. The draft resolution thus required that, for complaints concerning projects under consideration, the Panel's Chairperson, upon receiving the request, inform the President of the Bank, "with a copy to the Executive Directors." For projects under implementation, the Chairperson was required to inform the Executive Directors and the President. The distinction was not only procedural; it had important consequences spelled out in the draft with respect to the action following investigation.[110] Such a distinction was designed to avoid

---

107. *Resolution,* para. 16.

108. *Id.*

109. The *Operating Procedures* issued by the Panel on August 19, 1994, elaborates on these steps. *See* Annex I–1–2 to this book. The Panel also issued in August 1994 "Guidance on how to prepare a request for inspection," along with a "Model Form" for the request for inspection. On its part, Management issued BP 17.55 on the Inspection Panel, which addresses the internal steps to be followed by Bank staff in responding to a request for inspection.

110. Under para. 23 of the draft resolution dated September 9, 1993, the consequential difference that was to come after completion of the investigation by the Panel, was explained as follows:

confusion about the respective functions of the Management and the Board and to prevent getting the latter involved in operational actions that are correctly those of Bank Management. In particular, it was presumed that there would be no possibility for Board action with respect to a project before the loan financing that project was actually submitted to the Board for approval. Nonetheless, such a distinction was opposed in the Board's discussion of the text, especially as it was pointed out that certain issues, which arise early in the preparation and appraisal stages, could be of great sensitivity to the Executive Directors and their authorities. These are mainly issues related to the potential effect of the project on the environment and on the resettlement of population. As Bank policies regarding these issues could be violated in or before the project appraisal stage, Executive Directors insisted that the Board should be fully informed of the alleged violation and should be able to decide on whether an investigation was warranted, even with respect to complaints at this early stage. The distinction and its consequences were thus deleted in the final text of the Resolution.

After the President of the Bank receives notification of the request from the Panel's Chair, the Bank's Management will have to provide the Panel (within 21 days of the date of notification) with evidence that it is actually in compliance with the Bank's

---

In case of an inspection concerning a project under preparation, the Management will inform the Executive Directors within six weeks from receiving the Panel's recommendations of the action(s) taken or planned to be taken by Management with respect to such recommendations. The recommendations of the Panel and the actions completed during project preparation also will be discussed in the Staff Appraisal Report when the project is submitted to the Executive Directors for financing. In case of requests for inspection concerning projects for which financing was approved by the Executive Directors, the President, within six weeks of receipt of the Panel's report, will notify the Executive Directors of the actions he/she intends to take or which he/she recommends the Executive Directors to take on the basis of the report. In all cases, the Bank shall inform the party who requested inspection of the results of the examination of the request and the action taken in its respect, if any.

The distinction maintained in the draft was dropped in the final text of the *Resolution*.

policies and procedures, or that it is taking or intends to take measures to ensure such compliance. The Panel may find that the adequacy and specificity of such measures obviate the need for any inspection. Within 21 days of receiving such a reply from Management, the Panel, after consulting with the recipient of the loan involved and the Executive Director representing the borrowing (or guaranteeing) country,[111] must reach its conclusion on whether the request is eligible for investigation. This conclusion entails the Panel's recommendation to the Board as to whether an investigation is warranted. According to the Resolution, the Board's decision on this recommendation, whether positive or negative, must be communicated to the affected party within two weeks of its date, in the cases where the request was submitted to the Panel by such a party.[112] (As will be shown in Chapter Four, the Clarifications issued by the Board in 1996 extended this disclosure requirement to the Management response and shortened the period required for purposes of this disclosure to a maximum of three days.)[113]

It is conceivable that the Panel may find the request from the outset to be manifestly outside the scope of its mandate, and thus it would not warrant waiting for a response from Management. A reasonable reading of the text suggests that the Panel would not have to wait in such a case for a response from Management and could proceed directly to recommend to the Board that no action be taken. In case the request is manifestly frivolous, absurd, or outside the Panel's mandate, no recommendation would be needed. The Panel may simply refuse to have the request registered, to avoid the waste of time and effort, provided it informs the requesting party, the Board, and the President. Although this refusal is not provided for in the text of the Resolution, it would result, in the writer's view, from a common sense reading of the text. This conclusion, expressed in the first edition of this book, has indeed been followed in the Panel's practice in two cases so far.[114]

---

111. *Resolution,* para. 21.
112. *Resolution,* para. 19.
113. *See* Chapter Four, *infra,* at 169–170.
114. *See* Chapter Three, *infra,* at 105 and 114–115.

After the Board decides on whether the Panel should proceed with the investigation, the request for inspection, the Panel's recommendation, and the Board's decision will be made publicly available by the Bank.[115] Copies of these documents will be available to the public online through the Bank's InfoShop and the Bank's field office in the country concerned. The Resolution does not specify a period for such publicity, except for its earlier provision on the notification of the *affected party* of the Board's *decision* within two weeks of the date of the decision.[116] As mentioned, a shorter period (three days) has been required by the Board's 1996 "Clarifications" for the disclosure of Management response. It is expected that this shorter period will be the standard to be applied to other Panel-related documents as well.

A decision by the Board authorizing inspection "normally would not involve cessation of preparatory work on an operation," as was explained in the Management report to the Board dated September 10, 1993,[117] in answer to questions raised earlier in the discussion of the Board's Committee of the Whole. Management may decide, however, to suspend the Bank's preparatory work, or the Board may request it to do so pending the outcome of inspection in cases where the prevailing circumstances require such a measure. The Panel, in recommending inspection, may also indicate whether in its view suspension of preparatory work in whole or in part would be needed for the purpose of its inspection (if, for example, the continuation of such work would have the potential of making the alleged harm irreversible).

B.   *Investigation by the Panel*

The manner in which investigation by the Panel is to be conducted is also described in the Resolution. The Chairperson designates one or two members as having primary responsibility for

---

115. *Id.*, para. 25.
116. *Id.*, para. 19.
117. *See supra* note 5, para. 11.

a given inspection.[118] (It would be normally expected that the inspection of each request would be assigned initially to one Panel member.) The Panel, not the Chairperson, fixes a certain period for the assigned inspector(s) to report findings to the Panel.[119] Such a period is expected to vary according to the nature and complexity of the case.

Except for the safeguards outlined below, the Resolution is silent on the manner in which investigation will be carried out, leaving this matter to the discretion of the Panel. In its Operating Procedures issued in August 1994 before it received the first request for inspection, the Panel elaborated on "methods of investigation." It indicated that it would use a variety of investigatory methods, taking into account the nature of each request. The following methods were mentioned as examples: holding meetings with, or requesting submissions on specific issues from, the requester, the affected people, Bank staff, government officials, and representatives of both local and foreign NGOs; holding public hearings in the project area; visiting project sites; hiring independent consultants to research specific issues related to the request; researching Bank files; and "any other reasonable methods the Inspector(s) consider appropriate on the specific investigation."[120]

Upon receiving the preliminary report on the findings reached by the assigned inspector(s), the Panel will deliberate on it and reach its conclusion. Such a conclusion is normally expected to be reached by the consensus of the members of the Panel, as is the case with its procedural decisions generally and with its earlier recommendation on whether to proceed with the inspection. If consensus cannot be reached, the Panel's report will state "the majority and minority views."[121] Conceivably,

---

118. *Resolution,* para. 20.

119. *Id.*

120. *See Operating Procedures,* Annex I–1–2 to this book, para. 45.

121. *Resolution,* para. 24. The text of the *Resolution* speaks of the Panel's findings. The term *recommendation* was mentioned in earlier drafts but was replaced by *findings* on the suggestion of an Executive Director to avoid confusion with the Management recommendation on the steps to be taken in light

there could be three different views in the Panel. In this case, these disparate views will be stated in the report, although this situation is not explicitly envisioned in the Resolution. The Panel's conclusions will be preceded by a statement of the facts that led to them; in other words, the conclusions have to be reasoned. The Panel's report to the Board and the President has to discuss "all relevant facts" and should specifically indicate "whether the Bank has complied with all relevant Bank policies and procedures."[122]

Certain safeguards are provided in the Resolution to ensure that the investigation will be carried out properly. These include the access given to the members of the Panel to all the Bank staff (that is, to all those in the employment of the Bank, whether they are regular staff, consultants, or local field office staff) as well as to "all pertinent Bank records."[123] In particular, Panel members are required, as needed, to consult with the Director-General, Operations Evaluation Department, and with the Internal Auditor. Consultation with the former was a subject of some discussion in the Board meeting that adopted the Resolution. Some Board members from the beginning wanted the Panel to operate "under the umbrella" of the office of the Director-General, Operations Evaluation.[124] When the difference was explained between the "inspection function," which deals with projects before their completion, and the "operations evaluation function," which typically deals with completed projects, and after hearing the views of the Director-General, Operations Evaluation, the Board agreed to mention in the Resolution only that the Panel "shall consult" with the Director-General. The words *"as needed"* were added in this context to avoid the impression that such consultation was

---

of these findings. An attempt to replace the word "findings" by the word "recommendations" was made by the Panel and supported by certain NGOs during the first review of the *Resolution,* as explained in Chapter Four, at 165–166.

122. *Id.,* para. 22.

123. *Id.*

124. This was suggested in the "Four Executive Directors' Proposal" referred to in Chapter One, Section V, and advocated by some of the authors of the proposal in later discussions.

mandatory in all cases.[125] Consultation with the Internal Auditor, as needed, was also provided for on that occasion.

Other safeguards are mentioned in the Resolution to ensure that the Panel is fully aware of the views of the borrower and of the Executive Director representing the country that is the borrower or the guarantor of the loan giving rise to the investigation. Certain safeguards are also meant to ensure that the investigation does not undermine the Bank's relationship with that country or encroach on its jurisdiction. Specifically, Panel members must consult with both the borrower and the Executive Director during the investigation and must receive the consent of the country where actual inspection is to be carried out before such inspection takes place. This is *not* meant to make the inspection function itself subject to the prior consent of any country. Nor does it require a special consent for visits of Bank representatives, including Panel members, that do not involve investigative activities exceeding normal supervision and evaluation. (Such visits by Bank officials are authorized by an explicit provision in the General Conditions applicable to all loans.)[126] It only requires that investigative activities by the Panel, such as those listed in the Panel's Operating Procedures, other than a mere visit to the project site, will not take place in the territory of a country without its prior approval. Beyond this important limitation, the inspection process may otherwise proceed even if that country or any

---

125. The views of the Director-General, Operations Evaluation, were also sought at an earlier stage by the Joint Audit Committee of the Board on a comparison between the Four Executive Directors' Proposal and the Management proposal. In the Board discussion of September 1993, the Director-General, who is appointed by the Board and reports to it (with an administrative link to the President) expressed the view that the two functions (inspection and operations evaluation) had the same corporate objective and shared the same tool kit and professional relationship and that, to the extent possible, there should be a commonality of views between them, although an arm's length relationship was needed with respect to specific inspection to ensure that the integrity of the Operations Evaluation Department (which may cover the same projects in the post-completion stage) was not affected.

126. *See* General Conditions Applicable to Bank Loan Agreements, at Section 9.01(c) and General Conditions Applicable to IDA Credit Agreements, at Section 9.01(b).

other country is opposed to it. After all, the purpose of the investigation is to see whether the Bank, not the country, has complied with, or has committed a serious violation of its operational policies and procedures. As will be shown in Chapter Four, attempts have been made in the second review of the Panel experience to do away with the consent requirement in practice.[127] While the Board now expects Panel members to visit the country in the initial stage (that is, before investigation is authorized) only when necessary, it expects borrowing countries to accept their visits for inspection work in their territories as a matter of course.

In carrying out their investigations, Panel members are likely to face legal issues relevant to the rights and obligations of the Bank, the borrower, the guarantor (if the borrower is not a member country), and the affected parties. However, the Panel is not a court of law and has no power to interpret the Bank's Articles of Agreement, loan agreements, project agreements, guarantee agreements, and other agreements between the Bank and its borrowers. Nor does its power extend to determining the legal rights and obligations of the Bank under these instruments or under the Bank's policies and procedures. The Panel is required by explicit provisions in its constituent Resolution to "seek the advice of the Bank's Legal Department on matters related to the Bank's rights and obligations with respect to the request under consideration." (This requirement was highlighted in the outcome of both the first and second review of the Panel's experience.) In providing its advice, the Legal Department must limit itself to the legal questions put before it and avoid taking a position on the specific subject matter of the inspection.

C. *Follow-up Action*

Once the Executive Directors and the President receive the report on the findings of the Panel, Management will have up to six weeks from that date to submit its own report to the Board.

---

127. *See infra,* at 187–188.

This report should include Management's recommendations in response to the Panel's findings, whether the project giving rise to the complaint was under preparation or under implementation.[128] The Board will discuss the Panel's report and Management's recommendations before deciding on the directives to issue to Management in this respect. No time limit is set in the Resolution for Board action, and the Panel's report remains confidential at this stage.[129] As in the case of the Board decision on whether to allow the Panel to proceed with the inspection, in the cases where inspection is requested by an "affected party" (or its representative), the Bank must inform such party of the actions agreed to by the Board "within two weeks of the Board's consideration of the matter."[130] If such Board consideration takes more than one meeting,[131] this period would reasonably be expected to run from the date when the Board decision is reached, although the Bank may choose to keep the affected party informed as the matter progresses. In any case, the Panel's report and the Bank's response (that is, the Board's decision on Management recommendations) will have to be made publicly available "within two weeks after consideration by the Executive Directors of the report." It is thus presumed that the affected party will be informed of these documents simultaneously with or shortly before the general public.

---

128. *Resolution,* para. 23.

129. The proceedings of the Executive Directors are confidential, according to the Board's Rules of Procedure. That there are 24 Directors and 24 Alternates who report to 181 member governments has made it difficult, in practice, to maintain the confidentiality of reports circulated to Board members. Maintaining such confidentiality to the extent possible has nonetheless been deemed essential by the Board for protecting its members from outside pressure by special interest groups. According to the Resolution establishing the Panel, the report submitted by the Panel on the investigation is to be made publicly available only "after consideration by the Executive Directors of the report." *Resolution,* para. 25.

130. *Resolution,* para. 23. As will be explained in Chapter Four, *infra,* at 170, the two-week period has been reduced to three days.

131. In the case of the *Narmada Project* (Chapter One, Section II, *supra*), several Board sessions discussing successive Management reports were held before the matter was settled.

The matter will not be closed at this point. For projects under consideration, if the Bank continues its work on the financing of the project, the "Project Appraisal Document," a document which is circulated to Board members along with the President's Memorandum recommending the approval of a Bank loan or guarantee, must include the findings of the Panel and the actions taken by Management and the borrower to address these findings (assuming that the findings required such actions). The issue is bound to be reviewed by the Board at the time of loan approval, with a view to seeing, in the light of the information provided in the "Project Appraisal Document," whether adequate corrective measures have been taken. For projects under implementation, the borrower remains bound by its obligations under the loan agreement until the loan is fully repaid.[132] Disbursement under the loan would continue unless, of course, an "event of suspension" specified in the loan document occurred and the Bank found such action to be justified.[133] If the measures agreed by the Board require action by the borrower and the latter is not willing to take such action, the borrower may decide to cancel the undisbursed part of the loan (as was the case in the *Narmada Project* following the *ad hoc* inspection).[134] Otherwise, a conclusion will have to be reached by the Bank on whether the borrower's failure to act constitutes a violation of its agreement with the Bank, in which case the Bank will have available to it the remedies provided for in the General Conditions applicable to its loans (that is, suspension of

---

132. This is so by virtue of explicit provisions in the standard General Conditions Applicable to Bank Loans Agreements (Section 6.06) and to IDA Credit Agreements (Section 6.06).

133. This point was explicitly mentioned in the Management report to the Board dated September 10, 1993. *See supra* note 5, para. 11. The General Conditions applicable to Bank loans give the Bank the power to suspend disbursement, *inter alia*, when the borrower (or guarantor) fails to perform any obligations under the loan (or guarantee) agreement and when an extraordinary situation arises making it improbable that the project can be carried out or that the borrower (or guarantor) will be able to perform its obligations (Sections 6.02(c) and (e), IBRD; and Sections 6.02(b) and (d), IDA).

134. *See* Chapter One, *supra*, at 6.

disbursement of loan proceeds, cancellation of the loan, and the [unprecedented] acceleration of the maturity of the loan, including demand of immediate repayment of the full amount outstanding). Given the cooperative nature of the Bank and its ongoing long-term relationships with its borrowing members, matters are expected to be settled through negotiation more often than through resort to such remedies.

VI. Composition of the Panel

The Panel consists of three members who are appointed by the Bank's Board upon the nomination of the Bank's President. Such a nomination must be preceded, however, by consultation with the Executive Directors.[135] During the Board discussion of the Resolution (September 21–23, 1993), a suggestion was made that a search committee, consisting of Board members and Management representatives, select candidates for submission to the Board. This proposal was not approved, however. Instead, the draft was amended to require the President to consult with the Directors before making nominations. In practice, the President of the Bank asked the Executive Directors to propose names to him for nomination to the first Panel, then he submitted to them a short list of fourteen candidates for comments. This process resulted in shortening the list to seven, from which the President circulated his nomination of three candidates.

During the same Board discussion, several Executive Directors urged that at least one Panel member be from a borrowing country and that the Panel's composition reflect balanced representation. Although the Resolution requires Panel members to be of different nationalities, without further elaboration, the initial expectation, reflected indirectly in the first short list of nominees, was that one would be from North America, one from Europe, and one from a developing country. This need not always be the case, however. In subsequent Board discussions at

---

135. *Resolution,* para. 2.

the time the first Panel members were selected, several Executive Directors expressed disappointment that persons from important borrowing regions were not included and hoped that a better balance would be reached in future selections. This concern was reiterated on other occasions, but subsequent practice remains consistent with the initial composition.

Earlier drafts of the Resolution provided that the period of service on the Panel would be three years, except for the first members who would have staggered terms of two, three, and four years, and that members may serve for two terms. This was challenged in the Board's Committee of the Whole discussion on August 26, 1993, when one, non-renewable term was emphasized as a safeguard for the independence of the Panel. As a result, the September 9 draft mentioned that after the staggered periods of the first Panel (three, four, and five years) each vacancy will be filled for a period of five years, but no member will serve for more than one term. This requirement has remained intact in the final text.[136] Because the experience of the inspection function was to be reviewed by the Board "after two years from the date of the appointment of the first members of the Panel,"[137] and such review may, at least in theory, lead to the abolition of this function, the Resolution, at the suggestion of an Executive Director, included a provision that the appointment of Panel members, which always exceeds two years, will be "subject to the continuity of the inspection function."[138] This was meant to be reflected in the inspectors' terms of employment. In reality, of course, the continuity of the Panel has not been questioned. On the contrary, the Board renewed its support and appreciation of this function on several occasions, including the two reviews of the Resolution in 1996 and 1998/99. The Panel members, whose initial terms were three and four years, respectively, have been replaced according to the procedure mentioned above. This procedure has been criticized

---

136. *Resolution,* para. 3.
137. *Id.,* para. 27.
138. *Id.,* para. 3.

by some Washington-based NGOs that felt that consultation with them was not meaningful (they were informed of the process in some detail, but no names were discussed with them).[139]

Independence of Panel members was emphasized in the Management report submitted to the Board's Committee of the Whole as "a condition of effectiveness, objectivity, and credibility."[140] The qualifications provided for in the Resolution include "their ability to deal thoroughly and fairly with the requests brought to them, their integrity and their independence from the Bank's Management, and their exposure to development issues and to living conditions in developing countries."[141] "Knowledge and experience of the Bank's operations," which was included in the requirements in the early drafts of the Resolution, is mentioned in the text only as desirable, to alleviate a concern expressed in the discussion of the Board's Committee of the Whole on August 26, 1993, and in the Board's meeting of September 21, 1993. Making it a condition, it was argued, would favor only the appointment of former Bank officials, but it would suffice to have only one of the members of the Panel with knowledge of Bank operations. It was clear that such knowledge would be useful for inspectors, but it was agreed it should not be a condition of eligibility. This conclusion also varied from the requirements explained earlier in the report to the Board's Committee of the Whole, where knowledge of the Bank figured prominently in the qualifications of Panel members.[142] In actual practice, only one member of

---

139. *See also* Chapter Five, *supra,* at 202–203.

140. *Functions and Operations of an Inspection Function* (R93–122/1), August 6, 1993, para. 9 (limited circulation).

141. *Resolution,* para. 4.

142. In that report, the inspectors' qualifications were stated as follows:

- "sufficient knowledge and understanding of the Bank, its work, and its culture, to work comfortably and effectively in its environment;

- sufficient objectivity to be able to see the Bank's strengths and weaknesses in perspective;

- sufficient exposure to development issues to have a broad multidisciplinary grasp of the technical aspects of Bank operations; and

the Panel, a former staff member, has had hands-on experience with the Bank's work, and this experience took place more than thirty years before his appointment to the Panel, when the Bank was different in many ways.

As a further guarantee of the independence of inspectors, the Resolution clearly excludes from appointment anyone who worked for the Bank Group (including not only the IBRD but also all its affiliates), as a *staff member* (a term that includes consultants and "local staff") or an Executive Director, or alternate or advisor to an Executive Director, unless two years have elapsed since the end of such service.[143] Earlier drafts (prior to the last, September 9, 1993, draft) had a waiting period of five years, but this was reduced to two years following discussions in the Board's Committee of the Whole in August 1993. These discussions also resulted in the addition of a provision disqualifying a Panel member from participation in the hearing and investigation of "any request related to a matter in which he/she has a personal interest or had significant involvement in any capacity,"[144] because

---

- sufficient experience of living and working in developing countries to have a sympathetic understanding of the economic and political realities that shape the Bank's relationship with its borrowers."

Supra note 140, para. 9.

The required qualifications were rephrased in the President's Memorandum to the September 1993 meeting of the Board to read as follows:

"The credibility of the Inspection Panel will depend on its independence and on the objectivity and professional quality of the Inspectors. Inspectors should have experience of living or working in developing countries in order to have an understanding of the economic and political realities that shape the Bank's relationship with its borrowers, and a broad multi-disciplinary grasp of the technical aspects of Bank operations; knowledge and understanding of Bank operations and procedures would also be useful."

Supra note 5, para. 13 (emphasis added). The Resolution, as stated above, mentions that knowledge of the Bank is "desirable," para. 4.

143. *Resolution,* para. 5.

144. *Resolution,* para. 6. The words "significant involvement" in this text replaced the words "has been personally involved with" in the draft resolution dated September 9, 1993, as the latter wording was found by Executive Directors to be too restrictive.

this was seen as more important than a long waiting period before appointment.[145]

Moreover, the Resolution provides for two other safeguards to ensure that Panel members would not be subject to Management influence through sanctions or rewards. First, members of the Panel "may be removed from office only by decision of the Executive Directors, for cause."[146] Members are given immunity from arbitrary termination of service and from any Management action in this respect. Second, "members of the Panel may not be employed by the Bank Group, following the end of their service on the Panel."[147]

These requirements show that great attention must be given to the choice of Panel members. They should be persons whose knowledge, experience, integrity, and independence generate confidence on the part of all the parties concerned within and outside the Bank. Without such confidence, the credibility of the function, its very *raison d'être*, will be called into question. In addition, the choice should take into account the ability of the individuals concerned to work together as a team that would command respect of both the Bank and its critics.

All Panel members will work on a full-time basis when the workload justifies such an arrangement, as will be recommended

---

145. Some Directors found the waiting period unnecessary, especially for Executive Directors and their Alternates, in view of the many safeguards in the Resolution ensuring the independence of Panel members. This view did not prevail, however.

146. *Resolution*, para. 8.

147. *Id.*, para. 10. It should be noted that on the first occasion of appointment of Panel members, Management initially asked the Board to modify the latter condition for two of the proposed candidates who, given their relatively young age and that their appointment was to be for non-renewable terms of three and four years, respectively, had some reservations about serving under that condition. The condition was to be modified to prohibit these members from any employment with the Bank within five years of the end of their service on the Panel and from any *regular* staff employment after this five-year period, thus allowing for their possible future employment as consultants to the Bank. Concerns expressed by some Executive Directors, however, led to full conformity with the Resolution (*i.e.*, appointment of all members of the Panel under the general ban of future employment in the Bank in any capacity).

by the Panel and approved by the Bank's Board.[148] Meanwhile, only the Chairperson will work on a full-time basis, and the other two members will be called upon when actual requests for inspection or other Panel business require their attendance. The first chairperson was known at the time of the appointment as the person designated in the Resolution as the "Panel member initially appointed for five years,"[149] the other two were appointed for three and four years, respectively. Until all Panel members serve on a full-time basis, the terms of employment of each member should therefore reflect work conditions that may shift from a full-time to a part-time basis or vice versa, depending on who is elected as Chairperson. During the Board discussion of the text of the Resolution in September 1993, the annual rotation of the chair was emphasized to avoid a situation where the Panel would be dominated by the same Chairperson to the detriment of its multilateral character. The text of the Resolution does not require such a rotation, however; it only states that, following the first year of the Panel, "the members of the Panel shall elect a Chairperson for a period of one year."

Finally, although the Resolution provides that the Panel members "shall be officials of the Bank," it qualifies this by the phrase "in the performance of their duties, taking into account that initially at least two of them will be working on a part-time basis."[150] The Resolution states that, as inspectors, they will enjoy the privileges and immunities accorded to Bank officials, will be subject to the requirements of the Bank's Articles of Agreement concerning their exclusive loyalty to the Bank, and will be subject to the Bank's applicable Staff Principles.[151]

---

148. *Id.*, para. 9.

149. *Id.*, para. 7.

150. *Id.*, para. 10.

151. The *Resolution* specifies in this respect the obligations stated in subparagraphs (c) and (d) of paragraph 3.1 and paragraph 3.2 of the Principles of Staff Employment. These require that staff members shall: "3.1 (c) conduct themselves at all times in a manner befitting their status as employees of an international organization. They shall avoid any action and, in particular, any public pronouncement or personal gainful activity, that would adversely or unfavorably reflect on their status or on the integrity, independence, and impartiality that are

VII. Administrative and Financial Aspects of the Panel's Work

A.   *Status of the Panel*

As explained earlier, the Panel is not merely a list of persons to be called upon to participate in an inspection when the need arises. As is shown in Annex III, this different approach has been followed in both the Inter-American Development Bank and the Asian Development Bank.[152] Nor is the Panel a full-time operating Bank facility (until its workload justifies this status).

Initially, the Panel was envisaged as a compromise between these two situations, a compromise necessitated by the impossibility of predicting the number of requests the Panel will receive and by the desire to avoid the large cost of appointing its members on a full-time basis for a job that could be exercised only on a few occasions. Although the idea of an agreed list to be activated when the need arises was proposed by some Executive Directors during the Board's discussion of the Resolution, it was felt that a stronger presence would be needed to give credibility to this new facility and to provide a basis for an institutional working relationship between it and the Bank's Management and Board. The Resolution thus assumes that, of the Panel's three members, only the Chairperson will work on a full-time basis at Bank headquarters. The other two will be called upon on a case-by-case basis until the workload reaches a stage where the Board finds it reasonable, on the recommendations of the Panel, to allow the three inspectors to work on a

---

required by that status;" and "(d) observe the utmost discretion in regard to all matters relating to the Organizations both while they are staff members and after their service with the Organizations has ended. In particular they shall refrain from the improper disclosure, whether direct or indirect, of information related to the business of the World Bank or the IFC." And that: "3.2 all rights in any work produced by staff members as part of their official duties shall belong to the World Bank or the IFC unless such rights are explicitly relinquished."

152. *See infra,* at 491 *seq.*

full-time basis.[153] Practical arrangements have been made to facilitate the work of the Panel in spite of this situation, and the three inspectors have been provided with electronic mail and fax facilities at their homes or offices to allow them to remain in touch with the Bank and with each other on a continuous basis.

There is no doubt that the idea of a full-time Chairperson was based on emphasizing the visibility of the new facility, rather than on any prediction regarding the volume of its work at the outset.[154] No similar arrangement exists, for instance, for the Bank's Administrative Tribunal, which deals with staff disputes and handles dozens of such disputes every year.

B.   *The Executive Secretary*

The Panel's Chairperson is not the only official of the Panel expected to be available in the Bank's headquarters from the outset. The Resolution provides that the President of the Bank will appoint, after consultation with the Executive Directors, an Executive Secretary for the Panel.[155] The Secretary is chosen from Bank staff members, presumably to ensure full familiarity with the Bank's policies, procedures, and working methods. He or she also need not work on a full-time basis "until the workload so justifies."[156] The requirement of consultation with the Board before the appointment of the Executive Secretary was introduced in the September 1993 Board discussion of the draft

---

153. *Resolution,* para. 9

154. An earlier version of the Management report to the Board on the Panel stated that "it was more likely than not that the [complaints] will be more substantial at the outset than later." *See supra* note 140, para. 27. If such prediction was accurate, it would not be consistent with the Resolution's arrangement for the initially part-time work of the other two inspectors. Obviously, the number and nature of the complaints submitted to the Panel will be the practical determinants of whether only the Chairperson or the full Panel will work on a full-time basis. So far, the need has not arisen to change the arrangement envisaged initially.

155. *Resolution,* para. 11.

156. *Id.*

resolution after some Directors went further to suggest that the Executive Secretary be appointed by the Board.[157]

C.   *Remuneration and Other Costs*

The Resolution provides that "once [the members of the Panel] begin to work on a full-time basis, they shall receive remuneration at a level to be determined by the Executive Directors upon a recommendation of the President, plus normal benefits available to Bank fixed-term staff."[158] This provision applies to the Chairperson of the Panel while he/she serves as such. During the Board discussion of the Resolution, Management indicated that its budget estimates for the Panel's cost assumed full-time inspectors at grades 27–28 in the then applicable Bank salary scale, which are the highest grades for Bank staff below the vice presidential level. On that basis, and on the assumption that the three inspectors would make five trips a year of different distances and would need office space, support staff, and occasionally some consultants, Management assumed that the Panel's annual budget (which would include the cost of the Executive Secretary) would be about $1.5 million, a figure that caused some Executive Directors to urge cost restraint.[159] The Panel's budget in FY99 (July 1, 1998, to June 30, 1999) reached $1.7 million.[160]

---

157. The first Executive Secretary of the Panel was appointed on April 4, 1994. He is Mr. Eduardo G. Abbott, a Chilean national, who served as a member of the Bank's Legal Department since 1978. As of August 1, 1994, Mr. Abbott has worked on a full-time basis on Panel matters. Later on, the Secretariat was further strengthened by the appointment of Ms. Antonia M. Macedo, a national from New Zealand, as Assistant Executive Secretary.

158. *Resolution,* para. 10.

159. The Board approved on April 21, 1994, that the remuneration of full-time members of the Panel will be fixed at the ceiling of level 28 of the Bank's salary scale [(R94–56, IDA/R94–60), April 5, 1994]. The first Chairman was appointed, however, at level 29, equal to that of a Vice President of the Bank, in recognition of his seniority.

160. *See Review of World Bank Programs and FY Budgets* (R98–143), June 23, 1998, Annex 10, at 26.

The Resolution, assuming two inspectors will not be working full time at the outset, provides that "they shall be remunerated on a *per diem* basis and shall be reimbursed for their expenses on the same basis as the members of the Bank's Administrative Tribunal." The *per diem* payment for such members is at present US $1,100.

The Management's report to the Board's Committee of the Whole meeting of August 26, 1993, emphasized the need for an institutional system for the Panel. Although recognizing the importance of avoiding the cost of a full-time unit before the need for it existed, it concluded with the following statement:

> "It would not seem appropriate to make a decision on this function largely or even significantly on the basis of costs alone. The important thing is to structure the function in such a way that, if the workload is modest, costs can be adjusted to match it. If the costs turn out to be larger, it would only be because there is a substantial and continuous volume of legitimate complaints, and hence a need for the function. In that case, it is hard to conceive the cost arising as anything but an essential cost of doing business in the way that now seems appropriate to the Bank community and its shareholders."[161]

D.   Annual Report

The Resolution requires the Panel to furnish an annual report to the President and the Executive Directors concerning its activities and mandates the publication of such a report by the Bank. Given the importance of its subject matter to varied audiences, it is expected that requests will be made for the publication of this report in several languages.

---

161. *See Functions and Operations of an Inspection Function*, Draft Paper (R93–122/1), August 6, 1993, at para. 29.

E.   *Location of the Panel in the Bank's Organizational Structure*

The Resolution is silent on the administrative location of the Panel, which was described in all preceding drafts as an independent inspection panel.[162] During Board discussion of the draft Resolution of September 1993, Management indicated that the Panel would be located in the Secretary's Department (now named Corporate Secretariat) and that its "administrative link" with that department would not undermine the independent function of the Panel. This will be identical to the treatment of the Bank's Administrative Tribunal. Such administrative linkage means that the Executive Secretary of the Panel will, administratively, report to the Bank's Vice President and Secretary and that the latter will be responsible for the administrative aspects of the selection of Panel members and of the Panel's budget. It does not give the Vice President and Secretary the right to intervene in the work of the Panel. Such work will be subject only to the Resolution and, ultimately, to the Board's control through its decisions on whether to allow an inspection to take place and on the measures to be taken in response to the Panel's findings in a specific case.

---

162. The word *independent* was dropped at the suggestion of an Executive Director during the September 21, 1993, Board meeting on the basis that, although the Panel members are to exercise their function with full independence, the Panel remains part of the Bank and describing it as an "Independent Inspection Panel" may give the erroneous impression that it is an external supervisory authority. The Board has, however, emphasized the Panel's independence on several occasions, including, as will be shown, the two reviews of the Resolution conducted so far. *See* Chapter Four, *infra,* at 156 *seq.* and 173 *seq.*

3

A Study of the Resolution as Applied in Practice— The Experience of the Inspection Panel

Introduction

As of June 30, 1999, the World Bank Inspection Panel has received sixteen requests, of which it registered fourteen. It recommended an investigation in six of the registered cases, but declined to do so in six others.[1] The Panel's recommendation in the last two cases is still pending. In twelve out of fourteen registered cases, the Panel made a field visit before submitting its recommendation to the Board on whether inspection was justified.

The two requests that the Panel declined to register were clearly outside the scope of the Panel's mandate as described in the Resolution establishing it. The first of these requests concerned the Bank's continued lending to a country even though

---

1. For a detailed summary of the Panel's case work from the Panel's perspective, see the *First* and *Second Annual Report of the Inspection Panel,* the former covering the period from August 1, 1994, to July 31, 1996, and the latter from August 1, 1996, to July 31, 1997, and Alvaro Umaña Quesada (ed.), *The Inspection Panel: The First Four Years* (1998). *See also* Richard E. Bissell, Recent Practice of the Inspection Panel of the World Bank, 91 *American Journal of International Law* 741 (1997), and Sabine Schlemmer-Schulte, The World Bank's Experience with Its Inspection Panel, 58 *Zeitschrift für ausländisches öffentliches Recht und Völkerrecht (ZaöRV)—Heidelberg Journal of International Law* 353–388 (1998) (reporting and commenting on the cases before the Panel and their contribution to the development of international law). Lori Udall's study, *The World Bank Inspection Panel: A Three Year Review* (1997), presents a different analysis of the Panel's experience at 17–61.

the requesters' property was allegedly expropriated in that country. This request was not related to any specific Bank-financed project where the Panel could investigate the Bank's compliance with its own policies and procedures with respect to the design, appraisal, or implementation of a project. The other request that the Panel declined to register concerned an IFC investment, not an IBRD or IDA operation.

Out of the other fourteen requests, seven related to IBRD- and five to IDA-financed projects. One request, the first received by the Panel, related to a project appraised for financing by the IDA but for which no financing decision had been taken by the Board. One request, the last brought before the Panel, regarded a project to be financed by both IBRD and IDA. Thirteen of the requests concerned specific investment projects, of which eleven constituted large infrastructure projects (such as hydroelectric dams, power stations, natural resources management, the construction of a bridge, an irrigation and water drainage area, and a sanitation system); one request related to environment, and one dealt with land reform. Another request resulted from a sector adjustment operation. In all the requests concerning infrastructure projects, non-compliance with Bank policies and procedures covering primarily environmental issues and social interests of affected people was alleged by the complainants. (Two requests concerned the same infrastructure project.)

Twelve of the fourteen registered requests have been disposed of. Remedial action plans agreed upon between the Bank and borrowers relating exclusively to actions to be taken by the borrowers (and/or other entities responsible for project execution) were made as a result of six of the registered requests. Five of these plans were made before the Board met to decide on the Panel recommendation on whether to investigate. (Three had been agreed upon between Management and the borrower after the Panel had issued its recommendation to the Board; two were agreed upon before Management presented its response to the Panel.) The sixth plan was made after the Board authorized investigation, but before the Panel had reached its findings. In addition, during the Board discussion of a Panel's recommendation in a recent case, Management announced that it would work with the government, in consultation with affected people, to address the issues identified by the Panel. This announcement led the Board to conclude that no further inspection was required in that case and that, instead, Management, acting with the government, would prepare a report in consultation with beneficiaries regarding future project implementation and that the Panel would be kept informed and would separately give its comments on the report once it was completed.

Geographically, registered requests covered two projects in Bangladesh, three projects in Brazil, and two projects in India. With the exception of the first request received by the Panel that related to a project in Nepal, then appraised but not financed by the IDA, each of the other registered requests related to a Bank- or IDA-financed project in Argentina/Paraguay, Lesotho/South Africa (two separate requests concerning the same project), Nigeria, and Tanzania, respectively.

Of the six cases in which the Panel recommended investigation, the Board formally authorized it in two cases: *Arun III*, Nepal, and *NTPC*, India (of which one, the *NTPC investigation*, was limited to the Bank's headquarters after the Panel had visited the site at an earlier stage). In a third case, *Yacyretá*, Argentina/Paraguay, the Board asked the Panel to make assessments that, *de facto*, required the Panel to investigate.[2] In two other cases, *PLANAFLORO* and *Itaparica*, both in Brazil, in lieu of authorizing investigation, the Board requested the Panel to assist it in the review of the progress in the implementation of remedial action plans agreed between the Bank and the borrower involved. In one more case, *Jamuna Bridge*, Bangladesh, where the Panel had not recommended investigation, the Board asked the Panel to follow up on the progress in the implementation of a remedial action plan. In another case, *India Ecodevelopment*, the Board asked that the Panel be involved in the plan expected to result from discussion between Management

---

2. *Compare* Umaña, *supra* note 1, at 317, where he states that the Board had authorized investigation in one case only. The same is reported by Udall, *supra* note 1, at 1. For an explanation, *see* Chapter Five, at 219 *seq*.

and the borrower. The Panel's actual and potential involvement in the assessment of project performance under remedial action plans has amounted so far to seven cases, including the cases where no prior inspection by the Panel, formal or *de facto,* had taken place. In most of these cases, such involvement has not been limited, however, to reviewing the Bank's compliance with its operational policies and procedures. As mentioned before, the Panel's recommendation with respect to the last two cases is still pending.

The following summary provides the background of the requests submitted to the Panel in the order they were received. In the course of the requests dealt with under the procedures of the Resolution establishing the Panel, certain practices have evolved. The interpretations of and practices developed under the Resolution are reflected in the Board's actions in specific cases. They are also reflected in the points included in the "Clarifications of Certain Legal Aspects of the Resolution," which the Board issued in October 1996 on the occasion of the completion of its first review of the Resolution, then revised when it reviewed the Panel's experience again in 1998/99, as detailed in the following chapter. A few controversial issues remained without a definite answer, however, even though the Panel took a position on them. These include the eligibility of adjustment operations for inspection, the scope of harm to be assessed in the case of such operations, and the admissibility of anonymous requests.

I.   Planned Arun III Hydroelectric Project/Nepal

The first request (registered in October 1994) related to a proposed hydroelectric project in Nepal (Arun III) that was under consideration, but not yet financed, by the IDA.[3] The project

---

3. *See Request for Inspection: Panel Recommendation—Nepal Arun III Proposed Hydroelectric Project* (IDA/SecM94–378), December 16, 1994 (including in Attachment (1) the text of the request).

included the construction of a dam, a hydroelectric power plant, an access road to the dam and plant, and a hydroelectric power scheme with transmission lines from the plant to other parts of the country. A local NGO representing four citizens of Nepal, including two who "asked for anonymity," complained about non-compliance by the IDA with a number of its policies, including applicable ODs on "disclosure of information," "environmental assessment," "involuntary resettlement," and "indigenous people."

In its response to the Panel in November 1994, Management stated that it had followed the applicable policies and procedures with respect to the design and appraisal of the proposed project.[4]

In December 1996, the Panel, following the Resolution, found that apparent violations of IDA policies existed and recommended an investigation in the areas of environmental assessment, involuntary resettlement, and treatment of indigenous people.[5] Its analysis was based on the Bank's records, conversation with staff, and a field visit.

Before the Board had received the Panel recommendation to carry out an investigation, IDA Management (the Regional Vice President) made a presentation to the Board on the proposed project, which included information not previously provided in Management's written response submitted to the Panel.[6] Upon the Board's request, the Panel was furnished with the new information and asked to indicate its reaction to the Board.[7] After consideration of the documents received and in light of further discussions with Management, the Panel reiterated its original recommendation for an investigation of possible violations of the three IDA policies it had focused on.[8]

Before taking a decision on the Panel's recommendation, and noting that the first stage of the process envisaged in the Resolution was exclusively about eligibility, the Board asked for a

---

4. *Id.* (Attachment (2) of the Panel's Recommendation.)
5. *Id.* (Panel Recommendation.)
6. *See First Annual Report of the Inspection Panel, supra* note 1, at 15.
7. *Id.*
8. *Id.*

legal opinion from the General Counsel on the eligibility requirements. In this legal opinion, this writer discussed in some detail the scope of the role of the Panel in the preliminary stage of whether to recommend an inspection in general, without commenting on the Panel's report and recommendations on the actual case at hand. One interesting point marked on that occasion was whether the term "affected party" covers any two or more persons affected by the Bank's alleged violation of its policies and procedures. As explained in Chapter Two, this was resolved by the Board's agreement that "a community of persons" assumes the sharing of some common interests or concerns.[9]

In February 1995, the Board authorized an investigation in the Arun III project with respect to the issues of environmental assessment, involuntary resettlement, and indigenous people as recommended by the Panel.[10] However, before the Panel completed its investigation, Management submitted to it a remedial action plan to address these issues.[11]

A month later, in June 1995, the Panel sent a report to the Board pointing out failures in the original appraisal of the project, but concluding that the remedial actions proposed by Management would satisfactorily meet the Bank's policy requirements if diligently followed.[12] Even though economic analysis of the project was not part of the terms of reference that the Panel set for itself and the Board approved, the Panel nevertheless expressed some concerns about that question as well.

The matter became moot after the Bank's new President (as of June 1, 1995), James D. Wolfensohn, commissioned a comprehensive review led by Maurice Strong, whom he had appointed as Senior Advisor. The conclusion of this review cited the "potential of significantly higher cost overruns, the uncertainty

---

9. *See* Chapter Two, *supra,* at 59–61.

10. This decision was taken in the Meeting of the Executive Directors of the Bank and IDA held on February 2, 1995 (XM95–1), February 10, 1995, at para 5.

11. *Memorandum by Management to the Inspection Panel proposing remedial measures,* dated May 23, 1995.

12. *Request for Inspection: Panel Investigation Report—Nepal Arun III Proposed Hydroelectric Project* (INSP/SecM95–3), June 22, 1995.

regarding co-financing [by other lenders] as well as implementation and management aspects of the project relevant to its size and risk."[13] Mr. Strong, on his part, found that the project "did not meet the standards of the industry." The President decided in August 1995 not to proceed with the project.

II. Compensation for Expropriated Assets/Ethiopia

In March 1995, the Panel received a second complaint on behalf of two Greek citizens who alleged that IDA had violated a specific policy by continuing to lend to Ethiopia despite the latter's failure to compensate them for the expropriation some twenty years earlier of property belonging to their family.[14] The policy referred to by the complainants required IDA (and the Bank) "not to lend for projects in a country if it considers that the position taken by it with respect to alien owners of expropriated property is substantially affecting its international credit standing."[15]

The request was not registered by the Panel. The reason cited for this decision was that the requesters had failed to exhaust local remedies for their compensation claim and, consequently, had not shown that the failure of the government to compensate them was caused by IDA's continued lending to Ethiopia.[16]

Management submitted a note to the Board stating that the basis for non-registration of the request should have been that

---

13. *President's Memorandum in response to the Panel's Investigation Report* dated June 21, 1995, and circulated to the Board as INSP/SecM95-5, dated August 2, 1995. *See also* Udall, *supra* note 1, at 20–21.

14. *See First Annual Report of the Inspection Panel, supra* note 1, at 56 (summarizing the details of the Request for Inspection: Compensation for Expropriation and Extension of IDA Credits to Ethiopia).

15. OMS 1.28 (May 1986) on *Disputes over Defaults on External Debt, Expropriation, and Breach of Contract* required the Bank. This OMS has been replaced in May 1996 by OP 7.40, which states that "when there are disputes over expropriations that, in the opinion of the Bank, the country is not making reasonable efforts to settle and that are substantially harming the country's international credit standing, the Bank considers whether to continue lending for new projects in the country."

16. *See First Annual Report of the Inspection Panel, supra* note 1, at 56.

the request fell outside the scope of the Panel's mandate.[17] Neither the requesters' claim nor the allegedly violated policy related to the design, appraisal, or implementation of a project, whereas inspection under the Resolution is limited to these areas. This note, which simply restated a requirement clearly stipulated in the Resolution, did stir a controversy, however, and led many Western NGOs to accuse Management of interfering in the work of the Panel and grossly encroaching on its independence.

On the suggestion of Executive Directors, a discussion between Management and the Panel took place on the issues of which policies and procedures and which projects would be covered by the Panel's mandate under the Resolution. The results were recorded in a note from the General Counsel to the Panel's Chairman which indicated that (i) the Panel's mandate is limited to reviewing compliance with Bank policies and procedures with respect to the design, appraisal, and/or implementation of projects as provided for in the Resolution; and (ii) "the term 'project' has been broadly defined in the Bank's practice and is not limited to specific investments" and that the term should not have "a narrower meaning in the context of the Inspection Panel than it otherwise has in the Bank's practice."[18]

In his reply, the Chairman of the Panel specifically understood the latter statement to mean that "SALs, SECALs and other sector operations were clearly included."[19] The two memoranda were circulated to Board members with a statement

---

17. *Memorandum from the President ad interim to the Executive Directors, Request for Inspection: Compensation for Expropriation and Extension of IDA Credits to Ethiopia* (IDA/R95–83), dated May 30, 1995.

18. *Memorandum by Ibrahim F. I. Shihata to Ernst-Günther Bröder, Scope of the Mandate of the Inspection Panel as defined in Resolution No. 93–10 (IDA 93–6) establishing the Panel (the Resolution)*, dated June 8, 1995. In this note, reference was made to the General Counsel's legal opinion on "Project and Non-Project Financing under the IBRD Articles of Agreement" (SecM84–1053), dated December 21, 1984.

19. *Memorandum from Ernst-Günther Bröder to Ibrahim Shihata, Request for Inspection: Compensation for Expropriation and Extension of IDA Credits to Ethiopia*—Meeting on Memorandum of the President *ad interim* to the Executive Directors and Mr. Shihata's Memorandum to Mr. Bröder of the same date, dated June 9, 1995.

indicating that "it is clear from this exchange that agreement has been reached to the effect that. . . . (ii) the term 'project' as used in the Resolution . . . has the same meaning as used in Bank practice."[20] The Panel concluded from this understanding that the term "project" included, in principle, programs and activities other than specific physical works.[21] As will be shown, it extended the coverage to adjustment loans when the occasion arose.

In July 1995, the Board decided to approve the decision not to register the request, expressly incorporating the point made earlier by Management in its decision.[22] As will be seen, the 1996 "Clarifications" confirmed this approach.[23]

III. Emergency Power Project/Tanzania

The third request, submitted to the Panel in May 1995, was mainly based on two grounds: (1) Failure to follow provisions in the IDA Articles of Agreement that prohibit the IDA from financing a project if, in its opinion, private financing for that project was available on reasonable terms (Article V, Section I (2)) and from being influenced by political considerations (Article V, Section 1(g)) and require that the project be recommended to the Board by a competent committee; and (2) failure to follow the IDA's environmental policies.[24] A group of U.S. and Tanzanian citizens (as, respectively, owners and employees of a corporation incorporated in Tanzania) presented that request concerning an IDA-financed power project in Tanzania.

20. *Memorandum by the Vice President and Secretary to the Executive Directors and Alternates, Scope of the Mandate of the Inspection Panel: Compensation for Expropriation and Extension of IDA Credits to Ethiopia*, dated June 16, 1995.

21. *See First Annual Report of the Inspection Panel, supra* note 1, at 57.

22. Minutes of the Meeting of the Executive Directors held on July 6, 1995 (M95–43; IDA/M95–43), July 14, 1995, at para. 3.

23. Chapter Four, *infra*, at 169.

24. *See Request for Inspection—Tanzania: Power VI Project, Panel Recommendation* (INSP/SecM95–6), August 16, 1995 (including in Annex 1 the text of the request itself).

The project related to the construction of an emergency power plant in Dar-es Salaam, Tanzania, as part of the government's plan to develop the country's energy sector and, especially, move from the utilization of imported fuel to domestically produced gas. The requesters' company had proposed its services to the government for installation of the turbines needed for the realization of the power plant, but its turbines had been found by the IDA to be technically unsound from an engineering, economic, and financial point of view.

In its July 1995 response, Management stated that (a) the requesters were not eligible, (b) one of the allegations in the request was inadmissible, and (c) no violation of Bank policies had occurred.[25]

Regarding the requesters' eligibility, Management stated that the U.S. private requesters had not demonstrated that they had at least a substantial presence in Tanzania to fulfill the requirement of the Resolution that a requester should be "in the territory of the borrower." Management also questioned the existence of a commonality of interest among the requesters in view of their different capacities as owners and employees in the corporation from which, in Management's view, only divergent, but not common interests, could result. Management also questioned whether the project had any direct impact on the requesters. Regarding the inadmissibility of a specific allegation in the request, Management asserted that failures related to the consideration of alternative private sector financing under IDA's Articles of Agreement could not be subject of a request for inspection since such failures, even if they existed, would not relate to non-compliance with Bank policies and procedures applicable to the project. Finally, Management rebutted alleged failures to follow requirements under the IDA's Articles of Agreement and its environmental policies.

---

25. *See Request for Inspection: Panel Recommendation—Tanzania: Power VI Project* (INSP/SecM95–6), August 16, 1995 (including in Attachment (2) Management's response).

The Panel undertook a field review to ascertain the request's eligibility.[26] As the Panel noted in its recommendation of August 1995, the field review established the requesters' eligibility and the request's general admissibility to its satisfaction. In terms of the alleged failures, however, the Panel did not find that failures by the IDA existed. By contrast, it found that the Board of IDA, by approving the credit, had clearly concluded that private financing was not available on terms reasonable for the recipient, since it was informed by both Management and the requesters of the availability of financing by another source. The Panel also concluded that the requesters had failed to demonstrate that their interests were likely to be affected in a material way as a result of any violations by the IDA of its environmental policies.[27] Therefore, the Panel did not recommend an investigation.

In September 1995, the Board, on a no-objection basis, took notice of and approved the Panel's recommendation not to investigate.[28]

IV. Rondonia Natural Resources Management Project—PLANAFLORO/Brazil

The fourth request, which was registered in June 1995, related to the IBRD-financed Rondonia Natural Resources Management Project (PLANAFLORO) in the state of Rondonia in Brazil. A group of NGOs from that state, acting as agents of Rondonia residents, complained about non-compliance with a number of IBRD policies, including the environment-related policies on "forestry," "wildlands," "indigenous people," and "NGO participation."[29] The request also alleged non-compliance with other

---

26. *Id.*, at para. 6. (Panel Recommendation.)

27. *Id.*, at para. 15. (Panel Recommendation.)

28. *Minutes of the Meeting of the Executive Directors of the Bank and IDA on September 21, 1995* (M95–55; IDA/M95–55), September 26, 1995, at para. 6.

29. *See Request for Inspection—Brazil: Rondonia Natural Resources Management Project, Panel Recommendation* (INSP/R95–2), August 18, 1995 (including in Annex 1 the text of the request). For Management's initial response to the request, *see* Annex 2 of the Panel's Recommendation.

Bank policies (that is, policies on "investment lending," "accounting, financial reporting, and auditing," "project monitoring and evaluation," "procurement," "use of consultants," "project supervision," "borrower compliance with audit covenants," and "suspension of disbursements").

Management's response of July 1995 contended that the request was not eligible because there was (a) no material harm suffered by the requesters, and (b) no direct attribution of such harm to Bank actions or omissions.[30] In Management's view, the project aimed at reversing several decades of environmental mismanagement of the Rondonia area through an improved approach to natural resource management and conservation. Any harm described in the request, such as the occurrence of natural resource degradation or depletion, was of too general a nature to constitute harm suffered by the requesters or to be linked to the Bank's actions or omissions in connection with the project. Besides, Management asserted that it had complied with the environment-related policies on forestry, wild lands, indigenous people, and NGO participation as well as with all other policies referred to in the request, rebutting all claims of non-compliance by the requesters in detail. Management, however, generally shared some of the requesters' concerns, namely that the project was not proceeding as quickly as expected. To alleviate the latter concerns, Management provided information on its strategy to help improve and accelerate project implementation, including specific remedial actions agreed to with the borrower.[31]

In August 1995, the Panel recommended to the Board, on the basis of an initial field study, that an investigation was warranted into potential violations of several policies related to the design, appraisal, and supervision and monitoring of the execution of PLANAFLORO.[32] Although the Panel acknowledged that Management had provided extensive information and a fair and realistic assessment of most of the project's difficulties and

---

30. *Id*. in Annex 2 of the Panel's Recommendation.
31. *Id*.
32. *Id*. at para. 14. (Panel Recommendation.)

delays, the Panel was not convinced that there had been full compliance with Bank policies and procedures. Nor was the Panel satisfied that the proposed remedial measures were adequate.

The Panel did not, however, recommend an investigation of the Bank's compliance with its procurement guidelines because of an earlier confirmation by the Board that all procurement issues were outside the Panel's mandate. This confirmation had been issued after the Panel had asked the Board for it in the course of a separate query from an NGO. After having received the Board's approval of this approach, the Panel clarified in its response to the inquiring NGO in April 1995 that the provision of the Resolution excluding complaints against "procurement decisions of borrowers" from the scope of the Panel's mandate extended also to procurement decisions by the Bank.[33] Quoting from the first edition of this book,[34] and noting that there was a separate mechanism for addressing complaints related to procurement, the Panel concluded that procurement decisions by the Bank, while not expressly mentioned in the Resolution, were excluded from the Panel's jurisdiction.[35] The 1996 "Clarifications" later confirmed that conclusion by stating that no procurement action is subject to inspection by the Panel, whether taken by the Bank or by the borrower.[36]

After receipt of the Panel's recommendation, the Board, after a lengthy discussion, asked the Panel in September 1995 to conduct an additional review to further substantiate the materiality of damages and to establish whether such damages were caused by deviation from Bank policies and procedures. This step may have, in fact, amounted to authorizing an investigation, albeit a preliminary one, before the eligibility of the request was established by the Board. It was not based on the provisions of

---

33. *See First Annual Report of the Inspection Panel, supra* note 1, at 55–56.

34. Ibrahim F.I. Shihata, *The World Bank Inspection Panel* 51–52 (1994). *See also* Chapter Two, *supra* at 52–54.

35. *See First Annual Report of the Inspection Panel, supra,* note 1, at 55–56.

36. *See* 1996 *Clarifications,* reprinted in Annex I–2 to this book, in the section on "eligibility and access."

the Resolution that limit the first phase of the process to ascertaining the eligibility of the request before the carrying out of investigation and, as explained in the previous Chapter, expect the Panel's work at this stage[37] to be completed on a *prima facie* basis within 21 days.[38] In the case at hand, however, the Board concluded that it needed more factual information to enable it to reach a decision on whether further investigation should be carried out. The decision had some basis in the Operating Procedures adopted by the Panel.[39] The practice was later codified in the 1996 "Clarifications."[40] It was seriously questioned and reversed, however, in the second review of the Resolution, as elaborated in Chapter Four.[41]

In November 1995, before submission of the Panel's additional report, Management informed the Panel of the status of the project's implementation; in particular, it presented to the Panel a detailed remedial action plan to be agreed upon with the Government of Brazil.

In December 1995, the Panel submitted its additional report to the Board.[42] In this additional report, the Panel maintained that Bank failures existed both in the design and implementation of the project, in particular because the situation for many intended beneficiaries was worse than it had been two years ago when the project had started.

According to the Panel, the deterioration of the situation was the result of completing the road access components of the project before completing its zoning part. Unlawful burning, logging, and encroachment in areas reserved for indigenous people

---

37. *See* Chapter Two, *supra*, at 49–51.

38. *See Resolution Establishing the Panel*, reprinted in Annex I–1–1 to this book, at para. 19.

39. *See* paras. 34–35 of the *Operating Procedures* adopted by the Panel on August 19, 1994 and Chapter Two, *supra*, at note 66.

40. *See* 1996 *Clarifications*, reprinted in Annex I–2 to this book, in the section on the "Panel's Function" and Chapter Four, *infra*, at 165.

41. *See* Chapter Four, *infra*, at 187–188.

42. *See Request for Inspection—Brazil: Rondonia Natural Resources Management Project, Panel Report on Additional Review* (INSP/R95–4), December 12, 1995.

and rubber collectors did thus take place, preventing those people from making their living as usual based on trees, flora, and fauna. It also emphasized that the borrower's action plan agreed upon with Management would not necessarily solve the existing problems because many of the remedies envisaged were not detailed, but were to be defined in the future.

The Board decided in January 1996 not to authorize an investigation but to review the execution of the action plan prepared by the borrower and Bank staff after six to nine months, with the assistance of the Panel. This decision was taken after the Board received the Panel's additional report and a new report by Management[43] on the status of the project's implementation, which included the aforementioned action plan. The review was completed in December 1996 to the Board's satisfaction.[44]

The handling of this particular request by the Panel, Management, and the Board has a special relevance to the evolution of the Panel's experience. By requesting the Panel to carry out an additional review, it contributed to the "preliminary assessment" process that was later codified in the above-mentioned "Clarifications" of the Resolution issued by the Board in 1996. As will be shown, the potential problems of that approach foreshadowed debates that later called for a second review of the Resolution.

This was the first case where a remedial action plan agreed between the borrower and Management was submitted to the Board before the latter considered the Panel's recommendation on the investigation. (In the Arun III case, the remedial plan was submitted to the Board after it authorized full investigation, but

43. *See Brazil: Rondonia Natural Resources Management Project, Management Report on the Status of Implementation* (SecM95–1271), December 20, 1995.

44. *See Brazil: Rondonia Natural Resources Management Project, Management Report on the Status of Implementation* (SecM96–1159), December 2, 1996, and *Brazil: Rondonia Natural Resources Management Project, Inspection Panel Report on Review of Progress in Implementation* (INSP/SecM97–7), March 26, 1997, which were discussed in the Meeting of the Board of Executive Directors on April 3, 1997, according to the Informal Notes of the Meeting.

before the Panel had submitted its findings.) The Resolution does not envisage the preparation of remedial action by the borrower and does not mention that an action plan remedying Bank failures may be submitted by Management at this point in time. As explained in detail in Chapters Two and Four,[45] it only gives Management the opportunity to adopt remedial measures concerning the Bank's own failures on two different occasions: before the request for inspection is heard by the Panel, and after an investigation is completed.

PLANAFLORO did not remain the only case in which Management presented a remedial action plan that the borrower agreed to carry out shortly before the Board had to decide on the Panel's recommendation. The submission of a remedial action plan of this type at this point in time became a trend in Management behavior. As will be shown in the following chapter,[46] this has confused the issue of Bank failures with that of the borrower. It also created a dilemma for the Board, which could not ignore the introduction of new remedies that, if deemed sufficient to address the harm, would obviate the need for inspection and thus make it superfluous. Meanwhile, the issue of *the Bank's* compliance with its operational policies would be sidelined on the assumption that no failure was attributed to the Bank.

V.   Pangue/Ralco Hydroelectric Complex/Chile

The fifth request, received by the Panel in November 1995, came from a Chilean NGO, representing people living in the area in which the Pangue/Ralco complex of hydroelectric dams on a river in Chile was to be built.[47] The requesters alleged the violation of a number of IFC and Bank policies. However, the Panel

---

45. *See* Chapter Two, *supra*, at 49–51, Chapter Four, *infra*, at 175–176, and Chapter Five, *infra*, at 223–225.

46. *See* Chapter Four, *infra*, at 180–181, and Chapter Five, *infra*, at 220–221, and 225–226.

47. *See Request for Inspection—IFC Financing of Hydroelectric Dams in the Biobío River in Chile* (INSP/SecM95-8), December 1, 1995.

informed the requesters and the Board of its decision not to register the complaint because it found that the request clearly lay outside its mandate since it concerned not an IBRD- or IDA-financed project, but one financed by the IFC.[48]

At the request of the IFC President (who is also the President of the Bank), outside consultants were appointed to examine the complaints. They wrote a lengthy report on the violations attributed to IFC that was subsequently published by IFC. On the advice of outside counsel, only the comments, findings, and recommendations related to IFC were made public to protect IFC from possible legal actions (given the report's specific allegations of violations by the enterprise in charge of the project that had not been established through a judicial process). The publication also included a rebuttal by IFC of many of the accusations leveled against it, along with intended corrective measures where they were justified.[49]

In spite of its affiliation with the Bank, IFC is a legally separate organization that supports private investment without government guarantee. Its activities are not subject to the Resolution establishing the Panel. However, this case gave momentum to calls on the Bank Group to extend the inspection function to the IFC. As will be explained in the following chapter, IFC Management has already submitted options for an inspection mechanism for its activities, noting that the nature of such activities requires differentiation from the Bank's Panel.[50]

VI. Jamuna Bridge Project/Bangladesh

The sixth request was received from a Bangladeshi NGO, representing the "char people" (that is, people who live on mid-channel islands that emerge periodically from the Jamuna River bed as

---

48. *See First Annual Report of the Inspection Panel, supra* note 1, at 21.

49. *See Pangue Project—Jay Hair Review Report* (IFC Report No. 2067), dated July 15, 1997. The report indicated that portions of it were deleted for the reason stated above.

50. *See* Chapter Four, *infra*, at 157 *seq.*

a result of accretion).[51] The request was registered by the Panel in August 1996. According to it, the IDA had failed to comply with its policies on "environmental assessment," "resettlement," and "participation of NGOs." The project concerned involved the financing of the construction of a multipurpose bridge over the Jamuna River. In particular, the requesters alleged they had not received compensation for the damages incurred as a result of their resettlement. In fact, it was claimed that the initial resettlement plan did not even acknowledge the existence of the char people.

Management's response of September 1996 referred to an erosion and flood policy adopted by the borrower in agreement with the Bank that included a system of compensation of the char dwellers affected by river erosion.[52] This erosion and flood policy was, however, adopted only after the request was registered and while Management was drafting its response.

The Panel reviewed the requesters' concerns, according to the Bank's records, both at Bank headquarters and at the bridge site. It concluded that the construction of the river channel through river training (that is, river alignment works) was likely to result in destruction or permanent flooding of the islands on which the char dwellers lived and earned a living. The Panel also examined the "erosion and flood policy" agreed upon with the IDA that was designed to compensate for any adverse effects of the destruction or flooding of the islands. In light of the latter policy, the Panel found that an investigation was not warranted at that stage, a view which it expressed to the Board in its report of December 1996.[53] According to the Panel, the "erosion and flood policy" potentially constituted an adequate framework for the mitigation of or compensation for harm. Compliance by Management with the Bank's policies and procedures would be

---

51. See *Request for Inspection—Bangladesh: Jamuna Bridge Project, Panel Recommendation* (INSP/SecM96-14), December 2, 1996 (including in Annex 1 the text of the request). For Management's initial response, *see* Annex 2 of the Panel's Report and Recommendation.

52. *Id.* (reproducing Management's response in Annex 2).

53. *Id.* at para. 56. (Panel Recommendation.)

assured if balanced supervision and constant monitoring by Management were forthcoming.

In April 1997, the Board approved the Panel's recommendation not to investigate. However, the Board asked Management to provide a progress report on the project's implementation for its review. It also stated that it would invite the Panel to participate in that review.[54]

In May 1998, Management submitted its progress report on the implementation of the erosion and flood action plan, noting that the bridge was opened one year ahead of the loan's closing date and that the project's progress in terms of environmental and socioeconomic programs for affected people was satisfactory.[55]

In August 1998, the Panel presented its report on the progress of the implementation of the erosion and flood action plan.[56] Focusing on the progress towards mitigating the adverse effects of the project on char people and the adequacy of the project's remedial measures, the Panel concluded that, despite some remaining problems, the remedial measures in place for compensating the char people appeared adequate if certain adjustments were made. Once again, the issue of whether the Bank had violated its operational policies was overshadowed by the borrower's corrective measures in favor of the affected people.

VII. Yacyretá Hydroelectric Project/ Argentina/Paraguay

The seventh request registered in October 1996 was more complex. A Paraguayan NGO alleged, both on its own behalf and on behalf of people living in the project area (who requested that

---

54. *Minutes of the Meeting of the Executive Directors of the Bank and IDA* (M97–19; IDA/M97–18), April 15, 1997, at para. 3.

55. *See Bangladesh: Jamuna Bridge Project, Management's Report on the Progress of the Implementation of the Erosion and Flood Action Plan* (SecM98–422), May 21, 1998.

56. *See Bangladesh: Jamuna Bridge Project, Inspection Panel Report on the Progress of the Implementation of the Erosion and Flood Action Plan* (INSP/SecM98–13), August 17, 1998.

their names "be made available only to the Inspection Panel members but otherwise remain confidential"), that the IBRD had, among other things, failed to follow its policies on "resettlement," "indigenous people," "wildlands," "project supervision," and "environmental assessment" in the design and implementation of the Yacyretá Hydroelectric Power Plant project.[57] This project is physically located in Argentina and Paraguay and benefits both countries. It is co-financed by the Bank and the Inter-American Development Bank (IDB). The Bank's loans were made to Argentina. The latter country will be the primary user of the electricity generated by the power plant to be built, together with a water reservoir, by closing the Parana River through which the boundary between Argentina and Paraguay runs. The project under this loan is carried out by a binational (that is, a joint public Argentinean-Paraguayan) entity, Entidad Binacional Yacyretá (EBY).

In its response of October 1996, Management challenged the eligibility of the request in a number of respects.[58] It argued first that, since the Bank loans for the Yacyretá project were made to Argentina and the requester was a Paraguayan entity, neither the requester, nor allegedly affected parties represented by it, were "in the territory of the borrower," as required by the Resolution. It added, however, that, due to the circumstances of this project, "Management understands the pragmatic interest in applying the Board Resolution flexibly on this point." Then Management took the position that the requester could not file a request on its own behalf because it had not itself been directly affected by any damage. Finally, it suggested that the "anonymity" of the requesters would impose serious constraints on Management's ability to fully respond to their concerns, particularly regarding the scope of the alleged harms and the seriousness of alleged violations and causation.

---

57. *See Request for Inspection—Argentina/Paraguay: Yacyretá Hydroelectric Project, Panel Recommendation* (INSP/R96–2), December 26, 1996 (including in Annex 1 the text of the request). For Management's initial response, *see* Annex 2 of the Panel's Recommendation.

58. *Id.,* reproducing Management's response in Annex 2.

The Panel, after conducting a field study, concluded in its report, dated December 24, 1996, that the requesters were eligible.[59] They were considered to be "in the territory of the borrower" because the project had a bi-national character. The Government of Paraguay, although not a recipient of the Bank loan, had also accepted some obligations under "owners agreements" jointly concluded between Paraguay, Argentina, and the Bank. In addition, a different loan, not cited by the requesters, had been made by the Bank to Paraguay in part to address the resettlement of people living in Paraguay in the area next to the project site. In what seems to be a recognition of the "pragmatic interest" referred to in Management's response, the Panel found that the Paraguayan NGO and the Paraguayan residents it represented were eligible requesters in the territory of the borrower, even though they were not residents of Argentina. The claim of this NGO was admitted by the Panel on the basis of its allegations regarding damage to biodiversity and other environmental conditions caused by an alleged violation of Bank policies, even in the absence of any evidence of damage to the NGO itself or to the persons it represents.[60] Furthermore, "anonymity" was found by the Panel not to be a valid reason for declaring a request ineligible. The Panel stated that it had to take into account the legitimate concerns of requesters regarding possible reprisals against them, presumably by government authorities. (While the Panel's report mentions that "[t]he Inspector verified the identity of the 'anonymous' requesters and obtained first-hand knowledge of some of the alleged material harm on the spot during his field visit," it was clear that the complainants were not anonymous to the Panel; their identity was only to be kept confidential.)

Besides these technical issues related to the requesters' standing, the Panel's "preliminary conclusion" was that the request was eligible for investigation. In spite of the preliminary nature of

---

59. *Id.* at paras. 13–39. (Panel Recommendation.) *See also Second Annual Report of the Inspection Panel, supra,* note 1, at 11.

60. For further comments, *see* Chapter Five, at 228.

this conclusion, the Panel's report stated, "the Panel is not convinced that there has been substantial compliance with the relevant policies and procedures."[61] It noted in particular that the main civil work components were almost complete, while only about a fifth of the housing in the resettlement component had been completed, and other activities and social mitigation measures lagged far behind. The Panel, therefore, recommended that the Board authorize an inspection.[62]

In its discussion of the Panel's report in February 1997, the Board did not, however, follow the Panel's recommendation. Its decision was based partly on the fact that Management and the borrower had meanwhile agreed on an action plan designed to take care of the problems associated with project implementation. Instead, the Board agreed, after an informal meeting, on a formula "negotiated" among its members. It invited the Panel to "undertake a review of the existing problems of the Yacyretá project regarding environmental and resettlement issues in order to provide an assessment of the adequacy of the action plan agreed upon between the Bank and the countries concerned (Argentina and Paraguay) within the next four months." The Board then added that it expected the Panel "to review consistency of the Bank's actions with its procedures while reviewing the action plan." The latter addition, which was not part of the original negotiated formula, was subject to objections on the grounds that such a review would amount to an investigation, whereas the purpose was the forward looking remedial exercise. It was agreed upon, however, at the end of the meeting. Later on, this addition raised a controversy as to whether the word "procedures" in this context also covers the Bank's policies. Although that controversy was not resolved in the Board, the Panel's review was certainly not limited to Bank procedures. According to the Panel, "Bank procedures, in practice, flow only from Bank policies and, therefore, it could include in its review

---

61. See *Request for Inspection—Argentina/Paraguay: Yacyretá Hydroelectric Project, Panel Recommendation* (INSP/R96–2), December 26, 1996, at para. 27.

62. *Id.* at para. 43.

of Yacyretá the issue of compliance with both procedures and policies of the Bank."[63] An important point raised in the Panel's report was missed in the Board discussion, that is, the eligibility of the request in the absence of any evidence of damage to the requester, but due to alleged damage to biodiversity and the environment (a position that clearly departs from the Board's denial, during discussion of the Resolution, of claims based on public interest).

While the Panel was reviewing the plan, it received a number of further requests from Argentinean requesters asking for inspection of specific aspects of project execution. They related to alleged damage to the people and communities, as well as the environment on the Argentine side of the reservoir. The Panel, in consultation with the Board, incorporated the new requests into the ongoing review.[64] The Panel's review coincided with an investigation that was being carried out at the time by the inspection mechanism of the IDB at the request of its Board.

In September 1997, the Panel presented the report on its review to the Board.[65] Neither the word "inspection" nor "investigation" was mentioned, but the review amounted, in substance, to an investigation of the complaints submitted by the requesters.

The Board discussed the Panel's report in December 1997 and concluded that the implementation of the action plan had made significant progress towards resolving the environmental and resettlement problems of the project. It requested Bank Management to continue its follow-up of the implementation of the action plan and to report to it on further progress in the matter within six months. After a discussion on whether the Panel ought to be involved in that follow-up, the Board decided not to involve the Panel in the follow-up this time but announced that it would determine later what further role it wished the Panel to play in this respect.

---

63. See Second Annual Report of the Inspection Panel, supra note 1, at 18.

64. See Request for Inspection—Argentina/Paraguay: Yacyretá Hydro-electric Project (INSP/R97–5), June 12, 1997.

65. See Request for Inspection—Argentina/Paraguay: Yacyretá Hydro-electric Project, Panel Review and Assessment (INSP/R97–10), September 18, 1997.

Another progress report was discussed in the Board in June 1998.[66] In that report to the Board, Management conceded that serious social and economic problems remained on the Paraguayan side of the project, although significant progress had been made on the Argentinean side. It was agreed that Management, together with the IDB, would develop another action plan in consultation with affected people to address the problems identified in Paraguay.

The last progress report was discussed in the Board in May 1999.[67] In that report, Management noted that implementation of the project was well on its way on the Argentinean side, while, on the Paraguayan side, implementation continued to be characterized by setbacks. The latter were, however, beginning to be overcome with intensive supervision and persistent pressure from the Bank. Increased supervision has resulted in virtual completion of main resettlement works and greater consultation with affected groups. As problems with the provision of infrastructure and social services for the families being resettled remained to be solved, completion of the implementation of the action plan would be delayed beyond 1999. Overall progress nevertheless has been made on the basis of actions jointly agreed upon between the governments of Argentina and Paraguay on the one hand, and the Bank and IDB on the other.

It should be noted that meanwhile, in mid-February 1997, 51 Argentinean brickmakers, who had been resettled during the course of the construction of the project, initiated separate law suits against the joint executing agency (EBY) for damages suffered as a result of the project. In September 1997, both the Bank and the IDB were added as co-defendants to the law suits. The Province of Misiones was later added as a co-defendant in August 1998. The alleged basis for the brickmakers' action against the

---

66. See *Informal Notes—Status of Action Program, Argentina/Paraguay: Yacyretá Hydroelectric Project,* Meeting of the Board of Executive Directors on June 23, 1998.
67. See *Argentina—Yacyretá Hydroelectric Project—Progress Report* (SecM99–333), May 14, 1999, discussed in an informal Board meeting on May 25, 1999.

Bank was its involvement as a co-financier of the project in the preparation of the resettlement and environmental action plans. The Bank filed preliminary motions with the court seeking dismissal of the law suits on the basis of the Bank's immunity and the plaintiffs' failure to state a claim against the Bank.[68] The latter failure was manifested by the fact that there was no privity between the Bank and the plaintiffs that could form a basis for a contractual cause of action, and the Bank did not undertake or breach any duty to the plaintiffs and did not cause harm that could be attributed to a Bank negligence. As required by Argentinean law, the Bank also filed answers on the merits. The case is pending.

The NGO, which had filed the request with the Bank, also brought a request for investigation through the IDB's inspection mechanism.[69] This request, which was received in December 1996, led IDB's Board of Executive Directors in April 1997 to decide that a panel of three experts selected from the IDB Independent Inspection Mechanism Roster should investigate the request. This was done after IDB's Management had adopted, in February 1997, a "Basic Program" to mitigate the social and environmental effects of the project. The panel of experts reported to IDB's Board in September 1997. It detected a variety of problems, regarding effective participation of affected people, resettlement, and the environment, which had the potential to erode the purposes of the project. The IDB panel expressed its view that measures in addition to those already in place and contemplated by the "Basic Program" would be needed to solve all problems. In October 1997, IDB's Management sent its response to the panel's report to its Board, agreeing in principle with the panel's assessment. So far, IDB's Board of Executive Directors has not yet made a final decision on further corrective measures to be taken. However, a high-level meeting

---

68. For details of the question of Bank immunity, *see* Chapter Five, Section II, *infra*, at 243 *seq*.

69. For detailed information on the arguments made in this request and its status, *see* IDB's inspection function web page at http://www.iadb.org/cont/poli/yacreta.htm.

of the governments concerned with IDB, at which IBRD representatives were also present, held in early December 1998, discussed future action related to this matter.

VIII. Jute Sector Adjustment Credit/ Bangladesh

The eighth request submitted to the Panel was filed in August 1996 by a group of owners of private jute mills in Bangladesh.[70] The requesters alleged that they had suffered economic losses because of the IDA's failure to follow its policies and procedures on "adjustment lending," "supervision of programs," and "suspension of disbursements" in the design and implementation of the Bangladesh Jute Sector Adjustment Program. This program was meant to restructure Bangladesh's jute manufacturing industry according to the needs of the world market. Measures taken for the purpose of restructuring included the elimination of excess capacity by closure and downsizing of a certain number of public mills, privatization of another number of these mills, and retrenchment of employees of closed, downsized, or privatized mills.

The requesters specifically alleged that they had suffered losses because, contrary to the initial intention of the program, the privatization and closing of public sector mills was delayed. In addition, public sector mills were provided with capital and could thus operate at full capacity, while private sector mills such as the requesters' were denied capital and had therefore to reduce their business.

As a result of internal problems in Bangladesh, the conditions for the disbursement of the second tranche of the credit, originally expected to take place in March 1995, were not met, and consequently the tranche was not released. In fact, the project suffered from a three-year delay in implementation. This was the

---

70. *See Request for Inspection—Bangladesh: Jute Sector Adjustment Credit, Panel Report and Recommendation* (INSP/R97–3), March 20, 1997 (including in Annex 1 the text of the request).

first, and so far the only, request for inspection related to an adjustment credit in the absence of any physical project.

In its response to the request, Management took the position that "complaints with respect to delays in the implementation of [an adjustment program were] outside the jurisdiction of the Inspection Panel" as such complaints would only concern actions that were the "responsibility of other parties, but not of IDA."[71]

In March 1997, notwithstanding the above argument, the Panel, on the basis of Bank records and a field visit, informed the Board that, in its view, the request was eligible because the requesters had suffered the alleged harm caused by the Bank's failure to ensure sufficient political commitment on the part of the borrowing government and to maintain certain macroeconomic policies as required under the Bank's policy on adjustment lending.[72] The Bank, said the Panel, might have also failed to supervise the general macro-economic framework under the supervision of programs policy.[73] In addition, according to the Panel, the Bank should have considered remedies other than the non-release of the second tranche of the credit, such as suspension and cancellation of the credit, as prescribed in the policy on suspension of disbursement.

The Panel disagreed with Management's position that the Panel had no mandate to review the implementation of adjustment credits. It requested the Acting General Counsel to explain the remedies available to the Bank under an adjustment loan in case the borrower fails to take the actions needed for implementing the adjustment program or takes actions inconsistent with that program. The Acting General Counsel listed a range of available remedies that apply to all Bank loans. On the basis of its "preliminary review," the Panel was satisfied that the request met all eligibility criteria, but it was not satisfied that Management complied with all Bank policies during the implementation of the

---

71. *Id.*, reproducing Management's response in Annex 2.
72. *Id.*, at paras. 87–89. (Panel Recommendation.)
73. *Id.*

project. Noting that the new Government of Bangladesh and the Bank were negotiating a revised time-table for the implementation of the program and an extension for the credit's closing date, the Panel stated that "close supervision during this extension with regard to financial discipline might at least meet some of the requesters' concerns." It added, however, that an extension of the closing date, without revisiting basic design concepts with the government and requesters, might not be an adequate solution and that the termination of the program without a new approach in place "would presumably meet none of [the requester's] expectations from the reform program." The Panel concluded that investigations in this context "would serve no useful purpose," and, therefore, it did not recommend it to the Board.[74]

In its meeting in April 1997, the Board agreed with the Panel's conclusion not to investigate, without further comment. The decision was taken on a no-objection basis (that is, without holding a meeting in which the important underlying issues could have been discussed). In June 1997, this credit was closed without disbursement of its remaining tranches.

By simply agreeing with the Panel's recommendation not to authorize an investigation of this case, the Board did not consider the implications of subjecting adjustment programs supported by Bank loans to the Panel's inspection, even though the Panel takes it for granted that this is the case now. This position is based on the not too specific note agreed upon with Management on the occasion of the second case mentioned earlier and confirmed in the 1996 "Clarifications," that is, that "the term 'project' as used in the Resolution . . . has the same meaning as used in Bank practice."[75] Assuming that this case will be taken as a precedent and that adjustment operations would be subject to the inspection function, the important questions raised in Chapter Two should then be considered.[76] As mentioned in that Chapter, these questions were not discussed at the time of the adoption of the

---

74. *Id.* at para. 89.
75. *See* this Chapter, *supra*, at 106.
76. *See* the discussion of this point, in Chapter Two, *supra*, at 37–41.

Resolution because it was generally assumed throughout its drafting that it was to deal with project operations. The term *project* is
broadly used in the Bank, but adjustment operations are not considered part of project lending in the Bank's usage.

IX.   Itaparica Resettlement and Irrigation Project/Brazil

The ninth request, received by the Panel in March 1997 and registered in the same month, concerned a resettlement and irrigation project in Itaparica, Brazil.[77] It was financed by two
successive Bank loans (even though the second loan was extended through an amendment of the original loan agreement). The
request was submitted by a local union of rural workers representing people living in the project area. It alleged IBRD violation of its policies on "dam and reservoir projects,"
"environmental assessment," "involuntary resettlement," and
"indigenous people." It may be noted that although the Bank did
not finance the construction of the Itaparica dam that gave rise to
the involuntary resettlement of people, the negative effects of
which, however, the Bank tried to mitigate by financing the resettlement and irrigation project.

   In its response of May 1997, Management asserted that the
request was time-barred because more than 95 percent of the
combined proceeds of the loans financing the project had been
disbursed as of the date the request was received.[78] (The
response characterized the two loans as one in view of the fact

---

77. *See Request for Inspection—Brazil: Itaparica Resettlement and
Irrigation Project, Panel Recommendation* (INSP/R97–7), June 27, 1997
(reproducing the request in Annex 1). For Management's initial response to the
request, *see* Annex 2 to the Panel's Recommendation.

78. A first loan for the Itaparica Resettlement and Irrigation Project was
approved in 1987 in the amount of US$132 million equivalent. A supplemen-
tal loan in the amount of US$100 million equivalent was approved in 1990.
Pointing to the aggregate loan of US$232 million equivalent and the fact that
$226.143 million of that aggregate amount (*i.e.*, 97.5 percent) had been dis-
bursed as of the registration date of the request, Management came to the conclusion that the request was ineligible.

that the supplemental loan was introduced by an amendment of the original loan agreement.) Regarding the alleged violation of Bank policies, Management contended that the Bank policies had been complied with, although the project was executed during a tumultuous period in Brazil with high inflation, political change, and shifting priorities all taking their toll on project execution. Delays, in particular, had been overcome by close supervision by Bank staff and the setting of benchmarks for project monitoring agreed upon between the Bank and the Government with the objective of accelerating project execution.

In June 1997, the Panel, which had carried out an initial field study, recommended investigation of the complaint.[79] It noted specifically that serious violations of the policies on involuntary resettlement, indigenous peoples, and supervision by Management could have occurred. In the view of the Panel, these possible violations warranted an investigation. It may be noted that the Panel rejected Management's view that the request was time-barred. It based its view on the argument that the existence of a single project with the same objectives and features for which consecutive financing in separate, successive loans had been made would (neither legally nor practically) mean that there would be a single loan of which the proceeds had to be combined.

Before the Board took a decision on the Panel's recommendation, some Executive Directors requested a legal opinion from the General Counsel on the question of whether the request was time-barred. In the legal opinion submitted in response to that request, the General Counsel took the view that the Resolution's rule, which barred requests for inspection when disbursement of at least 95 percent of the loan financing the project had taken place, did not apply to the actual case.[80] The project was initially financed by a Bank loan, which was fully disbursed. It was further

---

79. See *Request for Inspection—Brazil: Itaparica Resettlement and Irrigation Project, Panel Recommendation* (INSP/R97–7), June 27, 1997. (Panel Recommendation at para. 46.)

80. See *Legal Opinion of the Senior Vice President and General Counsel, Time-Limits on the Eligibility of Complaints Submitted to the Inspection Panel* (SecM97–693), July 28, 1997.

financed on a later date by a supplemental loan that had not been 95 percent disbursed (although it came close to that). The opinion concluded that, under such circumstances, the request would not be time-barred for the second loan even though it was financing the same project. In calculating the disbursed amount for this purpose, each loan had to be treated separately, regardless of whether the additional funds made available to the borrower were committed through a new, additional loan agreement or an amendment of the first agreement financing the project. An amendment of the agreement providing the first loan was a convenient device; it did not change the fact that a new loan was made to the borrower.

The Board decided in September 1997 not to authorize an investigation, noting that a remedial action plan had been prepared by the borrower after Management's initial response to the Panel. Implementation of the Plan would be fully financed by the Government of Brazil at a cost of $290 million. The Board concluded that the Bank should help supervise the implementation of the Brazilian Plan as requested by the Government. It noted specifically that both the action plan and the request for Bank supervision of its implementation were initiated by the Brazilian Government, and it decided to further review progress made in a year. It also decided to "invite the Panel to assist in that review, taking into account the findings of the ongoing OED study of the project when available."

In December 1998, Management submitted its report summarizing the progress achieved in project implementation since the 1997 September Board meeting.[81] Together with that report, Management presented the project's Implementation Completion Report (ICR) that provided a comprehensive assessment of the Itaparica resettlement since its beginning, including the evaluation of project outcomes. The progress report focussed on the main events that had taken place since December 1997, when the loan was closed, especially with respect to the

---

81. *See Brazil: Itaparica Resettlement and Irrigation Project—Implementation Progress Report* (SecM98–1005), December 24, 1998.

implementation of the Government of Brazil's action plan. The report noted significant progress made in the construction of the irrigation works, the construction of social infrastructure, the process of negotiations on resettlement options with affected people, the issuance of land titles for the rural population, the creation of cooperatives and/or farmers' associations, and the construction of service centers. Management further announced that it would continue to supervise the implementation of the project until December 1999 and submit by then, in addition to regular supervision reports, a final progress report. The December 1998 progress report, together with a technical note supplementing the report,[82] was discussed in the Board in May 1999 in an informal meeting.

In its technical note of May 1999, Management said that the chances of sustainability of the Itaparica project had increased with support by all levels of the Government of Brazil and improved supervision by the Bank, while significant and complex challenges remained to be addressed for a successful completion of the resettlement.

During this September 1997 meeting, where a lengthy discussion of this and the next request took place, the Board decided to hold a second review of the role of the Panel and the Resolution establishing it.

X.   NTPC Power Generation Project/India

The tenth request was received by the Panel in May 1997. Residents in the Singrauli area of India, where the National Thermal Power Corporation (NTPC) operates and is expanding a number of coal-powered generating facilities financed by the Bank, alleged non-compliance by the Bank with, among others, its policies on "environmental assessment," "involuntary

---

82. *See Brazil: Itaparica Resettlement and Irrigation Project—Technical Note, Supplement to Implementation Progress Report* (SecM98–1005/1), May 14, 1999.

resettlement," and "indigenous people."[83] The complaint was filed by one of the residents on her own behalf and on behalf of 33 other residents who requested that their names be made available only to the Panel members, but otherwise remain confidential.

In its response to the request, Management, for the first time, recognized partial failure to observe some of the Bank's policies involved. Following what had become a tradition by then, it submitted a detailed remedial action plan agreed upon with the borrower, which it attached to its response of June 1997.[84]

The Panel undertook a field visit. On the basis of that visit, together with a review of the records, it concluded that there would appear to be no grounds for an investigation into the allegation of failure to observe the Bank's policy on indigenous peoples. However, the Panel found *prima facie* evidence of harm indicating the possibility of serious violations by the Bank of other policies and procedures, specifically those on involuntary resettlement, environmental assessment, and supervision. It, therefore, recommended in July 1997 that the Executive Directors of the Bank's Board authorize an investigation into these aspects.

In September 1997, the Board approved the Panel's recommendation for an investigation by the Panel of the Bank's role in the power generation project. Conscious that the Panel had already undertaken a preliminary review at the project site, the Board decided that the investigation should be conducted at the Bank's headquarters in Washington. The Panel would report its findings to the Board within three months, and the Board would then decide whether any further action was appropriate. The Board also took notice of the action program of corrective measures agreed upon between Bank Management and the borrower

---

83. See *Request for Inspection—India: NTPC Power Generation Project, Panel Report and Recommendation* (INSP/R97-9), July 25, 1997 (including in Annex 1 the text of the request itself).

84. *Id. Memorandum to the Chairman of the Panel, India: NTPC Power Generation Project, Management Response to Request for Inspection,* June 3, 1997, reprinted in Annex 3 of the Panel's Report and Recommendation regarding this request.

and requested periodic progress reports on the implementation of that program.[85]

The Panel presented its report in December 1997, following the investigation it conducted at the Bank's headquarters.[86] In this report, the Panel confirmed that the violations of Bank policies and procedures regarding the involuntary resettlement, environmental assessment, and associated aspects of the project, of which it had found *prima facie* evidence in its earlier recommendation, were established by its desk study. The Panel's report noted that the failure "appear[ed] more serious than previously assumed."[87]

Management concluded that "valuable lessons were learned" from intensive reflection on the request and continued to place emphasis on the implementation of the action plan.[88]

The Panel's report and Management's response to it were discussed in the Board in February 1998. The Board agreed to wait before taking any decisions until the progress reports prepared by Management on implementation of the action plan together with a report by an independent monitoring panel and another by an independent institute for social impact assessment were completed.

---

85. Parallel to the Panel's investigation, Management delivered progress reports as requested by the Board. The first such report was circulated in January 1998; the second, third, fourth, and fifth reports were distributed in April, June, November, and December 1998 respectively. *See India: NTPC Power Generation Project, Status of Action Program, First Progress Report* (INSP/SecM98–1), January 12, 1998; *India: NTPC Power Generation Project, Status of Action Program, Second Progress Report* (INSP/SecM98–6), April 21, 1998; *India: NTPC Power Generation Project, Status of Action Program* (SecM98–501), June 16, 1998; *India: NTPC Power Generation Project, Status of Action Program, Fourth Progress Report* (SecM98–908), November 13, 1998, and *India: NTPC Power Generation Project, Status of Action Program, Fifth Progress Report* (SecM98–967), December 7, 1998.

86. *See Request for Inspection—India: NTPC Power Generation Project, Panel Report on the Investigation* (INSP/R97–15), December 24, 1997.

87. *Id.* at para. 18.

88. *See India: NTPC Power Generation Project, Management Report and Recommendation on Inspection Panel Report* (INSP/SecM98–2), February 4, 1998.

In June 1998, the Board considered Management's first progress reports on the implementation of the NTPC action program. It favorably noted the resumption of Bank supervision, the preparation of a new, complementary Singrauli development project, a social impact assessment by an independent institute whose conclusions Management would incorporate in a new action plan, and close monitoring of the project implementation by a newly created, special Bank unit. It was agreed that Management would keep the Board informed about the status of the action plans concerning the implementation of the NTPC project through future progress reports. In December 1998, the Board considered Management's next progress reports, noting that the issues raised in the Panel's report were being adequately addressed and that a final progress report on the resolution of the remaining issues should be prepared to conclude the matter.[89] The latter report was circulated to the Board in February 1999.[90]

XI. Ecodevelopment Project/India

The eleventh request for inspection was received by the Panel in March 1998. It related to the Ecodevelopment Project in India financed by an IDA credit and a grant from the GEF to improve park management and village ecodevelopment in seven areas, including the Nagarahole National Park in Karnataka. Unlike many other projects, the Ecodevelopment Project is by design a "process project," rather than a "blue print project." According to the more flexible design of a "process project," the improvement of the management of protected areas of significant global biodiversity follows a novel planning process according to which

---

89. *See Informal Notes, India: NTPC Power Generation Project, Status of Action Program—Fourth and Fifth Progress Reports,* December 10, 1998. *See also India: NTPC Power Generation Project, Status of Action Program—Fourth Progress Report* (SecM98–908), November 13, 1998, and *India: NTPC Power Generation Project, Status of Action Program—Fifth Progress Report* (SecM98–967), December 7, 1998.

90. *See India: NTPC Power Generation Project, Status of Action Program, Sixth and Final Progress Report* (SecM99–85), February 9, 1999.

people living in and around the protected areas are involved in the planning beyond the design phase of the project.

In this context, the "process design" of the project means that ongoing planning mechanisms are established while simultaneously results on the grounds are produced through project implementation. This approach may, by its nature, invoke the risk of non-compliance with Bank policies such as the one on indigenous peoples that requires consultations and plannings at the design stage of the project to be completed before implementation of the project can start. This feature, though apparent, was not explained at the time the project was presented to the Board for approval. The risks of the innovative approach were only generally highlighted and ways of reduction of its negative impact were mentioned.

The request was submitted by an Indian NGO representing tribal people living in the Nagarahole National Park. The requesters alleged that the IDA had violated their rights and interests as a result of violations of its policies on "indigenous peoples," "involuntary resettlement," and "forestry" as well as GEF policies in the design and implementation of the Ecodevelopment Project. They specifically emphasized that the project, as designed, failed to show that any tribal population lived in the core areas of the Nagarahole National Park, and that no specific indigenous peoples development plans were prepared with the informed participation of the affected tribal groups and NGOs. Furthermore, they feared that an anticipated forceful eviction of the tribal population from the project area would uproot them from their forest habitats (that is, their socio-cultural life base). The Panel registered this request in April 1998.[91]

Management responded in May 1998 that it had complied with the relevant policies and procedures in the implementation of the Ecodevelopment Project.[92] However, compliance with the

---

91. See *Request for Inspection—India: Ecodevelopment Project* (INSP/SecM98–5), April 3, 1998.

92. See *Request for Inspection—India: Ecodevelopment Project, Panel Report and Recommendation* (INSP/R98–4), October 27, 1998 (in Annex 2 reproducing Management's Response).

policy on indigenous peoples would specifically rest on the finalization of consultations agreed upon during project appraisal and the development of "microplans." The latter is a process of village-level planning through which individual families and groups can express their needs and get financial support for those needs. The microplan also ensures the involvement of the families and groups in the protected area management planning process prior to each set of investments at the village level. Regarding the alleged non-compliance with the policy on involuntary resettlement, Management stated that the policy was not violated either, since the project would not require anyone to move. Consequently, there would be no case of involuntary resettlement. As to the policy on forestry, Management pointed out that it would have complied with the few aspects of that policy relevant to the project. (Since the Nagarahole Protected Area would be a national park and not a forest reserve, the project, according to Management, would generally not be covered by the policy on forestry.)

In October 1998, the Panel, basing its report on a study of the records as well as an initial field visit, recommended to the Board to authorize an investigation.[93] The Panel's recommendation rested on its finding that certain key premises underlying the design of the project were flawed, including a lack of data. As a result, a significant potential for serious harm existed. In detail, the Panel noted that Management appeared to have been aware of the paucity of information at the appraisal stage and was therefore unable to predict the potential adverse impact of the project on the *adviasi*, the tribal people in the park. In the view of the Panel, GEF guidelines on participation were not followed either, and more detailed consultation, as required by the policy on indigenous peoples in the appraisal phase, was only intended to be undertaken during implementation of the project. The Panel also noted that no separate indigenous peoples' development plan was prepared during the appraisal stage, as required by the policy on involuntary resettlement. The Panel noted further that

93. *See id.* (Panel Recommendation.)

the microplanning process, which, according to Management, would ensure the proper inclusion of the concerns of tribal people at the implementation stage, did not come forth to the extent it was projected by Management. Only three microplans had been completed, and several more had been planned, all for communities outside the park. No microplans were under preparation, however, for the *adviasi* tribal people, of whom 97 percent wished to remain in their communities within the park. The Panel concluded its recommendation by emphasizing that, in order to comply with policies and monitor compliance with loan covenants, it would be necessary for Management to supervise the project thoroughly and make sure that serious future imbalance would be avoided.

In December 1998, the Board decided that no investigation was required at that time. In the Board meeting, Management explained in detail its intentions regarding the implementation of the project, which would also meet the points raised in the Panel's report. In view of this, the Board saw no need for investigation. Instead, it asked Management, together with the State Government of Karnataka and in consultation with the affected people, to address the concerns expressed in the Panel's report and prepare a report to the Board on how to address the Panel's conclusions and intensify the implementation of the project, especially as relating to the microplanning. It decided further that Management should keep the Panel informed. The Panel would separately give its comments on Management's report to the Board at the end of this process.

XII. Highlands Water Project/Lesotho/ South Africa

In May 1998, the Panel received its twelfth request relating to a planned second water project in Lesotho. The request was registered in the same month. The requesters were residents of the township of Alexandra, Guateng Province, in South Africa, to which water will be transferred under the project. They filed on their own behalf and more generally on behalf of the community of Alexandra, whose members would "rather remain anonymous." However, names of the requesters were provided to the Bank's Office in Pretoria on the basis of confidentiality. The requesters contended that their rights or interests were likely to be materially and adversely affected by omissions of IBRD in the design of the proposed project. The project involves the building of a dam in Lesotho and the supply of water to the Guateng province in South Africa.[94] Policies specifically alleged to have been violated by the Bank included the policies on "dam and reservoir projects," "economic evaluation of investment operations," "water resources," and "poverty reduction."[95]

Before Management issued its response, the Bank's Board approved the second phase of the Lesotho Highlands Water Project. The issue of presenting a loan for approval to the Board while a request pertaining to it was pending with the Panel became an issue for Management consideration. In the absence of express provisions to the contrary in the Resolution establishing the Panel, Management decided that, as a matter of principle, a request for inspection cannot by itself cause the Bank to freeze the approval by the Board of an operation in the absence of compelling reasons.[96] It therefore delayed Board consideration for approval and instead took the occasion to brief the Board on the circumstances surrounding the request and Management's views thereon. Management then rescheduled the Board meeting for project approval, and the Board, fully aware of the facts relating to both the project and the request for inspection, approved the loan, notwithstanding the pending request.[97]

---

94. See Request for Inspection—Lesotho/South Africa: Phase 1B of Lesotho Highlands Water Project, Panel Report and Recommendation (INSP/R98–2), August 19, 1998 (including in Annex 1 the text of the request itself).

95. Id.

96. See Chapter Two, supra, at 137. A different position was adopted for the Arun III project, under different circumstances.

97. See para. 23 of the Resolution, which requires, for projects inspected during preparation, that "[t]he findings of the Panel and the actions completed during project preparation also will be discussed in the Staff Appraisal Report when the project is submitted to the Executive Directors for financing."

In its response of June 1998 to the request, Management pointed out that, in its view, the request did not meet several of the eligibility requirements under the Resolution.[98] In support of this position, Management contended that the requesters were not "in the territory of the borrower." They were residents of a community in South Africa, while the borrower was a governmental agency of Lesotho. Management also noted that, as the community had resolved "to file the claims anonymously, [and] the requesters have not presented any written evidence that the Alexandra community has designated them as their representatives," their quality as representatives of Alexandra was questionable. Management emphasized further that the requesters had not taken any steps to bring their allegations of Bank failures to the attention of Management prior to lodging a request with the Panel. Regarding the alleged violations of Bank policies, Management stated that all policies had been complied with. In particular, an economic evaluation of the project was completed, and an environmental assessment had been carried out in consultation with affected people and NGOs in Lesotho. Design alternatives of the project were considered, and the requirements of the Bank's policy on poverty reduction were fully complied with.

In its August 1998 report and recommendation, which was delivered on the basis of a study of the records and an initial field visit,[99] the Panel, recognizing that the names of the individuals who submitted the request were given by them to the Bank in the very note that requested confidentiality, blamed Management for revealing to the Board that the request had been filed by "three individuals." It is not clear how this can be an "abuse of trust," as the Panel called it when the names were not given to the Board. The Panel rightly complained that the Bank's resident mission in Pretoria had faxed the request to Management headquarters rather than forwarding it directly to the Panel.

---

98. *See Request for Inspection—Lesotho/South Africa: Phase 1B of Lesotho Highlands Water Project, Panel Report and Recommendation* (INSP/R98–2), August 9, 1998, at Annex 2 including Management's response to the request.
    99. *Id.* (Panel Report and Recommendation.)

Regarding the eligibility of the request, the Panel noted that the requesters were "in the territory of the borrower" because the notion of the borrower should, in addition to the borrower itself, extend to the guarantors of a loan. As South Africa is a guarantor and the project in its entirety was, in the Panel's view, located in Lesotho and South Africa, the necessary territorial link according to the Resolution would be established. Moreover, the population of the Guateng Province in South Africa, where the requesters live, was referred to as beneficiaries of the water project in their capacity as future industrial and urban water users.

As to the alleged violation of Bank policies, the Panel noted that it would no longer look into a potential violation of the policy on evaluation of investment operations because the requesters had dropped their claim in this respect. Regarding the failure to consult with potentially affected people according to the Bank's environmental policy for dam and reservoir projects, the Panel noted that Management failed to consult to the necessary extent with such people until the end of April 1998. No violation was seen in terms of the obligations under the policy on water resources management and poverty reduction. "But the Panel [was] not satisfied that there [was] *prima facie* evidence linking [the] situation [of hardship suffered by the requesters] to the project, nor with the Bank's decision to proceed with financing [it]. . . . There [did] not appear to be a connection between these conditions and any observance or not by the Bank of its own policies and procedures." It, therefore, recommended to the Board not to authorize an inspection.[100]

On September 2, 1998, the Board approved the Panel's recommendation on a no-objection basis.

XIII. Drainage and Sanitation Project/ Nigeria/Lagos

In June 1998, the Panel received and registered the thirteenth request. It related to an IDA-financed drainage and sanitation

---

100. *Id.* at 18.

project in Lagos, Nigeria.[101] The requesters, the Social and Economic Right Action Center (SERAC), a local NGO, acting on behalf of itself and individuals, families, and community development associations, claimed that the rights or interests of communities in the project area had or would be adversely affected as a result of IDA's failure to comply with a range of policies, especially those on "involuntary resettlement," "poverty reduction," "gender dimensions of development," and "project monitoring and evaluation." Instead of improving the health standards and living conditions in the respective areas of Lagos by clearing and aligning existing stormwater drains as envisaged in the project plans, the request alleged that people living in the project area suffered and would continue to suffer destruction of their homes and businesses without compensation or resettlement or face the possibility of eviction. It further alleged that drainage channels had become receptacles for waste water that overflowed regularly into living spaces. People escaping from this situation had become squatters or lived in distant places far away from their employment.

In its response of July 1998, Management indicated it had complied with all Bank policies and procedures.[101] It pointed out in particular that, contrary to the requester's allegations, fewer than 300 people had been resettled and properly compensated in connection with the project, while no other forcible evictions occurred. The demolition of slum communities was outside the scope of the project and, therefore, had not been carried out under the project. Also, all necessary consultations connected to the resettlement and studies for the project design had been undertaken.

The Panel delivered its report and recommendations in November 1998.[103] On the basis of a study of the Bank's records

101. *See Request for Inspection, Nigeria/Lagos Drainage and Sanitation Project* (INSP/SecM98–10), June 26, 1998.

102. *See Memorandum from the President to the Chairman of the Inspection Panel, Nigeria—Lagos Drainage and Sanitation Project, Management Response to Request for Inspection*, dated July 27, 1998.

103. *See Nigeria: Lagos Drainage and Sanitation Project, Panel Report and Recommendation* (INSP/R98–5), November 10, 1998.

as well as a site visit, it did not recommend that the Board authorize an investigation. Although it had not found any violations by Management regarding the policies on "poverty reduction," "gender dimensions," and "project monitoring and evaluation," it had observed potential neglect related to compliance with the policy on "involuntary resettlement." In one of the communities included in the project, some resettled people had apparently not been compensated or properly resettled. As these people appeared to not have been living in the area at the time of loan processing, however, the Panel was satisfied with Management's assurances that the people who could be identified at the time of the project's execution would now be properly compensated under an agreement between the Bank and the borrower.

In November 1998, the Board, on a no-objection basis, took notice of, and approved the Panel's recommendation not to investigate.

XIV. Land Reform and Poverty Alleviation Pilot Project/Brazil

In January 1999, the Panel registered a request (dated December 10, 1998, and received on December 14, 1998) signed by more than 800 Brazilian rural workers and residents and a number of NGOs, labor unions of rural workers, religious welfare groups, church associations, and an academic institute regarding the Land Reform and Poverty Alleviation Pilot Project in Brazil that is financed by IBRD.[104] The project is testing a market-based land reform mechanism in the Northeastern Brazilian states of Bahia, Ceara, Maranhão, Pernambuco, and Minas Gerais. Under it, beneficiary associations of about 15,000 families of poor rural laborers and farmers, who are either landless or have insufficient land for subsistence, obtain financing to purchase agricultural properties they judge to be suitable and for

---

104. *See Request for Inspection—Brazil: Land Reform and Poverty Alleviation Pilot Project* (INSP/SecM99–1), January 12, 1999, including the notification of registration.

which they negotiate directly with willing sellers. Families also receive grants for complementary investments to raise the productivity and output of the properties they acquire. Completion of project implementation is planned within three years.

The complainants asserted in their request that the project would, in its design and implementation, violate the Bank's policies on "poverty reduction," "disclosure of information," and "involvement of NGOs in Bank Operations." In a letter dated December 21, 1998, submitted on behalf of the requesters to "supplement information" regarding the request, it was also contended that the Bank had violated its policy on "environmental assessment."

Specifically, the requesters complained that the project was not achieving its objectives. According to the requesters, the project was supposed to facilitate the agrarian reform as outlined under the Brazilian constitution. The latter would require expropriation of uncultivated lands against the payment of compensation to the owners (with 20-year government bonds) and the settlement of landless rural families to make agricultural use of it. According to the request, the project, instead of facilitating the implementation of the constitutionally mandated land reform, would render the latter ineffective. The means used under the pilot project would avoid expropriation because they would provide for the rural workers organized in associations to negotiate directly with the landowners the sale in cash of their unused land to the workers, using funds provided by the government with assistance through Bank financing.

The requesters further asserted that the project is not being implemented as a pilot project. The usefulness of a pilot project would be assessed during and after its implementation, and a decision for or against the financing of further similar projects would be made only after such an assessment. By contrast, the project in question would have contributed to the endorsement of a recently enacted Brazilian law that provided for a general replacement of the constitutionally required agrarian reform through expropriation of unused land by the establishment of a market in land. Furthermore, the Bank would have committed itself publicly to a loan of about $250 million per year to an expanded version of the Land Title Project without awaiting a more judicious evaluation of the pilot project upon its completion.

The requesters also asserted that the poorest would not be able to repay the financial debts they would incur in the medium- and long-term under the land-purchase program and would end up poorer than before. After the landless would own the land to be sold by landowners, the latter, according to the request, would repurchase that land under land-purchase associations they had formed themselves. Using the "market-approach" to land reform (that is, replacing administrative expropriation with negotiated land-purchase) would also substantially increase land prices and thus reward the large landowners who, instead of being paid in 20-year governmental agrarian reform bonds, would receive immediate cash payments.

The project would also not have been subject to the required environmental assessment.

Finally, it was alleged that the necessary documents for the participation of rural workers were not accessible to all concerned organizations, and not all organizations representing rural workers were consulted in the preparation of the project.

In March 1999, Management presented its response.[105] Management disagreed with the requesters that the project would not be achieving its objective. It pointed out that, by the end of January 1999, some 8,000 families had already received land and titles to a total of 204,000 hectares, or about 25 hectares per family. The remaining families would follow suit shortly. The pace in implementing the project and the actual demand for financing of the land purchases indicated that the voluntary, market-based approach to achieve redistribution of land assets in Brazil might indeed alleviate the country's rural poverty to a noticeable extent.

---

105. *See Brazil: Land Reform and Poverty Alleviation Pilot Project, Panel Report and Recommendation* (INSP/R99–4), June 2, 1999 (reproducing Management's response in Annex 2).

Management also emphasized that the project would be implemented as a pilot project. The agreement with the Brazilian Government to test a market-based land reform mechanism had emerged from earlier experience with demand-driven, community-based development programs that had yielded significant results. Poverty assessments and other studies in the country had further suggested trying market-based mechanisms to achieve land reform. Management acknowledged that views regarding land reform can differ and emphasized that the Bank's approach under the pilot project was not supposed to supplant all other land reform instruments, including expropriation available to the Brazilian Government. Expropriation, as Management understands it from the Brazilian Government, would not be constitutionally mandated. Management noted, nevertheless, that the Brazilian Government had already expressed its wish to expand the pilot and to involve other states within and outside northeast Brazil under further Bank-financed programs.

According to Management, the project does not violate the Bank's policy on poverty reduction. The policy's broad recommendations had all been observed in the project's design, and the request did not link any alleged harm to the violation of specific provisions of the policy. Similarly, the project, according to pre-project analysis, would have very good prospects for financial sustainability. Factors contributing to this sustainability included that lands selected by the rural landless families were often among the best available, while expropriated land would often be unproductive, underutilized, and of poorer quality. Additional grant resources would allow the families to make productive use of their newly acquired properties, including the purchase of technical assistance. Management also noted, with respect to the alleged increase in the prices of agricultural land, that, as a result of the project, land prices had actually been falling in recent years, and the pilot project was at any rate too small to exert a significant influence on the market.

Regarding the alleged violation of the Bank's policy on environmental assessment, Management noted that the project was environmentally screened. Upon screening, it was qualified as a project from the activities of which no significant adverse environmental impacts were expected to result.

Regarding the alleged failure by the Bank to disclose information, Management contended that it had disclosed all standard information on the project through its InfoShop in Washington, D.C., as requested under the relevant Bank policy. In addition, the Bank's field office assisted interested parties to access that InfoShop and obtain documents from it. Equally, copies of the Bank's Operational Manual that contains the policies and procedures were disseminated by the borrower, which also provided information on the project through the media. In terms of participation, Management emphasized that project beneficiaries were participating in the project through the community associations they had to form to negotiate land purchases and receive financing. As to participation by NGOs, Management noted that the local chapters of several NGOs (including some that signed the request) had been involved in the project's implementation.

In addition to its substantive comments on the request, Management's response questioned the eligibility of the request because, rather than demonstrate actual or potential harm to project beneficiaries by violation of Bank policies, it criticized the policy choice of the Brazilian Government in the area of land reform. Furthermore, Management contended that the requesters themselves were not eligible. None of the signatories of the request identifiable by name, organization, location, and national identity number was a project beneficiary. The request did not contain any evidence that any actual beneficiaries had designated the requesters to act as their agents in representing the request.

Management finally expressly offered to provide the Panel with materials obtained from participating Brazilian states that would provide evidence of the participants' belief in the sustainability and success of the project.

In June 1999, the Panel issued its report and recommendation to the Board.[106] On the basis of a study of the records

---

106. *Id.* (Panel Report and Recommendation).

and an initial field visit, the Panel did not recommend an investigation.

In connection with Management's concerns regarding the eligibility of the request, the Panel noted that at least 41 individuals who had filed the request were participating in the project and were, therefore, clearly eligible. As the rights or interests of the remaining requesters, who were not immediate project beneficiaries, were found by the Panel also amenable to be affected by a failure of the Bank to comply with its own policies, their complaints seemed justified. The Panel emphasized further that the representation of intended project beneficiaries, rural workers, and small farmers by the organizations that are signatories to the request should be recognized for the purposes of bringing a request before the Panel if the living conditions of the rural poor represented by these organizations were indeed at risk to deteriorate.

The Panel, however, expressly stated that it would not discuss the role of expropriation and the legality of alternative methods of agrarian reform programs because these issues would not directly relate to Bank policies and procedures. Focusing rather on the major eligibility requirement of *prima facie* evidence of acts or omissions of the Bank causing or likely to cause harm, the Panel analyzed in its report the evidence and information on specific policy violations before the Panel and the nature of the alleged actual or potential harm that had been caused or may in the future be caused by the Bank-financed project. Given the project's qualification as a project from which no significant adverse environmental impacts were expected as well as the absence of any evidence of real negative environmental impacts, the Panel concluded that no environmental harm was likely to result from the project. On the basis of its visit to selected project sites and its meeting with several beneficiaries and sub-project leaders, the Panel found that there was also no likelihood of a grave deterioration of the beneficiaries' personal situation in terms of cultivation and output projections of the land. In particular, no actual or potential price increases for agricultural land were likely to result from the project, nor were other living conditions at danger. While beneficiaries emphasized that technical assistance to improve their agricultural projects and marketing skills, working capital to facilitate the sustainability of their projects, and assistance to improve their management skills were of essence, the Panel found that these concerns were taken care of by Management's efforts to improve the terms and conditions of credits for land purchases for beneficiaries. The Panel further noted that Management had informed and consulted with potential project beneficiaries. In light of this assessment, the Panel did not recommend an investigation of the matters alleged in the request.

In mid-June 1999, the Board of Executive Directors approved of the Panel's recommendation on a no-objection basis.

XV. Swissbourgh Diamond Mines (Pty) Ltd & Others Regarding Highlands Water Project/Lesotho/South Africa

In May 1999, the Panel registered the fifteenth request brought before it by six companies registered in Lesotho and by South African nationals as individuals who were also shareholders in the Lesotho companies. The companies led by Swissbourgh Diamond Mines (Pty) Ltd claimed to have been deprived of their mining rights in an area of the Malibamats'o River valley, including their rights to fair, full, and prompt compensation for the illegal revocation of these rights, because of IBRD's non-compliance with its policies and procedures in connection with its financing of the Lesotho Highlands Water Project.

The conclusion of the loans financing the latter project (which was also the subject of the twelfth request before the Panel), was allegedly the reason why the requesters' leases to mine, which were granted in 1988 to the Swissbourgh Diamond Mines (Pty) Ltd and later sublet by the latter to the five other companies, were cancelled in 1991. The cancellations were made as the construction of the dams for the supply of water to the Guatang province in South Africa and of the hydroelectric power generation facility required the Highlands Development

Authority of Lesotho to hold a valid lease over the project area
without any private investor's claims to mine in respect of this
area. Although the first requester immediately obtained an interim court order setting aside the cancellations of leases and also
pursued main proceedings in court to void such cancellations
through final court judgment (proceedings that are still pending
before court), the Bank, allegedly in full knowledge of the unlawful expropriation and the ensuing disputes over it, entered into
the loan agreements financing the project and asked the borrower for project execution after conclusion of the agreements.

According to the requesters, the Bank failed to observe in this
context its policy and procedure on disputes over defaults on
external debt, expropriation, and breach of contract, and its procedure on disclosure of operational information.[107] Specifically,

---

107. The relevant parts of the Operational Manual Statement on *Disputes
over Defaults on External Debt, Expropriation and Breach of Contract* (OMS
1.28) (June 1978), applicable at the time of appraisal of Phase 1A of the project, read:

"The Bank will not lend for projects in a country if it considers that
the position taken by that country with respect to alien owners of
expropriated property is substantially affecting its international credit
standing. Nor will it appraise projects in such a country unless it has
good grounds for believing that the obstacles to lending will soon be
removed. Reasons for not proceeding with lending operations include:
(i) a denial of liability for compensation coupled with a refusal to submit the dispute to judicial or quasi-judicial determination; (ii) an
admission of liability for compensation in general terms coupled with
either an offer of compensation obviously inadequate in amount or
terms of payment and not subject to negotiation, or else a failure to
negotiate in good faith over such matters or to submit them to judicial or quasi-judicial determination; (iii) a failure, in the Bank's judgment, to make reasonable efforts to arrive at settlements; (iv) a failure
to pay and, if required, to transfer abroad compensation in accordance
with the terms of an agreed settlement, a judicial decree or an arbitral
award."

The relevant parts of the Bank's Operational Policy on *Disputes over
Defaults on External Debt, Expropriation, and Breach of Contract* (OP 7.40)
(May 1996), applicable at the time of appraisal of Phase 1B of the project, read:

"The Bank recognizes that a country may expropriate property of
aliens in accordance with applicable legal procedures, in pursuance in

the requesters alleged that the Bank should have suspended disbursement of funds in relation to the Lesotho project, should have reconsidered lending for new projects in the country in the meanwhile, and should not have appraised the project while the requesters' dispute over the expropriation was pending. They also suggested that the Bank should have promoted a prompt and adequate settlement of the requesters' dispute and provided the requesters with copies of all project information documents and staff appraisal reports concerning the project. According to the requesters, the Bank failed to take any of these steps although the requesters had raised their concerns with Bank staff. As a result of the Bank's alleged failures and especially its inaction to contribute to the solution of the dispute over the unlawful expropriation, the requesters maintain to have suffered financial damage, including loss of profit because they could no longer carry out mining activities pursuant to their leases on the land on which the project was implemented.

In its June 1999 response, Management contended to have been seen in full compliance with the requirements of the Bank's policies on disputes over defaults on external debts, expropriation and breach of contract, and disclosure of operational information. As prescribed by the first policy, the Bank had informed itself about the borrower's efforts to settle the dispute over the alleged expropriation of the requester, as well as assessed the potential harm resulting from the dispute to the country's international credit standing to see whether it needed to reconsider its financing in the country.

---

good faith of a public purpose, without discrimination on the basis of nationality, and against payment of appropriate compensation. When there are disputes over expropriations that, in the opinion of the Bank, the country is not making reasonable efforts to settle and that are substantially harming the country's international credit standing, the Bank considers whether to continue lending for new projects in the country. Further, the Bank may not appraise proposed projects in such a country unless it has good grounds for believing that the obstacles to lending will soon be removed. [. . .] The Bank seeks to promote prompt and adequate settlements, either negotiated between the parties on a mutually satisfactory basis or arrived at through mediation, conciliation, arbitration, or judicial determination."

According to information provided to the Bank by the borrower, the mineral leases had been granted illegally. The dispute over the matter had also been submitted to the courts, and the borrower had indicated to be prepared to abide by the courts' final decision over it. The latest judgment in the case, pronounced in late April 1999, declared the mining leases void *ab initio* and canceled their entry in the register of deeds. In light of this information, the Bank had concluded that the borrower had been making reasonable efforts to settle the dispute. Consequently, there was no substantial harm resulting from the alleged expropriation to Lesotho's international credit standing and, thus, no reconsideration of Bank financing in Lesotho was necessary. As to the alleged violation of the Bank's policy on disclosure of information, Management noted that, as required by policy, it had kept all project-related information available at the Bank's Infoshop (earlier the Public Information Center) and advised the requesters to contact the latter to obtain the information they asked for. Management added that the request, in its view, would even be ineligible, as it was submitted after two of the several subsequent loans financing the project had been closed during the life of which the alleged violations had taken place. The Panel's recommendation to this request is pending.

XVI.   Western Poverty Reduction Project/China

In mid-June 1999, as this book was being finished, the Panel registered the sixteenth request.[108] This request concerned a poverty reduction project with several, mainly infrastructure, components to be financed by IBRD and IDA and to be carried out in the Gansu and Qinghai Provinces and Inner Mongolia Autonomous Region in China. The project's components specifically include support for land and household development by

---

108.   *See Request for Inspection, Notice of Registration, China: Proposed Western Poverty Reduction Project* (INSP/SecM 99–6), June 19, 1999.

providing improved agricultural and livestock technology packages, the building of a new dam, the renovation of an existing dam, the construction of irrigation and drainage systems, the improvement of rural roads, the building of drinking water supply facilities, the extension of electric power lines, the provision of credit to establish non-state owned and household-based rural enterprises, the construction and upgrade of basic education and health facilities, and the support for the voluntary placement of rural laborers and rural poor.

The request was submitted by the International Campaign for Tibet (ICT), a U.S.-based NGO allegedly acting on behalf of people living in the project area. ICT claimed that its representational authority would be "based on its long-standing involvement in the project area and its mandate to advocate on behalf of the interests of the Tibetan people." ICT claimed further that it had "received letters from inside the project area seeking international assistance in raising concerns about the devastating impacts of this project on local peoples" and that their "claim meets the exceptional circumstances requirement [under the Inspection Panel Resolution] for non-local representation."[109]

In terms of the alleged harm potentially resulting from the project, ICT asserted that the project, if approved and implemented, would adversely affect the lives and livelihood of Tibetan and Mongolian ethnic peoples. Specifically, the resettlement of the new migrants would directly adversely impact 4,000 local people and "have [further] indirect impacts on the entire county including a serious risk of escalation of ethnic tension and resource conflicts." According to the request, the potential harm would result from the Bank's non-compliance with its policies on "disclosure of operational information," "environmental assessment," "indigenous peoples," "involuntary resettlement," and "pest management." The matter is pending Management's response and the Panel's recommendation.

---

109. For a general discussion of the circumstances that would allow for non-local representation, *see* Chapter Two, *supra*, at 64–66.

Post Script

After the manuscript of this book had been sent to the publisher, three developments that are worth reporting happened. The Panel submitted its recommendation not to authorize an investigation in the *Swissbourg Diamond Mines/Lesotho* case, which the Board approved on a no-objection basis; Management sent its response concerning the *China Western Poverty Reduction Project;* and a seventeenth request regarding the *Special Structural Adjustment Loan* in *Argentina* was registered by the Panel.

The Panel's July 1999 recommendation in *Swissbourg Diamond Mines/Lesotho* found the request eligible, especially as a third loan, financing the project and dated December 1998, had not yet been closed when the request was submitted. The Panel further found that Management did not comply with procedural requirements in the Bank's policy on disputes over defaults on external debt, expropriation and breach of contract. According to the Panel, Management had specifically violated a procedural provision requiring that "[i]f, at the time a loan is presented to the Executive Directors for approval, there are any substantial amounts in dispute between the borrowing country and suppliers or lenders to, or investors in, that country, the matter is mentioned in the Memorandum and Recommendation of the President/President's Report." However, according to the Panel's report, the lawsuit over the significant amount in damages claimed by the requesters from Lesotho was not referred to in the President's Report when the third loan financing the project was submitted to the Board for approval. Further procedural provisions were found to have been violated by Bank Management in the process of assessing whether the dispute over the expropriation was substantially harming the country's international credit standing and regarding the release of project information. Nevertheless, the Panel found no link between any actions and/or omissions of the Bank and the harm claimed by the requesters. Consequently, it did not recommend an investigation into the matters alleged in the request. The Board approved this recommendation on a no-objection basis.

Management's response to the request concerning the *China Western Poverty Reduction Project*, submitted in July 1999, concluded that the Bank had complied with its policies. It noted, however, that some of the qualitative aspects of the project's design could be improved, especially with regard to the social and cultural aspects of the project. Management announced that measures were being taken to ensure that these aspects are strengthened. Specifically, Management noted that there was no violation of the Bank's policy on indigenous peoples as that policy would not apply to voluntary population movements or ethnic demographic shifts as contemplated under the project. Management also explained that measures to address the requester's concerns of dilution of Tibetan and Mongol cultures (such as culturally sensitive education and health care systems and protection of the way of life of herders in the move-in area) would mitigate the cultural risks feared by the requesters. Through these measures the objectives of the Bank's policy on indigenous peoples would be fulfilled. Management also argued that a self-standing indigeneous people's development plan was not necessary because the needs of indigenous peoples were addressed through measures integrated in the project. Management further contended that a resettlement action plan addressed all needs of the few people that were involuntarily resettled under the project, as required by the Bank's policy on involuntary resettlement. Management also noted that the project was correctly screened and assessed for its environmental impact, as required under the respective Bank policy. Similarly, the Bank's policy on pest management had been observed by ensuring that the borrower would introduce certain strategies to minimize and monitor the use of chemical pesticides. Finally, Management maintained that all disclosure requirements of the respective Bank policy were fulfilled by making specific project information pertaining to the environment and the resettlement available to the affected people in China prior to project appraisal, the Bank calling for this information from the borrower before project appraisal, and sending it to the Infoshop. The Panel's recommendation is still pending.

The seventeenth request, registered in August 1999, was submitted by a group of attorneys from a center for legal and social studies in Argentina, an NGO representing about 418 beneficiaries of the Pro-Huerta program providing food and nutrition assistance to the absolute poor. The requesters alleged that IBRD violated the terms and conditions under which the Board of Executive Directors approved the *Special Structural Adjustment Loan* because the latter's last tranche is intended to be released despite the fact that the disbursement conditions set forth in the loan agreement are not met. Specifically, adequate levels of funding for a number of specific social programs (including the Pro-Huerta program) are allegedly not maintained, eventually resulting in the termination of the Pro-Huerta program. The requesters also alleged the violation of the Bank's policies on "poverty alleviation," "suspension of disbursement," and "disclosure of information." Management's response and the Panel's recommendation to this request are pending.

4

Board Reviews of the Inspection Panel's Experience

Introduction

The 1993 Board Resolution establishing the World Bank Inspection Panel provides that the Board will "review the experience of the inspection function . . . after two years from the date of the appointment of the first members of the Panel."[1] As the latter date was April 1, 1994, the envisaged Board review was to take place after April 1, 1996. In fact, the review started earlier in an informal way when the Panel submitted to the Board, on November 27, 1995, a working paper entitled "Practical Suggestions Based on Experience to Date,"[2] which the Board discussed in an informal meeting, on February 27, 1996. At this meeting it was agreed, in light of the divergent views expressed, that the formal review of the Panel's experience would be dealt with first by the Board's Committee on Development Effectiveness (CODE). As shown below, discussions in CODE, and then in the full Board, led to the adoption on October 17, 1996, of certain changes and interpretations of the Resolution that were conveniently described as "Clarifications."[3] Experience proved, however, that such clarifications did not reduce divisiveness in the Board's subsequent discussions on

---

1. *Resolution,* para. 27.
2. (INSP/95–3), November 27, 1995.
3. *See Clarifications of Certain Aspects of the Resolution Establishing the Inspection Panel,* dated September 30, 1996, and approved by the Executive Directors on October 17, 1996 (R96–204), reproduced in Annex I–2 of this book (hereinafter *Clarifications*).

whether to authorize investigations. When the Board finally reached a decision on the difficult cases of the *Itaparica Project* (Brazil) and the *NTPC Power Generation Project* (India) on September 9, 1997, this was coupled, as explained in the previous chapter, with an agreement among Executive Directors that a second Board review of the Panel's experience was to follow suit.

I.   The First Review—1996

When the February 1996 informal Board meeting took place, the Board had before it, in addition to the Panel's "working paper," four papers submitted by Management that had been previously given to the Panel. These included (i) "a non-exhaustive list of issues for discussion;"[4] (ii) a table summarizing the manner in which requests before the Panel were handled; (iii) a list summarizing the Panel's views (expressed in its November 1995 "working paper") and the views communicated by NGOs to Bank Management; and (iv) a note and a table comparing the Bank's Panel with the inspection panels established by the Inter-American Development Bank (IDB) and the Asian Development Bank (ADB) in 1994 and 1995, respectively.[5]

The Executive Directors, as mentioned, agreed that CODE would first review the matter in depth in light of Management's recommendations and the Panel's views and submit its own recommendations to the full Board. Detailed suggestions for changes in the Resolution were received in late March 1996 from NGOs, such as Oxfam International (headquartered in London) and International Rivers Network (located in Washington, D.C.), and were circulated by Management to CODE members without comment. On May 7, 1996, Management submitted to CODE

---

4. The issues listed in that paper included: form and composition of the Panel; the Panel's function; the role of the Board; extension of the Panel's function to private sector operations in IFC and MIGA; and disclosure issues.

5. For an updated version of this table, *see* Annex III of this book.

for the first time a paper on the review,[6] which was followed two days later by a memorandum from the Panel commenting on that paper.[7]

Management's paper explained that, as a document issued by Management, it appropriately had not included any comments on the Panel's performance. However, it welcomed "the Panel's contribution to the credibility and accountability of the Bank and its staff" and "highly appreciate[d] the spirit of cooperation shown by Panel members." The paper covered all the questions raised at the time, whether by Board members, the Panel, or NGOs, listing the Panel's and NGO's views on the issues covered by their comments before concluding with Management's position on each question. The paper included certain possible amendments to the Resolution that Management suggested that the Board might find appropriate.

Discussion in CODE revealed a broad preference among its members to keep the original Resolution establishing the Panel intact while providing for measures of flexibility in its implementation. It was felt that, rather than introducing amendments to the Resolution, the Board should consider the issuance of directives to guide its application in practice. Such directives, being issued by the Board, would have the same force as the Resolution and would, in fact, complement its text.

A.   *Possible Application of the Inspection Function to the International Finance Corporation (IFC) and the Multinational Investment Guarantee Agency (MIGA) Operations*

Management's paper to CODE noted that the Resolution did not exclude the *Bank's* private sector operations and agreed in

---

6. *Review of the Resolution Establishing the World Bank's Inspection Panel* (CODE 96–24), May 7, 1996.

7. *Memorandum to the Committee on Development Effectiveness—Subject: Review of the Resolution Establishing the World Bank's Inspection Panel*, dated May 9, 1996 (CODE 96–27), May 14, 1996.

principle that such operations in Bank affiliates may also be subject to inspection. Such inspection should, however, differ in certain respects from that provided for in the Resolution. For instance a broader list of potential Panel members might include additional experts more familiar with the private sector, of whom three would constitute a specific panel in each case by decision of the Panel's chair. Any inspection of private sector operations might also require stricter safeguards with respect to disclosure of documents, shorter procedures to avoid delay, and greater attention to the requirements of domestic law with respect to property and privacy rights. A separate paper was requested by CODE on the subject and was subsequently prepared by the IFC Management and discussed in CODE. It was agreed in that discussion that IFC and MIGA would consult with the business community, co-financiers, and Executive Directors representing borrowing countries and report back to CODE. Once CODE had completed its consideration of the inspection mechanism for IFC and MIGA projects, it was Management's intention, as declared at the time, to propose a common approach to inspection for all Bank Group private sector operations. In October 1997, CODE discussed an IFC report, "Consultations with Private Sector Clients and Co-financiers on the Possible Establishment of an Inspection Mechanism for IFC and MIGA."[8] The report showed that a majority of those consulted were not in favor of an inspection function and would not, at any rate, welcome inspection under the established procedures of the existing Panel. Discussion in CODE on this point was not conclusive; Management was asked to present different options to a subsequent meeting. Consequently, IFC Management submitted to CODE a joint IFC/MIGA paper on several options, including, among many others, the possibility to extend the mandate of the Bank's Inspection Panel to IFC and MIGA, with or without

---

8. *Consultations with Private Sector Clients and Co-financiers on the possible Establishment of an Inspection Function for IFC and MIGA* (CODE 97–50), August 19, 1997.

modifications to meet the special requirements of private sector operations.[9] The paper, however, emphasized the shortcomings of this option. Without prejudice to the outcome of the debate, the IFC and MIGA jointly proceeded with implementation of one of the options mentioned in the paper, namely the appointment of a compliance advisor/ombudsman.[10]

---

9. *IFC and MIGA, Options to Enhance Environmental and Social Compliance and Accountability in IFC and MIGA* (CODE 98–12), March 4, 1998.

10. The function of this position would be to advise and assist IFC and MIGA in dealing with sensitive or controversial projects, either at the request of the President or IFC's or MIGA's management or on the suggestion of the ombudsman himself. In performing this function, the ombudsman is expected to "consult with the President and coordinate with IFC's or MIGA's management." Also, the ombudsman would assist in dealing with complaints from external parties affected by IFC or MIGA projects. Outside complaints received by the President, IFC, MIGA, or the ombudsman would be investigated by the ombudsman "as appropriate;" such investigation is to be carried out "in consultation with affected parties, project sponsors, and IFC's or MIGA's management." A "flexible process aimed primarily at correcting project failures and achieving better results on the ground" is required. The ombudsman "may directly communicate with complainants and affected parties, while respecting the confidentiality of sensitive business information." He will report on findings and recommendations to the President, who will determine what actions are required. The ombudsman is also required to report his findings and recommendations directly to the affected parties. Such findings and recommendations will be disclosed to the public through the World Bank InfoShop, unless the President decides otherwise in consultation with the affected party. Finally, the ombudsman is to supervise audits of IFC's and MIGA's overall environmental and social performance and sensitive projects to ensure *ex-post* compliance with "policies, guidelines, and procedures." The ombudsman, who, unlike the Inspection Panel, is part of the President's office of IFC and MIGA (but not of their respective line management), may "provide advice to Management on environmental and social policies, procedures, guidelines, resources, and systems established to ensure adequate review and monitoring of IFC and MIGA projects." His role here is to provide comments, not to undermine Management responsibility for these issues. At the request of IFC's or MIGA's environmental and social staff, the ombudsman may also provide advice on specific project issues. A Search Committee exclusively consisting of six representatives of business and environmental groups was established by the President of IFC and MIGA to identify candidates for this position. *See IFC Press Release* No. 99/39. Ms. Meg Taylor, a national of Papua New Guinea, was appointed compliance/advisor/ombudsman for IFC and MIGA on March 31, 1999. *See* http://wblnoo11.Worldbank.org/News/i.

The newly established position differs from the Bank's Inspection Panel in two important respects. While the ombudsman is also meant to be an independent expert, he reports directly to the President of IFC or MIGA, as the case may be, not to the respective Board of Executive Directors of each organization. No authorization from such a Board is required for the performance of his investigative duties, either. In addition, his role is not limited to investigating complaints from local parties adversely affected by IFC or MIGA operations. He is also to "advise and assist" the two organizations in dealing with "sensitive or controversial projects." He may provide advice on their environmental and social policies and procedures. And he will supervise audits of their overall environmental and social performance (to ensure *ex post* compliance). These three functions are outside the scope of the World Bank Inspection Panel.[11]

Several arguments have been made for a different inspection mechanism for IFC and MIGA. These institutions exclusively finance or guarantee private sector operations without any government guarantee. (The Bank finances mainly government or public sector operations; when it finances the private sector through loans or guarantees, it must obtain a government guarantee.) Public accountability and transparency have not been traditionally emphasized as much for private sector operations in the absence of any governmental role. The IFC/MIGA ombudsman, for example, is required to respect the confidentiality of sensitive business information and his findings are not to be made publicly available as a matter of course. He will only recommend to the President the extent and form of possible disclosure. Because of their dealing with the private sector, IFC and MIGA financing or guarantee agreements may be subject to domestic law, unlike the Bank's loan and guarantee agreements that exclude the application of any conflicting provision in the law of the borrower. They have, therefore, to be attentive

---

11. As explained in Chapter One, *supra*, at 14–15, the Operations Evaluation Department (OED) in the Bank carries out *ex post* audit of management's operational performance.

to domestic law requirements, including those relating to the rights of the investors they deal with. The extent of IFC financing of equity does not cover the total amount and is often limited to a small percentage of the equity capital.[12] Partner private investors may not readily accept the intrusion and delay to be caused by an inspection process akin to that of the Bank. The IFC/MIGA ombudsman is thus entrusted with a "flexible process" that is "proactive and non-adversarial" and is aimed primarily at "correcting project failures and achieving better results on the ground." He will be dealing exclusively with private sector operations, thus developing an understanding of the needs of this sector. His advice will also be sought at an early stage in the project cycle with a view to resolving problems and identifying solutions, rather than establishing compliance or failure.

This does not necessarily mean that an independent inspection function is not possible or desirable for IFC. It only suggests necessary differentiation in the scope and procedures to be followed with respect to inspection of private sector operations.[13]

After considering the proposals submitted by Management and the Panel on all other matters and being aware of the views expressed by NGOs, CODE reached its conclusions on the review of the Panel's experience as stated in a subsequent Management paper endorsed by CODE and submitted to the

---

12. IFC equity financing is usually in the range of 5 percent to 15 percent of a project's equity. *See International Finance Corporation Annual Report*, 20 (1999).

13. The prospect of the establishment of such a function, in addition to the ombudsman, has significantly increased by the call, in the context of the Twelfth Replenishment of IDA resources, for "instituting an appropriate and independent inspection function suitable for the private sector." On March 4, 1999, the Managements of IFC and MIGA submitted a report to CODE on an "Integrated Accountability Mechanism for IFC and MIGA" (CODE 99–14), suggesting that after the ombudsman reaches his findings an adversely affected party should have access to a credible independent forum as a last resort. This forum is suggested to be the Bank's Inspection Panel, operating, however, under "a substantially different procedure, method, and time-table" tailored to the needs of the private sector. The Panel would then report its findings to the Board of IFC or MIGA, as the case may be.

Board.[14] At that time, the conclusions of that paper represented the consensus of CODE, the Panel, and Management. They were later reflected in the "Clarifications" approved by the Board in October 1996.[15]

B.   *The Panel's Function and Procedures*

1.   *The "Two-Stages Approach" and the Possible Need for "Preliminary Assessment" in the First Stage*

A suggestion considered by some NGOs to be important for the Panel's independence was to dispose of the *two-stages approach* and allow the Panel to proceed with the investigation without having to seek prior Board approval. However, the Board continued to think that the rationale underlying the original approach (that is, maintaining the Board's responsibility for the decision to proceed with the process and minimizing outside pressure on Panel members) was valid. The Panel itself did not ask for a change in the original approach; it only suggested extension of the time period of the first stage when needed, as will be explained. As for Management, it simply stated that because the matter related to the Board's relationship with the Panel, it was not appropriate for Management to comment on it. The requirement of *Board approval of the Panel's recommendation to investigate remained intact* in the 1996 review.

Noting that "the extent of information expected by the Board at the preliminary stage was sometimes equivalent to the content of an investigation" and that, as a practical matter, the 21-day period provided for in paragraph 19 of the Resolution would not be adequate for that purpose or for any preliminary assessment by it, the Panel asked for the extension of that period. The Panel specifically added that "extending the time period of

---

14. *See Review of the Resolution Establishing the Inspection Panel—Clarification of Certain Aspects of the Resolution* (R96–204), submitted to the Board on September 30, 1996, and discussed on October 17, 1996.
    15. *See* text in Annex I–2.

the preliminary stage reduces the need for a formal 'investigation/inspection' which can still be authorized by the Board as a last resort." In response, Management mentioned that the 21-day period authorized for the Panel at the preliminary stage was predicated on the assumption that the Panel would at that stage only ascertain on a *prima facie* basis the eligibility and admissibility requirements and during that short period would not pass any definite judgment on the merits of the request. Passing such a judgment at that early stage would, in the Management view, defeat the whole purpose of the second stage, either obviating the need for it and rendering it superfluous, or prematurely prejudging its outcome. The assumption was that the Panel should not reach a hasty finding on the merits. Once it was authorized to investigate, there was no time limit on its investigation. The period of such investigation would naturally vary depending on the complexity of each case.

Management suggested, therefore, that the Executive Directors should, in the light of the Board's actual experience, consider first whether the well-defined two-stages approach established in the Resolution, with its distinction between jurisdiction over the request and the merits of the request, should be maintained. If it were to be maintained, the 21-day period need not be changed or might be extended only slightly. If, however, as suggested by the Panel, it was deemed useful to consider the initial stage a period of a "preliminary assessment" of the *merits* of the request, which could obviate the need for the full investigation envisaged in the Resolution, the 21-day period provided for in the Resolution would clearly need to be extended. Because such a period might vary from case to case, and given the need to avoid delays, Management suggested that in case the "preliminary assessment" concept was approved by the Board, the Resolution might be amended to (a) clearly give the Panel the power of making a preliminary assessment of the merits of the request (and not just establishing its eligibility and admissibility) before the Board authorized full investigation, wherever the Panel deemed that to be useful, and (b) allow the Panel to extend the period of that preliminary assessment as might be needed for completing the assessment, up to a certain ceiling (for, say, 56 working days). However, Management stated that, although the distinction between the two stages established in the Resolution was installed by the Board for sound reasons, its soundness would be questionable if the Board were to expect the Panel to give it a definite assessment of the merits of the case at the early stage of establishing whether the Panel had jurisdiction over a specific request. The Resolution envisaged that the Panel would confine itself at the first stage to ascertaining the standing of the requester, the eligibility of the request, and whether it was barred under the Resolution. It further assumed that that preliminary stage would culminate in a recommendation by the Panel "as to whether the matter should be investigated." If such valid assumptions were not deemed to be practical by the Board, an amendment of the Resolution along the lines stated earlier would be justified.

In its comments on Management's paper, the Panel clarified that the "preliminary assessment" it proposed was needed to determine sometimes complex eligibility questions under the Resolution—including the establishment of the existence of harm.[16] Far from being a *disguised investigation*, the Panel argued, the proposed preliminary assessment attempted to find a realistic way of complying with the Resolution and meeting Board requirements for information. There was no suggestion by the Panel, as it saw the situation, that "the 'merits' (that is, whether the *allegations* that the Bank has violated policies and procedures and such violation has caused the damage) should be investigated in the preliminary period." On the contrary, the Panel wished to provide "a satisfactory factual basis"—as required under the Resolution—for a decision on whether an investigation needed to be carried out. The Panel added that "it was essential to retain the investigation stage," which follows the preliminary stage of ascertaining eligibility.

16. *See* Panel paper submitted to CODE, *supra* note 7.

2.   Time Limits During the First Stage

The Board decided that the Panel's recommendation should normally be completed within 21 days, as originally envisaged.[17] However, it gave the Panel the discretion it had asked for when it finds it appropriate to carry out "a preliminary assessment" of the alleged damage (in particular, when this could lead to a resolution of the matter without the need for a full investigation).[18] The Board asked that the Panel, in undertaking such a preliminary assessment, indicate to the Board the date on which it would present its findings and recommendation as to whether a full investigation was still required. If such a date was expected by the Panel to exceed eight weeks from the date of receipt of Management's response, the Panel would seek Board approval for the extension, possibly on a "no-objection" basis. The Board also made it clear, in that respect, that what was needed at that preliminary stage was not to establish that a serious violation of the Bank's policy had *actually* taken place and had resulted in damages suffered by the affected party. Rather, it was to establish whether the complaint was *prima facie* justified and warranted a full investigation because it was eligible under the Resolution.[19]

3.   Outcome of Inspection: Findings or Recommendations

Some NGOs and other commentators requested the Bank *give the Panel the power, not only to reach "findings" as a result of its inspection but also to make recommendations to the Board regarding the project under inspection as well as the Bank's applicable policies and procedures.* Management noted in its paper that confining the substantive function of the Panel to reaching such findings was a decision initially taken by the Board after careful analysis. It

---

17. *See* Clarifications, *supra* note 3, under the section on the Panel's function.

18. *Id.* The Board's position on this matter was reversed in the conclusions of the second review of the Panel's experience, as shown later in this chapter.

19. *Id.*

was feared at the time of establishing the Panel that endowing it with a substantive advisory function that went beyond the investigation of requests would require placing at its disposal technical and financial resources far beyond its existing facilities. More important, the proper lines between the role of the Panel and that of Management would be blurred if the Panel, rather than Management, recommended to the Board operational remedial measures or changes in Bank policies and procedures. In practice, Management discussed with Panel members changes in the proposed project in the case of the *Arun III Project*, which was not yet approved.[20] The Board invited the Panel to "assist the Board in its review of Management's progress" in a number of other cases, as shown in the previous chapter. Such flexibility, Management stated, had not been seen as inconsistent with the text of the Resolution and, although it is not provided for, it may continue to be followed without amending the Resolution. The Board agreed that the Panel's investigations should continue to result in "findings" (not in recommendations to the Board on the merits of the project or on the Bank's overall policies and procedures).[21] The Board would continue to act on the basis of recommendations of Management with respect to such remedial action as may be needed, in light of the Panel's findings.[22]

C.   *The Issues of Access to the Panel and Eligibility of Requests for Inspection*

Management had no objection to extending access to the Panel to "all affected parties, including a single individual," as

---

20. In her study of the Panel's first three years experience, Udall notes that in practice the Panel made recommendations on "project reform" in four cases including, besides Arun III (Nepal), the PLANAFLORO (Brazil), Jamuna Bridge (Bangladesh) and Jute Sector (Bangladesh). *See* Lori Udall, *The World Bank Inspection Panel: A Three-Year Review 74* (October 1997). In fact, the Panel pointed out in these cases the requirements of certain Bank policies and the need for steps to meet such requirements.

21. *Clarifications, supra* note 3, under the section of the Panel's function.

22. *Id.* The Board's position on this matter was reversed in the conclusions of the second review of the Panel experience, as shown later in this chapter.

suggested by NGOs (and as was originally mentioned in the first draft Resolution). It clearly stated that in case the Board decided to amend the Resolution to authorize requests submitted by an affected individual, the requirement that the request be submitted by a "community of persons" would be dropped, and the definition of such community would become immaterial. "Otherwise, the definition of the 'community of persons' requirement might better be clarified in the text of the Resolution."

On its part, the Panel strongly believed that, "*instead of focusing on formal technicalities* [related to the eligibility of the requesters], *the eligibility criteria would be better based on the existence of actual or possible damage or harm which is or may be possibly caused by a Bank-financed project, where the harm could be remedied if the Bank's policies and procedures are appropriately applied to the design, appraisal, or execution of such project.*"[23] In this respect, the Panel expressed its concern that if a more restrictive interpretation of the current eligibility requirements was made, access to the Panel would be limited to "the fortunate few that can rely on the advice of international lawyers and NGOs." Subsequently, in its comment on Management's paper to CODE, the Panel explained that, "*in practice, the Panel has avoided dwelling on alleged violations of policies and procedures in the preliminary stage.*"[24] This Panel's view, which differs from the requirements of that stage as explained in Chapter Two,[25] was to be expressed in stronger and broader terms on the occasion of the second review of the Panel's experience, as will be seen.[26]

The Board favored maintaining the present language of the Resolution with the understanding that the affected party, which the Resolution describes as "a community of persons, such as an organization, association, society, or other grouping of individuals," includes "any two or more persons who share

---

23. Note 2, *supra*. (Emphasis added.)
24. Note 7, *supra*. (Emphasis added.)
25. *See* Chapter Two, *supra*, at 49–51.
26. *See* this chapter, *infra*, at 191 *seq*.

some common interests or concerns,"[27] confirming an interpretation given on an earlier occasion by the Board on the
General Counsel's advice.[28]

The NGOs that wrote to the Bank also asked for broadening
access to the Panel to cover *requests submitted by foreign NGOs
and to local NGOs whose rights or interests had not been affected by
the project, or, more generally, to claims submitted in the public
interest.* Earlier, in its paper to CODE, Management did not
object to broadening access to any party as long as it was an
"affected party," that is, a party whose rights or interests might
be harmed or threatened by an alleged Bank action or omission
related to a specific project. Management noted that that would
not meet the broader demands of NGOs, but suggested that
NGOs that were not "affected parties" might, under the
Resolution, submit a request to an Executive Director. If the latter was convinced of the seriousness of the request, he could forward it to the Panel if he was not satisfied with the initial
Management reply. Neither CODE, nor the full Board, supported extending the inspection function beyond the scope provided
for in the Resolution.

The Board also declined the Panel's suggestion to authorize
inspection upon the request of the Bank's President, as had also been
proposed by some NGOs. Management described the proposal as
possibly "a useful option." However, many members of the
Board had noted that the Panel was established by the Board to

---

27. *Id.* under the section on eligibility and access.

28. *See Memorandum of the Senior Vice President and General Counsel, Role
of the Inspection Panel in the Preliminary Assessment of Whether to Recommend
Inspection,* dated January 3, 1995. Annex I–4 of this book. Some commentators
criticized that reading of the Resolution that is based on the Resolution's language. In their criticism, they wrongly assumed that the General Counsel's
advice meant that the interests of the complainants ought to be "affected in the
same way." Letter from Oxfam International to the Chairman of CODE
(CODE96–15), March 26, 1996, at 8. *See also* Daniel D. Bradlow, A Test Case
for the World Bank, 11 *The American University Journal of International Law
and Policy* 247, 262 (1996) (arguing that individual complainants may not meet
the commonality of interest standard if affected in a different manner). No such
requirement should be drawn, however, from the General Counsel's Legal
Memorandum, the text of the Resolution, or its Board-approved interpretation.

perform an independent function for the Board, which, in their view, could eventually be undermined by the Panel's reporting to the President in the cases referred by him for inspection.

The Board clarified that, even though the Resolution speaks of *"projects financed by the Bank,"* the request for inspection might relate either to a project under consideration by Bank Management (that is, a project in the design, preparation, preappraisal, or appraisal stage), or to a project already approved by the Board that would be or was being financed by the Bank.[29] Such a broader coverage was intended from the beginning. The Board also reconfirmed an earlier Board understanding (from July 1995) to the effect that the term "project," as used in the Resolution, had the same meaning as generally used in the Bank's practice,[30] without further explanation.

As also agreed in July 1995, it was clarified that the Panel's mandate did not extend to reviewing the consistency of the Bank practice with *all* of its policies and procedures but, as stated in the Resolution, was limited to cases of alleged failure to follow the Bank's operational policies and procedures *with respect to the design, appraisal, and/or implementation of projects,* including cases of alleged Bank failure to follow up on the borrowers' obligations under loan agreements, with respect to such policies and procedures.[31]

D.   Disclosure of Information

The Board agreed to make Management's response to the request for inspection, as well as the opinions of the General Counsel of the Bank on matters related to the Panel, available to

---

29. *See* Clarifications, *supra* note 3, under the section on eligibility and access.

30. *Id.* For details on the discussion regarding the meaning of the term "project" under the *Resolution, see also* Chapter Two, *supra,* at 36–37 and the *First Annual Report of the Inspection Panel,* at 57–58.

31. *See* Clarifications, *supra* note 3, under the section on eligibility and access. Emphasis in the original text.

the public promptly after the Board had discussed these documents.[32] Both changes were requested by NGOs and welcomed by Management. The Board also shortened the period of disclosure of all documents from two weeks to three days from the date of Board decision,[33] in response to NGOs' demands agreed to by Management. The further demand by NGOs to make public or at least to disclose to the requester Management's response once it was given to the Panel (that is, before it was seen by the Board) was not supported by Management, nor granted by the Board. Management explained in its paper to CODE that the timing of disclosure was meant to protect the integrity of the Board's decision-making process and the confidentiality of Board proceedings. Making its response to the request for inspection as well as the General Counsel's opinions on matters related to the Panel publicly available before the Board had acted on them, according to that argument, might unduly subject the Board's decision-making process to pressure from sources outside the Bank. Interestingly, however, Management suggested that if the Panel, after having received Management's response, felt that it should communicate with the requester (for example, to ascertain certain facts), there was nothing in the Resolution that prevented it from doing so.

E.   Composition of the Panel

No change in the *composition of the Panel* was proposed. Board members were aware of the "roster approach" adopted in IDB and ADB, but they agreed with Management's recommendation that the Panel's structure should not be changed. It was also agreed, however, that once a decision was made on the inspection of private sector operations, the question of the composition of the Panel might be revisited, unless a separate panel or function was to be established for that purpose.[34]

---

32. *Id.* under the section on outreach. In the case of the General Counsel's opinions, the Board reserved its right to decide against disclosure in a specific case.
33. *Id.*
34. *Id.* under the section on the composition of the Panel.

F.   *Authority to Interpret the Resolution*

The Board also accepted the clarification made in the Management paper to CODE and endorsed by the latter to the effect that the *authority to interpret the Resolution* was vested in the Board.[35] The Panel would apply the Resolution in specific cases as it understood it, subject to the Board's review when the matter was submitted for its consideration.[36] The Board reconfirmed the Resolution's requirement that the advice of the Bank's Legal Department be sought by the Panel "on matters related to the Bank's rights and obligations with respect to the request under consideration."[37]

G.   *Independent Outside Counsel?*

The *request of some NGOs that the Board should have a legal counsel to advise on Panel matters, separate from the Bank's General Counsel, was not granted.* It was recalled that the General Counsel is the Counsel of the Bank as a whole, not of one organ of it. He or she provides legal advice to both the President and the Board on all matters, and neither the President nor the Board has a role in the formulation of his or her views.[38] This position allowed the General Counsel to issue statements to the Bank's underwriters and external auditors without either of them questioning his statements. In any event, the General Counsel was not involved in the preparation of Management's response to the requests for inspection, and there was no scope, therefore, for the "conflict of

---

35. *Id.* under the section on the role of the Board.

36. *Id.*

37. *Id.*

38. For a comprehensive description of the role of the Bank's General Counsel, *see* Ibrahim F.I. Shihata, The Role of the World Bank's General Counsel, *Proceedings of the 91st Annual Meeting of the American Society of International Law* (ASIL) 214–222 (1997). For a further discussion of the role of the Bank's General Counsel in connection with the Inspection Panel process, *see* Sabine Schlemmer-Schulte, The World Bank's Experience with Its Inspection Panel, 58 *Zeitschrift für ausländisches öffentliches Recht und Völkerrecht— Heidelberg Journal of International Law* 353, 382–84 (1998).

interest" alleged by the commenting NGOs. The case of the *Itaparica Project* in Brazil proved the point; the General Counsel's legal opinion to the Board differed in its conclusions from the position taken in Management's response on the eligibility question. While certain NGOs' writings refer to this as the "one case" related to the Panel where the General Counsel's views differed from Management's,[39] they omitted the fact that he was asked by the Board to give legal opinions on Panel matters on only two occasions. It may also be recalled that on both occasions he dealt with questions of principle and declined to comment on the merits of the case at hand.

H.   *Providing Information on the Role of the Inspection Panel*

Also, the Board agreed that significant efforts should be made to *make the Inspection Panel better known in borrowing countries,* but it stated that the Bank should not provide technical assistance or funding to potential requesters, as suggested earlier by some NGOs.[40]

I.   *Procurement Decisions*

Finally, the Board clarified that the *exclusion of procurement decisions* from the Panel's jurisdiction was not limited to decisions taken by the borrower (as the letter of the Resolution suggests) but extends to all procurement decisions, including those taken by Bank Management, as originally intended.[41] It was noted in this respect that a separate mechanism existed for addressing procurement-related complaints.

---

39. *See, e.g.,* Udall, *supra* note 20, at 43.
40. *Clarifications* under the section on "Outreach."
41. *Id.* under the section on the eligibility and access. *See also* Chapter Two, *supra,* at 52–54.

II.   The Second Review—1998/1999

The difficulties experienced by the Bank's Board when it addressed Panel recommendations continued despite the 1996 "Clarifications." This was particularly evident in the Board's discussion of subsequent complaints related to the *Itaparica* and *NTPC* projects, which led the Executive Directors to agree on that occasion on the need for a second review of the Panel's experience as a whole.

A.   *Management and Panel Papers*

The first informal Board meeting on that review took place on November 13, 1997. The Board had before it (i) a Management paper dated November 6, 1997,[42] which was shared beforehand in draft with the Panel; (ii) a detailed study prepared previously by this author for another purpose,[43] and (iii) a paper from the Panel summarizing its experience and views.[44]

In its paper, Management suggested that the Board had two options. The first option would be to follow literally the original text of the Resolution. This would require Management to limit its submission on the steps it may take to address past failures by the Bank, if admitted, to the very initial stages or the latest stage of the process. This would give Management the opportunity to remedy the situation, first when a complainant approaches Management before submitting its complaint to the Panel, then in the 21-day period after Management receives the request

---

42. See *Second Review of the Inspection Panel Experience* (SecM97–873), November 6, 1997.

43. Ibrahim F.I. Shihata, *The World Bank Inspection Panel—Its Historical, Legal and Operational Aspects*, first submitted to the Expert Meeting on the World Bank Inspection Panel, held at the Raoul Wallenberg Institute of Human Rights and Humanitarian Law in Lund, Sweden, on October 23–25, 1997, to be published in Ibrahim F.I. Shihata, *The World Bank in a Changing World, Volume Three* (2000) (forthcoming).

44. *Some Lessons from the Inspection Panel's Three Years Experience* (INSP/SecM97–11), November 6, 1997.

submitted to the Panel or after the investigation is completed. The second option, which is closer to the Board's practice codified in the 1996 "Clarifications," would allow Management to prepare remedial plans on its failures at any time during the intermediate stage (between the date it receives the request from the Panel and the submission to the Board of the Panel's findings) but with certain refinements. The plan would, in this case, be submitted first by Management to the Panel, which would comment on its adequacy in its report to the Board. The Panel might then agree that the plan obviated the need for further action on its part or might still recommend a full investigation.

The Panel explained its own position in a separate paper, where it clearly described its *"raison d'être"* as providing "groups who believe they are or could be negatively affected by Bank projects with direct access to an independent international forum where they can submit their complaints and have them addressed."[45] As to the Panel's function stated in its constituent Resolution (that is, ascertaining Bank compliance with its operational policies and procedures if allegations are made to the effect that serious violations have been made, resulting or likely to result in material harm to the complainant), the Panel's paper stressed its understanding that "[it is] the Bank alone and not the government or borrower, that is to be the exclusive subject of any investigation."[46] However, according to the Panel's paper, some Executive Directors had seen the Panel "less as an instrument for achieving Management compliance with Bank policies and more so as an instrument for ensuring borrower's compliance with legal covenants for the projects in question." In what seems to this writer as mixing the Panel's basic function (ascertaining Bank's compliance or failure) with one condition for the exercise of that function (assessing the resulting material harm), the Panel's paper suggested that:

> *"[a]ccording to the Resolution, the Panel has two main functions: on the one hand it is asked to check*

---

45. *Id.*
46. *Id.*

*on Management's compliance with the Bank's oper-
ational policies; on the other, it is asked to assess
'material harm' on affected or potentially affected
populations. A review of past Board decisions reveals
that the Panel's role in checking compliance with
operational policies has been downplayed, while its
role in addressing actual or potential harm to local
populations and assessing remedial actions has been
emphasized."*[47]

Most interesting here is that what was described by the Panel
during the first review of its experience as a matter not to be
dwelled on at the preliminary stage, but, by implication, at the
stage of investigation,[48] became a matter of lesser importance in
the work of the Panel generally (that is, it was "downplayed," not
by choice of the Panel, but by a perceived attitude of the Bank's
Board).

The Panel's paper also referred to Management's practice to
submit *borrowers'* remedial action plans before the Board meets
to consider the Panel's recommendation on whether to investigate. It described that practice as having "effectively preempted
the process envisaged in the Resolution." To cure this, it
described two possible courses. The Board could revert to the
Resolution's requirements, realizing, however, that that "may
serve no other purpose than to delay the implementation of
remedial action, which clearly is the primary objective of the
Requesters." Or, the Board could authorize action plans to be
submitted under an extended time limit (longer than the 21 days

---

47. *Id. See* this point repeated recently in Alvaro Umaña Quesada (Ed.),
The World Bank Inspection Panel—The First Four Years, 1994–1998, at 326
(1998, World Bank Publication). Mr. Umaña, echoing what the Panel stated
during the first review, note 7 and the text accompanying note 20, *supra,*
referred to the Panel's verification of Bank's compliance with its policies as a role
"which can be described as a 'policing' function" and is "less useful to the Board
since the Panel's 'verdict' does not lead—nor should it lead—to any action
beyond correcting failures in project design or execution." *See also The
Inspection Panel Annual Report,* August 1, 1996 to July 31, 1997, at 18.

48. *See* this chapter, *supra,* at 162–164.

required for Management's response). The Panel in its report to the Board could then offer its views on "the eligibility of the claims and on the adequacy of the action plan and consultation processes." Although the Panel was aware that the action plans submitted so far dealt with measures to be taken by the borrower, not the Bank, no mention was made of action plans to correct Bank failures, and no emphasis was placed on the issue of Bank compliance.

Informal Board discussion showed a broad preference for the second option presented in Management's paper and stressed by the Panel's paper. However, these discussions revealed a great measure of dissatisfaction on the part of Executive Directors representing borrowing countries. They saw that the remedial plans were always concerned with measures to be taken by the borrower at the borrower's own expense, and not with corrective actions to be taken by the Bank, thus implying that failures were only attributable to borrowers. More important, the process, as they saw it, had departed from the purpose of the inspection function, which was meant to address the failures of the Bank and no other party.

B.   The "Commentary"

This led to an approach that this author formally proposed as a "Commentary" on the ongoing debate and that was circulated to the Board with a supporting note from the Bank's President in early 1998.[49] The purpose of that approach was to ensure full respect for the scope of the Panel's function established in the Resolution while benefiting from the practical position preferred by the Board under the 1996 "Clarifications." The proposed approach consisted mainly of tailoring the procedure to be followed to the nature of each response made by Management to

---

49. *See Second Review of the Inspection Panel Experience—A Commentary*, (SecM98–8), January 7, 1998. The *Commentary* is explained in some detail in the text, in view of its impact on the outcome of the second review, where many, but not all, of the points mentioned in the *Commentary* were adopted.

the request for inspection, while paying full regard to three important points: (i) The Resolution's requirement (Paragraph 14(a)) that complaints with respect to actions that are the responsibility of parties other than the Bank are excluded from the Panel's mandate, (ii) the Panel's power to suggest to the Board in the initial stage whether the complaint had met the eligibility requirements, regardless of any position on this matter taken by the complainant or Bank Management, and (iii), as a matter outside the realm of the Resolution, the need for the *Bank*, as a responsible international institution, to discuss with the borrower the harm resulting from Bank-financed projects with a view to resolving the issue, whether this harm is subject to the Panel's inspection mandate or not. The following scenarios had thus to be dealt with separately:

A first possible scenario envisaged that Management's response would be that *there was no serious violation of any Bank policy or procedure applicable to the operation involved.* Such a response should normally be made within the 21-day period provided for in the Resolution. Depending on whether or not it agreed with Management's position, the Panel would, in such a case, formulate its recommendation to the Board on whether an investigation was needed. The Panel would follow the requirements of the Resolution in this process, limiting itself to looking into alleged actions or omissions attributed to the Bank and to no other party.

A second possible scenario envisaged response by Management to the Panel to the effect that *the request did not meet the Resolution's requirements for reasons other than the absence of any serious violations,* such as that the complainant was not an affected party or that the loan was more than 95 percent disbursed. Again, in this case, the 21-day period provided by the Resolution should normally be adequate for providing such a response. The Panel would assess the eligibility of the complaint and formulate its recommendation on whether an investigation was needed. The Panel's assessment might agree or disagree with Management's response, but it would exclusively address actions or omissions attributed to the Bank. Under the Resolution as clarified in 1996, the Panel would normally make its recommendation within a 21-day period, but it has the possibility of extending that period up to eight weeks and may even seek a longer extension from the Board.

A third possible Management response was that *failures did exist, but they were exclusively attributable to the borrower or to other factors external to the Bank*. If the Panel agreed that there was no evidence that any failure could be attributed to the Bank, there would be no point in recommending an investigation. Investigation would be recommended, however, if the Panel did not agree with Management's position because it felt that the alleged harm could be attributed to the Bank in whole or in part. Possibly, however, the Panel would recommend investigation if it was unable to make a determination on the matter at that early stage. However, Management would be expected under that scenario to present to the Board a remedial action plan on the measures the borrower had agreed to take to remedy the situation. The 21-day period provided for in the Resolution might not suffice for the preparation of such a remedial plan. Management would need to discuss it with the borrower *and the affected parties* and reach agreement on it with the borrower before presenting it to the Board. In such a case, Management might be allowed an extension, up to eight weeks, from the day it received the complaint, for the preparation of the response including the action plan, if any. The Panel did not have a role under the Resolution with respect to an action plan that exclusively addressed measures to be taken by the borrower, not the Bank. Nothing, however, according to the commentary paper, would prevent the Board, if it so wished, from asking the Panel to assist in the review of the implementation of such a plan. However, that would be an *ad hoc* assignment outside the scope of the Panel's Resolution. In any event, the Board would consider the remedial plan only after it received the Panel's view on whether it agreed that there was no scope for inspection due to the absence of any failure on the part of the Bank.

A fourth possible response by Management was *that failures did exist which were exclusively attributable to the Bank*. In this case, the Bank's response should indicate the measures the Bank intended to take to rectify such failures. Management might need the above-mentioned extension of the 21-day period to prepare that response and consult with the borrower and the affected party on the corrective actions. The Panel, on its part, would assess the situation in light of Management's response and any *consultation* it might wish to make. It would have the extended period approved in the 1996 "Clarifications" (eight weeks, subject to possible further extension) for that purpose. Clearly, in that case the Panel would consider whether the Bank's response satisfactorily disposed of the matter and therefore obviated the need for inspection. Should that not be the case, the Panel would recommend a full investigation of the Bank's alleged failures.

A fifth possible answer was that *Management agreed that certain failures had occurred, some of which were attributable to the borrower and some to the Bank.* Typical of such situations are those where the borrower had not honored its obligations under the loan agreement, but poor supervision on the part of the Bank had resulted in the continuation of such a failure on the part of the borrower with resulting harm to affected parties. Because the Panel's mandate under the Resolution is related to the failures attributable to the Bank, and not to "actions that are the responsibility of other parties, such as a borrower," a distinction had to be made between the action required in each case, and the role of the Panel would be defined accordingly. In such situations, Management would prepare, within the extended period, *two separate sets of corrective measures:* those related to the Bank itself and meant to correct any failure on its part, and those agreed with the borrower and addressing what the borrower should do to correct its failures (and, failing this, what remedies were or would be taken by the Bank under the loan agreement as a result of continued violations). Although the first set of proposed corrective measures relating to the Bank's own failures would be addressed in the first instance to the Panel, the second set of measures were to be addressed directly to the Board and would be dealt with by the Board, as in the case when Management took the position that failures were exclusively attributed to the borrower or other external factors. Upon receipt of the remedial plan proposed by the Bank to correct its own failures, the Panel would determine, in the extended period already granted to it, whether an investigation was needed and, therefore, should be recommended to the Board. It might do so if it believed that the measures proposed by the Bank were not adequate to rectify all the Bank's failures or that the Bank's failures appeared in fact to exceed those characterized in Management response as Bank failures. In deciding whether to authorize the investigation, the Board would review the assessment made by the Panel and the earlier response by Management. Clearly, if such investigation was approved by the Board on the recommendation of the Panel, it would be limited to the Bank's actions and omissions alleged in the request for inspection to constitute violation of Bank policies, the harm resulting from such actions and omissions, and the adequacy of the Bank's plan to address its failure, if any. If the Bank's failure proved to be in the area of supervision of the borrower's obligations, the Panel might have to note that such obligations had not been met, without, however, making this matter the subject of its investigation.

The purpose of the above scenarios as presented in the "Commentary" was to capture different possibilities and tailor a practical procedure for each one, within the framework of the Resolution and its 1996 "Clarifications." The only addition to pre-existing procedures was the possibility of extending the 21-day period provided for in the Resolution for Management response. If additional scenarios were to arise in practice, they could be dealt with under the same understanding: the Panel would independently recommend whether investigation was needed in each case, but such investigation, if authorized by the Board, would be limited to the *Bank's* behavior and the adequacy of the *Bank's* response with respect to that behavior. Meanwhile, any *borrower's* failure discovered in the process would be remedied under an agreed plan between the Bank and the borrower, following appropriate consultation with the affected parties, and would be directly submitted to the Board for approval.

In this way, the Resolution would be fully respected in practice *and* the harm would also be redressed.

Questions on the above "Commentary" led to the issuance of further clarifications:[50] The "Commentary" did not, in fact, add new requirements to the Resolution as interpreted in 1996. It aimed at enabling the Panel to perform the function provided for in the Resolution, without allowing this function to be pre-empted by other actions. If applied as proposed, these procedures would result in addressing any failure regardless of its source, but without confusing different roles. There was nothing new in Management's recognition of failures on its part (as was partially done in the case of the *NTPC Project*) or in denying any such failure (as in practically all other cases submitted to the Panel.) Such assignment of failures, however, would not bind the Panel; it is free to disagree with it or to state that it was not in a position at that early stage to take a position on the matter. In either case, it could recommend investigation. Any remedial action addressing Bank failures would be submitted first to the Panel, which might agree or disagree with its adequacy. Affected people would be consulted about the content of any remedial plan affecting them, whether it addressed Bank's or borrower's actions. Although a plan of the latter type did not fall within the Panel's purview, the Board could ask the Panel, as it did on several occasions, to assist it in the review of progress in the plan's implementation. Nothing in the proposed procedures reduced the scope of the Panel's function as described in the Resolution. The independence and integrity of the Panel were fully preserved.

C.   *Panel's Response*

Just before the Board met on March 12, 1998, to informally discuss the above "Commentary," the Board received a paper from the Panel dated March 10, 1998, which expressed disagreement

---

50. Note from Ibrahim F.I. Shihata to the Executive Directors, February 17, 1998.

with the approach outlined in the "Commentary."[51] According
to that paper, the objective of not entangling the Panel in matters
related to the borrower's failure to honor its obligations was "not
in question." What was questioned was the "practicability" of
devising separate procedures depending on the nature of
Management's response (even though it was made clear that in
practice Management's response inevitably in each case either
denied or admitted, fully or partially, non-compliance). The Panel
stated that it would normally be in no position at that early stage
to agree or disagree with Management's position. (The proposed
procedures indicated, however, that if that was the case, the Panel
could recommend investigation, if other eligibility conditions
were met). The Panel's paper thus disagreed with the
Commentary's view of unbundling the issues involved and stated
that under the different scenarios the Board could be confronted
with two views (of Management and Panel, respectively) on how
responsibilities for alleged harm should be assigned (which, however, has actually happened in practically every case handled by
the Panel so far). As Management was a party to the matter in dispute and tended to assign responsibility to the borrower in previous cases, the Panel felt that it would not be fair to give it the
power of making an assignment of responsibility, even if it was
reflecting only Management views and was completely subject to
the Panel's evaluation. It was explained earlier, however, that it
was only natural, if not inevitable, that Management would take
a position in its response to the request regarding the complaints
leveled against its actions, and it was for the Panel, then the
Board, to ascertain the validity of that position.

Other comments by the Panel seemed to have been based on
a special understanding of the "Commentary" that cannot be

---

51. *Second Review of the Inspection Panel Experience—Inspection Panel's
Comments on Management's Paper* dated December 17, 1997 and submitted to
the Board on January 7, 1998, (INSP/SecM98-4, March 10, 1998). The
December 1997 *Commentary* (Management paper) was discussed in draft with
the chairman and another member of the Panel (the third member not being
available at the time) before its circulation to the Board on January 7, 1998, and
their suggestions of minor changes were accommodated.

supported by its language and certainly was not intended. The Panel's paper spoke of the impracticability of assigning failures between the Bank and the borrower *in certain percentages* (an idea that had not been mentioned in the "Commentary"). It also added that the "Commentary's" approach could effectively prevent the Panel from ascertaining whether the Bank had adequately supervised the project (an idea which contradicts the language of the "Commentary," whose purpose, on the contrary, was to assist the Panel in carrying out its main function, that is, verifying the Bank's compliance with its policies and procedures, including the assessment of the Bank's adequate supervision of project implementation). The Panel implied that Management had no right to raise issues of eligibility in its response to the request for inspection.[52] It assumed that the "Commentary" introduced more restrictive eligibility requirements than were provided for in the Resolution (in fact, it was strictly based on the text of the Resolution as interpreted by the Board). The Panel also criticized the description in the "Commentary" of the affected party as "a community of two or more persons who *have* common interests or concerns" (rather than "who *share* some common interest or concerns" as agreed in the 1996 "Clarifications"), but no different meaning was intended in that respect. Finally, the Panel, whose practice has shown less interest in the "technicalities of eligibility," suggested that the Board revive the "second option" discussed in November 1997 (the preliminary assessment by the Panel and possible remedial plans on steps to correct Bank failures in the first stage of the process), or that the Bank should consider a new option based on IFC's options paper to CODE[53] (that is, turning the inspection function into a Compliance Officer/Ombudsman function). According to the Panel's paper, this latter one-stage approach, "seems to validate Panel's opinion on the disadvantages of a formal quasi-judicial process that focuses on narrow eligibility requirements and assigning responsibility, and the advantages of

---

52. *See* a discussion of this view in the next chapter, at 225.
53. *Supra*, note 9 of this chapter.

a flexible process aimed at finding pragmatic ways to resolve identified problems."

D.   Board Review—The Working Group Report

The Board, after hearing from the Panel and Management on
March 12, 1998, decided to discuss the matter itself, albeit informally, rather than referring it to CODE, as was done in the first
review. Its divisive discussion led to an agreement on the chairman's suggestion to establish a Working Group consisting of six
Executive Directors to consider and recommend a solution to the
full Board. The Working Group was established on March 16,
1998, comprising Executive Directors representing both borrowing and non-borrowing members.

Unlike CODE, which discussed the first review in the presence of both Management and the Panel, the Working Group
heard the Panel and the General Counsel but kept its discussions
otherwise limited to its members. They concluded their task with
a report to the Board dated December 9, 1998.[54] Although the
report presented a compromise among the members of the
Working Group, it restored to a large extent the foundations on
which the Resolution establishing the Panel was based. The main
points of this report may be summarized and analyzed as follows:

1. The Working Group asked the Board to "strongly reaf-
firm the importance of the Inspection Panel process and its
contribution to improving the effectiveness of Bank policies
and procedures and increasing the accountability of Bank
Management and staff with regard to operational work of the
Bank, thus enhancing project quality."

2. "The Panel must be independent, and the integrity of the
Resolution must not be compromised." The Working Group
urged both "Bank Management and the Panel to adhere
strictly to the Resolution."

---

54. *See* (R98–297), December 9, 1998, reprinted as Annex I–3 of this
book.

3. The proposals of the Working Group listed below, if accepted by the Board, should supersede the paragraph entitled "The Panel's Function" in the October 17, 1996, "Clarifications." Relevant procedures of the Bank and the Panel should be modified accordingly.

4. Except for Management recommendations to the Board after the Panel completes its investigation and submits its findings, "Management at its initiative should not communicate directly with the Board on matters associated with the request." This means, *inter alia*, that any plan prepared by Management before the Panel has completed its inspection to correct the Bank's failure to observe its operational policies and procedures should be submitted to the Panel, not directly to the Board. As for remedial action plans to be agreed between the Bank and the borrower, the Panel's role, as will be seen, is much more limited.

5. After a request for inspection is forwarded by the Panel to Management, the latter "should provide evidence either that:

(i) it has complied with the relevant Bank's operational policies and procedures; or that

(ii) there are serious failures attributable exclusively to its own actions or omissions in complying, but that it intends to comply with the relevant policies and procedures; or that

(iii) the serious failures that may exist are exclusively attributable to the borrower or to factors external to the Bank; or that

(iv) the serious failures that may exist are attributable both to the Bank's non-compliance with the relevant operational policies and procedures and to the borrower or to external factors.

The Inspection Panel may independently agree or disagree, totally or partially, with any of such evidence or allegations provided by Management and will proceed accordingly."

6. If Management admits serious failures attributable exclusively or partly to the Bank, "it may provide, together with its

response, evidence that it has since complied or is taking steps to comply (that is, it may prepare a *Bank 'Compliance Plan'"* that "should contain only those actions that the Bank can implement by itself)."[55] As this plan will be submitted first to the Panel, the latter "should satisfy itself as to whether the Bank's compliance or Compliance Plan are adequate and reflect this assessment in its reporting to the Board."

7. "The Panel *shall determine* the eligibility of a Request for inspection independently of any views that may be expressed by Management."[56] This implies that Management may express in its response any views it may have regarding eligibility of the request, but that the Panel acts independently in reaching its own conclusion on this issue. The use of the words "shall determine" in its context does not negate the Board's role in approving or denying the Panel's recommendation to authorize investigation, but it practically qualifies it, as will soon be explained.

8. The Panel is expected to seek the view of the Bank's Legal Department with respect to matters relating to the Bank's rights and obligations (the Resolution requires this as an obligation on the Panel).

9. "For its *Recommendation* on whether an investigation should be carried out, the Panel should satisfy itself that *all* the eligibility criteria provided for in the Resolution have been met."[57] This clearly means that the Panel should not limit itself in this early stage to the issue of harm and leave the issue of violation of Bank policies to the investigation stage.[58] However, all eligibility conditions would be assessed on a *prima facie* basis only. Hence, "the original time limit, set forth in the Resolution for both Management's Response to the request and the Panel's Recommendation, should be strictly observed." The report did not address whether the

---

55. Emphasis added.
56. Emphasis added.
57. Emphasis added.
58. Compare the Panel's comments on the first review, *supra* note 7, and the second review, *supra* note 51.

21-day period would be adequate for Management's preparation of the Compliance Plan.

10. In the first stage of the process (before the Panel recommends investigation), the Panel may visit the project country "if it believes this is necessary to establish the eligibility of the Request." However, "any definite assessment" of material adverse effect attributable to the Bank's failure to respect its policies and procedures will be done after the Panel has completed its investigation.

11. As to the important question of the two-stages approach, the Working Group's "strong recommendation" was that the two stages would be maintained in principle but that the Board "will authorize an investigation without making a judgment on the merits of the claimant's Request and without discussion, except with respect to the technical eligibility criteria." The latter criteria were defined in the report to mean "criteria other than the existence of *prima facie* evidence of Bank's serious failure and the resulting material adverse effect." "If issues of interpretation of the Resolution arise, the Panel shall clear them with the Board." What all this meant was that the Working Group suggested that the Board normally would not review the merits of the Panel's conclusion on whether the specific eligibility requirements of a serious violation of Bank policies and procedures and a resulting material harm to the complainant were met in a specific case. Yet, as the Board maintains authority over the interpretation of the Resolution, questions of interpretation would first be cleared with the Board. In particular, issues related to the scope of the Panel mandate and the definition of what the Resolution means by the required eligibility criteria (other than the *prima facie* assumption of violation and harm) may be discussed by the Board, in light of the particular facts of the case at hand. As a result of this proposal, the Working Group suggested that the "preliminary assessment" concept introduced in the 1996 "Clarifications" (and earlier in the Panel's Operating Procedures) would no longer be needed, and that the Board's approval of the Working Group's report

would result in a formal revision of the 1996 "Clarifications" regarding this point.

12. The Working Group also stressed the "non-judicial," "evaluative" nature of the Panel's investigation. This of course was understood from the beginning. It should not be seen, however, as an invitation to the Panel to reach its findings lightly. These findings, as emphasized in the following chapter, will have a great impact, within and outside the Bank. Legal suits might be brought against the Bank before national courts, citing in part the Panel's findings and claiming compensation.[59] Findings on a "serious violation" of Bank operational policies and the resulting "material harm" ought therefore to be reached with utmost care after a full investigation of the facts.

13. The Working Group urged the Panel to keep a low profile during investigation "in keeping with its role as a fact-finding body on behalf of the Board." While the Panel's contacts with requesters and other affected people are acknowledged and consultation with them is welcomed, the Working Group suggested that the Panel's methods "should not create the impression that it might be investigating the borrower's performance." It asked the Board to indicate to both Panel and Management to decline media contacts "while an investigation is pending or underway."

14. The Panel's findings (as reflected in the report stating the conclusions of the Panel's investigation) "should focus on serious Bank failure to observe its operational policies and procedures with respect to project design, appraisal, and/or implementation," as indeed is required by paragraph 12 of the Resolution. The Panel should discuss "only those material adverse effects, alleged in the Request, that have totally or partially resulted from serious Bank failure of compliance." If the Panel finds that harm has occurred but was not due to Bank failures, "the Panel's Report will so state without entering into analysis of the material adverse effect or its causes."

---

59. See Chapter Five, *infra*, at 233–235.

This is consistent with paragraph 14 (a) of the Resolution, which excludes from the Panel's purview "complaints with respect to actions that are the responsibility of other parties, such as a borrower or potential borrower and that do not involve any action or omission on the part of the Bank."

15. In the Panel's assessment of material adverse effects, it should compare the current situation with that prevailing before the Bank-financed project existed. "Non-accomplishments and unfulfilled expectations that do not generate a material deterioration compared to the without-project situation should not be considered as material adverse effect." Although the assessment could be difficult to make in specific cases, the Panel will "carefully exert its judgement" and "be guided by Bank Policies and Procedures where relevant." (In fact, the Resolution does not specifically speak of "pre-project" and "post-project" situations. Rather, it defines the Panel's role in terms of investigating alleged serious violations of Bank policies related to the design, appraisal, or implementation of the project at hand that results or could result in a material adverse effect. Such effect or harm should be measured according to the ordinary meaning of these terms, that is, an actual or potential bodily harm or financial loss directly resulting from Bank violations, not simply from the non-accomplishment of project purposes.)

16. A major point in the Working Group's original report is the clear distinction between the "Compliance Plan" that the Bank may prepare to address its own failures, if any, and the remedial "Action Plan" to be agreed upon between the Bank and the borrower to improve project implementation. With respect to the latter plan, "Management should communicate to the Panel the nature and outcome of consultations with affected parties" and the Panel may submit to the Board a report on their view of the *adequacy of such consultation*. According to the Working Group, "[t]he Board should not ask the Panel for its view on other aspects of the Action Plans, nor would it ask the Panel to monitor the implementation of the Action Plan."

17. Finally, the Working Group emphasized that its proposals would enhance the effectiveness of the inspection function only if they were adhered to "by all parties in good faith" and if borrowers do not withhold their consent for the Panel's field visits. If these assumptions prove to be incorrect, the Working Group concluded, the Board should revisit the above proposals. Such a Board review falls, at any rate, within the Board's powers at any time.

E.   *The Aftermath of the Working Group Report*

The Working Group Report, like any other report of a Board committee to the full Board, was expected to be directly discussed in the Board and a date was set for this purpose. However, a few days after circulation of the report to Board members, the Bank President and the Executive Directors received a letter signed by two Washington-based NGOs, though written in the name of other U.S. and U.K. NGOs as well. The letter requested that the Board allow "public comment and participation" in any clarifications of, or changes in the Resolution and procedures of the Panel. Describing the review process as "conducted in secrecy," the letter demanded "consultation with the public" and postponement of the Board meeting to allow for such consultation.[60]

The following day, *The Wall Street Journal* carried a story with the exciting heading, "Effort Would Curb Watchdog of World Bank—Big Borrower Nations Seek Limit on Probing Harm to People and Ecology."[61] Although only two of the six members of the Working Group represented large borrowing countries and the four others are nationals of non-borrowing

---

60. Letter signed by David Hunter, Center for International Environmental Law, and Kay Treakle, Bank Information Center, dated January 11, 1999, Re: Public Comment on the Review of the Inspection Panel.

61. *The Wall Street Journal*, January 12, 1999, at A2 and A8. A similar story by the same writer, Michael Philips, appeared in *The Globe and Mail*, January 11, 1999, at B9.

countries, and although the report repeatedly called for strictly observing the Resolution establishing the Panel, the story depicted it as an attempt by big borrowers to give the Panel a much more limited role than that originally envisaged. Furthermore, it cited matters that were either not included in the report (such as restricting Panel visits to the project country) or originated in the Resolution itself, not in the Working Group's proposals (such as the barring of requests based on borrower's actions), as evidence of "the effort to hobble the . . . Panel." The story also quoted one of the writers of the letter of the previous day in support of its allegations.

1.   Reaction of the Inspection Panel

On January 20, 1999, the three members of the panel circulated to the Board their comments on the Working Group report.[62] After expressing appreciation for the Working Group's reaffirmation of the Resolution establishing the Panel and confirmation of the Panel's integrity and independence, the paper flatly stated that "many of the Working Group's proposals would have the exact opposite effect." Reaffirming the Panel's previously held position about the nature of its role, it stated that "for civil society, the redressal of alleged harm is the most important feature of the Panel process" and that "[r]equests for inspection are not based on the intellectual concern that Bank policies and procedures may have been violated. Rather, they are motivated by a keen desire that the Bank redress the adverse effects resulting from such violations." Based on this concept (fundamentally different from the Resolution's focus on what the Panel called an "intellectual concern," that is, ascertaining whether the Bank has complied with its policies and procedures), the paper did not mention that, pursuant to the Resolution, assessing harm is required only as an eligibility condition in the requests for

---

62. Inspection Panel Working Group: *Second Review of the Inspection Panel. 1998 Clarifications of Certain Aspects of the Resolution—Inspection Panel Comments* (INSP/SecM99–2), January 20, 1999.

inspection. Nor did it mention that "redressing harm" is not, under the Resolution, part of the Panel's inspection function.

The Panel's paper repeated its earlier objections first expressed in its comments on the 1998 "Commentary,"[63] especially the perceived impracticality and unfairness of Management's preliminary indication in its response to a request for inspection whether in its view the alleged harm had resulted from a Bank failure or other causes (even though, as explained before, this is inevitably done in each response, and in any case, the Panel is the arbiter of any position taken by Management in this respect). Management's indication of whether the harm is due to its or somebody else's failure was called "finger pointing," as if the accused party, Management, ought to take the accusation as a given, without expressing its own views to the Panel. (Clearly, the Panel is under no obligation to accept Management views. It may take any position it wishes and may recommend investigation if it was not in a position at this early stage to make a *prima facie* assessment.)

The Panel's paper also assailed the idea of two separate plans, one to remedy Bank failures, if any, and another to address action required from the borrower. It proposed instead that "Management and the Borrower should be asked to cooperate in the preparation of a single remedial plan." Understandably, the Panel's paper criticized the limited role given by the Working Group to the Panel in assessing the remedial action plan to be agreed with the borrower. (The Resolution does not mention borrowers' action plans and does not give the Panel any role with regard to such action plans.)[64] Reverting to a suggestion made in the 1998 "Commentary," the Panel proposed that "the Board retain its current option to involve the Panel in appropriate follow-up processes."

Surprisingly, the Panel's paper did not welcome the Working Group's "strong suggestion" that the Board approve the Panel's

---

63. *See* this chapter, *supra*, at 181 *seq.*
64. *See* Chapter Two, *supra*, at 50–51. *See also* this chapter, *supra*, at 175–176, Chapter Five, *infra*, at 222–224.

recommendation to investigate without discussion. Instead, it criticized the timid recommendation that Board members, who, according to the Resolution, must approve each investigation, should limit their intervention, if any, to raising questions regarding "technical eligibility criteria." The paper thus proposed that "if the notion of a 'Preliminary Assessment' is abandoned in favor of a short initial report as proposed, it would seem to be more in keeping with the spirit of the proposals that the Panel should simply submit its report to the Board for information and then proceeds to the next step, if any." The Panel did not mention that their latter proposal would introduce a fundamental change to the process envisaged in the Resolution that may only be introduced through its amendment.

The Panel's paper strongly criticized the Working Group's suggestion that harm should be compared with the "without the project situation." It did not recall that the Resolution speaks of harm resulting from a serious violation of Bank operational policies applicable to the project at hand. It is this "harm resulting from policy violations," which could not exist in the absence of the project, rather than any other criterion, that should guide the work of the Panel in this area, until the Resolution is amended. As for the time limits in the Resolution that the Working Group asked all parties to strictly observe, the Panel suggested, "for pragmatic reasons . . . that the possibility of seeking an extension as provided in the 1996 "Clarifications" should be maintained."

Clearly, a basic difference existed between the Panel's view of its role (which responds to the practical concerns of the affected parties without limiting itself to the assessment of Bank behavior) and the Working Group's attempt to reestablish this role as defined in the Resolution.

2.   Intervention by NGOs

The Board meeting to discuss the Working Group's report was first scheduled for January 20, 1999. The request by some NGOs for consultation led to a change of the date. On January 26,

1999, members of the Working Group had an "informal discussion" with representatives of some U.S. and U.K. NGOs, where the Working Group explained the findings of its report and NGO representatives expressed their concerns. Following this, the Board meeting to discuss the Working Group's report was rescheduled to March 16. To the knowledge of this writer, this was the first time a report submitted by a Board Committee to the Board was discussed with private parties outside the Bank before the Board had the chance to consider the report. This unprecedented step was followed, however, by another unprecedented event, an informal meeting between the full Board and a larger number of NGOs representatives held on March 24, 1999, after the proposed Board meeting to discuss the Working Group's report was postponed again, to April 20.

Before the Board meeting with the NGOs, several inaccurate press articles reported negatively on the Working Group's report.[65] Objections were also received from NGOs echoing previous comments made during the first review as well as the Panel's own comments on the Working Group's report. Among the NGO comments, detailed suggestions were received from Brazilian and Mexican NGOs. Three well-known members of the U.S. Congress, one senator, one congressman, and one congresswoman, also wrote a joint letter to the Bank President criticizing the Working Group's report and making specific suggestions along the lines previously received from U.S. NGOs. Specifically, they requested (i) elimination of the preliminary review process that requires Board authorization of investigations (or the approval being deemed to be given upon submission of the Panel's recommendation unless otherwise decided by a "two-thirds vote of the Board"), (ii) preparation of remedial action plans only after the Panel process is completed, (iii) judging harm by measuring the claimant condition against the condition the claimant would be in had the Bank's policies not been violated,

---

65. *See, e.g., Inter Press Service* (IPS) report *New Battle Looms Over World Bank Watchdog,* January 26, 1999; *The Wall Street Journal, World Bank to Seek Comment on a Plan to Leash Watchdog,* February 3, 1999, at A14.

and (iv) requiring unimpeded Panel access to project sites to be a condition of Bank loan agreements.

Some concerned individuals also sent their comments, among which two should particularly be noted. Daniel Bradlow, a professor of law at American University in Washington, D.C., repeated the concerns of several NGOs and the Inspection Panel. In his otherwise learned comments, he argued in particular that Management's response to a request for inspection should not include any factual record to support its answer on whether it has complied or intends to comply with Bank policies and procedures. This, according to him, would best enable the Panel to freely establish the factual record regarding the allegations included in the request.[66] Coming from a professor of law, this suggestion may be particularly troublesome. The fact that the party to which alleged violations are attributed may present its point of view in no way deprives the investigator from reaching his independent conclusion. Nor does the fact that Management knows more about the project deprive the Panel, which has access to all Bank files and all Bank staff, from ascertaining whether the information provided by Management is accurate. Any lawyer knows that unfairness does not result from the attempt by a party facing allegations of misconduct or abuse of powers to present its version of the factual record or that such a party may be in a better position to know the facts. Rather, unfairness results from depriving a party from defending its position according to the facts available to it. What matters here is that the Panel should itself have access to all the records and should be able to exercise an independent judgment after having heard the views of both the requesters and Management. It should be borne in mind that what is required from the Panel at the first stage is only a position on questions of eligibility, including only *prima facie* evidence of Bank violations and resulting harm, not a full investigation of the request.

66. Comments by Professor Bradlow on the Inspection Panel Working Group Report Entitled Second Review of 1998—Clarifications of Certain Aspect of the Resolution, dated March 10, 1999.

Another interesting intervention came from Professor Devesh Kapur, also an academic, but one with profound knowledge of the Bank, due to his co-authorship of a book on the Bank's history whose authors were given an extensive period of time and full access to all Bank files before they produced their impressive work.[67] Unlike other commentators, Professor Kapur supported a "more restrictive regime for the Inspection Panel," which he saw as "adding further to the powers of the North, especially the U.S., vis-à-vis developing countries." According to Kapur, "[t]he parallels between the Bank's Inspection Panel and the Independent Counsel statute in the U.S. are striking. Both were driven by good liberal intentions responding to real abuses (although in the Bank's case even the circumstances surrounding the birth of the Inspection Panel would not meet the smell test of governance it applies to its borrowers); both were hijacked to partisan political ends; both ended up causing damage; both need to be either laid to rest or severely modified, and both prove the adage that the best can be the enemy of the good."[68]

3.   Board/NGOs Informal Meeting

In the March 24, 1999, informal meeting between the Board and representatives of NGOs and other civil society constituencies from developing and developed countries, the Chair of the Working Group emphasized that their report was fully in support of the Inspection Panel. According to him, the Group thought to have successfully reconciled the diverse opinions among borrowing and non-borrowing countries on the working of the Panel. In particular, its report strengthened the Panel's function as originally envisaged under the Resolution by prohibiting Management to agree with the borrower on a remedial action plan at a

---

67. *See* Devesh Kapur, John P. Lewis, and Richard Webb, *The World Bank—Its First Half Century* (1997).

68. Comment by Devesh Kapur on the Draft Report on the Inspection Panel sent to the Working Group on February 23, 1999.

stage where the Resolution does not foresee such early action. It also clarified the Panel's mandate by referring to a response by the Bank regarding its own failures as a compliance plan and to borrowers' responses to their failures as action plans. The report also expressed trust in the Panel's work by confirming that an investigation would normally be authorized by the Board if the Panel so recommends.

NGOs and civil society representatives voiced their satisfaction with the Inspection Panel and its work as the only mechanism for affected people in many borrowing countries to bring complaints for harm resulting from Bank-financed projects. (Implying again that their concern is redress of such harm regardless of its cause—a noble concern, no doubt, that is worthy of the Bank's attention but is different from the Panel's function as defined in the Resolution establishing it.) The establishment of the Panel was praised as a move towards "democratization" of a public international institution. There was also broad consensus among the NGOs representatives that the Panel was not sufficiently known and that access to it was still difficult.

Several representatives specifically asked that Board approval of the Panel's recommendation in favor of an investigation should be automatic or that the power to decide that an investigation be carried out should be exercised directly by the Panel.

Several speakers argued that the roles of the requesters and Management in the Panel process were not balanced. According to them, requesters should be given further opportunities to express their views in the Panel process, particularly after adoption by Management of compliance plans. Prior consultation with affected people on such plans was also requested. Some speakers suggested that Management's compliance plan should be prepared only after the Panel's investigation was completed.

The Working Group report's distinction between a compliance plan and an action plan was said by some commentators to be impossible in practice because, in their view, the Bank and the borrower were jointly responsible for every project.

The report's reference to the "without-project" situation as a basis for comparison to assess material adverse effect was also criticized. In the view of commentators this approach would narrow the opportunities to bring requests to the Panel.

A participant criticized the report's recommendation to not allow the Panel to contact the media during in-country investigation because this would, in his view, prevent the community from knowing about the ongoing investigation. Another participant criticized the report's statement that the Inspection Panel was expected to seek the views of the Bank's Legal Department on the Bank's rights and obligations, even though this was a requirement of the Resolution. Some participants, apparently not aware of the Panel's position on the Jute Sector Adjustment Loan to Bangladesh, called for broadening the scope of the Panel's mandate beyond the Bank's project work to assess failures to comply with Bank policies in non-project activities and, specifically, to include adjustment lending in the Panel's mandate.

One participant, confusing anonymity with confidentiality, stressed the importance for affected people to be able to bring "anonymous" requests because of possible adverse repercussions from governments. Another participant argued in favor of a more "curative" approach in the Bank's operations in order to make the Panel ultimately irrelevant but make the Bank's operations more efficient and the people, as the ultimate beneficiary in Bank-financed projects, more satisfied.

Members of the Inspection Panel attended the meeting. The chairman of the Panel, James MacNeill, stated that the Panel was in favor of "streamlining the initial phase of the Inspection Panel process," an increased Panel involvement in the borrower's remedial action plans, and measures to facilitate greater access to the Panel. He reiterated the Panel's objection to the "without-project" basis for the measurement of material harm suffered by the requesters.

Following the informal discussion, the Bank received comments from "The NGO Working Group on the World Bank," representing a number of NGOs in different countries, as well as from two Washington-based NGOs. These comments focused once again on the need to define the technical eligibility criteria that may be discussed in the Board at the initial stage and objected to the proposed standard of harm based on a comparison with the pre-project situation. The comments also asked the Board to do away with the requirement of prior Board authorization of the investigation or to deem Board approval to be granted upon the Panel's recommendation to investigate.

4.   Revision of the Working Group's Report

In light of the comments received, the Working Group reissued its report with the following modifications:

1. The reference to a Bank "compliance plan" related to the correction of its failures, if any, was replaced by the simple language of the Resolution (para. 18) to the effect that Management "shall provide the Panel with evidence that it has complied or intends to comply with the Bank's relevant operating policies and procedures." The report properly left it to the Panel to assess in its report to the Board the adequacy of the evidence contained in Management's statement on its compliance or intention to comply.

2. Strict observance of the time limit of 21 days for Management to respond to the request, then for the Panel to report to the Board on whether an inspection was needed, remained a requirement in the report. However, an exception for a possible extension in either case was allowed "for reasons of *force majeure*" and with Board approval.

3. The technical eligibility criteria that might be discussed at the Board in the initial stage were clearly enumerated to include the following verifiable objective facts that are required by the Resolution and need no subjective evaluation:

(a) the affected party consists of two or more persons in the borrower's territories (Resolution, para. 12). (As discussed earlier, the language of the Resolution that was meant to apply is more elaborate. It has been clarified in 1996 by the Board—and was clarified again in the same manner in the Board's final conclusions of the second review);

(b) the request includes an assertion of serious violation by the Bank of its policies and procedures, "which is alleged to have or is likely to have a material adverse effect on the requester" (Resolution, para. 12 and 14 (a));

(c) the request asserts that the subject-matter has been brought to Management's attention and that, in the requester's view, Management has failed to respond adequately by demonstrating that it has followed or is taking steps to follow the Bank's policies and procedures (Resolution, para. 13);

(d) the matter is not related to procurement (Resolution, para. 14 (b));

(e) the related loan has not been closed or substantially closed (Resolution, para. 14 (c)); and

(f) the Panel has not previously made a recommendation on the matter, or, if it has previously made a recommendation, then there is an assertion in the request of new evidence or circumstances not known at the time of the request (Resolution, para. 14 (d)).

4. The language on the Panel's conduct of its work was changed. After repeating the original language acknowledging the importance of contacts between the Panel and the requesters and the gathering of information through consultation with affected people, the new language explained "the need to conduct such work in an independent and low-profile manner" and called on both the Panel and Management to limit their comments to the media to the process, not the substance, of inspection. Such comments would only be made "under those circumstances in which, in the judgment of the Panel or Management, it is absolutely necessary to respond to the media." The new language added that the Panel, or Management, as the case may be, "should make clear that the Panel's role is to investigate the Bank and not the borrower."

5. The comparison with the pre-project situation in assessing material adverse effect was maintained, but with the addition that in using that situation as a base case, the Panel will be

"taking into account what baseline information may be available." The many objections to the concept by outside commentators had not swayed the Working Group away from the conviction that harm cannot be assessed in the abstract, but in relation to the conditions prevailing before the project existed.

6. The report, as revised, made a clear distinction between (i) Management's report to the Board after the Panel had completed its inspection and reached its findings (which would include Management's recommendations to the Board on how any negative findings may be addressed, as required by para. 23 of the Resolution), and (ii) the "Action Plans" that may be agreed upon between the borrower and the Bank. However, the new language added: "Such Action Plans, if warranted, should normally be considered by the Board in conjunction with the Management's Report (submitted under para. 23 of the Resolution)."

7. The revised report added a new paragraph entitled "Outreach," which stated that the Working Group "underlines the need for Management to make significant efforts to make the Inspection Panel better known in borrowing countries," as specified in the 1996 "Clarifications." This reminder to Management came as a response to comments made by NGOs, especially local NGOs, who complained about the dearth of information on the Panel despite the assurances given in the 1996 "Clarifications."

8. The revised report also emphasized "the importance of prompt disclosure of information to claimants and the public, as stipulated in the Resolution (paras. 23 and 25) and in its 1996 'Clarifications'" and, for the first time, recommended that information provided to claimants be translated into their own language.

5.   Board Decision on the Second Review

The Board meeting held on April 20, 1999, did not witness any of the divisive debates typical of previous Board discussions of

Panel-related issues. Just before the meeting, the U.S. Chair circulated a statement that welcomed "the modest progress" reflected in the Working Group's proposals but repeated three concerns: that the Board remains "at the center of decision-making" on authorizing investigation; that the Panel is asked to assess harm on the basis of a "without project" standard (which the U.S. statement indicated that it "probably does not pass the test of reasonableness"); and doubts about the practicability and usefulness of "the proposal for unbundling" of the reasons for project failures. However, "despite the substantial misgivings," the statement indicated that the U.S. Chair was "prepared to accept the report, albeit with major reservations indicated above," and urged the Board "to implement the Working Group's recommendations effective today, April 20."

In the Board meeting, questions of clarification were raised by the Chairman of the Panel to which answers were given by the Chairman of the Working Group and by the Chairman of the Board (the Bank's President). A host of comments supportive of the report were also made by other Board members. The Board accepted the report of the Working Group, and the Chairman of the Board reiterated his and Bank Management's support of the Panel and the hope that the new clarifications included in the Working Group's report will enable the Board and the Panel to address future complaints smoothly and effectively. He also asked that a statement be prepared to reflect the Working Group's recommendations that would state clearly the Board's conclusions of the review after taking into account the further clarifications made during the discussion. The text of this statement, entitled "Conclusions of the Board's Second Review of the Inspection Panel," appears in Annex I–3 of this book.

The substantive changes introduced in the final document, in comparison to the revised report of the Working Group, are as follows:

(i) the term *force majeure,* justifying extension of the 21-day time limit given to Management, then to the Panel, in paragraphs 18 and 19, respectively, of the Resolution is now defined to mean "reasons beyond the control of Management or the Panel" (as the case may be) (item 8 of the "Conclusions");

(ii) the criterion related to the identity of the affected party was properly described in terms of the Resolution and the 1996 "Clarifications" to read "any two or more persons with common interests or concerns and who are in the borrower's territory";

(iii) the criterion related to the assertion in the request of a serious violation resulting in material adverse effect was reworded to clarify the intended meaning, that is, the issue that may be discussed by the Board at this stage is not whether the violation took place and the harm existed or was likely to occur, but only to make sure that the request "does assert in substance" such violation and harm. It is, in other words, a requirement related to the content of the request as presented to the Panel, not to the actual facts of the complaint. (Similar clarifications were made in the language of items 9(c) and (f) of the "Conclusions," without any attempt to change their meaning);

(iv) the "Conclusions" made it clear that the Board requires that the information to be disclosed to claimants be provided *by Management* to claimants in their language. The words "to the extent possible" were added in view of the possible practical difficulties that may arise (unavailability of translators to the language; multitude of languages, unwritten languages, etc.); and

(v) the words "absolutely necessary" were changed to "necessary" in the description of the circumstances in which the Panel or Management may respond to the media. The meaning was adequately served without the adverb.

Other changes were merely editorial, introduced only for the sake of clarity or brevity.

The "Conclusions" were then circulated to the Board and were approved without any objection.

5

Assessment of the Inspection Panel's Constituent Resolution and the Experience in Its Application

Introduction

By giving affected parties direct access to an independent unit within the World Bank's structure (the Inspection Panel), the Bank's Executive Directors opened a new chapter in the status of private groups (affected entities and communities of persons) *vis-à-vis* the Bank. Before discussing the potential effects of this important contribution of the Panel and its impact on issues of Bank accountability and liability, it may be useful to provide an evaluation of the Resolution establishing the Panel (and the two documents resulting from the Board review of its application) and the actual experience of the Panel in the first five years of its existence. Such an evaluation may prove helpful to any future assessment of the inspection function, whether undertaken by the Bank's Board or by outsiders, in light of the Panel's work in the years to come.

I. Assessment of the Inspection Function as Defined in the Resolution and Complementary Documents and as Performed in Practice

A. *Early Criticism*

Before the Panel started its activities, at least seven features of the inspection function were strongly criticized by Western NGOs and some other commentators. These relate to an alleged lack of adequate independence of the Panel members, limited access to the Panel, limited scope of its activities, a presumed advisory nature of its role, possible preemption of that role by Management's early remedial action, perceived lack of, or delay in, the disclosure of its processes and decisions, and the possible termination, or limitation, of the inspection function after a two-year period. Each of these criticisms deserves further clarification and rebuttal.

1.   Is the Independence of the Panel Adequately Secured?

Even before it had started its work, the Panel was characterized by one critic as a "subordinate organ" of the World Bank's President and Board[1] in view of the fact that its members are nominated by the former and appointed by the latter. Some earlier proposals, it should be recalled, suggested the creation of an "Independent Appeals Commission" located outside the Bank,[2] or a completely separate "watchdog agency" that "must be insulated from the conflicts of interest inherent in the Bank's multiple roles as development agency, lending institution, debt collector, and representative of developed country interests."[3]

Although the Panel established in the Bank is part of the Bank's organizational structure, its functional independence is

---

1. *See* Krishna Sumi, *The World Bank—Development Financing, Environment and Human Rights Issues* (1994, in Japanese) (hereinafter Sumi). References here are based on an English summary published in Tokyo by *The Weekly Economist,* February 8, 1994. *See also* David B. Hunter & Lori Udall, The World Bank's New Inspection Panel: Will It Increase the Bank's Accountability?, *Center for International Environmental law: CIEL Brief* No. 1, at 2–3 (April 1994).

2. *See supra* Chapter One, Section IV (C). Some commentators speak of the existing Inspection Panel as an "independent appeals panel," thereby creating the wrong impression that it might be a forum where World Bank decisions can be appealed, *see* Lori Udall, The World Bank and Public Accountability, in *Struggle for Accountability* 392 (J.A. Fox and L.D. Brown, eds., 1998).

3. Jonathan Cahn, Challenging the New Imperial Authority: The World Bank and the Democratization of Development, 6 *Harvard Human Rights Journal* 159, 190 (1993).

secured by a number of safeguards previously elaborated on in this book. Bank staff members cannot be appointed as Panel members before a lapse of two years after the termination of their service. Panel members serve only for one non-renewable term; they cannot be reappointed as staff members, and their remuneration is predetermined at fixed amounts not subject to individual changes.[4] Furthermore, the Panel will have a budget of its own (as part of the budget of the Corporate Secretary's Department in the Bank) and a separate secretariat (consisting at present of its own Executive Secretary, Assistant Executive Secretary, and support staff). Neither the location of the Panel within the Bank's organizational chart, nor the fact that its Executive Secretary worked at the beginning (for a few months only) on a part-time basis, affects the functional independence of the Panel. The fear that only former Bank staff would be appointed to the Panel has proved to be unjustified. (Only one of the members initially appointed worked for a brief period for the Bank more than three decades ago; his term will terminate at the end of July 1999.) Even the complaint that NGOs would play no role in the nomination of Panel members[5] proved exaggerated in practice. The President's consultation with the Executive Directors prior to making his nominations gave them the opportunity to express all relevant concerns known to them, including those of NGOs. In addition, Management did inform the most concerned NGOs of the process followed in advance of the nomination of the two replacements selected so far. Both of those new Panel members have had extensive experience with NGOs' work, and one of them (the current chairman of the Panel) actually headed a large environmental NGO in his country at the time of his appointment.

Strong evidence of the Panel's independence may also be found in the fact that there was often disagreement between the Panel and Management regarding the eligibility and evaluation of requests. Such disagreement was freely expressed in the Panel's

---

4. *See* Chapter Two, at 96–97.
5. *See* Sumi, *supra* note 1.

recommendations and Management's responses.[6] Similarly, the Panel took exception to Management's views expressed on the occasion of the two reviews by the Board of the Panel's experience.[7]

In the words of Alvaro Umaña Quesada, who served as a member of the Panel for four years and was its chairman in the last of those years "[t]he Panel has, despite tremendous pressure, functioned as an independent structure, as it was intended,"[8] and the Bank President "has been a strong supporter of the Panel."[9]

2.   Do Relevant Parties Have Limited Access to the Panel?

From the beginning, access to the Panel was found by certain commentators to be "excessively restricted" because of the condition that only groups in the borrowing country whose rights or interests are directly and adversely affected are eligible to lodge complaints, to the exclusion of claims by an affected individual as well as by groups outside the borrowing country concerned.[10] It should be recalled, however, as explained earlier, that an

---

6. For details, *see* the Panel's reports on the requests submitted to it and *supra,* Chapter Three.

7. *See* Chapter Four, *supra. Compare,* however, Lori Udall, *The World Bank Inspection Panel—A Three Year Review,* 67 (October 1997).

8. Alvaro Umaña Quesada (ed.), *The World Bank Inspection Panel: The First Four Years* (1994–1998), at 323. Mr. Umaña did not elaborate on the "pressure" he refers to or its source. This writer is not aware of such pressure having been exerted by Bank Management. The practice of submission of action plans listing borrower's corrective actions has been criticized by the Panel, and previously by this author, for the reasons mentioned. This practice, however, could hardly have qualified as "tremendous pressure" on the Panel. Management has often disagreed with the Panel's assessments, especially on eligibility issues, as the Panel has disagreed with Management on many issues. Such disagreement cannot be described as pressure from either party on the other. On a number of occasions, this writer invited the Panel to meet with the regional management concerned with a specific project to ensure a better understanding of the facts and issues involved. Again, there was no pressure from either party on the other in these meetings.

9. *Id.* at 324.

10. *See* Sumi, *supra* note 1.

Executive Director may also request investigation by the Panel. If individuals or groups who do not meet eligibility conditions have a serious complaint that warrants investigation by the Panel, they can bring it to the attention of any one of the Bank's 24 Executive Directors. The judgment of an Executive Director about whether to pursue the matter is likely to depend on its seriousness and on whether, after discussing the question with Management, it is clear that an independent investigation by the Panel would still be needed. As mentioned in Chapter Four, when the issue of whether single individuals or only communities of persons would have standing before the Panel was discussed in the context of the first Board review of the Panel's experience, Management was open to the possibility of complaints by affected individuals. The "Clarifications" resulting from that review emphasized, however, the original, Board-introduced requirement that requests can be submitted to the Panel by two or more individuals who share some interests or concerns. This was not seen as a limitation on the inspection function, but rather as a safeguard against frivolous claims that otherwise may limit the time the Panel may devote to handling serious complaints.

The criteria for standing and eligibility to make requests for inspection, explained in Chapter Two, expressly require that those who submit such requests be directly affected, except for the Executive Directors who have a special "custodial" role based on their institutional responsibility for the observance by the Bank of its own policies and procedures.[11] While not excluding the possibility of collaboration between locally affected claimants and external partner organizations in case of need,[12] the Panel

---

11. On the role of the Executive Directors, *see generally* the Memorandum of the Vice President and General Counsel, *The Role of the Executive Directors of the Bank Under the Bank's Articles of Agreement and in the Bank's Practice*, (BPC87–2), October 5, 1987. *See also* Richard Gerster, Accountability of Executive Directors in the Bretton Woods Institutions, 27 *Journal of World Trade Law* 87, 104–05 (1993).

12. Such collaboration may be envisaged in the "exceptional case where the party submitting the request contends that appropriate representation is not locally available and the Executive Directors so agreed at the time they

was not created as a forum for *actiones populares*, that is, legal suits presented in the public interest by a person or persons acting on behalf of the public at large.[13]

Finally, the exclusion of a request for inspection submitted by a single individual was based only on practical grounds, as explained earlier.[14] It thus need not be theorized as a denial of the "subjective rights" approach prevalent in some academic discussions, especially in the environmental field.[15] Although such a denial was consciously pursued in the 1992 *Rio Declaration on Environment and Development*,[16] which studiously avoided references to individual "rights,"[17] the drafting history of the Resolution on the Panel shows that individual requests were originally provided for and subsequently deleted only in response to a concern expressed during Executive Directors' discussions that the Panel could be distracted by too many such requests.[18]

---

consider the request for inspection" (*see Resolution,* para. 12 and Chapter Two, *supra,* at III(B)). For illustrations of cooperation among local and foreign NGOs on environmental issues, *see* David A. Wirth, Legitimacy, Accountability, and Partnership: A Model for Advocacy on Third World Environmental Issues, 100 *Yale Law Journal* 2645 (1991). *See also* I. Udall, *supra* note 7, at 75. In practice, foreign NGOs assisted in the drafting of a number of requests submitted to the Panel.

13. The much-debated issue of representation of public (community) interests in cases involving environmental harm therefore does not arise here. *See generally,* Michelle Leighton Schwartz, International Legal Protection for Victims of Environmental Abuse, 18 *Yale Journal of International Law* 355 (1993). *Compare,* however, the Panel's position in the Yacyretá case, Chapter Three, *supra,* at 118–119.

14. *See supra* Chapter Two, at 59–61.

15. For a critique, *see* Gunther Handl, Human Rights and Protection of the Environment: A Mildly 'Revisionist' View, in *Human Rights, Sustainable Development and the Environment,* 117 (A. Cancado Trinidade, ed., 1992).

16. Report of the United Nations Conference on Environment and Development (Rio de Janeiro, 3–14 June 1992), U.N. Doc. A/CONF. 151/Rev. 1, Vol. I, at 3–8 (1992).

17. *See* Jeffrey D. Kovar, A Short Guide to the Rio Declaration, 4 *Colorado Journal of International Environmental Law and Policy* 119 (1993); and Dinah Shelton, What Happened in Rio to Human Rights?, 3 *Yearbook of International Environmental Law* 75 (1992).

18. The Bank's approach may be compared to recent developments of collective action in environmental and consumers' law matters in European countries. *See, e.g.,* Catherine Kessedjian, L'action en justice des associations de

3.   Is the Panel's Mandate Unduly Limited in Scope?

The Panel's substantive jurisdiction is, for the reasons explained in Chapter Two,[19] limited no doubt to matters that are attributed to the Bank and for which the Bank can take corrective measures. Giving the Panel an unrestricted right to further investigate whether the actions of Bank borrowers are consistent with all international agreements on human rights and the environment without any limitation, as advocated by certain NGOs[20] and authors,[21] would give the Panel the role of a guardian and enforcer of international agreements concluded outside the Bank and a judge of whether they have been violated by the states parties to them. Not only is this a role different from the one for which the Panel was established; it would also entangle the Bank, and not just the Panel, in areas clearly outside its mandate (as far as *political* matters are concerned).[22] The Panel can certainly investigate specific environmental and human rights issues (for example, rights of those involuntarily resettled as a result of a Bank-financed project, rights of indigenous people in project areas, and so forth) to the extent that these are covered by the Bank's own policies and raised by affected parties.

International agreements, whether on the environment, human rights, or other matters, are binding on the states parties to them and the international organizations created or regulated by these agreements. It is the responsibility of such states,

---

consommateurs et d'autres organisations représentatives d'intérêts collectifs en Europe, 33 *Riviera di diritto internazionale privato e processuale* 281–300 (1997).

19. *See* Chapter Two, Section II.

20. *See* the proposal to establish an "Independent Appeals Commission" referred to in Chapter One, Section IV (C) and suggestions made by some NGOs in the course of the first review of the Panel's experience, Chapter Four, *supra*, at 156 *seq. See also* Udall, *supra* note 7, at 5–6.

21. *See* Sumi, *supra* note 1.

22. *See* Ibrahim F.I. Shihata, *The World Bank in a Changing World*, Volume I (1991), Chapter Two: The World Bank and Human Rights; *ibid., The World Bank in a Changing World*, Volume II (1995), Chapter Eighteen and Chapter Nineteen and *ibid., The World Bank in a Changing World*, Volume III (forthcoming 2000), Chapter Four on Democracy and Development and Chapter Five.

through their actions within and outside the Bank, to meet their international obligations under these agreements. The Bank is bound by its Articles of Agreements, the agreements to which the Bank is a party, its own rules and policies consistent with its Articles and agreements, and relevant rules of customary international law that are relevant to international organizations like the Bank.

In the environment field, the Bank went a step further. It has been Bank policy since 1984 that the Bank does not finance (i) "projects that contravene any international environmental agreement" to which the country on whose territory the project is located is a party, and (ii) "projects which would significantly modify natural areas designated by international conventions as World Heritage Sites or Biosphere Reserves."[23] As long as this principle remains part of Bank policy, the Panel's mandate will cover claims regarding its violation. However, the Panel, as repeatedly explained during the Board's discussion that led to the adoption of the Resolution, is not a supra-national organization endowed with the power to enforce international agreements among Bank member states—agreements to which the Bank is not a party and that do not bestow such function on the Bank. Other mechanisms exist or should exist for the enforcement of such international agreements. The Panel, as envisaged in the Resolution, is simply a mechanism to help ensure that the Bank's operational actions will be consistent with its own operational policies (and procedures), including the above-stated policy regarding certain international environmental agreements. The Panel also has a mandate to investigate whether the Bank has properly followed up on the borrowers' obligations *under Bank loan agreements*.

Demands were also made to broaden the Panel's mandate by empowering it to make recommendations regarding the projects

---

23. This language first appeared in OMS 2.36 on *Environmental Aspects of Bank Work*, para. 9 (e)(May 1984). *See also* OP 4.36 *Forestry*, para. 2 (September 1993). OP 4.01 on *Environment Assessment* also has a similar provision.

it investigates and, more generally, the Bank's operational policies.[24] It has been explained in the previous chapter why these
demands were not acceptable to the Board and how, in any event,
the Panel commented in some cases on the substance of the projects it investigated or "preliminarily assessed."[25]

4.   Should the Panel Have Decision-Making Powers?

The Panel has also been criticized for its inability to make its own
decisions on whether investigations are warranted and to offer
relief to complainants as a result of such investigations.[26]
However, the Bank's own governance rules require that decisions
be made by the decision-making organs of the Bank that are
defined in its Articles of Agreement. The Panel is not one such
organ. Its intervention in operational matters by the issuance of
binding decisions would conflict with the Bank's present governance structure and could cause serious problems to the management of its business. The Panel's role should not be
underestimated, however. The Panel is not, as several commentators erroneously have described it, an "advisory body."[27] Rather,
it is a fact-finding body. Its function is not to provide advice to
the Bank, except for its recommendations to the Board on the
preliminary issue of whether an inspection should be undertaken.
Its main role is to investigate complaints and come to a finding,
that is to a conclusion as to whether the Bank has observed its
policies and procedures. If its finding is that the Bank has not

---

24. These demands were made by NGOs on the two occasions of the
Board's review of the Panel's experience (as explained in Chapter Four) and
appear also in several writings. *See, e.g.,* Udall, note 7, *supra,* at 65, and Daniel
Bradlow, International Organizations and Private Complaints: The Case of the
World Bank Inspection Panel, 34 *Virginia Journal of International Law* 553,
610 (1994) (suggesting that the Panel process could "encourage the Bank to
consider a more open and participatory rule-making procedure" for the adoption of policies).

25. *See* Chapter Three, at 102 *seq., supra.*

26. *See* Hunter and Udall, *supra* note 1, at 3. Sumi suggests that the Panel's
"recommendations" be followed by staff unless a specific decision to the contrary is made by a two-third majority vote of the Board.

27. *See, e.g.,* Bradlow, *supra* note 24, at 575.

been in compliance with its policies and procedures, this will obviously be a powerful conclusion that neither the Bank's Management nor Board can ignore (in spite of the fact that the Panel does not have all the safeguards of a judicial process). As one commentator has noted, "the strength of the Panel's advisory powers [sic] comes from the combination of its independence and the fact that the Bank will make the complaints, all the Panel's recommendations and findings, and the decisions of the Executive Directors publicly available."[28]

It is only regrettable that this fact-finding role of the Panel with respect to the issue of compliance was downplayed in favor of establishing harm until the second Board review addressed that issue. Ascertaining the harm inflicted on affected parties is certainly required as a precondition for performing inspection. To focus on it, while downplaying the main function of verifying the Bank's compliance or failure with respect to its policies, has no doubt humanitarian motives; but it represents to this writer a clear departure from the text and objective of the Resolution establishing the Panel, as explained in other parts of this book.[29] Establishing the existence or potential existence of the material harm is a condition in the exercise by the Panel of its main function. Ignoring this to the point of making "harm" rather than "Bank compliance" the principal issue can open the door wide to claims against the Bank even when no violation of a legal obligation was ever attributed to the Bank or established by a court of law. It can also lead to absurd results, particularly in adjustment operations that the Panel has included in its mandate by registering a request related to one such operation. (As shown earlier, the Panel's recommendation not to carry out inspection in that case did not allow for a Board discussion of the issues of eligibility of adjustment operations.)[30] The almost inevitable harm resulting

---

28. Daniel D. Bradlow, *An Overview of the World Bank Inspection Panel,* a paper prepared for the Workshop on the World Bank Inspection Panel held at the American University, Washington, D.C., on March 28, 1994, at 7 (limited circulation).

29. *See* Chapter Two, at 71–72, Chapter Four, at 191–193, and this chapter at 219–222.

30. *See* Chapter Two, *supra,* at 37–41 and Chapter Three, at 124–127.

from such operations to losers in the reform process can hardly be blamed on the Bank, if it has properly followed its policies and procedures, including those related to the social effect of adjustment on vulnerable groups.

With all the care taken in the Resolution's language to ensure the professional and personal integrity and credibility of the Panel members, it is only to be expected that their findings will receive great attention by both the Bank's Management and Board. Such findings, while legally not binding on the Bank's decision-making organs, will undoubtedly have an overwhelming impact. As correctly noted, "[i]f these recommendations and findings of the Panel are not respected or generally adopted by the Board, the Panel runs the risk of being viewed as irrelevant by non-Bank actors."[31] More importantly, perhaps, the Bank would run the risk of not being an accountable institution.

Certainly, the publication of the Panel's findings and reports will provide "non-Bank actors" with "an opportunity to evaluate the work of the Panel and the Bank's response to its findings. . . ."[32] It is difficult, however, to see how the same commentator has reached the conclusion that "if all the Panel's recommendations are accepted, without debate, by the Board, the Panel runs the risk of being viewed as too subservient to the Bank."[33]

It should be recalled, here, however, that the Bank's ability to apply legal remedies against its borrowers (for example, suspension and cancellation of the loan) is governed by the loan agreements and the General Conditions applicable to them. Such remedies may be based on the borrower's violation of its contractual obligations under loan agreements, not by the Bank's failure to observe its operational policies. A finding by the Panel may lead indirectly to the adoption of such remedies, but only to the extent that an event of default on the part of the borrower has existed. It will then be for the Bank to decide whether to apply

---

31. Daniel D. Bradlow, The World Bank Votes to Establish an Inspection Panel, 6 *Third World Debt in the 1990s*, at 2, 3 (1993).

32. *See* Bradlow, *supra* note 28, at 7–8.

33. *See* Bradlow, *supra* note 28, at 3.

the remedies available to it. This may particularly happen in the context of a complaint that the Bank has previously failed in its follow-up on the borrower's obligations.[34]

5.   Does the Possibility of Remedial Action by Management Obviate the Need for Investigation?

As explained in previous chapters, the Bank's Management, after being informed of a complaint submitted to the Panel, may admit the error attributed to it and provide the Panel with the measures the Bank intends to take to correct it. This would constitute a plan for remedies to be adopted *by the Bank* with regard to *Bank actions or omissions.* Under such circumstances, the Panel may conclude that there would be no need for investigation, unless the proposed Bank compliance actions were deemed by the Panel to be inadequate in addressing the complaints.[35] As explained in Chapter Four,[36] the obviation of the need for inspection in such cases has been seen by the Panel as a positive development to the extent that it allowed for correcting *Bank failures* in a speedy manner. This process has, however, been criticized from the beginning on the basis that it gives the Bank an opportunity to handle problems before they become subject to investigation without the complainant being given the opportunity to respond.[37] This criticism ignores the fact that the plan concerning Bank actions is meant to address

---

34. *See Resolution,* para. 12. *Compare* Sumi, *supra* note 1, where he calls for empowering the Panel to recommend suspension of lending for the project in question "during the period up to completion of investigation and to cancel the loan in cases where a high degree of infringement of human rights or destruction of the environment is taking place." The latter suggestion gives the Panel the powers of a court of law over legal disputes arising under loan agreements contrary to the provision in the General Conditions Applicable to Bank loans (Article X, Section 10.04), which provide for international arbitration between the Bank and the borrower when such disputes cannot be settled through negotiations.

35. *See supra,* Chapter Two, Section II(B).

36. *See* Chapter Four, *supra,* at 174–176 and the first edition of this book, at 100.

37. *See* Bradlow, *supra* note 28, at 8.

the Bank's own failures and would be subject at any rate to the Panel's review. If the Panel finds such actions to be inadequate, it can recommend an investigation. Failures in the implementation of such plans by violation of the measures included under them could also be subject to a new request for inspection by the same complainant, as this would be a different subject-matter than the original complaint. If, on the other hand, the Panel finds that Management's actions satisfactorily addressed the complaint as far as the Bank was concerned, the objective of the Panel's function would have been served.

The above actions introduced by Management on its own should not be confused with the remedial action plan that may be agreed upon between the borrower and Bank Management that sets forth measures to be taken *by the borrower* and that may include changes in the project's scope or timetables agreeable to the Bank. As elaborated in the previous chapter, such latter plans, while they may better await the results of the Panel's investigation, fall outside the Panel's mandate as defined in the Resolution. The recent requirement, agreed upon in the second review of the Panel experience, that the Panel's view on whether affected parties were adequately consulted in the preparation of these latter plans, ensures, however, that the Board will be informed of the Panel's position on this matter in each case.

6.   Timing of Making the Panel's Reports Publicly Available

The Resolution establishing the Panel has also been criticized for not making the Panel's recommendation (on whether an investigation is warranted) and findings (on the result of the investigation) available to the complainant at the same time they are presented to the Board and in the same language of the community to which the complainant belongs.[38] Disclosure of Board decisions on inspection matters is required in the Resolution to be made within two weeks after the Board's

---

38. *See* Sumi, *supra* note 1.

decision on the matter in each case,[39] but this period has been shortened to three days since the October 1996 "Clarifications," at least for Management's initial response to the Panel.[40] (The language issue is not addressed by the Resolution, but it has been resolved in the "Conclusions" of the second review.) Critics contended that the Resolution "excludes the public from participating until after the Executive Directors consider the [Panel's] reports."[41] Making the reports public at an earlier date would not in itself give the public a formal role in the process, however; it will only open the door for pressure on Board members by the media and interested NGOs, as witnessed every time such reports were leaked before Board meetings.

The Panel, it should be noted, is not a political or judicial organ. It can, however, hear any individual or group who may contribute to the inspection of a specific case, before it reaches its conclusions. The Resolution does not require that such hearing necessarily be conducted in a closed session; only it was not intended that hearings held in furtherance of the Panel's assessment in the case of a concrete request would be used to open the door for the lobbying of Panel members or for other attempts by third parties to influence their work. Confidentiality of the Board's proceedings is a different matter. It is required by the Board's Rules of Procedure to preserve the integrity of its deliberative process and to protect the Executive Directors against undue pressure from other parties who may have special interests in a particular outcome.[42] An open institution is not required to subject its Board to outside pressure by parties with special interests in the result of its deliberations.

---

39. See *Resolutions,* paras. 19, 23, 25.

40. See 1996 *Clarifications,* reprinted in Annex I–2 in this book, under the section entitled *Outreach* and Chapter Four, *supra,* at 170.

41. See Hunter and Udall, *supra* note 1, at 3.

42. See Rules of Procedure of the Executive Directors of IBRD and IDA, Section 7. See *also* The World Bank Policy on Disclosure of Information, 13 (World Bank, 1994), reprinted in Annex II–13 of this book.

7.   Was the Review of the Inspection Function as Described in the Resolution Too Restrictive?

The provision in the Resolution requiring the Executive Directors to review the Panel's experience in two years was also criticized as possibly allowing, as a result of the review, for the termination of the Panel's function or for further restricting this function. Experience shows that these concerns have not been justified. This criticism led, however, to the suggestion by some writers that such a review be carried out not only by the Bank's Board but also by "representatives from the borrowing countries and NGOs."[43]

The Board's review of new Bank initiatives after a period of implementation is a regular feature of the Board's work. It is meant to enable the Board, which represents all member countries, to introduce necessary or desirable improvements in the light of experience and should not be viewed with suspicion. Other writers have indeed seen in the review a cause for the Panel "to be prudent and deliberate in its actions" and for NGOs "to carefully select the complaints they bring to the Panel" so that they may "demonstrate both the need for an independent inspection panel and the contribution that it can make to improving the operations of the Bank."[44] There is nothing, of course, to prevent NGOs or others from undertaking their own evaluation of the Panel's experience and making it available to the Bank. This happened, in fact, after three years of the Panel's experience.[45]

In both Board reviews of the Inspection Panel's experience, all the views expressed by NGOs and concerned individuals were made available by Management to Board members. In the second review, the Board responded favorably to NGOs' request for a discussion with them before the Board met formally to consider the matter. As seen in the previous chapter, the Board formal meeting was twice postponed to allow for such consultation. This

---

43. *See* Sumi, *supra* note 1.
44. *See* Bradlow, *supra* note 28, at 9.
45. *See* Udall, *supra* note 7.

unprecedented step is not known in the work of any international financial institution.

B.   Analysis of the Panel's Experience

It is interesting to note from the cases submitted to the Panel and summarized in Chapter Three above, that investigation was authorized by the Board explicitly in two cases, the *Arun III Project* in Nepal, which had not been financed by the Bank at the time of inspection (and where Bank financing was eventually withdrawn), and the *NTPC Power Generation* project in India, where inspection took place only at the Bank's headquarters. The Board virtually authorized inspection in a third case, the *Yacyretá* dam project in Argentina/Paraguay, but it stood short of stating so explicitly. Thus, of the six requests found by the Panel to justify investigation, Board authorization was clearly denied in two cases, *PLANAFLORO* in Rondonia, Brazil, and *Itaparica*, also in Brazil, and found not to be necessary in a third case (*Ecodevelopment*, India). In all these three cases, the Panel was given a supervisory role in the review of progress under plans to be carried out by the borrower. The main reason for the denial of Bank authorization in the two Brazilian cases, according to Board discussions, was that remedial action plans were found by the Board to be satisfactory. In the third case, the Board felt that the borrower and Management were working towards resolving the issues raised by the Panel in a project that, by its nature, required evolution of measures and plans while the project was being implemented.

In the view of this writer, there are two reasons for the evolution of a practice that did not fully meet initial expectations suggested by the wording of the Resolution.

The straightforward approach provided for in the Resolution requires the Panel to limit its role at the initial stage to ascertaining whether eligibility criteria are met. As explained earlier, this has to be done only on a *prima facie* basis at this stage. However, as elaborated in Chapter Two, the Panel has adopted from the beginning (August 19, 1994) a procedure of "preliminary review," which the Panel introduced on its own initiative in its Operating Procedures. As stated subsequently in a "working paper" prepared by the Panel in 1995, on the occasion of the first review of its experience, the Panel later felt that the Board, by repeatedly asking it to take further time to produce additional reports during the first stage, had practically modified the Resolution's requirements.[46] The Panel described that "modification" as "a pragmatic approach, developed by the Board in response to very real problems."[47] It also noted on that occasion that "the extent of information expected by the Board at the preliminary stage is sometimes equivalent to the content of an investigation."[48] A Board majority seemed to have found in that approach (later to be called "preliminary assessment") a convenient method that could satisfactorily address the situation, without requiring the Board to authorize the full "investigation" envisaged in the Resolution whenever warranted. However, the purpose of the Panel's investigation according to the Resolution (that is, to ascertain Bank compliance with its own policies and procedures in the cases where serious violations result in adverse material effect to the party requesting inspection) seems to have suffered. The Panel, in its own words, "avoided dwelling on alleged violations of [Bank] policies and procedures in the preliminary stage" and emphasized that "the focus of the preliminary review should be on identifying existing or potential damage."[49]

Management was also quick in each case to produce a remedial action plan where the borrower was to take the required

---

46. *See Review of the Inspection Function—Practical Suggestions Based on Experience to Date,* Working Paper for the World Bank Executive Directors prepared by the Inspection Panel in November 1995 and Chapter Four, *infra.*

47. *Id.*

48. *Id.*

49. Memorandum to the Committee on Development Effectiveness, *Review of the Resolution Establishing the World Bank's Inspection Panel* (CODE96–27), May 14, 1996). In this document, the Panel expressed its view that an investigation of alleged violation of Board policies can take place only after the existence of possible harm has been established. *Compare* the second sentence in para. 13 of the *Resolution.*

actions. The preparation by Management of plans that require the borrower, rather than the Bank, to take measures to correct past failures focused attention on the borrower's failures and the measures to be taken by the borrower to correct them. The subject-matter of inspection, according to the Resolution, was downplayed under the assumption by Management that no failure was attributable to the Bank and the Panel's conviction that such a "policing function" was of questionable value anyway.

Not surprisingly, Executive Directors representing the borrowing countries involved have typically seen the process as an embarrassment to their government, exposing its mistakes and interfering in the relationship between the affected people and their government. Opposition groups within these countries also used the inspection process in some instances to pressure the government. An attitude against investigation whenever it could be avoided thus evolved among borrowing countries and created a divisive climate every time the Board had to discuss a Panel recommendation to investigate a complaint. Even when investigation was authorized, the term investigation/inspection had to be avoided in one case (*Yacyretá*), and the process had to be limited to inspection at the Bank's headquarters in another *(NTPC)*. As a result, outside commentators and even the Panel speak only of one Board authorization having been issued so far.[50]

The Panel's attitude towards Bank compliance evolved further during the second review of the Panel's experience, as shown in Chapter Four. After suggesting during the first review that that issue be relegated to the investigation stage, the Panel, probably also reflecting its own preferences, concluded in its paper to the Board at the beginning of the second review that "past Board decisions reveal that the Panel's role in checking compliance with operational policies has been downplayed, while its role in addressing actual or potential harm to local populations and assessing remedial actions [by the borrower] has been

---

50. *See* Chapter Three, at 101–102.

emphasized."[51] In other words, what was to be relegated to the second stage (at the time of the first review) became, at the time of the second review, a matter that the Panel felt was downgraded altogether by the Board. As shown in the previous chapter, the outcome of the second review has, however, preserved the original function of the Panel, as described in the Resolution.

The "preliminary assessment" procedure, first adopted by the Panel (under the name of "preliminary review") and effectively endorsed by the Board in 1996, was probably based on a certain understanding of paragraph 13 of the Resolution that may differ from its literal and intended meanings. This paragraph reads as follows:

> "The Panel shall satisfy itself *before a request for inspection is heard* that the subject-matter of the request has been dealt with by the Management of the Bank and Management has failed to demonstrate that it has followed, or is taking adequate steps to follow the Bank's policies and procedures. The Panel shall also satisfy itself that the alleged violation of the Bank's policies and procedures is of a serious character." (Emphasis added.)

As the language of the first sentence speaks of a condition that has to be fulfilled before a request for inspection is "heard," it clearly makes the prior submission of the subject-matter of the request to Management and the lack or inadequacy of Management's reply to the complainant conditions for the admissibility of the request by the Panel, as explained in detail in Chapter Two.[52] It also envisages that Management's adoption at this earliest stage of what the Panel would see as adequate steps to follow the Bank's policies and procedures could cause the Panel not to recommend investigation. However, as repeatedly

---

51. *Review of the Inspection Panel Experience—Inspection Panel Paper* (INSP/SecM97–11), November 6, 1997. *See also* Chapter Four, *supra,* at 174–176.

52. *See* Chapter Two, *supra,* at 49–51 and 72–73.

noted in this book, in every case where a remedial action plan was prepared by Management, it related to corrective measures to be taken *by the borrower*. It was also done *after* the request for inspection was submitted to the Panel and (in all but one case—*Arun III*) before the Board was to discuss the Panel's recommendation to investigate. The submission of such a plan could not, therefore, bar the request from being "heard" or eventually investigated by the Panel. Yet, it created a dilemma for many Board members who saw in the plan a satisfactory solution that addressed the underlying complaints and spared all parties the travails of an investigation. The result, however, was seen by the Panel to preempt the process envisaged by the Resolution[53] and was criticized by many outsiders as an attempt to shortcut that process, effectively not letting the Panel proceed with investigation when the eligibility conditions were met. That this was accurately the case only with respect to two out of the total of six requests recommended for inspection seems to have been ignored. (As we have seen, the qualifications attached by the Board to its authorization of inspection in two of the three cases where it occurred led some unduly not to consider them actual cases of inspection, thus giving the impression that only one case was investigated out of the recommended six.)

Under a literal reading of the Resolution, remedial steps may be adopted by Management before the matter reaches the Panel. They may also be adopted after the Panel undertakes its investigation and reaches its findings. In the latter case, Management is required to submit to the Board its recommendations in response to such findings.[54] The Resolution does not require the adoption by Management of an action plan in the intermediate stage between the registration of a request for inspection and the submission of the Panel's findings. It expects Management, however, to indicate in its response to the request referred to it by the Panel the steps it has taken or intends to take to correct whatever failures it would admit in the Bank's own

---

53. *See* note 42, *supra.*
54. *See* the *Resolution,* para. 22.

behavior. While thus not excluding the possibility of an early plan to correct *Bank* failures, if any, the Resolution envisages that Management would provide the Panel with a response within 21 days to enable the Panel to decide whether the request was eligible for investigation, and that the Panel would make a recommendation to the Board only on this question within a similar period. If Management submits to the Panel a list of corrective measures related to Bank actions or omissions, the Panel would naturally evaluate the adequacy of such measures. It may, however, find that such evaluation would have to await a full investigation of the complaints.

As already mentioned, an action plan on remedial measures to be taken *by the borrower* alone is likely to divert attention from the main issue of whether the *Bank* has followed its policies and procedures. Yet, it could, as a practical matter, make a full investigation superfluous from the viewpoint of many Board members. This has in fact contributed to the Board's practice in a number of cases of declining to authorize the investigation recommended by the Panel and to request instead progress reports on the implementation of the plan. The occurrence of the possibility of an action plan at that stage and its possible preemption of the Panel's role were, in fact, among the criticisms leveled against the Resolution from the beginning.[55] However, this criticism was not justified for a simple reason. The action plan conceived at the time of the Resolution was to include only measures to be taken by the Bank to remedy failures admitted by it. Also, the Panel would be in a position to comment on the adequacy of such a plan before the Board discussed it. As explained earlier, the obviation of the need for inspection in such cases was seen early on as a positive development to the extent that it would allow for correcting *Bank failures* in a speedy manner.[56]

It may thus be surmised that the preparation of borrower-related remedial action plans as developed in practice may have

---

55. *See* the first edition of this book, at 100. *See also* Chapter Four, *supra*, at 175–176 and this Chapter at 225–226.

56. Chapter Two, at 49–51, and the first edition of this book, at 100.

practically served the purpose of the affected parties[57] but not always that of the inspection function. It has also caused much frustration and misunderstanding, especially for those watching the process from the outside. This matter was discussed at length in the second review of the Panel's experience. Its candid discussion by the Executive Directors in 1998 and 1999 has developed a solution which, as explained in the previous chapter, may well serve the purposes of affected parties *and* the inspection function.

1.   *Management Practices Criticized by the Panel*

The Panel has in particular criticized two Management practices: (i) questioning the eligibility of the complainants or their request, and (ii) preparing early action plans for borrowers to follow. Both questions have been dealt with in the 1998/1999 review.

As to the first question, this writer has always maintained that Management in its response may alert the Panel to issues of eligibility it deems relevant, but the Panel must assess these issues independently of Management views. It would be counterproductive to argue otherwise. Management has a stake in the functioning of the Panel according to the Board Resolution establishing it and should not be deprived of addressing all relevant issues in its response. The Panel, on its part, would determine what to recommend to the Board according to its own convictions. Because the purpose of the first stage of the Panel's process is to establish eligibility of the complaints, any comments by Management could also prove to be useful to the Panel in making its own assessment. There is no interference in the Panel's independence as long as it maintains the final say as to what to recommend to the Board. This conclusion has been implicitly reflected in the outcome of the second review.

As to the second question, the Panel's criticism was perfectly justified, all the more so when the borrowers' remedial plans were submitted directly to the Board without prior knowledge of the

---

57. This has been questioned, however, in view of the long time it takes to implement these plans. *See* Umaña, *supra* note 8, at 326–27.

Panel. It was understandable, however, from the viewpoint of Bank staff, to act swiftly to cause the borrower to address the harm claimed by the complainants, especially when they saw that such harm had occurred but did not, in their view, result from their actions or omissions. This is, from the staff's viewpoint, part of their duty to supervise the project and assist the borrower in correcting its failures, regardless of how such failure became known to Management. As a result of the second review, Management must now distinguish between any corrective measures covering Bank compliance and the remedial Action Plan that includes measures agreed with the borrower and to be taken by the borrower. The first may be submitted by Management to the Panel as part of its response to the request, so that the Panel may give its views to the Board on its adequacy. It may also be included in Management's recommendations after the Panel completes its inspection. As to the other type of plan, the Panel should be informed of the nature and outcome of consultation with affected parties in the preparation of such a plan and may report to the Board its views on the adequacy of these consultations (but not on the plan as a whole). This latter distinction may prove difficult to make in some cases in practice.

For the reasons already explained, the inspection function became increasingly unpopular with borrowing government officials, who saw it evolving from a mechanism to ensure Bank compliance with its operational policies to an instrument that exposes their failures to the public and pressures the Bank to insist through remedial action plans on strict compliance with previously agreed covenants and to introduce new obligations on borrowers. It is not, therefore, as some have argued, resistance by governments to the term "investigation" and its connotations that have caused the problem; the issue is, of course, more substantive in nature. The investigation, which was meant to cover Bank actions and omissions, has ended up, in the view of government officials, covering instead government actions and omissions. The directives issued by the Board as a result of the second review should alleviate or reduce borrowers' concerns in this respect.

2.   Systemic Problems

In addressing the merits of certain complaints (especially the *PLANAFLORO* project in Rôndonia, Brazil, and the *Yacyretá* project in Argentina/Paraguay), the Panel has identified some "systemic problems"[58] that have also been mentioned in some OED reports.[59] They resulted from what the Panel saw as a greater attention paid by staff to the physical infrastructural or mechanical components of projects, compared to their social and environmental components. Although Bank loans typically financed the former components, the Panel found that they left the latter to be financed by the borrower. Staff also tended, according to the Panel, not to give the same attention to social and environmental operational policies as they did to other operational policies. Both phenomena have changed, however, in more recent years, thanks in part to the Panel's findings. The Bank increasingly finances social and environmental components of projects, either in the same loan or through a separate loan. The recent categorization of operational policies, referred to in Chapter Two,[60] is meant *inter alia* to highlight for the staff the importance of observing the Bank's social and environmental policies.

---

58. *See* Umaña, *supra* note 8, at 326.

59. *See* OED, *Recent Experience with Involuntary Resettlement: Overview*, Report No. 17538, June 2, 1998, at 65–71; *ibid., Poverty Assessment: A Progress Review*, Report No. 15881, August 7, 1996, at 32–38. In the first report, the OED noticed, however, that "[s]ince the early 1990s, there has been a distinct trend toward improved planning, including preparation of Resettlement Action Plans." In the second report, OED highlighted the relative imbalance in Bank concern over economic as opposed to social and environmental *policies*. Furthermore, in its report *The Social Impact of Adjustment Operations: An Overview*, Report No. 14776, June 30, 1995, at 70–71, OED emphasized that macroeconomic stabilization and supply-side policies are not by themselves enough to achieve faster growth and poverty reduction, implying the need for developing an information base to strengthen poverty and social development analysis.

60. *See* Chapter Two, *supra*, at 45–46.

3.   Issues for Further Consideration

Some of the Panel's practices may deserve to be carefully discussed in the Bank's Board with a view to either confirming them or alerting the Panel to possible conflict with the Resolution. These practices were not addressed in the Board either because the Board focussed on more controversial points in the case at hand or because the Panel did not recommend investigation and the Board approved the recommendation on a no-objection basis (that is, without a Board discussion).

One of these practices (that is, accepting the standing of a requester NGO on the basis of alleged harm to the environment, not specifically to the NGO involved [as stated in *Yacyretá*]), amounts to accepting claims based on public interest. This may not be consistent with the Resolution's requirement of a direct material harm borne or to be borne by the complainant itself. A more direct link between the potential harm to the environment and the specific NGO involved is required under the Resolution.[61]

The Panel has also considered an adjustment operation as readily falling within its mandate, (the *Jute Sector Adjustment* loan to Bangladesh). As discussed earlier, the Resolution assumes inspection of project operations. While the term "project" has a broad meaning in the Bank's practice, and it was agreed that this broad meaning is conveyed by the term used in the Resolution, adjustment operations are not considered part of project lending in this practice.

---

61. The latter position was adopted by the European Court of Justice under Article 173, para. 4 of the EEC Treaty, which, like the Inspection Panel Resolution, requires direct harm suffered or to be suffered by the claimant in order for him to have *locus standi* before the court. *See Greenpeace and Others v. Commission* (C–321/95 P, 1998 WL 171598; CEA 1998). *Compare* the position taken by the U.S. Supreme Court in 1972, in the absence of legislative text to the contrary, to the effect that "[a]esthetic and environmental well-being, like economic well-being, are important ingredients of the quality of life in our society, and the fact that particular environmental interests are shared by the many rather than the few does not make them less deserving of legal protection through the 'judicial process.'" *Sierra Club v. Morton* 405 U.S. 7Q7 (1972).

The general practice of not discussing in the Board a Panel recommendation not to investigate a certain complaint may also need to be reviewed. There could be cases where this recommendation is based on the fact that the Bank did not commit any violation of its policies, even though harm has been done and could be attributed to the Bank's own policies. In such cases, there is a need to discuss the Bank policies involved, with a view to ensuring that they would not cause such harm in the future. Without a Board discussion of the issue, it could easily escape attention and deprive the inspection function of one of its important advantages.

In analyzing the Panel's experience, one should not lose sight of its positive effects. A former chairman of the Panel has recently noted that: "[t]he most salient lesson from the cases considered earlier [by the Panel] is that concerned local citizens now have a new way to relate to the World Bank and to monitor the transparency and accountability of its operations."[62] This is certainly one important lesson without precedent in the work of international organizations. Not less important, however, are the greater attention that Bank staff pay now to the Bank's policies and procedures and the greater concern the Bank and its borrowers have with the strict compliance of borrowers with their legal obligations under loan documents. A broader lesson of great importance is perhaps the need to pay greater attention to both the institutional capacity of borrowers to meet Bank conditionality and the capacity of the Bank to devise its conditions and supervise their implementation in a realistic manner, taking into account the practical limitations of each case.

C.   Costs and Benefits to the Bank and Its Members

1.   Perceived Risks to the Bank and Its Members

Many of the risks perceived during the discussion in the Bank's Board of the draft Resolution establishing the Panel were

---

62. *Id*. Umaña, *supra* note 8, at 325.

considered by this writer as either not real or outweighed by the benefits of this initiative to the Bank and its borrowing members.[63] It may be useful to reiterate these concerns and see the extent to which they have been justified in practice.

i.   Possible Deterrent Effect on Bank Staff

The first perceived risk was that the establishment of the Panel might have a deterrent effect on the Bank's staff, causing them to be over-concerned with following the rules and procedures and less innovative in their work. In particular, it was noted that projects that involve resettlement of population or have environmental effects may, as a result, be unreasonably delayed or dropped altogether. Job security, it was feared, would prevail under these new circumstances over job productivity. The same fear caused some Executive Directors during the discussion to call on the Bank's Management to adopt clear rules that would not subject Bank staff to disciplinary actions except in cases of intentional violation of the Bank's policies and procedures.

Innovation does not have to take place at the expense of applicable rules, however. While the Bank's staff are expected to be innovative and are encouraged to question rules when they feel they no longer serve their purpose,[64] they are neither encouraged nor expected to violate Bank policies or procedures as long as these are in force. Violation of such policies or procedures could entail disciplinary action, whether the Panel exists or not.[65] If the presence of the Panel makes the staff more careful in their

---

63. *See* the first edition of this book, at 103.

64. "Resourcefulness and creativity" are indeed among the competencies against which the performance of Bank staff is measured. In particular, managerial staff are evaluated *inter alia* according to whether the manager "challenges conventional wisdom and actively pursues new approaches" and "takes prudent risks in situations where delay could have high costs for the client or the Bank." *See* The World Bank, *Competencies for Managerial Jobs,* item 16 (1994). This latter document has been superseded by others, but the emphasis on innovation has since, if anything, greatly increased.

65. *See* Staff Rules, Rule 8.01, Section 3.

work or causes them to question the need for some existing rules or policies that need to be reconsidered, that would be a welcome contribution to the Bank's work.

ii.   Possible Internationalization of Domestic Disputes in Violation of the Borrowing Country's Jurisdiction

Another perceived risk is that a complaint by an affected party (to the effect that the Bank is not following up on a violation by a borrowing country of its obligations under a loan agreement) could transform a domestic dispute between the affected party and its government into an international dispute between this government and the Bank. Such internationalization, the argument went, would limit the country's jurisdiction over persons and events in its territory.

Some of the practices referred to earlier in this book may have proven that risk to be real. To the extent that such internationalization occurs, however, it will be the result of international obligations of the borrowing country under the agreements with the Bank. Neither the complaint nor the Panel's findings create in this situation new obligations for the borrowing country. They may merely alert the Bank to the borrower's obligations under its loan agreement. Their focus, however, should be on the Bank's obligations, including its duty to see to it that the borrower's obligations are being carried out. Because these obligations are meant to serve the agreed objective of the project for which the loan is made, their fulfillment would presumably be in the borrower's interest. Any limitation on the country's domestic jurisdiction would only be due to what the country initially undertook to do under the loan agreement. The Panel will in any event be concerned with the Bank's actions and omissions. It has no authority to address the borrower or call on it to behave in any particular manner towards individuals or entities subject to its jurisdiction. Any doubt that may have existed on this point may not now be justified in light of the conclusions of the second review of the Panel's experience.

*iii.   Possible Expansion or Abuse of the Panel's Functions
        beyond the Limits Defined in the Resolution*

In the first edition of this book, it was stated that:

> "[T]here is no basis to fear that the members of
> the Panel will disregard the limits set on their
> function by the Resolution establishing the Panel,
> whether these relate to the standing of com-
> plainants, the subject-matter of inspection or the
> projects in respect of which investigation may be
> authorized. On the contrary, Panel members can
> only be expected to exert their function judi-
> ciously with great attention to all the procedural
> and substantive requirements provided for in the
> Resolution. As explained earlier, these were
> designed to ensure that the inspection function
> will not exceed the purpose for which it has been
> established."[66]

What was not foreseen, however, was that the Board would
repeatedly call on the Panel to produce additional reports to firmly establish the harm suffered by affected people at the initial
stage and that Management would step in with plans for actions
to be taken by borrowers before a decision was made on whether
investigation was warranted. The result was a growing conviction
on the part of Panel members to the effect that the main emphasis should be placed on assessing the damage and the ways to
address it while giving less attention to the main issue (under the
Resolution) of assessing the degree of Bank's compliance with its
operational policies. It is hoped that the recent "Conclusions" of
the second review of the Panel's experience will assist the parties
concerned to act in a manner fully consistent with the Resolution.
    Pressure is likely to continue from sources outside the Bank,
mainly from NGOs in developed countries, to broaden the

---

66. *See* the first edition of this book, at 105.

eligibility for requesters of inspection, the scope of such inspection, and the power of the inspectors with respect to remedial actions.

From the beginning, some commentators envisaged that the Panel would make recommendations on the compensation to be paid to affected parties or on changes in the project design,[67] even though the Resolution lends no support to such a conclusion. Some of those who correctly understood the role of the Panel as envisaged are asking for changes to enlarge that role. A few members of the U.S. Congress indicated in congressional discussions and in correspondence with the Bank that they expect such enlargement to take place.

It is therefore possible that the concerns expressed so far by the above-mentioned sources may be translated over time into requests from certain member countries to change the scope or the nature of the inspection function. It is the responsibility of the Bank's Board and Management to ensure that changes will be introduced if they are deemed, after careful analysis, to be necessary or desirable, and in an objective manner consistent with the Bank's governance under its Articles of Agreement.

iv. Possible Legal Action Against the Bank or the Borrower Based on the Panel's Findings

Fears were expressed at the time the Panel was conceived that findings confirming the Bank's non-observance of its own policies and procedures could expose the Bank to the risk of legal suits before national courts initiated by or on behalf of affected parties. As mentioned earlier, suits have, in fact, been brought against the Bank in one case (*Yacyretá*), where the government, the Bank, and IDB were sued for alleged damages, without reliance, however, on the Panel's report.

Although in most cases liability, if it existed at all, would fall on the borrower whose actions or omissions on the ground had caused the damage, there is a risk that the Bank may be sued for

---

67. *See, e.g.*, Bradlow, *supra* note 28, at 11.

alleged damage resulting directly from its own failure. Such a risk may not materialize except in rare cases, but it cannot be ruled out, especially in litigious environments where resort to courts by activist groups is a normal practice.

The Bank maintains that, as a public international organization, pursuing international public purposes (for example, facilitating reconstruction in the territories of its members and development in less developed member countries, promoting international investment and trade, and thus raising living standards and reducing poverty on a worldwide scale), the Bank enjoys immunity from legal action before national courts except where this immunity is explicitly waived. This matter is dealt with in detail in Section II of this chapter. It is important to emphasize two points, however: (i) violation by the Bank of its policy, even if established by the Panel, is not necessarily a violation of applicable law that entails liability for ensuing damages; and (ii) since the Panel is not a court of law, its findings on Bank violations cannot be taken *ipso facto* as a conclusive evidence against the Bank in judicial proceedings. If the Panel's findings were to be taken as a basis of Bank legal liability, drastic amendments to the Resolution would be needed to give both the complainant and the Bank typical judicial safeguards.

Whether the Panel's assessment may indirectly contribute to the determination that borrower actions constitute a fault under domestic law is a separate question. While the borrower's actions clearly do not fall within the Panel's mandate under the Resolution, the Panel's findings with respect to Bank actions and the factual basis of such findings might be cited in a claim against the borrower, with or without joining the Bank as co-defendant, before domestic courts. It should also be noted here that the Panel is not a judicial body that follows judicial rules of evidence in reaching its conclusion and, at any rate, has no mandate in assessing the borrower's behavior *per se*. This is all the more reason that the Panel should limit its conclusions to the Bank's actions and omissions and should not base definite findings on the merits of the complaints before it completes its investigation. As to the Panel's recommendation to investigate, the Panel can only reach such a recommendation on a *prima facie* evidence subject to further investigation. Given the preliminary nature of the Panel's conclusions at this stage, its recommendation to the Board to carry out inspection should be formulated in a manner to avoid any implication of actual violation by the borrower of its legal obligations. Acting otherwise would not only be outside the Panel's mandate; it may expose the Bank to legal disputes with its borrowers who would see themselves subjected to trial *in absentia*, without due process. Fairness to both the Bank and the requesters also requires the Panel to take particular care not to reach definitive conclusions at this early stage. This point is emphasized in the conclusions of the second review.

2.   Possible Benefits to the Bank and Its Members

The Inspection Panel's activities, perhaps its mere presence, was meant to enhance the Bank's efficiency, to the benefit of its borrowers. The Panel's accessibility to a broad range of affected parties was also meant to broaden the scope of the Bank's accountability. These two factors can only increase the Bank's credibility in both its borrowing and non-borrowing member countries and provide the basis for their continued support, which is vital for its future. Other benefits may also ensue.

i.   Effect on the Bank's Efficiency

As explained in Chapter One, the Bank, prior to the establishment of the Panel, developed several review and evaluation mechanisms that were meant to provide it with the feedback necessary to enhance its knowledge and technical capabilities. The Panel's function is different from these mechanisms. It differs from staff supervision of project execution in that it provides an opportunity for in-depth inspection, after an actual complaint has been received, by three independent experts. Unlike the Bank's operational staff, Panel members have not been involved in the project's design, appraisal, or supervision and thus have no interest in the staff's prior action. It is also different from the post-implementation review by the Operations Evaluation Department, in that it allows for independent inspection from the beginning of the project cycle and, therefore, for possible remedial action before project completion. The efficiency effects of the Panel's work are therefore relevant both to the project at hand and to future Bank activities in general.

In fact, the mere presence of the Panel has contributed to making the Bank's operational staff more diligent in the observance of Bank policies. The usual zeal of presenting projects for Board approval in a manner and pace that meet the lending program's targets has been tempered by Management's greater concern with project implementation and by the zeal of the staff not to put the institution in the embarrassing position of being found in violation of its own policies and procedures. Since these policies and procedures are meant to ensure quality in the Bank-financed projects and to serve broader institutional objectives approved by Bank members (through the Executive Directors), the greater attention paid to them is likely to serve the Bank, its members as a whole, and in particular the borrowers concerned.

Inspection can also raise issues not otherwise known or appreciated and might cause the Bank to adopt more effective or clearer standards in the pursuit of its objectives. In the process, it can enhance the awareness of the borrowers involved of deficiencies in their own processes and attitudes that need to be corrected. The publication of the results of the panel's work should also enable all those concerned with the development process—governments, international financial institutions, NGOs, and others—to draw lessons from this experience and to have them reflected in their subsequent policies and actions. The end result should increase the efficiency of the Bank and of development finance in general. This of course assumes that the Panel will always be properly used as envisaged and will carry out its function with the high degree of competence, integrity, and independence expected from it. It also assumes that the Bank staff will make every effort to facilitate the Panel's work and benefit from its results.

ii. Effects on the Bank's Accountability

The concept of accountability, in its traditional meaning, denotes answerability for the performance of a person or an office, within an institution. More recently, the concept of accountability has emerged in discussions on international development law in connection with calls for transparent, participatory, and evaluatory systems of monitoring the progress of sustainable development.[68]

Much confusion seems, however, to exist in current writings on the Bank's accountability and, more generally, on the accountability of multilateral organizations. Many such writings ignore the structure of accountability institutionalized in these organizations by their constituent instruments (that is, their internal system of accountability), while focusing only on accountability to the public at large or to the NGOs that assert representation of public interest (that is, external accountability).[69]

In the case of the World Bank, the staff are accountable to the President who appoints them. The President is appointed by the Executive Directors and is accountable to them.[70] The Executive Directors are appointed or elected according to a

---

68. *See, e.g.,* Peter Slinn, Law, Accountability and Development, *Third World Legal Studies* vii–xx (1993) (noting the emergence of the notion of accountability in connection with debates on the role of law in the development process).

69. *See, e.g.,* James C.N. Paul, Law and Development into the '90s: Using International Law to Impose Accountability to People on International Development Actors, *Third World Legal Studies* 1–16 (1992) (arguing that international agencies, notably the World Bank, should be held accountable for the harm they inflict upon people through their development activities and give these people the opportunities of redress and rights to seek compensation). *See also* remarks by Daniel D. Bradlow, Richard Bissell, Jo Marie Griesgraber, Harold K. Jacobson, Sabine Schlemmer-Schulte, and David A. Wirth at the Panel Discussion on "The Accountability of International Organizations to Non-State Actors" on the occasion of the 1998 Annual Meeting of the American Society of International Law (ASIL) in *Proceedings of the 92nd Annual Meeting of ASIL* 359–373 (1998) (expressing different views on the meaning and scope of and reasons for introducing mechanisms of accountability of international organizations to non-state actors).

70. *See* IBRD Articles of Agreement, at Article V, Section 5(a) and IDA Articles of Agreement, at Article VI, Section 5(a).

system whereby each of the five members with the largest number of shares appoints one Executive Director and the Governors appointed by other members elect the other (19) Executive Directors every two years through constituencies of Governors.[71] With the exception of certain powers reserved to the Board of Governors, all the powers of the Bank, which, in principle, are vested in the Board of Governors, have been delegated to the Executive Directors who, as Bank officials, are accountable to the Board of Governors. All member countries are represented individually in the Board of Governors, each by a Governor and an Alternate Governor. These are typically ministers of finance or development who are accountable to their parliaments, the members of which are accountable to the public which elects them.

This structure of accountability befits the international character of the Bank that all members are required to respect.[72] It differs somewhat from *direct* accountability to the public or the government of any particular member country. But it is a sophisticated structure of accountability befitting an international institution. Many commentators, however, seem to assume that the only meaningful accountability is direct accountability to the public (or, more precisely, to those who claim to represent it) and, seeing that this is lacking in international organizations, accuse them, and the Bank in particular, of lack of accountability.[73]

The Bank's system of accountability enables any member country which disputes the manner in which the Bank applies its Articles of Agreement to submit any question of interpretation of these Articles to the Executive Directors for decision, subject to possible appeal by any member to the Board of

---

71. *See* IBRD Articles of Agreement, at Article V, Section 4(b). The Executive Directors of the IBRD serve *ex officio* as Executive Directors of IDA.

72. *Id.* Article V, Section 5(c) (IBRD) and Article 6, Section 6(c) (IDA).

73. *See, e.g.*, Peggy A. Rodgers, Looking a Gift Horse in the Mouth: The World Bank and Environmental Accountability, 3 *Georgetown International Environmental Law Review* 457 (1990); Jonathan Cahn, Challenging the New Imperial Authority: The World Bank and the Democratization of Development, 6 *Harvard Human Rights Journal* 159 (1993).

Governors.[74] Disputes between the Bank and its borrowers that are not settled through negotiation can be submitted to international arbitration.[75] Furthermore, an Executive Director can at any time raise with Management or before the Board any relevant issue, especially issues of concern to the government or governments that appointed or elected him/her or to private parties. Ultimately, the parliaments of member countries, through their authorization and appropriation of funds to the Bank and through their approval of the amendment of its charter, when required, can exercise a form of parliamentary review that complements the institution's system of accountability.[76]

With the establishment of the Inspection Panel, the Bank has created an additional accountability mechanism responding to the concerns of third parties affected by Bank Operations. The Inspection Panel thus introduces a possible direct relationship between private affected parties and the Bank. In other words, far from making the Bank accountable for the first time, as some observers have inaccurately stated, the inspection function adds to a system of accountability based on the institutional hierarchy of the organization another system initiated by complaints by affected parties. This new measure of accountability does not substitute for the *upward system of accountability* that exists; it simply assists it to function more efficiently by adding a *downward system of accountability* reaching out to affected parties. Decisions on remedial actions that may result from this new system remain in the hands of the Executive Directors who are responsible for the general operations of the Bank. The Panel simply gives the affected parties a voice in questioning the Bank's actions. It also provides, through its findings, the Executive Directors and the President with *independently ascertained facts*

---

74. *See* IBRD Articles of Agreement, at Article IX, and IDA Articles of Agreement, at Article X.

75. *See* General Conditions Applicable to Loan and Guarantee Agreements of the IBRD, at Article X, Section 10.04 (and of IDA).

76. Such review should be distinguished from inappropriate influences on the organization's policy-making by the Legislature of a single member country, in disregard of the collective will of the organization's governing bodies.

that enable them to perform their duties and to ensure the Bank's compliance with its policies and procedures. In this manner, the additional mechanism neither detracts from nor dilutes the existing system of accountability. On the contrary, it is meant to strengthen it and increase its efficiency.

As will soon be explained, this accountability mechanism of the Inspection Panel, while giving third parties rights of access to an independent fact-finding forum, does not amount to a judicial review capable of providing legal remedies. In other words, resort to the Panel does not by itself give affected people rights of redress from the Bank, such as the right to seek financial compensation. As a legal matter, the latter right can only be based on the concept of liability.[77]

iii.   Other Benefits

The Bank's independent inspection function could have other, perhaps unintended, benefits. It gives the Bank the opportunity to defend itself before a credible forum against mounting accusations of critics who often lack accurate information but feel free to blame project failures on the Bank. For this reason, the Bank's Management had confidently welcomed the exercise by the Panel of its investigative function. The Bank should have nothing to lose in this process. Whether the facts to be found by the Panel cleared the Bank from the accusations leveled against it or pointed out where the Bank had failed, inspection could be and in fact has been helpful to the institution. In both situations, the Bank demonstrates to all the parties concerned and to the public at large that it is a credible, responsive institution worthy of the broad and continued support it receives from its members.

------

77. For a discussion of legal liability as different from and narrower than accountability, *see* Section II of this chapter, *infra*. *See also* Sabine Schlemmer-Schulte, The World Bank Inspection Panel: Accountability to Non-State Actors, Vol. 2, No. 1, *Translex* 11–14 (April 1999) (discussing the dimension of international responsibility of the Bank in addition to its accountability and legal liability to third parties).

II.   Issue of Liability of the Bank and Its Staff for Harm Attributed by the Panel to the Bank's Non-Compliance with Its Policies and Procedures

A.   Basis of Liability

The Bank's policies and procedures do not by themselves constitute binding rules of domestic or international law.[78] The standards incorporated in such policies often exceed both domestic law requirements (for example, for resettlement of populations in case of large infrastructural projects) and international law standards (for example, for the environment). While Bank staff are required by Bank rules to apply these policies and procedures, they do not themselves implement the projects financed by the Bank. Their obligation, therefore, as explained in Chapter Two, is to see to it that Bank policies and procedures that require action by borrowers are properly reflected in the project design as well as in the legal documents and that borrowers' obligations to carry out such action are executed as agreed. There is no legal obligation on the part of the Bank or its staff to guarantee that the project it finances will succeed or will not cause any harm to any party. The obligation is to exert best efforts to ensure the project's success by reflecting Bank policies in the loan documents and carefully supervising the borrower's implementation of the measures required under these documents.[79] Typically, such measures aim, among other things, at avoiding or minimizing any harm that may afflict people and the environment as a result of the project.

Questions, however, will inevitably be raised regarding the liability of the Bank and its staff where a harm is clearly attributed

---

78. When such policies are reflected in the provisions of a loan agreement between the Bank and a certain borrower, the rules of this agreement are clearly binding on the two parties to it. For details on the legal nature of the Bank's policies, *see* Chapter Two, *supra*, at 41 *seq.*

79. *See* Chapter Two, *supra*, at 43–44.

by the Panel, in whole or in part, to the Bank's failure to observe its policies and procedures. Some observers have suggested that the Bank should, at a minimum, bear the cost of remedial actions taken by the borrower in such cases.

In this context, a distinction has to be made between the Bank's liability to its borrowers and its liability to third parties, such as the parties affected by the projects it finances. By virtue of provisions in the General Conditions applicable to Bank loan agreements, the rights and obligations of the Bank, the borrower, and the guarantor (if any) are enforceable in accordance with their terms, notwithstanding any conflicting law in the borrowing country. Furthermore, disputes between the Bank and the borrower may be resolved by negotiations and, failing this, through international arbitration.[80] (In practice, such disputes have always been resolved through negotiations.) The inspection function does not interfere with this process; it relates exclusively to the inspection of the extent of the Bank's observance of its policies and procedures and any harm that may be afflicted on affected parties in the territories of the borrower as a result of serious violations by the Bank. It does not investigate the harm that may be suffered by the borrower itself.

As for the Bank's possible legal liability to affected parties in the territory of the borrower as a result of the Panel's findings, it has to be noted once again *first* that the Inspection Panel is not a court of law that bases its findings on strict judicial procedures and rules of evidence, and *second* that, as a public international organization, the Bank and its staff have immunity in their operations from legal action before national courts, except when this immunity has been waived.

---

80. *See* Article X, Sections 10.01 and 10.04 of the General Conditions Applicable to IBRD Loan and Guarantee Agreements, dated January 1, 1985. A similar provision (Article X, Sections 10.01 and 10.03) appears in the General Conditions applicable to IDA credit agreements. By virtue of provisions in all such agreements, the General Conditions constitute an integral part of the agreement. Agreements between IBRD or IDA, on the one hand, and a borrowing country, on the other hand, are treaties, registered as such at the U.N.

B.   *The Issue of Immunity*

The immunity of international organizations from legal actions related to their operations is based on customary international law that accords immunity to all public international organizations in the pursuit of their public purposes.[81] The purpose of such immunity is to allow these organizations to carry out the international public functions entrusted to them without interference from the authorities (including judicial authorities) of a single member country. As such, it is an important safeguard needed to ensure the multilateral character of international organizations. The actions of such organizations must reflect the collective will of their members as expressed by the governing bodies of each organization pursuant to its rules, not the will of any of their members acting unilaterally. The principle of immunity is codified in the 1947 Convention on the Privileges and Immunities of the Specialized Agencies of the United Nations, subject only to the waiver by the agency concerned.[82] The Bank is a specialized agency of the United Nations,[83] and the waiver provided for in its Articles of Agreement is repeated in this context.[84] This waiver is an exception from the Bank's general immunity as an international organization pursuing public purposes (mainly development assistance to member countries). Explicit provisions on the Bank's immunities appear in many of the establishment agreements entered into between the Bank and

---

81. *See* Derek W. Bowett, *The Law of International Institutions*, 349–50 (1982); Finn Seyersted, *Jurisdiction over Organizations and Officials of States, The Holy See and Intergovernmental Organizations*, 14 *International Comparative Law Quarterly* 493, 526 (1965); Wilfred C. Jenks, *International Immunities*, 40–41 (1961); and Restatement of the Foreign Relations Law of The United States (Revised), § 467 Comment & Reporters' Note 4 at 73 (Tentative Date No. 4) (1983).

82. 33 U.N.T.S. 261–302, Article 3, Section 4.

83. *See* Agreement between the U.N. and the IBRD approved by the Board of Governors on September 16, 1947, and between the U.N. and the IDA approved by the Board of Governors on February 24, 1961.

84. *See* Convention, *supra* note 82, at Annex V (1).

countries where it has field offices.[85] The Bank has asserted this immunity in the few cases in which it was sued before national courts. There has been no case in any country in which a *final* judicial decision denied the Bank immunity when asserted.[86]

---

85. For instance, a declaratory provision in the Establishment Agreement with the Government of Argentina reads as follows: "The Bank shall enjoy immunity from every form of legal process, except in cases arising out of or in connection with the exercise of the Bank's powers to issue or guarantee securities. It is understood that, as provided in Article VII, Section 3 of the Articles of Agreement, no action shall be brought by the Government or persons acting for or deriving claims from the Government [...]."

86. As noted in Chapter Three (the text accompanied by note 66), the Bank faces legal suits initiated by individual brick makers which are pending before an Argentinean court where the questions of Bank immunity and the plaintiff's failure to state a claim against the Bank have yet to be decided upon. Two other cases were brought against the Bank, also in Argentina. The case of *Patagonian Rainbow, S.A. vs. Neuquén, Provincia del y otro s/ordinario*, was directly filed before the Supreme Court (because the defendants include the Province of Neuquén) and is pending. The World Bank, IDB, and the Banco de la Nación were joined as co-defendants. The other case, *Alimentos de los Andes, S. A.*, which involved the same defendants, excepting the Province, and including instead the Bank of the Province of Neuquén, was filed before the Federal Court of the First Instance of Civil and Commercial Matters. On November 27, 1997, this court denied the World Bank's motion to dismiss on the basis that the Bank's immunity, like that of sovereign states, did not extend to the case at hand. On appeal, the Court of Appeals affirmed the decision, noting that the Bank's immunities did not cover the "issuance or guarantee of securities"(which is true, but has no relevance to the case). The case is now pending before the Supreme Court of Argentina. (In the first case, the plaintiff asked for an increase of the loan amount from the provincial bank and, in the second, sought the performance of loan agreements with the provincial bank. The latter bank was relying in both cases on a loan from the Banco de la Nación that in turn had received loans from the World Bank and IDB for on-lending for projects of the type involved.)

In an earlier case, *SGEEM v. IBRD*, a French company sued the IBRD before a French court in 1989 because disbursement of Bank loans and IDA credits to Zambia were suspended, with the result that payments due to the French company under a contract financed by an IDA credit were not made by Zambia. The French court, before deciding on the jurisdictional issue (Bank and IDA immunity and lack of privity of contract between the Bank or IDA and the French company), scheduled a hearing on the merits, but no decision was reached on either count. The suspension of disbursement was lifted for other reasons; Zambia paid the company and the case was discontinued.

All the final decisions in other cases where Bank or IDA immunity was asserted confirmed such immunity. The last example is an opinion by the High Court of Justice of Ghana in *Felicia Adjei and Others vs. The Attorney General and Others*, suit No. 811/96, opinion issued on July 30, 1996.

In a case against the IFC (a Bank-affiliated, but legally separate, organization), the U.S. District Court for the District of Columbia recently denied IFC's immunity with respect to certain acts under an interpretation of the U.S. International Organizations Immunities Act (IOIA).[87] This Act grants to international organizations in the United States "the same immunity from suit and every form of judicial process as is enjoyed by foreign governments."[88] When the IOIA was enacted in 1945, foreign governments enjoyed absolute immunity, but in 1967 a new legislation, the Foreign Sovereign Immunities Act (FSIA),[89] created exceptions to the immunity of foreign governments. The main exception is that *commercial* activities carried out by a foreign state in the United States do not benefit from sovereign immunities. Another exception consists of cases based on certain *tortious acts and omissions* by foreign states or their employees acting within the scope of their employment, unless the tortious act qualifies as a "discretionary function."[90] The FSIA "is generally silent about international organizations"[91] and does not refer to them in the context of immunity issues.

The case in point was brought before the U.S. District Court (one judge) by a former IFC employee who first sued her director for alleged infliction of emotional distress, assault, and battery, then joined IFC in the suit as a co-defendant.[92] Under the assumption that the FSIA does circumscribe the immunity available under the IOIA, the court, taking the facts to be as alleged for the purpose of the jurisdictional issue, ruled against the immunity of IFC and its staff member. Some of the latter's acts were alleged to have constituted a tortious act that was not,

---

87. 22 U.S.C. §§ 288–288j.

88. *Id.* at §§ 288 a(b).

89. 28 U.S.C. § 1602–1611.

90. *Id. at* § 1605 (a)(5).

91. *Broadbent v. Organization of American States*, 628 F.2d 27 (D.C. Cir. 1980).

92. *Rendall-Speranza v. Nassim*, 942 F. Supp. 621 (D.D.C. 1998); *Rendall-Speranza v. Nassim and the International Finance Corporation*, 932 F. Supp. 19 (D.D.C. 1996).

in the view of the court, a discretionary function. However, the U.S. Court of Appeals for the District of Columbia reversed that decision.[93] The reversal was based on the grounds that the claims against IFC and its staff member were barred by the statute of limitations except for the claim against the staff member for battery that allegedly took place on a date subsequent to the other alleged acts. The court held that the latter claim was barred by immunity of the employee under § 288 d(b) of the IOIA.[94] The court did not refer in this respect to the tortious act exception under the FSIA and upheld the immunity of *staff* acting in their official capacity without exception. As to the immunity of the IFC, the court did not find it necessary to decide whether the FSIA exception extends to international organizations under the IOIA because the claim was barred on other grounds.

Even though the IFC cited its Articles of Agreement and customary international law at length in its submissions, the District Court based its (now reversed) decisions exclusively on the two above-mentioned U.S. Acts.[95] This is regrettable—the IFC Articles, as a treaty ratified by the United States, are also part of the U.S. law.[96] Its provisions on the immunity of its officials from legal actions do not allow for exceptions of alleged tortious acts. International law, of which the IFC is a subject, does not authorize exceptions of this kind that could deprive international organizations of their freedom to act under their

---

93. *Rendall Speranza v. Nassim,* 107 F. 3d 913; 1977.

94. §288 d(b) of IOIA provides that officers and employees of [international] organizations shall be immune from "suit and legal process relating to acts performed by them in their official capacity and falling within their functions as such representatives, offices, or employees."

95. *Compare IBRD v. District of Columbia,* 996 F. Supp. 31, 34–5, where the District Court cited the IBRD Articles in its decision on the Bank's immunity from taxes on its operations.

96. *See* 7 U.S.T. 2198, T.I.A.S. No. 3620; Public Law No. 350, Chapter 788, of the 84th Congress of 11 August, 1955; and the Executive Order No. 10680 signed on October 1956 designating IFC as an international organization benefiting from certain privileges and immunities in terms of Public Law No. 291 of the 79th Congress of 29 December 1945.

rules, independently from interference by the authorities of a single member. At any rate, the specific provisions of the IFC Articles should prevail over the general provisions of FSIA, even if the latter were otherwise applicable to international organizations, as concluded by the District Court. Such a general extension of the FSIA exceptions to international organizations was at best a controversial matter. As noted by a U.S. Federal Court on an earlier occasion, "[n]either rationale of the restrictive notion of immunity [of foreign states under FSIA] would seem to apply to international organizations."[97] More recently, the Federal Court of Appeal for the District of Columbia (3rd circuit) clearly ruled that the immunity of international organizations was not subject to the commercial activities exception provided for in the FSIA, but only to the limits which might be introduced by the U.S. President according to the IOIA itself.[98]

1.   The Bank's Immunity Before U.S. Courts

Immunity of the Bank itself was confirmed in the few cases brought against the Bank in several countries, including cases before the U.S. courts. Judicial and legislative practice in the United States will be explained in some detail here because it is more likely that future cases against the Bank, if any, may be mostly brought in the United States. Two earlier cases before U.S. courts are worth mentioning in particular: the *Mendaro*

---

97. *See Broadbent v. Inter-American Development Bank, supra* note 91, at 32, note 20. In that case, the court also saw no need to decide definitively on the issue because the international organization (OAS) was immune from liability even under FSIA. The FSIA refers in a few respects to international organizations. *See also Atkinson v. IDB*, 156 F.3d 1335, 1339–42. "The FSIA is 'beside the point' [for international organizations' immunity purposes] because it does not reflect any direct focus by Congress upon the meaning of the earlier enacted provisions of the IOIA." The argument could be made that if the tort exception was meant to apply to such organizations, the text of the Act would have referred to this explicitly, as it does in other contexts.

98. *See Atkinson v. IDB, supra* note 97.

case,[99] initiated against the Bank by a former staff consultant, and the *Morgan* case,[100] initiated by a "temporary employee" who worked for the Bank under a contract between the Bank and an employment agency. In both cases, the U.S. Federal court dismissed the suits on the basis of the Bank's immunity. In the words of the *Mendaro* court,

> *"[t]he facially broad waiver of immunity contained in the Bank's Articles of Agreement must be narrowly read in light of both national and international law governing the immunity of international organizations."*[101]

Later, in the *Morgan* case, where the claimant had no recourse to the Bank's Administrative Tribunal because he was not a staff member, the U.S. court nevertheless upheld the Bank's immunity. The clear conclusion in both cases is that the waiver of such immunity provided for in the Bank's Articles is limited to actions "arising out of [the Bank's] external *commercial* contracts and activities."[102]

The Bank's Articles of Agreement have an explicit provision on the immunity from legal process of the Bank's Governors, Executive Directors, Alternates, and staff with respect to acts performed by them in their official capacity, except when the Bank

---

99. *Mendaro v. World Bank*, 717 F.2d 610 (1983). *See also Chiriboga v. International Bank for Reconstruction and Development*, 616 F. Supp. 963 (D.D.C., 1985) and an earlier precedent, not involving the World Bank, in *Broadbent v. Organization of American States*, 628 F. 2d 27 (D.C. Cir., 1980).

100. *Morgan v. International Bank for Reconstruction and Development*, 752 F. Supp. 492 (D.C.D.C., 1990). The claimant was allowed access to the Bank's Administrative Tribunal after he had lost the case before U.S. courts.

101. *Mendaro, supra* note 99, at 611.

102. *Id.* at 620 (emphasis added). *Compare Lutcher S.A. Cellulose e Papel v. Inter-American Development Bank*, 382 F. 2nd 454 (D.C. Cir., 1967) where the Court of Appeals denied immunity of IDB and permitted a suit by a *private* borrower alleging IDB wrongfully lent money to plaintiff's competitors and failed to carry out alleged promises to make a market study before participating in further loans to industry. The Court found that the complaint "does not raise large or delicate international policy issues." *Id.* at 460.

waives this immunity.[103] Such immunity is established by the Articles, a treaty binding on Bank members, without any exceptions other than waiver by the Bank itself.

The Bank's Articles of Agreement also contain a general provision providing that the Bank may be sued in certain circumstances. This "facially broad waiver" reads as follows:

> "*Actions may be brought against the Bank only in a court of competent jurisdiction in the territories of a member in which the Bank has an office, has appointed an agent for the purpose of accepting service or notice of process, or has issued or guaranteed securities. No actions shall, however, be brought by members or persons acting for or deriving claims from members. The property and assets of the Bank shall, wheresoever located and by whomsoever held, be immune from all forms of seizure, attachment or execution before the delivery of final judgment against the Bank.*"[104]

This provision was meant to enable the Bank to borrow from financial markets by making it possible for its creditors to sue it before national courts. Such borrowings are conducted as commercial transactions subject to national law, and the disputes arising under them are subject to the jurisdiction of national courts. Outside the area of borrowing and similar commercial activities, the Bank, as a defendant, has consistently asserted immunity from the jurisdiction of national courts, accepting only international arbitration (in the cases of disputes arising under its loan and guarantee agreements,[105] or under supply or construction contracts). The Bank has also successfully asserted immunity in cases

---

103. *See* IBRD Articles of Agreement, at Article VII, Section 8(i), and IDA Articles of Agreement, at Article VIII, Section 8.

104. *See* IBRD Articles of Agreement, at Article VII, Section 3, and IDA Articles of Agreement, at Article VIII, Section 3.

105. *See* General Conditions Applicable to Bank Loans, at Article X, Section 10.04.

brought by staff and former staff members before national courts and has only accepted to be sued by them before its Administrative Tribunal established in 1980.[106] The narrow interpretation of the waiver provided for in the Article VII, Section 3, quoted above, was supported by the U.S. State Department Legal Adviser, and, as demonstrated above, by U.S. courts.[107]

In 1980, a letter from Roberts B. Owen, U.S. Department of State Legal Advisor, to Leroy D. Clark, Equal Employment Opportunity Commission General Counsel, commenting on Article VII, Section 3 of the IBRD Articles, stated:

> "*The language of the Article does not specify the exact scope of actions which may properly be brought against the Bank under its provision. However, at the time the Articles of Agreement were negotiated, Article VII (3) was intended as a limited waiver of immunity specifically to permit suits by private lenders against the Bank in connection with the Bank's issuance of securities, and to specify the venue for such actions, in order to facilitate the Bank's access to capital markets. Cf. Restatement (Second), Foreign Relations Law of the United States, § 84, Reporter's Note at 275 (1965). It was not designed (and should not now be construed) to subject the Bank to the full range of our domestic jurisdiction or to expose the Bank's international personnel and administrative actions to review by our courts and administrative agencies.*"[108]

---

106. *See Resolution of the Board of Governors No. 350,* dated April 30, 1980, establishing the World Bank Administrative Tribunal, effective July 1, 1980, with retroactive jurisdiction to January 1979.

107. The principle of general immunity from legal process except in cases arising from the exercise of borrowing powers is explicitly mentioned in the subsequent charters of international financial institutions. *See, e.g.,* Article 52.1 of the Agreement Establishing the African Development Bank.

108. (Citation deleted.) The letter is dated June 24, 1980. Similar letters were issued in other cases; the last such letter was jointly issued by the U.S. State

The U.S. courts normally give serious consideration to the opinion of the State Department in matters of foreign affairs. In the *Mendaro* case, for instance, the Legal Adviser's opinion was among the bases upon which the Court of Appeals founded its decision.[109] In *IBRD v. District of Columbia*, the practice that "courts must give great weight to the Executive branch's interpretation of international agreements" was emphasized again.[110]

In the *Mendaro* case, the court concluded that "it is evident that the World Bank's members could only have intended to waive the Bank's immunity from *suits by its debtors, creditors, bond holders, and those other potential plaintiffs to whom the Bank would have to subject itself to suit in order to achieve its chartered objectives.*"[111] The same conclusion could be drawn from the U.S. International Organizations Immunities Act of 1945, which provides that international organizations designated by the President "shall enjoy the same immunity from suit and every form of judicial process as is enjoyed by foreign governments, except to the extent that such organizations may *expressly* waive their immunity for the purpose of any proceedings or by the terms of any contract."[112]

2.   The Bank's Immunity outside the United States

The position of the U.S. State Department Legal Advisor and of U.S. courts in the above-cited cases is generally consistent with

---

Department and the U.S. Department of the Treasury on November 29, 1997, to the Chief Finance Officer of DC, expressing the U.S. position that the retroactive assessment of tax on account of World Bank cafeteria operations was "inequitable and inconsistent with Article VII, Section 9 of the Bank's Articles as incorporated in U.S. Law." See *IBRD v. District of Columbia*, 996 F. Supp. 31, where the decision was in favor of Bank immunity. See also *Atkinson v. IDB*, 156 F.3d, at 1337–38.

109. *Mendaro, supra* note 99, at 620–21.

110. 996 F. Supp., at 38.

111. *Mendaro, supra* note 99, at 615 (emphasis added).

112. Pub. L. 79–291, as amended, 22 U.S.C. § 288 (emphasis added). The World Bank was designated pursuant to this act by Executive Order No. 9751 on July 11, 1946 (3 C.F.R. § 558 (1943–48 compl.)).

practice in other member countries since the establishment of the World Bank. It is therefore consistent with the Vienna Convention on the Law of Treaties (and of the Vienna Convention on the Law of Treaties between States and International Organizations and between International Organizations), which state that "[a]ny subsequent practice in the application of the treaty which establishes the agreement of the parties regarding its interpretation" shall be taken into account.[113]

The narrow interpretation of the Bank's waiver of immunity is also consistent with the prevalent theory and practice outside the United States with respect to *state immunity*, which excludes from such immunity only acts *ratione gestiones* (that is, of commercial or business character).[114] Neither the Bank's lending operations, nor, clearly, the issuance and observance of its policies and procedures are commercial activities pursued for profit purposes. On the contrary, these represent the core of the international public purposes for which the Bank was established (that is, supporting development in the territories of its members and promoting international investment and trade).[115]

---

113. Article 31 (3)(b) of the Vienna Convention on the Law of Treaties of May 23, 1969, entered into force on January 27, 1980, 1155 U.N.T.S. 331 (1980) and Article 31 (3)(b) of the Vienna Convention on the Law of Treaties between States and International Organizations or between International Organizations of March 21, 1986, not yet entered into force, U.N. Doc. A/CONF. 129/15, reprinted in 25 *I.L.M.* 543 (1986).

114. *See* Peter D. Trooboff, Foreign State Immunity: Emerging Consensus on Principles, 200 *Recueil des Cours* 235 (1986, V); Georges R. Delaume, The Foreign Sovereign Immunities Act and Public Debt Litigation: Some Fifteen Years Later, 88 *American Journal of International Law* 257, 259–260, 277–79 (1994) (referring to U.S. and U.K. legislation and to Swiss and other European judicial doctrine). The U.S. Foreign Sovereign Immunities Act provides for the exception of *tortious acts*, as explained. *See also*, the European Convention on State Immunity adopted under the auspices of the Council of Europe in 1972 (516 U.N.T.S. 205) and the United Nations Draft Convention on Immunity of States and their Properties prepared by the International Law Commission (ILC) (*http://www.un.org/law/ilc/texts/jimm.htm* visited on Jan. 11, 1999). Under both texts, States enjoy in principle immunity unless exceptions, in particular relating to commercial activities in which the sovereign engages, apply.

115. *See* IBRD Articles of Agreement, Article 1 (Purposes).

No case has ever been decided on the merits by national courts concerning damages to third parties resulting from a Bank action or omission in the context of its loan or guarantee operations.[116] The Articles of Agreement are definitive on the Bank's immunity from actions "brought by members or persons acting for or deriving claims from members." They are equally clear, as already mentioned, on the immunity of Bank officials from legal proceedings regarding acts performed in their official capacity. The Articles also give to the Bank's Executive Directors the sole power to interpret the Articles' provisions, including those determining the scope of Bank immunities.

C.   *Situation in the Absence of Immunity*

The problem arises when national law provides for exceptions applicable to all international organizations, and a local court ignores the particular provisions of the charter of a specific organization (as the District Court judge concluded in the above-cited *Rendall-Speranza* case involving IFC).[117] It cannot, therefore, be stated with certainty what types of legal action against the Bank national courts might rule to fall within their jurisdiction. However, findings by the Inspection Panel would not relate to the Bank's commercial activities but to the degree of its compliance with its own policies and procedures. National courts, even if they agree with the findings, are not expected therefore to consider them a valid basis for a legal action subjecting the Bank to liability, in violation of its general immunity for activities that are not commercial in nature. To rule otherwise would be to allow national courts to become involved in the internal functioning of a public international organization. This would be contrary to the rationale of the concept of immunity of international organizations as understood in contemporary international law. It would also contradict Article VII, Section 1, of

---

116. *See* note 86, *supra.*
117. *See* notes 92 to 93, *supra,* and accompanying text.

the Bank's Articles of Agreement that endows the Bank with its
immunities "[t]o enable the Bank to fulfill the functions with
which it is entrusted."

Assuming, however, for the sake of discussion, that the
Bank's immunity in the circumstances discussed above is not recognized, the question of legal liability must then be discussed in
light of applicable law in each case. In principle, such liability will
be based on fault (intended harmful action or omission), or negligence under applicable law, unless that law imposes strict or
absolute liability (regardless of fault) in certain situations. The
mere failure by the Bank to observe its policies would not
amount to fault under applicable law, unless it happened that the
Bank's standards were identical to applicable law standards and
their violation was deemed a violation of applicable law. As previously emphasized, Bank policies typically require high standards beyond what borrowers or their foreign financiers
otherwise need to observe under national or international law.
In any event, the obligations the Bank would have to meet under
such laws, assuming they were applicable to it, would be different from the obligations of the party that actually implemented
the project. They would be limited to the exceptional cases of
lender liability where this type of liability may be recognized in
principle and established in a particular case through a judicial or
arbitral process. This point should not, of course, preclude the
Bank as a "partner in development" from assisting the borrower
in alleviating the harm in all possible situations. The remedial
action plans to be agreed upon with borrowers and any complementary Bank lending such plans may entail would normally represent the action expected from the Bank in such circumstances,
in addition, of course, to any internal measures the Bank may
take with respect to its control systems and the staff responsible
in case of misconduct.

D.   Lender Liability?

Lender liability for damage caused by a borrower to third parties
in the use of borrowed funds is not a common principle in

different legal systems in the absence of a direct contractual relationship between the lender and the affected party or a tortious
act attributed to the lender.[118]

In the United States,[119] lender liability, including liability of
the lender to third parties, has developed from case law from
the late 1960s onward and is confirmed in certain areas by
statutory law.

Cases of lender liability to third parties were, in principle,
based on control doctrine. A loan agreement may permit a lender
to exercise control (for example, over a financially troubled borrower) and the lender could in such cases be held liable for damages caused by improper interference, including those caused to
third parties. Courts have discussed control in circumstances in
which the lender exercised financial domination,[120] required

---

118. "It must be noted that the concept of lender liability for environmental harm originated in the United States and Canada and is, at present,
unknown to English law. It is also not likely that the concept will take root in
English law." *See* John Jarvis, Michael Fordham, and David Wolfson, *Domestic
Environmental Liability,* in *Banks, Liability and Risk* 155 (Ross Cranston, ed.,
2nd ed., 1995). Recent reform of environmental legislation in a number of
countries (Germany, Sweden, Finland, and Norway) has not included provisions
for lender liability for environmental damage. *See* Hennig Mennöh,
Environmental Liability of Companies and Managers in Germany, *International
Business Lawyer* 230 (May 1997) (discussing the new German Environmental
Liability Act of 1991), and Ari M. Huhtamäki and Jan Kleinemann, *Lender
Liability in the Nordic Countries,* in *Banks, Liability and Risk* 244–45 (Ross
Cranston ed., 2nd ed. 1995) (noting that seemingly no attention has been paid
by any of the Scandinavian legislators to the possibility of lenders becoming the
ones found liable for damages).

119. For details on the development of the concept of lender liability under
common law and statutory law, *see* Troy H. Gott and William L. Townsley III,
Lender Liability: A Survey of Theories, Thoughts and Trends, 28 *Washburn
Law Journal* 238 (No. 2, 1988), and Melissa Cassedy, The Doctrine of Lender
Liability, 40 *University of Florida Law Review* 165 (1988).

120. *See In re Process-Manz Press, Inc.,* 236 F. Supp. 333 (N.D. Ill. 1964)
(lender controlled borrower corporation through 100% stock pledge), *rev'd on
other grounds,* 369 F. 2d 513 (7th Cir. 1966), *cert. denied sub nom. Limperis v.
A. J. Armstrong Co.,* 386 U.S. 957 (1967); *Berquist v. First Nat'l Bank (In re
American Lumber Co.),* 5 Bankr. 470 (D. Minn. 1980) (lending bank fore-
closed on security interests and refused to honor checks); *Gay Jenson Farms Co.
v. Cargill, Inc.,* 309 N. W. 2d 285 (Minn. 1981) (lender corporation became
principal by active participation in borrower's daily business).

restrictive covenants,[121] influenced employee hiring decisions,[122] and interfered with management decisions.[123] Statutory definitions establishing guidelines for control have built on common law definitions.[124] This applies in particular to the most important introduction of lender liability by legislation in the environment field.

Environmental liability of lenders was first comprehensively regulated by the Comprehensive Environmental Response, Compensation and Liability Act of 1980 (CERCLA).[125] According to CERCLA, lenders, as "owners or operators" of polluting vessels and facilities (that is, in a strong position of control) may be held strictly liable for their debtor's environmental liability.[126] Excluded from this liability, however, are "secured

---

121. *See Canadair Ltd. v. Seaboard World Airlines,* 43 Misc. 2d 320, 250 N.Y.S. 2d 723 (Sup. Ct. 1964) (lenders control through chattel mortgage and equipment trust agreements); *see also In re Clearfield Bituminous Coal Corp.,* 1 S.E.C. 374 (1936) (lender exercised contractual right to veto creation of liens on extraordinary debt).

122. *See State Nat'l Bank v. Farah Mfg. Co.,* 678 S.W. 2d 661 (Tex. Ct. App. 1984) (lender blocked former CEO's return to position); *see also Krivo Indus. Supply Co. v. National Distillers & Chem. Corp.,* 483 F. 2nd 1098 (5th Cir. 1973) (lender's auditor sent to borrower to establish control procedures); *Chicago Mill & Lumber Co. v. Boatmen's Bank,* 234 F. 41 (8th Cir. 1916) (lender arranged to have former employee elected borrower's president).

123. *See Harris Trust & Sav. Bank v. Krieg (In re Prima Co.),* 98 F. 2d 952 (7th Cir. 1938) (lender induced borrowers to make decisions based upon loan acceleration clause), *cert. denied* 305 U.S. 658 (1939); *In re Teltronics Servs., Inc.,* 29 Bankr. 139 (Bankr. E.D.N.Y. 1983) (lender forced termination of employees); *State Nat'l Bank v. Farah Mfg. Co.,* 678 S.W. 2d 661 (Tex. Ct. App. 1984) (lenders coerced board of directors reelection policy formulation).

124. *See* Gott and Townsley, *supra* note 119, at 257 *seq.* (analyzing both statutes and case law of lender liability based on the control theory).

125. 42 U.S.C. § 9601–9656.

126. The U.S. Environmental Protection Agency (EPA) defined "owner or operator" to mean anyone participating in the management of a contaminated facility or owning an interest in it. *See* 57 Fed. Reg. 18,382 (April 29, 1992). *See also* Tracy K. Evans, Lender Liability, 16 *Annual Review of Banking Law* 40 (1997); Douglas A. Henderson, Lender Liability for Environmental Contamination—Recent Guidance from EPA and Department of Justice, 113 *Banking Law Journal* 918 (1996); and Richard E. Slaney, Lender Liability under CERCLA: The Rise, Fall and Rebirth of the EPA Rule, 101 *Commercial Law Journal* 389 (1996).

lenders," a term that covers any lender who, "without participating in the management of a vessel or facility, holds indicia of ownership primarily to protect his security interest in the vessel or facility."[127] Courts seemed to have narrowly defined the security interest exemption.[128] To protect lenders from exposure to "liability for problems they did not cause,"[129] CERCLA was circumscribed by a subsequent Act (the Asset Conservation Lender Liability and Deposit Insurance Act of 1996).[130] The latter Act, confirming a previous controversial rule by the U.S. Environmental Protection Agency (EPA), excludes from liability lenders that do not participate in the management of the borrower's enterprise. It also provides that lenders holding "an indicia of ownership primarily to protect [their] security interest" are not "owners or operators" for liability purposes under CERCLA. Pursuant to the 1996 Act, a lender "participate[s] in management only if, while the borrower is still in possession of the vessel or the facility, the lender exercises decision-making or managerial functions excluding environmental compliance."[131] Similar provisions appear now in some state legislation in the United States.[132]

Outside the environment field, a secured lender was held by U.S. courts not liable when he did not operate the plant of the borrower as a business enterprise.[133] A lender was found in another case to "owe no duty to protect third parties from the credit risk of an insolvent borrower."[134]

---

127. CERCLA, note 125, *supra, at* § 101 (20) (A).

128. *See, e.g., United States v. Maryland Bank & Trust Co.,* 632 F. Supp. 573 (D. Md. 1986); *United States v. Fleet Factors Corp.,* 901 F.2d 1550, 1557 (11th Cir. 1990), *certiorari denied,* 498 U.S. 1046 (1991).

129. *Federal Legislative Review,* Secured Lenders 89 (July–August, 1996).

130. Enacted as subtitle E of the Economic Growth and Regulatory paperwork Reduction Act of 1996, *Public Law No.* 104–208, 1996 U.S.C.C.A.N. (110 Stat. 3009), at 1166.

131. *Id.*

132. *See* California Senate Bill 1285, Cal. Health and Safety Code 25548 (West 1996); Idaho Senate Bill 1516, Idaho Code § 39.7201–7210 (1996).

133. *Adams v. Erwin Weller Co.,* 87 F3d 260 (8th Cir. 1996).

134. *Athey Product Corp. v. Harris Bank Roselle,* 89 F. 3rd. 430 (7th Cir. 1996).

It is worth noting in this respect that when the Bank enters into a loan agreement with any of its borrowers, its lending does not involve any action by the Bank as an "owner or operator" of a facility. Nor does the Bank hold any security interests in the projects it finances. Indeed, the Bank and its staff are prohibited from participating in the management of such projects.

To the extent that the Bank's own liability is established by a court of law in a specific case, as a result of the Bank's violation of a *legal* obligation applicable to it, a remote possibility no doubt, the Bank, as a responsible international organization, would of course be expected in such circumstances to take appropriate measures to comply and address the situation. This should not, however, be confused with the failure of the Bank to observe any of its policies or procedures that do not amount to a legal obligation *vis-à-vis* the affected party with whom the Bank has no contractual relationship. The Bank attempts through its policies and actions to protect the interests of such affected parties. Such attempts, even if they proved unsuccessful, should not be taken as a valid basis for holding the bank legally liable for the harm caused by other parties. Aside from the important issue of Bank immunities, the Bank's liability for harm to affected parties must be based on a legal cause of action that such parties can take up against the Bank before a court of law. Such cause of action may be based on a contractual relationship or a tort under applicable law. It cannot arise in the absence of either of these bases, except in a situation of strict or absolute liability that can hardly be envisaged in the case of the Bank's operations.

Concluding Remarks

I. An Overview of the Panel's Experience

There is no doubt that difficulties have been encountered in the Panel's performance of its function, and "all the parties are still climbing the learning curve."[1] These difficulties were manifested at the end of 1998 in varying degrees of dissatisfaction by practically all the parties concerned with the experience. The Panel was not satisfied with Management's practice of agreeing with borrowers on remedial action plans before the Panel submitted its recommendation to the Board and saw this as preempting its function. The Panel also was not happy with Management's invocation of eligibility issues in its initial response to the request for inspection. More important, the Panel felt frustrated each time the Board denied its recommendation for inspection. Some members of the Board wanted to eliminate altogether the requirement of Board approval of inspection in each case, while other members insisted on this requirement as a "crucial safeguard." Borrowing countries and their representatives were dissatisfied with what they saw as an unauthorized conversion of the process to the investigation of their actions and omissions, rather than those of the Bank. They were particularly unhappy about the publicity and the ensuing embarrassment associated with the inspection process. Affected parties, according to some spokesmen, complained about the lack of consultation with them, especially with respect to remedial plans, and not informing them of the outcome in their own language. Bank staff felt at times that the Panel was more concerned with the issue of harm, regardless of its cause, than with material harm resulting from the Bank's serious violation of its operational policies and procedures as

---

1. Alvaro Umaña (ed.), *The World Bank Inspection Panel: The First Four Years* (1994–1998), 325.

required by the Resolution. Some staff also felt that the Panel had recommended investigation even when important eligibility conditions were missing. NGOs, especially those based in Washington, had broader complaints concerning what they saw as a narrow mandate of the Panel frustrated by actions of both Management and Board.

These negative perceptions notwithstanding, the inspection process has been quite positive on the whole. The fear that the creation of the Panel would invite hundreds of mostly unsubstantiated complaints has not materialized. The record of the Panel shows that only sixteen requests have been submitted so far, of which two were not registered. Out of the fourteen others, the Panel found serious reasons to recommend inspection in six cases only (two cases are still pending). Although such inspection took place, in one way or another, in three cases, all but one of the other cases were subject to a detailed "preliminary review" or "preliminary assessment" to meet the Board's quest for what the Panel saw sometimes as an "equivalent to the content of an investigation." In spite of the timing shortcomings of the remedial action plan technique, it has helped borrowers to cope with important social and environmental issues in a fast and, as progress reports showed, generally effective manner. Compared with inspection carried out by outside *ad hoc* inspectors, both in the Bank and IFC, the Panel's inspection showed greater knowledge of development issues and a higher degree of sensitivity to the difficult balances that have to be maintained. The frustration of the various parties concerning past practice have been thoroughly addressed in the second review of the Panel's experience by the Bank's Board. The conclusions reached by the Board provide, on the whole, an attempt to get the Board, Management, and Panel to honor in practice the requirements of the Resolution establishing the Panel as it was originally written in 1993. There is no evidence of interference by any source within the Bank in the Panel's performance of its day-to-day work, and the record is clear that the Panel has the full support of the Bank's President. In the two reviews by the Board of the Panel's experience, the Panel received warm words of appreciation and respect, not only from the Board but also from Management.

The details provided in this book may have helped the reader to understand the complexities involved and, more important, how these complexities have been addressed and resolved. The outcome of the second review of the Panel's experience, in particular, will most likely raise the level of satisfaction of all the parties concerned, at least of those inside the Bank. As a living phenomenon, the Panel will further evolve, as the Bank as a whole will certainly do, to serve the ultimate purpose of supporting development that is both socially sound and environmentally sustainable. The Panel has already given the most simple and poverty-stricken people in several countries a voice in matters affecting them—one that is seriously listened to by the Panel, the Bank's top Management, and its Board. This in itself is an important change in the work of an inter-governmental organization.

II.   The Panel's Impact on the Evolution of International Law and Policy

The effects of the establishment and operation of the Inspection Panel will not be limited to the Bank and its borrowing members. Over time, they are likely to influence a number of areas of international law and policy far beyond the scope of the Bank's activities.

The establishment of the Panel, it should be noted, came at a time of growing interest in the role of individuals and private groups in international affairs. The traditional view of international law as the law governing relations between sovereign states as its sole subjects[2] has gradually given way to the recognition of the international juridical personality of certain non-state entities,

---

2. For a critical analysis of the 18th century origins of this view, *see* Mark W. Janis, Jeremy Bentham and the Fashioning of 'International Law,' 78 *American Journal of International law* 405 (1984); and Philip Allott, *International Law and International Revolution: Reconceiving the World* (1989).

namely, public international organizations. Increasingly, individuals and private entities in certain circumstances are also accorded rights and subjected to obligations under international law.[3] However, the phenomenal expansion of the rights of individuals and private groups derived directly from international law is a relatively recent development. This development is most manifestly reflected in rights of access and hearing granted to claimants other than states before an increasing number of international courts and tribunals.

At the global level, such facilities include sophisticated arbitration and conciliation mechanisms open to foreign investors against their host states, most notably, the International Centre for Settlement of Investment Disputes (ICSID).[4] At the regional level, they include such fora as the Court of Justice of the European Communities, the European Commission of Human Rights, the European Court of Human Rights (under its present Rules of Court), and the Inter-American Commission on Human Rights.[5] Bilateral arrangements, such as the U.S.-Mexico Claims Commission of the 1920s and the current Iran–U.S. Claims Tribunal, provide further examples of this trend.[6]

---

3. *See* Rosalyn Higgins, Conceptual Thinking about the Individual in International Law, in *International Law: A Contemporary Perspective* 476–78 (R. Falk et. al., eds. 1985).

4. ICSID was established by the 1965 Convention on the Settlement of Disputes between States and Nationals of Other States, prepared by the World Bank. *See* Aron Broches, *Arbitration Under the ICSID Convention* (ICSID Publication, October 1991); Ibrahim F.I. Shihata, ICSID Arbitration, in *Private Investment Abroad—Problems and Solutions in International Business in 1993* Chapter Sixteen, at 16-1-16-25 (C. Holgren, ed., 1994).

5. *See* Paul Mahoney and Soren Prebensen, The European Court of Human Rights, in *The European System for the Protection of Human Rights* 621, 630–31 (R. MacDonald et al., eds., 1993). *See also*, P.K. Mennon, The International Personality of Individuals in International Law: A Broadening of the Traditional Doctrine, 1 *Journal of Transnational Law and Policy* 51 (1992). *See also*, John H. Whitefield, How the Working Organs of the European Convention Have Elevated the Individual to the Level of Subject of International Law, 12 *ILSA Journal of International Law* 27 (1988); Akos G. Toth, The Individual and European Law, 24 *International and Comparative Law Quarterly* 659 (1975).

6. Under both arrangements, the commission and tribunal respectively were to hear claims of individuals against a state. *See* the 1923 Convention between the U.S. and Mexico referring general claims of citizens of both states

There is a widespread tendency to describe this evolution in terms of developing and strengthening international procedural safeguards for the protection of human rights, with a focus on judicial remedies against the violation of such rights based directly on international legal principles.

However, with the exception of the courts of the European Communities, existing international review mechanisms that have been invoked as possible precedents for the World Bank Inspection Panel are concerned exclusively with the activities of *States,* rather than international organizations. This applies, in particular, to mechanisms in the field of human rights—including the procedures developed within international organizations for this purpose, such as the U.N. Commission for Human Rights[7] and, more recently, the office of the U.N. High Commissioner for Human Rights,[8] and the facilities of the International Labour Organization[9]—as well as the judicial and semi-judicial review mechanisms referred to earlier.

By contrast, review mechanisms of the actions and omissions of international organizations have traditionally been limited to

---

against the other state to a commission and the 1923 Convention between the U.S. and Mexico referring claims of U.S. citizens against Mexico for losses or damages suffered through revolutionary acts between 1910 and 1920 to a commission, both reprinted in *Treaties and Other International Agreements of the United States of America 1776–1949* (Charles I. Bevans, ed., 1972). *See* further the Algiers Declarations establishing the Iran–U.S. Claims Tribunal reprinted in Rahmatullah Khan, *The Iran-United States Claims Tribunal—Controversies, Cases and Contributions* (1990), at 268. For references on the Iran–U.S. Claims Tribunal, *see* Nassib G. Ziadé, Selective Bibliography on the Iran–United States Claims Tribunal, 2 *ICSID Rev.—FILJ 534* (1987).

7. *See* Marc I. Bossuyt, The Development of Special Procedures of the U.N. Commission for Human Rights, 6 *Human Rights Law Journal* 1979–210 (1985); Theodor Meron, *Human Rights Law-Making in the United Nations: A Critique of Instruments and Process* (1986); and A. Williams, The United Nations and Human Rights, in *International Institutions at Work* (P. Taylor & A.J.R. Groom, eds., 1988), at 114–29.

8. *See* U.N. General Assembly Resolution 48/141, Dec. 20, 1993.

9. *See* Ernest A. Landy, *The Effectiveness of International Supervision: Thirty Years of I.L.O. Experience* (1966); and Victor Y. Ghebali, *The International Labour Organization: A Case Study on the Evolution of U.N. Specialized Agencies* (1989).

the review of staff appeals in personnel matters through an administrative tribunal and/or a less formal mechanism, such as a staff "appeals committee" or an "ombudsman."[10] The Bank, which has had a staff appeals committee since 1977, established its Administrative Tribunal in 1980, and, in addition, the office of the staff Ombudsman in 1981.

What was often overlooked was the lack of other, non-adjudicatory, mechanisms that address the *operational* activities of international organizations and aim at introducing greater efficiency in these activities by strengthening the accountability system of such organizations. The World Bank's Inspection Panel provides this type of mechanism, introducing a non-judicial process to assist in ensuring compliance with the internal operational policies and procedures of one of the largest and most effective international organizations. The deterrent effect of this process may be gained by the mere presence of the Panel. Its remedial effects, though ultimately brought about by an organ of the organization itself (the President or the Executive Directors), will also be driven by the Panel through the findings it will reach in each case.

The compelling need for review mechanisms for the operations of international organizations, especially international financial institutions, has made the inspection function replicable so far in two other institutions (though the details differ). This is likely to add demands on other organizations to follow suit. Once accountability to the affected public is postulated as an efficient complementary element in the overall accountability system of an international organizations, it is difficult to see why such an element should be restricted to the World Bank or to multilateral development institutions. Obviously, this would not be the case if the function were to contradict or dilute existing systems of governance and accountability in the organization involved or otherwise hinder its efficient operation.

---

10. *See* Chittharanjan F. Amerasinghe, *The Law of the International Civil Service as Applied by International Administrative Tribunals* 3, 49–81 (Vol. I, 1988).

The concepts of public participation and civic action are also receiving increased recognition in international circles, as demonstrated at the 1992 United Nations Conference on Environment and Development,[11] and as now reflected in World Bank operational policies.[12] Non-governmental organizations in all countries are clearly playing an effective role that is only expected to grow.[13] In a future where governments' actions, including their actions within international organizations, are likely to reflect the growing influence of non-State actors, international organizations will have to adapt their working methods to this new environment. The World Bank Inspection Panel, a reflection of this reality, attempts to reconcile the legitimate concerns of the people who may be affected by Bank-supported projects and the institution's legitimate concern for efficiency.

The establishment of the Panel may serve another related, though unintended, purpose, namely the development of the law of international trusts in the direction of recognizing the interests of ultimate beneficiaries by conferring on them the right to invoke certain procedures regarding the duties of the trustee. International trusts financed by outside donors and administered by an international organization abound at present. The World Bank alone has been trustee for hundreds of trust funds established by agreements between donors and the Bank. These trust arrangements assume that the legal ownership of the funds involved is held by the trustee but funds uncommitted at the expiry of the trust are to be returned eventually to

---

11. *See* Principle 10 of the Rio Declaration on Environment and Development, and Chapter 23 of Agenda *21*; UN Doc. A/CONF. 151/26/Rev. 1, Vol. I, at 5,373 (1992).

12. *See, e.g.,* OD 4.01 on *Environmental Assessment* (October 1991); OD 4.30 on *Involuntary Resettlement* (June 1990); and Good Practice (GP) 14.70 *Involving Non-Governmental Organizations in Bank Supported Activities* (March 1998). *See generally* Robert Picciotto, *Participatory Development: Myths and Dilemmas* (World Bank Publication, 1992); *The World Bank Participation Sourcebook* (World Bank Publication, 1996).

13. *See* Jessica T. Mathews, Power Shift, *Foreign Affairs* (January/February 1997).

the donor.[14] The recipient of the financial assistance provided through a trust fund is typically not a party to the arrangement, except in new types of international trusts where donors and recipients participate in the overall governance of the trust fund, as is the case of the "Interim Multilateral Fund" established under the Montreal Protocol, from which the Bank-administered Ozone Projects Trust Fund is financed.[15] Participation of recipient countries has also been institutionalized in the restructured Global Environment Facility (GEF), the trust fund of which is administered by the Bank.[16] GEF-financed projects administered by the Bank would, under the suggestion made in this book, be subject to the Panel's jurisdiction, insofar as compliance with the Bank's policies and procedures applicable to GEF projects is concerned.[17] In this sense "it may be argued that even 'secondary' trust beneficiaries other than states (in particular, locally affected groups) are now empowered to invoke the Bank's fiduciary duties—to the extent that these have been embodied in rules subject to review by the Panel."[18] Although this does not vest in such beneficiaries "beneficial ownership" of the trust funds,[19] it would bring the international trusts involved a step closer to domestic trusts as known in common law legal

---

14. *See* OD 14.40 on Trust Funds and Reimbursable Programs (December 1990).

15. *See* Jason M. Patlis, The Multilateral Fund of the Montreal Protocol: A Prototype for Financial Mechanisms in Protecting the Global Environment, 25 *Cornell International Law and Trade* 1, 31–36 (1992). *See also* Operational Policy and Bank Procedure (OP/BP) 10.21 on Investment Operations Financed by the Multilateral Fund for the Implementation of the Montreal Protocol (November 1993).

16. Negotiation on the restructuring of the GEF resulted in agreement in March 1994 on a new organizational structure whereby an Assembly of all the participant countries would have an overall oversight over the GEF which would be governed by a separate Council of 32 members in which developed, developing, and transition countries are represented.

17. *See supra* Chapter Two, Section I(A).

18. Peter H. Sand, *Trust for the Earth: New International Financial Mechanisms for Sustainable Development,* 18 (Paper submitted to the Symposium on Sustainable Development and International Law, Baden bei Wien, April 14–16, 1994).

19. *Accord id.*

systems.[20] This would represent a progressive development of international trust law.

In conclusion, in the context of such increased openness by the Bank to the parties ultimately affected by its operations, it is important to recall the initial managerial motive of the Inspection Panel that coincided with the mounting demands on the Bank.[21] Rather than deferring to an abstract democratic ideal of participation—though in full harmony with it—the procedural involvement of affected local people in the work of the Panel aims at two practical concerns: protecting the rights and interests of those parties that may be unintentionally undermined by Bank actions or omissions in violation of its policies, and improving the very process of environmentally and socially sustainable development, which is at the center of the Bank's mandate as interpreted at present.

---

20. For an early analysis of the concept of international trust funds and a comparison of their legal treatment with that of trust funds common law legal systems, *see* Sir Joseph Gold, Trust Funds in International Law: The Contribution of the International Monetary Fund to a Code of Principles, 72 *American Journal of International Law* 856–66 (1978).

21. *See supra*, Chapter One, Section I(A).

Annexes

Annex I
Documents Relating to the Inspection Panel

Annex I–1–1

Resolution Establishing the Inspection Panel —
September 1993

**International Bank for Reconstruction and Development
International Development Association**

Resolution No. IBRD 93–10
Resolution No. IDA 93–6

"The World Bank Inspection Panel"

The Executive Directors:
Hereby resolve:

1. There is established an independent Inspection Panel (here-inafter called the Panel), which shall have the powers and shall function as stated in this resolution.

Composition of the Panel

2. The Panel shall consist of three members of different national-ities from Bank member countries. The President, after consulta-tion with the Executive Directors, shall nominate the members of the Panel to be appointed by the Executive Directors.

3. The first members of the Panel shall be appointed as follows: one for three years, one for four years and one for five years. Each vacancy thereafter shall be filled for a period of five years, pro-vided that no member may serve for more than one term. The term of appointment of each member of the Panel shall be sub-ject to the continuity of the inspection function established by this Resolution.

4. Members of the Panel shall be selected on the basis of their ability to deal thoroughly and fairly with the requests brought to them, their integrity and their independence from the Bank's Management, and their exposure to developmental issues and to living conditions in developing countries. Knowledge and experience of the Bank's operations will also be desirable.

5. Executive Directors, Alternates, Advisors and staff members of the Bank Group may not serve on the Panel until two years have elapsed since the end of their service in the Bank Group. For purposes of this Resolution, the term "staff" shall mean all persons holding Bank Group appointments as defined in Staff Rule 4.01 including persons holding consultant and local consultant appointments.

6. A Panel member shall be disqualified from participation in the hearing and investigation of any request related to a matter in which he/she has a personal interest or had significant involvement in any capacity.

7. The Panel member initially appointed for five years shall be the first Chairperson of the Panel, and shall hold such office for one year. Thereafter, the members of the Panel shall elect a Chairperson for a period of one year.

8. Members of the Panel may be removed from office only by decision of the Executive Directors, for cause.

9. With the exception of the Chairperson who shall work on a full-time basis at Bank headquarters, members of the Panel shall be expected to work on a full-time basis only when their workload justifies such an arrangement, as will be decided by the Executive Directors on the recommendation of the Panel.

10. In the performance of their functions, members of the Panel shall be officials of the Bank enjoying the privileges and immunities accorded to Bank officials, and shall be subject to the requirements of the Bank's Articles of Agreement concerning their exclusive loyalty to the Bank and to the obligations of subparagraphs (c) and (d) of paragraph 3.1 and paragraph 3.2 of the

Principles of Staff Employment concerning their conduct as officials of the Bank. Once they begin to work on a full-time basis, they shall receive remuneration at a level to be determined by the Executive Directors upon a recommendation of the President, plus normal benefits available to Bank fixed-term staff. Prior to that time, they shall be remunerated on a *per diem* basis and shall be reimbursed for their expenses on the same basis as the members of the Bank's Administrative Tribunal. Members of the Panel may not be employed by the Bank Group, following the end of their service on the Panel.

11. The President, after consultation with the Executive Directors, shall assign a staff member to the Panel as Executive Secretary, who need not act on a full-time basis until the workload so justifies. The Panel shall be given such budgetary resources as shall be sufficient to carry out its activities.

Powers of the Panel

12. The Panel shall receive requests for inspection presented to it by an affected party in the territory of the borrower which is not a single individual (i.e., a community of persons such as an organization, association, society or other grouping of individuals), or by the local representative of such party or by another representative in the exceptional cases where the party submitting the request contends that appropriate representation is not locally available and the Executive Directors so agree at the time they consider the request for inspection. Any such representative shall present to the Panel written evidence that he is acting as agent of the party on behalf of which the request is made. The affected party must demonstrate that its rights or interests have been or are likely to be directly affected by an action or omission of the Bank as a result of a failure of the Bank to follow its operational policies and procedures with respect to the design, appraisal and/or implementation of a project financed by the Bank (including situations where the Bank is alleged to have failed in its follow-up on the borrower's obligations under loan agreements with respect to

such policies and procedures) provided in all cases that such failure has had, or threatens to have, a material adverse effect. In view of the institutional responsibilities of Executive Directors in the observance by the Bank of its operational policies and procedures, an Executive Director may in special cases of serious alleged violations of such policies and procedures ask the Panel for an investigation, subject to the requirements of paragraphs 13 and 14 below. The Executive Directors, acting as a Board, may at any time instruct the Panel to conduct an investigation. For purposes of this Resolution, "operational policies and procedures" consist of the Bank's Operational Policies, Bank Procedures and Operational Directives, and similar documents issued before these series were started, and does not include Guidelines and Best Practices and similar documents or statements.

13. The Panel shall satisfy itself before a request for inspection is heard that the subject matter of the request has been dealt with by the Management of the Bank and Management has failed to demonstrate that it has followed, or is taking adequate steps to follow the Bank's policies and procedures. The Panel shall also satisfy itself that the alleged violation of the Bank's policies and procedures is of a serious character.

14. In considering requests under paragraph 12 above, the following requests shall not be heard by the Panel:

(a) Complaints with respect to actions which are the responsibility of other parties, such as a borrower, or potential borrower, and which do not involve any action or omission on the part of the Bank.

(b) Complaints against procurement decisions by Bank borrowers from suppliers of goods and services financed or expected to be financed by the Bank under a loan agreement, or from losing tenderers for the supply of any such goods and services, which will continue to be addressed by staff under existing procedures.

(c) Requests filed after the Closing Date of the loan financing the project with respect to which the request is filed or after the loan financing the project has been substantially disbursed.[1]

(d) Requests related to a particular matter or matters over which the Panel has already made its recommendation upon having received a prior request, unless justified by new evidence or circumstances not known at the time of the prior request.

15. The Panel shall seek the advice of the Bank's Legal Department on matters related to the Bank's rights and obligations with respect to the request under consideration.

Procedures

16. Requests for inspection shall be in writing and shall state all relevant facts, including, in the case of a request by an affected party, the harm suffered by or threatened to such party or parties by the alleged action or omission of the Bank. All requests shall explain the steps already taken to deal with the issue, as well as the nature of the alleged actions or omissions and shall specify the actions taken to bring the issue to the attention of Management, and Management's response to such action.

17. The Chairperson of the Panel shall inform the Executive Directors and the President of the Bank promptly upon receiving a request for inspection.

18. Within 21 days of being notified of a request for inspection, the Management of the Bank shall provide the Panel with evidence that it has complied, or intends to comply with the Bank's relevant policies and procedures.

19. Within 21 days of receiving the response of the Management as provided in the preceding paragraph, the Panel shall determine whether the request meets the eligibility criteria set out in paragraphs 12 to 14 above and shall make a recommendation to the Executive Directors as to whether the matter should be

---

1. This will be deemed to be the case when at least ninety five percent of the loan proceeds have been disbursed.

investigated. The recommendation of the Panel shall be circulated to the Executive Directors for decision within the normal distribution period. In case the request was initiated by an affected party, such party shall be informed of the decision of the Executive Directors within two weeks of the date of such decision.

20. If a decision is made by the Executive Directors to investigate the request, the Chairperson of the Panel shall designate one or more of the Panel's members (Inspectors) who shall have primary responsibility for conducting the inspection. The Inspector(s) shall report his/her (their) findings to the Panel within a period to be determined by the Panel taking into account the nature of each request.

21. In the discharge of their functions, the members of the Panel shall have access to all staff who may contribute information and to all pertinent Bank records and shall consult as needed with the Director General, Operations Evaluation Department and the Internal Auditor. The borrower and the Executive Director representing the borrowing (or guaranteeing) country shall be consulted on the subject matter both before the Panel's recommendation on whether to proceed with the investigation and during the investigation. Inspection in the territory of such country shall be carried out with its prior consent.

22. The Panel shall submit its report to the Executive Directors and the President. The report of the Panel shall consider all relevant facts, and shall conclude with the Panel's findings on whether the Bank has complied with all relevant Bank policies and procedures.

23. Within six weeks from receiving the Panel's findings, Management will submit to the Executive Directors for their consideration a report indicating its recommendations in response to such findings. The findings of the Panel and the actions completed during project preparation also will be discussed in the Staff Appraisal Report when the project is submitted to the Executive Directors for financing. In all cases of a request made by an affected party, the Bank shall, within two weeks of the Executive Directors' consideration of the matter,

inform such party of the results of the investigation and the action taken in its respect, if any.

Decisions of the Panel

24. All decisions of the Panel on procedural matters, its recommendations to the Executive Directors on whether to proceed with the investigation of a request, and its reports pursuant to paragraph 22, shall be reached by consensus and, in the absence of a consensus, the majority and minority views shall be stated.

Reports

25. After the Executive Directors have considered a request for an inspection as set out in paragraph 19, the Bank shall make such request publicly available together with the recommendation of the Panel on whether to proceed with the inspection and the decision of the Executive Directors in this respect. The Bank shall make publicly available the report submitted by the Panel pursuant to paragraph 22 and the Bank's response thereon within two weeks after consideration by the Executive Directors of the report.

26. In addition to the material referred to in paragraph 25, the Panel shall furnish an annual report to the President and the Executive Directors concerning its activities. The annual report shall be published by the Bank.

Review

27. The Executive Directors shall review the experience of the inspection function established by this Resolution after two years from the date of the appointment of the first members of the Panel.

Application to IDA projects

28. In this resolution, references to the Bank and to loans include references to the Association and to development credits.

Annex I–1–2

Operating Procedures of the Inspection Panel —
August 1994

Operating Procedures of the Inspection Panel as Adopted by the Panel on August 19, 1994

Contents

Introduction

The Inspection Panel (the "Panel") is an independent forum established by the Executive Directors of the International Bank for Reconstruction and Development ("IBRD") and the International Development Association ("IDA") by IBRD Resolution No. 93–10 and the identical IDA Resolution No. 93–6 both adopted by the Executive Directors of the respective institutions on September 22, 1993 (collectively the "Resolution"). References in these procedures to the "Bank" includes the IBRD and IDA.

The Panel's authority is dictated by the Resolution: within that framework, these Operating Procedures are adopted by the Panel to provide detail to the operational provisions. The text is based on the Resolution and takes into account suggestions from outside sources.

In view of the unprecedented nature of the new inspection function the current procedures are provisional: the Panel will review them within 12 months, and in light of experience and comments received, will revise them if necessary; and will recommend to the Executive Directors ("Executive Directors") amendments to the Resolution that would allow a more effective role for the Panel.

Composition

The Panel consists of three Inspectors. At the outset, one Inspector, the Chairperson, will work on a full-time basis: the other two will work part-time. This arrangement is provisional. The Panel's workload will be dictated by the number and nature of requests received. If necessary, the Panel will recommend alternative arrangements to the Executive Directors.

Purpose

The Panel has been established for the purpose of providing people directly and adversely affected by a Bank-financed project with an independent forum through which they can request the

Bank to act in accordance with its own policies and procedures. It follows that this forum is available when adversely affected people believe the Bank itself has failed, or has failed to require others, to comply with its policies and procedures, and only after efforts have been made to ask the Bank Management ("Management") itself to deal with the problem.

Functions

The role of the Panel is to carry out independent investigations. Its function, which will be triggered when it receives a request for inspection, is to inquire and recommend: it will make a preliminary review of a request for inspection and the response of Management, independently assess the information and then recommend to the Board of Executive Directors whether or not the matters complained of should be investigated. If the Board decides that a request shall be investigated, the Panel will collect information and provide its findings, independent assessment and conclusions to the Board. On the basis of the Panel's findings and Management's recommendations, the Executive Directors will consider the actions, if any, to be taken by the Bank.

Participants

During the preliminary review period—up to the time the Panel makes a recommendation to the Board on whether or not the matter should be investigated—the Panel will accept statements or evidence from (a) the Requester, i.e. either the affected people and/or their duly appointed representative, or an Executive Director; (b) Management; and, (c) any other individual or entity invited by the Panel to present information or comments.

During an investigation, any person who is either a party to the investigation or who provides the designated Inspector(s) with satisfactory evidence that he/she has an interest, apart from any interest in common with the public, will be entitled to submit information or evidence relevant to the investigation.

Administration

The Panel has approved separate Administrative Procedures which are available from the Office of The Inspection Panel.

I. Subject Matter of Requests

Scope

1. The Panel is authorized to accept requests for inspection ("Request(s)") which claim that an actual or threatened material adverse effect on the affected party's rights or interests arises directly out of an action or omission of the Bank as a result of a failure by the Bank to follow its own operational policies and procedures during the design, appraisal and/or implementation of a Bank financed project. Before submitting a Request steps must have already been taken (or efforts made) to bring the matter to the attention of Management with a result unsatisfactory to the Requester.

Limitations

2. The Panel is not authorized to deal with the following:

   (a) complaints with respect to actions which are the responsibility of other parties, such as the borrower, or potential borrower, and which do not involve any action or omission on the part of the Bank;

   (b) complaints against procurement decisions by Bank borrowers from suppliers of goods and services financed or expected to be financed by the Bank under a loan/credit agreement, or from losing tenderers for the supply of any such goods and services, which will continue to be addressed by Bank staff under existing procedures;

   (c) Requests filed after the Closing Date of the loan/credit financing the project with respect to which the Request is filed or when 95% or more of the loan/credit proceeds have been disbursed; or

(d) Requests related to a particular matter or matters over which the Panel has already made its recommendation after having received a prior Request, unless justified by new evidence or circumstances not known at the time of the prior Request.

II. Preparation of a Request

3.   The Panel's operational proceedings begin when a Request is received. This section of the procedures is primarily designed to give further guidance to potential Requesters on what facts and explanations they should provide.

A. Who Can File a Request?

4.   The Panel has authority to receive Requests which complain of a violation of the Bank's policies and procedures from the following people or entities:

(a) any group of two or more people in the country where the Bank financed project is located who believe that as a result of the Bank's violation their rights or interests have been, or are likely to be adversely affected in a direct and material way. They may be an organization, association, society or other grouping of individuals; or

(b) a duly appointed local representative acting on explicit instructions as the agent of adversely affected people; or

(c) in exceptional cases, referred to in paragraph 11 below, a foreign representative acting as agent of adversely affected people; or

(d) an Executive Director of the Bank in special cases of serious alleged violations of the Bank's policies and procedures.

B. Contents of a Request

5.   In accordance with the Resolution, Requests should contain the following information:

(a)   a description of the project, stating all the relevant facts including the harm suffered by or threatened to the affected party;

(b)   an explanation of how Bank policies, procedures or contractual documents were seriously violated;

(c)   a description of how the act or omission on the part of the Bank has led or may lead to a violation of the specific provision;

(d)   a description of how the party was, or is likely to be, materially and adversely affected by the Bank's act or omission and what rights or interests of the claimant were directly affected;

(e)   a description of the steps taken by the affected party to resolve the violations with Bank staff, and explanation of why the Bank's response was inadequate;

(f)   in Requests relating to matters previously submitted to the Panel, a statement specifying what new evidence or changed circumstances justify the Panel revisiting the issue; and

(g)   if some of the information cannot be provided, an explanation should be included.

C. Form of a Request

Written

6.   All Requests must be submitted in writing, dated and signed by the Requester and contain his/her name and contact address.

Format

7.   No specific form is necessary: a letter will suffice. A Requester may wish to refer to the guidance and use the model form specifying required information. (Attached as Annex 1.)

Language

8.   The working language of the Panel is English. Requests submitted directly by affected people themselves may be in their local language if they are unable to obtain a translation. If requests are not in English, the time needed to translate and ensure an accurate and agreed translation may delay acceptance and consideration by the Panel.

Representatives

9.   If the Requester is a directly affected person or entity representing affected people, written signed proof that the representative has authority to act on their behalf must be attached.

10. If the Request is submitted by a non-affected representative, he/she must provide evidence of representational authority and the names and contact address of the party must be provided. Proof of representational authority, which shall consist of the original signed copy of the affected party's explicit instructions and authorization, must be attached.

11. In addition, in the cases of non-local representation, the Panel will require clear evidence that there is no adequate or appropriate representation in the country where the project is located.

Documents

12. The following documents should be attached:

   (a)   all correspondence with Bank staff;

(b) notes of meetings with Bank staff;

(c) a map or diagram, if relevant, showing the location of the affected party or area affected by the project; and

(d) any other evidence supporting the complaint.

13. If all the information listed cannot be provided an explanation should be included.

D. Delivery of Request

14. Requests must be sent by registered or certified mail or delivered by hand in a sealed envelope against receipt to the Office of the Inspection Panel at 1818 H Street, N.W., Washington, D.C. 20433, U.S.A. or to the Bank's resident representative in the country where the project is located. In the latter case, the resident representative shall, after issuing a receipt to the Requester, forward the Request to the Panel through the next pouch.

E. Advice on Preparation

15. People or entities seeking advice on how to prepare and submit a Request may contact the Office of the Inspection Panel, which will provide information or may meet and discuss the requirements with potential requesters.

III. Procedures on Receipt of a Request

16. When the Panel receives a Request the Chairperson, on the basis of the information contained in the Request, shall either promptly register the Request, or ask for additional information, or find the Request outside the Panel's mandate.

A. Register

17. If the request, appears to contain sufficient required information the chairperson shall register the Request in the Panel

Register; promptly notify the Requester, the Executive Directors and the Bank President ("President") of the registration; and transmit to the President a copy of the Request with the accompanying documentation, if any.

Contents of Notice

18. The notice of registration shall:

(a) record that the Request is registered and indicate the date of the registration and dispatch of that notice;

(b) the notice will include the name of the project, the country where the project is located, the name of the Requester unless anonymity is requested, and a brief description of the Request;

(c) notify the Requester that all communications in connection with the Request will be sent to the address stated in the Request, unless another address is indicated to the Panel Secretariat; and

(d) request Management to provide the Panel, within 21 days after receipt of the notice and Request, with written evidence that it has complied, or intends to comply with the Bank's relevant policies and procedures. The notice shall specify the due date of the response.

B. Request Additional Information

19. If the chairperson finds the contents of the Request or documentation on representation insufficient, he/she may ask the Requester to supply further information.

20. Upon receipt of a Request, the chairperson shall send a written acknowledgement to the Requester, and will specify what additional information is required.

21. The Chairperson may refuse to register a Request until all necessary information and documentation is filed.

C. Outside Scope

22. If the chairperson finds, that the matter is without doubt manifestly outside the Panel's mandate, he/she will notify the Requesters, of his/her refusal to register the Request and of the reasons therefor; this will include but not be limited to the following types of communications:

  (a) Requests which are clearly outside the Panel's mandate including those listed above at paragraph 2;

  (b) Requests which do not show the steps taken or effort made to resolve the matter with Management;

  (c) Requests from an individual or from a non-authorized representative of an affected party;

  (d) any correspondence, including but not limited to letters, memoranda, opinions, submissions or requests on any matter within the Panel's mandate which are not requests for an inspection; and

  (e) Requests that are manifestly frivolous, absurd or anonymous.

Records

23. The number of such Requests and communications received shall be noted in the Register on a quarterly basis and the yearly total included in the Annual Report.

D. Need for Review

24. In cases where additional information is required, or where it is not clear whether a Request is manifestly outside the Panel's mandate, the Chairperson shall designate a Panel member to review the Request.

E. Revised Request

25. If the Requester receives significant new evidence or information at any time after the initial Request was submitted,

he/she may consider whether or not it is serious enough to justify the submission of a revised Request.

26. If a revised Request is submitted, the time periods for Management's response and the Panel recommendation will begin again from the time such Request is registered.

IV. Management's Response

27. Within 21 days after being notified of a Request, Management shall provide the Panel with evidence that it has complied, or intends to comply with the Bank's relevant policies and procedures. After the Panel receives Management's response, it shall promptly enter the date of receipt in the Panel Register.

28. If there is no response from Management within 21 days, the Panel shall notify the President and the Executive Directors and send a copy to the Requester.

Clarification

29. In order to make an informed recommendation, the Panel may request clarification from Management; in the light of Management's response, request more information from the Requester; and provide relevant portions of Management's response for comment. A time limit for receipt of the information requested shall be specified; and

(a) whether or not such clarification or information is received within the time limit, make its recommendation to the Executive Directors within 21 days after receipt of Management's response; or

(b) in the event it is not possible for the Requester to provide the information quickly, the Panel may advise the Requester to submit an amended Request; the Executive Directors and Bank management will be notified that the process will begin again when the amended Request is received.

V. Panel Recommendation

30. Within 21 days after receiving Management's response, the Panel shall make a recommendation to the Executive Directors as to whether the matter should be investigated.

A. Basis

31. The Panel shall prepare its recommendation to the Board on the basis of the information contained in:

(a)   the Request;

(b)   Management's response;

(c)   any further information the Panel may have requested and received from the Requester and/or Management and/or third parties; and

(d)   any findings of the Panel during this stage.

B. Required Criteria

32. If, on the basis of the information contained in the Request, it has not already been established that the Request meets the following three conditions required by the Resolution, the Chairperson, in consultation with the other Panel members may, if necessary, designate a Panel member to conduct a preliminary review to determine whether the Request:

(a)   was filed by an eligible party;

(b)   is not time-barred; and

(c)   relates to a matter falling within the Panel's mandate.

Criteria for Satisfactory Response

33. The Panel may proceed to recommend that there should not be an investigation, if, on the basis of the information contained in the Request and Management's response, the Panel is satisfied that Management has done the following:

    (a) dealt appropriately with the subject matter of the Request; and

    (b) demonstrated clearly that it has followed the required policies and procedures; or

    (c) admitted that it has failed to follow the required policies and procedures but has provided a statement of specific remedial actions and a time-table for implementing them, which will, in the judgment of the Panel, adequately correct the failure and any adverse effects such failure has already caused.

Preliminary Review

34. If, on the basis of the information contained in Management's response and any clarifications provided, the Panel is satisfied that Management has failed to demonstrate that it has followed, or is taking adequate steps to follow the Bank's policies and procedures, the Panel will conduct a preliminary review in order to determine whether conditions required by provisions of the Resolution exist.

35. Although it may not investigate Management's actions in depth at this stage, it will determine whether Management's failure to comply with the Bank's policies and procedures meets the following three conditions:

    (a) whether such failure has had, or threatens to have, a material adverse effect;

    (b) whether, the alleged violation of the Bank's policies and procedures are, in the judgment of the Panel, of a serious character; and

(c) whether remedial actions proposed by Management do not appear adequate to meet the concerns of the Requester as to the application of the Bank's policies and procedures.

Initial Study

36. If the Chairperson considers, after the preliminary review and consultation with the other Panel members, that more factual data not already provided by the Requester, Management or any other source is required to make an informed recommendation to the Executive Directors, he/she may designate a Panel member to undertake a preliminary study. The study may include, but need not be limited to, a desk study and/or a visit to the project site.

C. *Contents*

37. On the basis of the review, the Panel shall make its recommendation to the Board as to whether the matter should be investigated. Every recommendation shall include a clear explanation setting forth reasons for the recommendation and be accompanied by:

(a) the text of the Request and, where applicable, any other relevant information provided by the Requester;

(b) the text of Management's response and, where applicable, any clarifications provided;

(c) the text of any advice received from the Bank's Legal Department;

(d) any other relevant documents or information received; and

(e) statements of the majority and minority views in the absence of a consensus by the Panel.

D. *Submission*

38. The recommendation shall be circulated by the Executive Secretary of the Panel to the Executive Directors for decision. The Panel will notify the Requester that a recommendation has been sent to the Executive Directors.

VI. Board Decision and Public Release

39. The Board decides whether or not to accept or reject the Panel's recommendation; and, if the Requester is a non-local representative, whether exceptional circumstances exist and suitable local representation is not available.

Notification

40. The Panel shall promptly inform the Requester of the Board's decision on whether or not to investigate the Request and, shall send the Requester a copy of the Panel's recommendation.

Public Information

41. After the Executive Directors have considered a Request the Bank shall make such Request publicly available together with the Panel's recommendation on whether to proceed with the inspection and the decision of the Executive Directors in this respect.

VII. An Investigation

A. *Initial Procedures*

42. When a decision to investigate a Request is made by the Board, or the Board itself requests an investigation, the Chairperson shall promptly:

(a) designate one or more of the Panel's members (Inspector(s)) to take primary responsibility for the investigation;

(b) arrange for the Panel members to consult, taking into account the nature of the particular Request, on:

(i) the methods of investigation that at the outset appear the most appropriate;

(ii) an initial schedule for the conduct of the investigation;

(iii) when the Inspector(s) shall report his/her (their) findings to the Panel, including any interim findings; and

(iv) any additional procedures for the conduct of the investigation.

43. The designated Inspector(s) shall, as needed, arrange for a meeting with the Requester and schedule discussions with directly affected people.

44. The name of the Inspector(s) and an initial work plan shall be made public as soon as possible.

B. Methods of Investigation

45. The Panel may, taking into account the nature of the particular Request, use a variety of investigatory methods, including but not limited to:

(a) meetings with the Requester, affected people, Bank staff, government officials and project authorities of the country where the project is located, representatives of local and international non-governmental organizations;

(b) holding public hearings in the project area;

(c) visiting project sites;

(d) requesting written or oral submissions on specific issues from the Requester, affected people, independent experts, government or project officials, Bank staff, or local or international non-governmental organizations;

(e) hiring independent consultants to research specific issues relating to a Request;

(f) researching Bank files; and

(g) any other reasonable methods the Inspector(s) consider appropriate to the specific investigation.

Consent Required

46. In accordance with the Resolution, physical inspection in the country where the project is located will be carried out with prior consent. The Chairperson shall request the Executive Director representing such country to provide written consent.

C. Participation of Requester

47. During the course of the investigation, in addition to any information requested by the Inspector(s), the Requester (and affected people if the Requester is a non-affected Representative or an Executive Director) or Bank staff may provide the Inspector(s) either directly or through the Executive Secretary with supplemental information that they believe is relevant to evaluating the Request.

48. The Inspector(s) may notify the Requester of any new material facts provided by Bank staff or by the Executive Director for, or authorities in the country where the project is located.

49. To facilitate understanding of specific points, the Panel may discuss its preliminary findings of fact with the Requester.

D. Participation of Third Parties

50. During the course of the investigation, in addition to any information requested by the Inspector(s), any member of the

public may provide the Inspector(s), either directly or through the Executive Secretary, with supplemental information that they believe is relevant to evaluating the Request.

51. Information should not exceed ten pages and include a one-page summary. Supporting documentation may be listed and attached. The Inspector(s) may request more details if necessary.

VIII. Panel Report

Contents

52. The report of the Panel (the "Report") shall include the following:

    (a) a summary discussion of the relevant facts and of the steps taken to conduct the investigation;

    (b) a conclusion showing the Panel's findings on whether the Bank has complied with relevant Bank policies and procedures;

    (c) a list of supporting documents which will be available on request from the Office of the Inspection Panel; and

    (d) statements of the majority and minority views in the absence of a consensus by the Panel.

Submission

53. Upon completion of the Report, the Panel shall submit it to:

    (a) the Executive Directors: accompanied by notification that the Report is being submitted to the President on the same date; and

    (b) the President: accompanied by a notice against receipt that within 6 weeks of receipt of the Report, Management must submit to the Executive Directors for their consideration a report indicating Management's recommendations in response to the Panel's findings.

IX. Management's Recommendations

54. Within 6 weeks after receiving the Panel's findings, Management will submit to the Executive Directors for their consideration a report indicating its recommendations in response to the Panel's findings. Upon receipt of a copy of the report, the Panel will notify the Requester.

X. Board Decision and Public Release

55. Within 2 weeks after the Executive Directors consider the Panel's Report and the Management's response, the Bank shall inform the Requester of the results of the investigation and the action decided by the Board, if any.

56. After the Bank has informed the Requester, the Bank shall make publicly available:

(a) the Panel's Report;

(b) Management's recommendations; and

(c) the Board's decision.

These documents will also be available at the Office of the Inspection Panel.

57. The Panel will seek to enhance public awareness of the results of investigations through all available information sources.

XI. General

Business Days

58. "Days" under these procedures means days on which the Bank is open for business in Washington, D.C.

Copies

59. Consideration of Requests and other documents submitted throughout the process will be expedited if an original and two

copies are filed. When any document contains extensive supporting documentation the Panel may ask for additional copies.

Consultations

60. The borrower and the Executive Director representing the borrowing (or guaranteeing) country shall be consulted on the subject matter before the Panel's recommendation and during an investigation.

Access to Bank Staff and Information

61. Pursuant to the Resolution and in discharge of their functions, the members of the Panel shall have access to all Bank staff who may contribute information and to all pertinent Bank records and shall consult as needed with the Director General, Operations Evaluation Department, and the Internal Auditor.

Legal Advice

62. The Panel shall seek, through the Vice President and General Counsel of the Bank, the written advice of the Bank's Legal Department on matters related to the Bank's rights and obligations with respect to the Request under consideration. Any such advice will be included as an attachment to the Panel's recommendation and/or Report to the Executive Directors.

Confidentiality

63. Documents, or portions of documents of a confidential nature will not be released by the Panel without the express written consent of the party concerned.

Information to Requester and Public

64. The Executive Secretary shall record in the Register all actions taken in connection with the processing of the Request, the dates thereof, and the dates on which any document or notification under these procedures is received in or sent from the Office of the Inspection Panel. The Requester shall be informed promptly. The Register will be publicly available.

65. A notice that a Request has been registered and all other notices or documents issued by the Panel will be available to the public through the Bank's PIC in Washington, D.C.; at the Bank's Resident Mission in the country where the project is located or at the relevant regional office; at the Bank's Paris, London and Tokyo offices; or on request from the Executive Secretary of the Panel.

Annex 1
Guidance on How to Prepare a Request for Inspection

The Inspection Panel needs some basic information in order to process a Request for Inspection:

1. Name, contact address and telephone number of the group or people making the request.
2. Name and description of the Bank project.
3. Adverse effects of the Bank project.
4. If you are a representative of affected people attach explicit written instructions from them authorizing you to act on their behalf.

These key questions must be answered:

1. Can you elaborate on the nature and importance of the damage caused by the project to you or those you represent?
2. Do you know that the Bank is responsible for the aspects of the project that has or may affect you adversely? How did you determine this?
3. Are you familiar with Bank policies and procedures that apply to this type of project? How do you believe the Bank may have violated them?
4. Have you contacted or attempted to contact Bank staff about the project? Please provide information about all contacts, and the responses, if any, you received from the Bank. You must have done this *before* you can file a request.
5. Have you tried to resolve your problem through any other means?
6. If you know that the Panel has dealt with this matter before, do you have new facts or evidence to submit?

Please provide a summary of the information in no more than a few pages. Attach as much other information as you think necessary as separate documents. Please note and identify attachments in your summary.

You may wish to use the attached model form.

Annex 2
Model Form: Request for Inspection

To: The Inspection Panel:
1818 H St., N.W., Washington, D.C. 20433, U.S.A.

We, _____, and _____, and other persons whose names and addresses are attached live/represent others, living in the area known as: _____
_____ [and shown in the attached map or diagram] claim the following:

1. The Bank is financing the design/appraisal and/or implementation of a project [name and brief description]

2. We understand that the Bank has the following policy(ies) and/or procedures [list or describe]:

3. Our rights/interests are [describe]:

4. The Bank has violated its own policies/procedures in this way:

5. We believe our rights/interests have been, are likely to be adversely affected as a direct result of the Bank's violation. This is, or is likely to cause us to suffer [describe harm]:

6. We believe the action/omission is the responsibility of the Bank.

7. We have complained/made an effort to complain to Bank staff by [describe]:

Please attach evidence or explanation.

8. We received no response; or

We believe that the response(s) (attached/not attached) is unsatisfactory because [describe why]:

9. In addition we have taken the following steps to resolve our problem:

We therefore believe that the above actions/omissions which are contrary to the above policies or procedures have materially and adversely affected our rights/interests and request the Panel to recommend to the Bank's Executive Directors that an investigation of these matters be carried out in order to resolve the problem.

As advised in your Operating Procedures, this Request for Inspection is brief. We can provide you with more particulars.

Date: _____

Signatures: _____

Contact Address: _____

_____

_____

Attachments: [Yes][No]
We authorize you to make this
Request public [Yes][No]

Annex I–1–3

*Administrative Procedures of the Inspection Panel —
July 1998*

Administrative Procedures of the Inspection Panel

(As Amended by the Panel on July 10, 1998)

Contents

Introductory Notes

Introductory Notes

A. The Inspection Panel (the "Panel") was established by the Executive Directors of the International Bank for Reconstruction and Development ("IBRD") and the International Development Association ("IDA") by IBRD Resolution No. 93–10 and the identical IDA Resolution No. 93–6, both adopted by the Executive Directors of the respective institutions on September 22, 1993 (collectively the "Resolution"). These provisional Administrative Procedures ("Procedures") are adopted by the Panel pursuant to paragraph 24 of the Resolution establishing the Panel. They are designed to implement certain powers and obligations of the Panel. They are intended to be complementary both to the provisions of the Resolution and to the Operating Procedures adopted by the Panel on August 19, 1994. The Procedures should similarly be considered as complementary to any ad hoc procedures adopted by the Panel for the conduct of a particular investigation pursuant to the Operating Procedures. In light of experience these Procedures may be revised as considered necessary by the Panel.

B. References in these Procedures to the "Bank" include the IBRD and IDA and references to the "Executive Directors" mean the Executive Directors of the Bank.

C. Please note that all headings are for ease of reference only. They do not form part of these Procedures and do not constitute an interpretation thereof.

Part I—Panel Meetings

Dates and Location

1. The Panel shall hold an Annual Meeting and other meetings as circumstances require. Meetings shall be convened at dates and locations fixed by the Chairperson.

Notices

2. The Executive Secretary shall use any rapid means of communication to give notice to Panel members of the time and place of each meeting not less than 21 days in advance of the date fixed, except that in urgent cases notice shall be given not less than 7 days prior to such date.

Quorum

3. A quorum for any meeting shall be 2 members of the Panel.

Agenda

4. Under the direction of the Chairperson, the Executive Secretary shall prepare a brief agenda for each meeting and transmit it with notice of the meeting. Additional items may be placed on the agenda by any Panel member at no less than 3 days notice.

Attendance

5. (a) Meetings shall be attended by Panel members, the Executive Secretary and staff designated by the Chairperson.

   (b) The Panel may invite any other persons.

   (c) At the Chairperson's discretion, meetings may be conducted by conference call.

Chair

6. The Chairperson, or in his/her absence a Panel member designated by the Chairperson, shall preside over all meetings of the Panel.

Decisions

7. (a) Election of the Chairperson, decisions on procedural matters, recommendations to the Executive Directors, reports of investigations, and adoption of the Annual Report shall be reached by consensus, and in the absence of consensus the majority and minority views shall be recorded in the minutes of the meeting.

   (b) Decisions on administrative matters shall be reached by consensus and in the absence of consensus will be decided by the Chairperson.

   (c) When, in the judgment of the Chairperson, an administrative or procedural action must be taken by the Panel which cannot be postponed until the next meeting or does not warrant the calling of a special meeting, the Chairperson, after consulting with the Panel members by any rapid means of communication, shall act or take such decision without meeting. Such actions will be confirmed by the Panel at its next meeting.

Secretary and Minutes

8. (a) The Executive Secretary shall act as Secretary of the Panel's meetings.

   (b) Except as otherwise specifically directed by the Panel, the Executive Secretary, in consultation with the Chairperson, shall be in charge of making and supervising all arrangements for Panel meetings.

   (c) At the request of any Panel Member: (i) the Executive Secretary shall prepare summary records of the proceedings of the Panel and provide the members with copies; (ii) verbatim records of his/her statements shall be included by the Executive Secretary in the summary records.

(d) Draft minutes shall be circulated to Panel members as promptly as possible after meetings. Such minutes shall be approved by the Panel on a no objection basis or at their next meeting. Verbatim records will be included in the summary record if a Panel member requests that his/her remarks be written down.

(e) Draft minutes shall be circulated to Panel members as promptly as possible after meetings. Such minutes shall be approved by the Panel on a no objection basis or at their next meeting.

Annual Report

9. The Annual Report on the operations of the Panel shall be approved at the Annual Meeting. The Report will be published by the Bank. Copies of the Report will be available on request from the Office of the Inspection Panel.

Part II—The Panel

Independence

10. The Panel is an independent forum. Any attempt to interfere with the functioning of the Panel for political or economic reasons or exert political or other influence on the Panel shall be made public.

11. The Panel members shall serve on the Panel in their individual capacity.

Impartiality

12. Recommendations and findings of the Panel shall be strictly impartial: only facts relevant to the Request or investigation under consideration shall be relevant to their decisions. Consideration of political factors shall be strictly prohibited.

Responsibility

13. The Panel members shall be responsible for the general operations of the Panel.

Communications

14. In general the Panel members shall communicate by any rapid means of communication as frequently as the workload demands. In connection with each Request for Inspection ("Request(s)") in progress, the part-time Panel member designated to conduct a preliminary review and/or an investigation will receive all documents and records of communications. The other Panel member(s) will receive notice of the documents received and a summary of activities on a weekly basis.

Election of Chairperson

15. The Chairperson of the Panel shall hold office for one year and will be elected by the Panel members annually at the Annual Meeting.

Resignation of Panel Members or the Chairperson

16 (a) If a Member resigns from, or is unable to serve on, the Panel, the other Panel Members will constitute the Panel until a new Member is appointed by the Executive Directors.

(b) If the Member that resigns or becomes unable to serve on the Panel is the Chairperson, the other Members shall decide who among them will serve as Acting Chairperson until such time as the Executive Directors appoint a new member, and an election of a new Chairperson can take place.

17. If the Chairperson resigns or is unable to act as a Chairperson but remains as a Panel Member, all the Panel Members may elect a new Chairperson for the remainder of his/her term or for the full one-year term referred to in paragraph 7 of the Resolution.

Recommendation for Full-Time Work

18. The Chairperson, with the agreement of the other Panel members, may recommend to the Executive Directors, the employment on a full-time basis of one or more of the part-time Panel members when, in his/her judgment, this is justified by the workload.

Disqualification

19. A Panel member shall not participate in the preliminary review and investigation of any Request related to a matter in which he/she has a personal interest or had significant involvement in any capacity. A Panel member shall disclose to the Chairperson any circumstances, which might be deemed to affect his/her impartiality or independence.

20.   A Panel member who becomes aware, in the course of a preliminary review or investigation, of any circumstances which may disqualify him/her must immediately inform the Chairperson.

Part III—The Chairperson

Responsibility

21. The Chairperson shall be responsible for the daily operations of the Panel, external relations, organization of the Panel members and allocation of tasks, and the functions and administration of the Secretariat.

Publicity

22. The Chairperson shall be the spokesperson for the Panel and, after consultation with the Panel members, make all formal

public statements on behalf of the Panel as a whole. Panel members making any other statements must make it clear they are doing so in a personal capacity.

Delegation of Authority

23. The Chairperson may delegate his/her authority to any other Panel member or, after consultation with the Panel, may delegate any of his/her administrative authority and functions to the Executive Secretary.

Acting Chairperson

24. The Chairperson shall appoint another Panel member or the Executive Secretary to act in his/her absence or in the event of his/her inability to act. The functions of the Executive Secretary, if appointed, shall be limited to administrative and routine procedural matters.

Appointment of Inspector(s)

25. The Chairperson shall designate the Panel member(s) to be primarily responsible for the conduct of a preliminary review or initial study or investigation.

Inability of Inspector(s) to Complete an Initial Review or Inspection

26. If the Inspector(s) designated by the Chairperson should resign or be unable to complete an initial study or investigation, the Chairperson shall promptly designate another Panel member to replace him/her.

27. Any such succeeding Inspector shall continue to conduct the initial study or investigation according to the same procedures and requirements as his/her predecessor.

28. If no other Panel member is able to undertake responsibility for completion of an investigation, the Chairperson or any Panel member shall propose another candidate(s) who shall meet the same eligibility criteria as contained in the Resolution appointing Panel members and who shall be appointed by the Executive Directors acting on the unanimous recommendation of the Panel.

Secretariat: Authority of the Chairperson

29. The Executive Secretary and the members of the staff, whether on direct appointment or on secondment, shall act solely under the direction of the Chairperson and the Panel.

30. The Chairperson shall have authority to impose disciplinary measures in accordance with the provisions of the Bank's Staff Manual and other applicable instruments.

Part IV—The Secretariat

The Executive Secretary

31. Under the general direction of the Chairperson, and in addition to what is otherwise specifically provided for in the Resolution and in these Procedures, the Executive Secretary shall be responsible for support and daily administration of the Panel's operations; the operation and administration of the Secretariat, and organization of staff.

Acting Executive Secretary

32. In consultation with the Chairperson, the Executive Secretary may appoint an Assistant who shall act for him/her in his/her absence or in the event of his/her inability to act.

Appointment of Staff Members

33. The Executive Secretary, in consultation with the Chairperson, shall select the members of the staff of the Secretariat. Appointments may be made directly or by secondment from the Bank in accordance with the provisions of the Bank's Staff Manual and other applicable instruments.

Independence

34. The Executive Secretary and the staff of the Secretariat shall be committed to the functions and role of the Panel. Any attempt by Bank member countries, non-governmental and other organizations, the Executive Directors, or Bank staff to interfere with or influence staff of the Secretariat in the discharge of their functions shall be reported to the Panel.

Part V—Requests for Inspection: General Administrative Functions

General

35. The Panel's Operating Procedures provide general guidance on the submission and processing of Requests.

Procedures for a Preliminary Review

36. The Chairperson, in consultation with the other Panel members as needed, shall in light of the nature and complexity of the Request, decide how a preliminary review shall be conducted.

The Register and Depository Functions

37. The Secretariat shall establish and maintain a Register for Requests to record notices and summaries of all other significant

data concerning the commencement, conduct and disposition of a Request. The Register shall be open to the public.

38. The original text of the said notices and summaries, as well as all documents submitted or prepared in connection with any Request, shall be deposited in the archives of the Panel.

Means of Communication

39. The Chairperson shall be the official channel for written communications and may delegate this function to the Executive Secretary. Evidence and documents shall be introduced into the proceeding by transmitting them to the Chairperson or Executive Secretary, who shall retain the original for the Panel files and arrange for distribution of copies and notices.

Place of Meetings and Proceedings

40. The Secretariat shall be responsible for making and supervising arrangements for proceedings held in Washington, D.C. or elsewhere.

Time Limits and Notices

41. The Executive Secretary shall be responsible for computing time limits specified in the Resolution or by the Panel and for the dispatch of all notices relating to a Request.

Supporting Documentation

42. The Executive Secretary shall compile a document bank (a compilation of essential documents from all sources). After the document bank has been established, the parties to the Request

or any other persons will be expected not to attach copies of any document in the bank to their reports, evidence or submissions etc., but to refer to it, giving the document number: this is to avoid adding to the paper load.

43. When any additional material is made available to a Panel member during the preliminary review period, or to the Inspector(s) leading an investigation, he/she shall promptly inform the other Panel members and provide copies of such material on request. The Chairperson, in consultation with the other Panel members, will determine whether such additional material shall be added to the document bank.

Confidentiality

44. Documents of a confidential nature will not be released without the express written consent of the party concerned.

Part VI—An Investigation: Lead Inspector

Responsibilities

45. Upon designation by the Chairperson, the Inspector(s) with primary responsibility for an investigation shall prepare and present for consideration and adoption by the Panel, a proposal containing but not limited to:

(a) procedures for the conduct of the investigation;

(b) an initial estimate of the professional and administrative support needed to carry out the investigation and the budgetary resources required for these purposes.

46. The Inspector(s) in charge will make every effort to carry out the investigation within the initial budgetary allocation approved by the Panel.

47. If in the course of the investigation, the Inspector(s) decides that the initial procedures are inadequate he/she shall promptly prepare an amended proposal for consideration by the Panel.

48. The Executive Secretary, under the direction of the Chairperson, shall be responsible for:

(a) administrative and logistical support,

(b) administration of the budgetary allocations for each case.

Employment of Consultants/Experts/Researchers

49. The Inspector(s) shall have responsibility for the appointment of any consultants and/or researchers and/or technical experts he/she considers necessary to carry out the investigation. The selection and employment of consultants shall be made in accordance with the principles and procedures applicable to the hiring of consultants by the Bank. In addition the Panel shall establish an independent roster of consultants.

50. The Executive Secretary, under the general direction of the Chairperson, shall be responsible for administration of the employment of such consultants/researchers/technical experts.

Oral Hearings

51. The Inspector(s) having primary responsibility for an investigation shall decide in each case whether oral hearings are necessary for gathering information relevant to the particular matter.

Preparation of Report

52. The Inspector(s) shall prepare a Report and submit it to the Panel through the Chairperson for consideration and adoption.

53. The Secretariat shall assist the Inspector(s) in the preparation of the Report.

Resources of Secretariat

54. If, during an investigation the Inspector(s) considers that
there are not enough Secretariat staff to assist him/her in carrying out the investigation, he/she shall recommend to the
Chairperson the employment, and specify the qualifications
required, of extra temporary staff. The Chairperson shall decide
whether extra Secretariat staff is required.

Part VII—Budget

55. The expenses of the Panel and the Secretariat shall be provided by the Bank, which shall give the Panel such budgetary
resources as shall be sufficient to carry out its activities. The Panel
will inform the Bank of the level of resources required to carry
out its mandate.

Part VIII—Miscellaneous

Immunities and Privileges: Certificates of Official Travel

56. The Executive Secretary may issue certificates to the following persons indicating that they are traveling in connection with
a proceeding under the Resolution: members of the Panel, officers and employees of the Secretariat; and as needed to
Requesters, consultants, witnesses and experts appearing in any
proceedings authorized by the Panel.

Business Days

57. "Days" under these procedures means days on which the
World Bank is open for business in Washington, D.C.

Language

58. The working language of the Panel shall be English.

Publications

59. The Panel shall request the Secretariat to prepare, publish and/or disseminate any material it considers will help in the understanding of its role and the preparation of Requests by affected parties.

Annex I-2

Board Classifications Resulting from the First Review of the Panel's Experience — October 1996

1996 Review of the Resolution Establishing the Inspection Panel

Clarification of Certain Aspects of the Resolution

The Resolution establishing the Inspection Panel calls for a review after two years from the date of appointment of the first panel members. On October 17, 1996, the Executive Directors of the Bank and IDA completed the review process (except for the question of inspection of World Bank Group private sector projects) by considering and endorsing the clarifications recommended by Management on the basis of the discussions of the Executive Directors' Committee on Development Effectiveness (CODE). The Inspection Panel and Management are requested by the Executive Directors to observe the clarifications in their application of the Resolution. The clarifications are set out below.

The Panel's Function

Since the Resolution limits the first phase of the inspection process to ascertaining the eligibility of the request, this phase should normally be completed within the 21 days stated in the Resolution. However, in cases where the Inspection Panel believes that it would be appropriate to undertake a "preliminary assessment" of the damages alleged by the requester (in particular when such preliminary assessment could lead to a resolution of the matter without the need for a full investigation), the Panel may undertake the preliminary assessment and indicate to the Board the date on which it would present its findings and recommendations as to the need, if any, for a full investigation. If such a date is expected by the Panel to exceed eight weeks from the date of receipt of Management's comments, the Panel should seek Board approval for the extension, possibly on a "no-objection" basis. What is needed at this preliminary stage is not to establish that a serious violation of the Bank's policy has actually resulted in damages suffered by the affected party, but rather to establish whether the complaint is *prima facie* justified and warrants a full investigation because it is eligible under the Resolution. Panel investigations will continue to result in "findings" and the Board will continue to act on investigations on the basis of recommendations of Management with respect to such remedial action as may be needed.

Eligibility and Access

It is understood that the "affected party" which the Resolution describes as "a community of persons such as an organization, association, society or other grouping of individuals" includes any two or more persons who share some common interests or concerns.

The word "project" as used in the Resolution has the same meaning as it generally has in the Bank's practice, and includes projects under consideration by Bank management as well as projects already approved by the Executive Directors.

The Panel's mandate does not extend to reviewing the consistency of the Bank's practice with *any* of its policies and procedures, but, as stated in the Resolution, is limited to cases of alleged failure by the Bank to follow its operational policies and procedures *with respect to the design, appraisal and/or implementation of projects,* including cases of alleged failure by the bank to follow-up on the borrowers' obligations under loan agreements, with respect to such policies and procedures.

No procurement action is subject to inspection by the Panel, whether taken by the Bank or by a borrower. A separate mechanism is available for addressing procurement-related complaints.

Outreach

Management will make its response to requests for inspection available to the public within three days after the Board has decided on whether to authorize the inspection. Management will also make available to the public opinions of the General Counsel related to Inspection Panel matters promptly after the Executive Directors have dealt with the issues involved, unless the Board decides otherwise in a specific case.

Management will make significant efforts to make the Inspection Panel better known in borrowing countries, but will not provide technical assistance or funding to potential requesters.

Composition of the Panel

No change in the composition of the Panel is being made at this time.

Role of the Board

The Board will continue to have authority to (i) interpret the Resolution; and (ii) authorize inspections. In applying the Resolution to specific cases, the Panel will apply it as it understands it, subject to the Board's review. As stated in the Resolution, "[t]he Panel shall seek the advice of the Bank's Legal Department on matters related to the Bank's rights and obligations with respect to the request under consideration."

October 17, 1996

Annex I–3

Board Conclusions of the Second Review
of the Panel's Experience — April 1999

Conclusions of the Board's Second Review of the Inspection Panel

The Executive Directors approved today, April 20, 1999, with immediate effect, the report of the Working Group on the Second Review of the Inspection Panel, as revised in light of the extensive consultations that took place after the report was first circulated.

The report confirms the soundness of the Resolution establishing the Inspection Panel (IBRD Resolution No. 93–10, IDA Resolution No. 93–6 of September 22, 1993, hereinafter "the Resolution") and provides clarifications for its application. These clarifications supplement the clarifications issued by the Board on October 17, 1996 and prevail over them in case of conflict. The report's recommendations approved by the Board are as follows:

1. The Board reaffirms the Resolution, the importance of the Panel's function, its independence and integrity.

2. Management will follow the Resolution. It will not communicate with the Board on matters associated with the request for inspection, except as provided for in the Resolution. It will thus direct its response to the request, including any steps it intends to take to address its failures, if any, to the Panel. Management will report to the Board any recommendations it may have, after the Panel completes its inspection and submits its findings, as envisaged in paragraph 23 of the Resolution.

3. In its initial response to the request for inspection, Management will provide evidence that

    i. it has complied with the relevant Bank operational policies and procedures; or that

ii. there are serious failures attributable exclusively to its own actions or omissions in complying, but that it intends to comply with the relevant policies and procedures; or that

iii. the serious failures that may exist are exclusively attributable to the borrower or to other factors external to the Bank; or that

iv. the serious failures that may exist are attributable both to the Bank's non-compliance with the relevant operational policies and procedures and to the borrower or other external factors.

The Inspection Panel may independently agree or disagree, totally or partially, with Management's position and will proceed accordingly.

4. When Management responds, admitting serious failures that are attributable exclusively or partly to the Bank, it will provide evidence that it has complied or intends to comply with the relevant operating policies and procedures. This response will contain only those actions that the Bank has implemented or can implement by itself.

5. The Inspection Panel will satisfy itself as to whether the Bank's compliance or evidence of intention to comply is adequate, and reflect this assessment in its reporting to the Board.

6. The Panel will determine the eligibility of a request for inspection independently of any views that may be expressed by Management. With respect to matters relating to the Bank's rights and obligations with respect to the request under consideration, the Panel will seek the advice of the Bank's Legal Department as required by the Resolution.

7. For its recommendation on whether an investigation should be carried out, the Panel will satisfy itself that all the eligibility criteria provided for in the Resolution have been met. It will base its recommendation on the information presented in the request, in the Management response, and on other documentary evidence. The Panel may decide to visit the project country if it believes that this is necessary to

establish the eligibility of the request. In respect of such field visits, the Panel will not report on the Bank's failure to comply with its policies and procedures or its resulting material adverse effect; any definitive assessment of a serious failure of the Bank that has caused material adverse effect will be done after the Panel has completed its investigation.

8. The original time limit, set forth in the Resolution for both Management's response to the request and the Panel's recommendation, will be strictly observed except for reasons of *force majeure*, i.e. reasons that are clearly beyond Management's or the Panel's control, respectively, as may be approved by the Board on a no objection basis.

9. If the Panel so recommends, the Board will authorize an investigation without making a judgement on the merits of the claimants' request, and without discussion except with respect to the following technical eligibility criteria:

(a) The affected party consists of any two or more persons with common interests or concerns and who are in the borrower's territory (Resolution para.12).

(b) The request does assert in substance that a serious violation by the Bank of its operational policies and procedures has or is likely to have a material adverse effect on the requester (Resolution paras. 12 and 14a).

(c) The request does assert that its subject matter has been brought to Management's attention and that, in the requester's view, Management has failed to respond adequately demonstrating that it has followed or is taking steps to follow the Bank's policies and procedures (Resolution para. 13).

(d) The matter is not related to procurement (Resolution para. 14b).

(e) The related loan has not been closed or substantially disbursed (Resolution para. 14c).

(f) The Panel has not previously made a recommendation on the subject matter or, if it has, that the request

does assert that there is new evidence or circumstances not known at the time of the prior request
(Resolution para. 14d).

10. Issues of interpretation of the Resolution will be cleared
with the Board.

11. The "preliminary assessment" concept, as described in
the October 1996 Clarification, is no longer needed. The
paragraph entitled "The Panel's Function" in the October
1996 "Clarifications" is thus deleted.

12. The profile of Panel activities, in-country, during the
course of an investigation, should be kept as low as possible
in keeping with its role as a fact-finding body on behalf of the
Board. The Panel's methods of investigation should not create the impression that it is investigating the borrower's performance. However, the Board, acknowledging the
important role of the Panel in contacting the requesters and
in fact-finding on behalf of the Board, welcomes the Panel's
efforts to gather information through consultations with
affected people. Given the need to conduct such work in an
independent and low-profile manner, the Panel—and
Management—should decline media contacts while an investigation is pending or underway. Under those circumstances
in which, in the judgement of the Panel or Management, it is
necessary to respond to the media, comments should be limited to the process. They will make it clear that the Panel's
role is to investigate the Bank and not the borrower.

13. As required by the Resolution, the Panel's report to the
Board will focus on whether there is a serious Bank failure to
observe its operational policies and procedures with respect
to project design, appraisal and/or implementation. The
report will include all relevant facts that are needed to understand fully the context and basis for the panel's findings and
conclusions. The Panel will discuss in its written report only
those material adverse effects, alleged in the request, that
have totally or partially resulted from serious Bank failure of
compliance with its policies and procedures. If the request
alleges a material adverse effect and the Panel finds that it is

not totally or partially caused by Bank failure, the Panel's report will so state without entering into analysis of the material adverse effect itself or its causes.

14. For assessing material adverse effect, the without-project situation should be used as the base case for comparison, taking into account what baseline information may be available. Non-accomplishments and unfulfilled expectations that do not generate a material deterioration compared to the without-project situation will not be considered as a material adverse effect for this purpose. As the assessment of material adverse effect in the context of the complex reality of a specific project can be difficult, the Panel will have to exercise carefully its judgement on these matters, and be guided by Bank policies and procedures where relevant.

15. A distinction has to be made between Management's report to the Board (Resolution para. 23), which addresses Bank failure and possible Bank remedial efforts and "action plans," agreed between the borrower and the Bank, in consultation with the requesters, that seek to improve project implementation. The latter "action plans" are outside the purview of the Resolution, its 1996 "Clarification," and these clarifications. In the event of agreement by the Bank and borrower on an action plan for the project, Management will communicate to the Panel the nature and outcomes of consultations with affected parties on the action plan. Such an action plan, if warranted, will normally be considered by the Board in conjunction with the Management's report, submitted under Resolution para. 23.

16. The Panel may submit to the Executive Directors for their consideration a report on their view of the adequacy of consultations with affected parties in the preparation of the action plans. The Board should not ask the Panel for its view on other aspects of the action plans nor would it ask the Panel to monitor the implementation of the action plans. The Panel's view on consultation with affected parties will be based on the information available to it by all means, but additional country visits will take place only by government invitation.

17. The Board underlines the need for Management to make significant efforts to make the Inspection Panel better known in borrowing countries, as specified in the 1996 "Clarifications."

18. The Board emphasizes the importance of prompt disclosure of information to claimants and the public, as stipulated in the Resolution (paras. 23 and 25) and in its "1996 Clarifications." The Board requires that such information be provided by Management to claimants in their language, to the extent possible.

19. The Board recognizes that enhancing the effectiveness of the Inspection Panel process through the above clarifications assumes adherence to them by all parties in good faith. It also assumes the borrowers' consent for field visits envisaged in the Resolution. If these assumptions prove to be incorrect, the Board will revisit the above conclusions.

Annex I–4

January 3, 1995

Role of the Inspection Panel in the Preliminary Assessment of Whether to Recommend Inspection

Legal Opinion of the Senior Vice President and General Counsel

Introduction

The Purpose of this Memorandum

During their meeting on December 20, 1994, the Executive Directors heard a statement from the Vice President, South Asia on the Arun III Project in Nepal. In their comments several Executive Directors emphasized the role of the Board in the inspection process and asked for my views on the scope of the role expected from the Panel at the initial stage of recommending inspection. Following this meeting, an Executive Director circulated a note requesting, my "comments on the Panel's report" which recommended that the requests for inspection related to the Arun III Project be investigated.[1] This memorandum is written in response to the questions raised by these Executive Directors.

The purpose of this memorandum is to explain what the Executive Directors' Resolution 93–10 establishing the Panel (the Resolution) requires from the Panel at the early stage preceding the Executive Directors' decision on whether to authorize investigation of a request for inspection. Such an explanation may

---

1. Memo from Mr. Evans, Executive Director, dated December 21, 1994.

be useful in guiding the work of the Panel and the Executive Directors triggered by such a request.[2] By contrast, this memorandum is not meant to pass any judgment on the Panel's actual preliminary report on the Arun III Project dated December 16, 1994.[3] Nor is it meant to influence the position to be taken by the Executive Directors on the recommendations of this report. Only the Board of Executive Directors is to pass judgment on the Panel's report and to act on its recommendations.

Establishing Eligibility: The Panel's Jurisdiction (Competence) and the Admissibility of the Request for Inspection

The Panel is not a judicial body. Yet, as described in the Resolution, its preliminary assessment of whether inspection is warranted could be likened to the process whereby a tribunal establishes its "jurisdiction" and the "admissibility" of the claim before it. In both cases, the conditions of invoking the forum's competence or jurisdiction have to be met and the claim has to be admissible before the forum, but neither implies a conclusion on the merits of the claim. This means that the Panel has to satisfy itself at this early stage that both the "request" and the "requester" are eligible under the Resolution and are not barred by any provision in the Resolution. Eligibility has three dimensions: one related to the person of the complainant (i.e., to establish the Panel's competence *ratione personae*), one to the subject matter (*ratione materiae*), and one to the timing of the request in relation to the project cycle (*ratione temporis*). Even when the Panel's jurisdiction is established, the Panel has to make sure that the request before it is admissible, i.e., not excluded by an explicit provision in the Resolution.

---

2. For further details on this matter, *see* Ibrahim F.I. Shihata, *The World Bank Inspection Panel* 39–64 (1994).

3. IDA/SecM94–378.

I.   Ascertaining, the Panel's Competence *Ratione Personae*—Establishing the "Standing" of the Complainant

If the request for inspection is not submitted by the Board of Executive Directors or by an Executive Director, it can be eligible only if submitted by an "affected party" as this term is defined in the Resolution. Such an affected party must fulfill the following requirements, pursuant to paragraph 12 of the Resolution:

1.   The affected party has to be "in the territory of the borrower." Such local party can act in its name or through a local representative. Employment of a foreign representative for this purpose may be acceptable "in exceptional cases" subject to two conditions: Proof that appropriate representation is not locally available, and approval by the Board of Executive Directors of such foreign representation at the time it authorizes inspection. A representative, whether local or foreign, must present to the Panel written evidence that he/she is acting as agent of the party on behalf of which the request is made. If the complainant is a juridical person, the territorial requirement would normally mean that it should have its principal place of business in the country where the project is located.

2.   The affected party has to be a "community of persons." The Resolution first requires that the affected party has to be "not a single individual." This has been interpreted in some writings as "any two or more persons." However, the Resolution describes it differently, explicitly elaborating on this phrase in paragraph 12 as follows: "i.e., a community of persons such as an organization, association, society or other grouping, of individuals." This suggests that complaints submitted individually by a number of persons, each acting in his own, single capacity will not meet the requirement. The group of individuals need not, however, have a juridical personality as an association, corporation, etc.; it has only to be a group which represents a commonality of interests.

3. The affected party has to be directly and adversely affected. This is reflected in the Resolution in two main requirements which clearly exclude complaints by a person or group
acting on behalf of the public at large (*actio popularis*). First,
"the affected party must demonstrate that its rights or interests have been or are likely to be directly affected by an action
or omission of the Bank." This language is flexible on the
nature of the harm, which could affect not only the legal
titles, powers and privileges (rights) of the party but also its
substantiated claims to such titles, powers and privileges
(interests). It is not flexible, however, in its requirement of a
direct causality between the alleged harm to the complainant
itself and the Bank's own actions or omissions. Second, it
should be established that such actions or omissions of the
Bank, which, as shown below, must represent an alleged serious failure of the Bank to follow its policies and procedures,
should have had or threaten to have "a material adverse
effect" on the affected party. While the materiality of the
effect is left to the judgment of the Panel, and eventually to
the judgment of the Executive Directors when they act on the
Panel's recommendations, the "adverse effect" is described in
paragraph 16 of the Resolution in terms of "the harm suffered by or threatened to such party or parties by the alleged
action or omission of the Bank." The burden of proof that a
material harm has been or is likely to be suffered falls on the
affected party, and so does the burden of proof that a causal
link exists between the Bank's alleged failure and such material harm. While the Panel is not expected to act with the
same scrutiny of a court of law in ascertaining these facts at
this early stage of assessment, it is clear from the Resolution
that the Panel must be reasonably satisfied that such elements
are met before it recommends an investigation.

The eligibility of the party requesting inspection is required
by the Resolution and it is the duty of the Panel, under
Paragraph 19 of the Resolution, to ascertain this eligibility,
whether or not Management asks it to do so.

II. Ascertaining the Panel's Competence
Ratione Materiae

The Resolution describes the eligible complaint as one that meets four requirements and is not otherwise excluded by an explicit provision in the Resolution. The requirements which the Panel has to ascertain are the following:

1. The complaint has to be based on an alleged "failure of the Bank to follow its operational policies and procedures with respect to the design, appraisal and/or implementation of a project financed by the Bank (including situations where the Bank is alleged to have failed in its follow-up on the borrower's obligations under loan agreements with respect to such policies and procedures)...." While the text of paragraph 12 requires, as a condition in the inspection function, that the affected party demonstrate that its rights or interests have been or are likely to be adversely affected by such "a failure" on the part of the Bank, the reference at the early stage of determining eligibility of the claim can only be to any alleged failure, as clearly mentioned in paragraphs 13 and 16 of the Resolution. In other words, the affected party need not establish such a failure at this stage to the satisfaction of the Panel. If the failure were to be actually established before investigation takes place, there would be no need for such investigation. The Panel must, however, satisfy itself from the outset that Management's response to the complaints submitted by the affected party did not adequately dispose of the matter, as required by the Resolution (Paragraph 13) and elaborated on in Section III below.

2. The alleged failure must be of a certain gravity. Paragraph 13 of the Resolution requires that "[t]he Panel shall also satisfy itself that the alleged violation of the Bank's policies and procedures is of a serious character," thus leaving it to the Panel to determine whether the violation is serious enough as to warrant its recommendation to investigate. The Executive Directors are the final arbiters on this matter as they alone

decide whether investigation will take place.

3.   The alleged failure must relate to the Bank's own policies and procedures which, according to the Resolution (Paragraph 12), "consist of the Bank's Operational Policies, Bank Procedures and Operational Directives, and similar documents issued before these series were started, and does not include Guidelines and Best Practices and similar documents or statements." Although this does not explicitly include other policies and procedures which may be incorporated in the Bank's Articles of Agreement or in specific Board decisions but not reflected in the above-mentioned instruments, it is reasonable to include these as well.[4] In all cases, the policies and procedures alleged to have been violated must be applicable to the project at hand, pursuant to their respective provisions on the scope of their application.

4.   The alleged failure must, as explained earlier, be such as to have or to be likely to have an adverse material effect on the complainant, i.e., a harm which is suffered or can be suffered by the complainant and which, in the judgment of the Panel, is material enough as to warrant investigation of the complaint.

III. Ascertaining the Panel's Competence *Ratione Temporis* and Establishing that the Complaint Is Not Barred for Other Reasons

There are five situations where the Resolution (Paragraphs 13 and 14) excludes complaints from the Panel's competence for time-related or other reasons. The first of these situations requires a preliminary, substantive judgment on the part of the Panel:

1.   Paragraph 13 of the Resolution requires the Panel to "satisfy itself before a request for inspection is heard that the subject-matter of the request has been dealt with by the

---

4. Shihata, *supra* note 2, at 47.

Management of the Bank and Management has failed to demonstrate that it has followed, or is taking adequate steps to follow the Bank's policies and procedures." The purpose of this requirement is clear: To allow Management the opportunity to address and remedy any shortcomings, thus obviating the need for inspection. The requirement does not mean that the Panel should exclude a complaint merely because it was addressed by Management. The Panel must reach a preliminary conclusion as to whether Management's actions were such as to dispose of the need for inspection. The Panel may thus recommend investigation even though Management has previously addressed the complaint if the Panel is not convinced of Management's response to the effect that it has fully complied with the Bank's policies and procedures. The same may occur even when Management admits failure and explains the actions taken or to be taken to correct it, if the Panel agrees that such actions are not adequate for compliance with the Bank's policies and procedures or new complaints arise with respect to the manner in which such actions are being, or have been implemented.

2. The Panel cannot, pursuant to Paragraph 14(a) of the Resolution, recommend investigation of a complaint with respect to actions which are the responsibility of parties other than the Bank, such as the borrower or potential borrower. This is a clear consequence of the fact that the Panel is a facility of the Bank, the function of which is limited to inspecting the Bank's failure to follow its own policies and procedures.

3. Under Paragraph 14(b) of the Resolution, the Panel is barred from accepting complaints from suppliers, contractors or losing bidders against procurement decisions under Bank-financed projects. The text of the Resolution refers to decisions made by the borrower (procurement decisions being for the borrower to make), but the purpose of the exclusion extends it to the clearance by the Bank of the borrower's procurement decisions when such clearance is required.[5]

---

5. For details, *see id.* at 51–52.

4. Paragraph 14(c) of the Resolution excludes "requests filed after the Closing Date of the loan financing, the project" or "after the loan financing the project has been substantially disbursed," i.e., "when at least ninety-five percent of the loan proceeds have been disbursed." Such time-barred complaints are not relevant to the Arun III Project at this stage as the IDA credit has not been made yet.

5. Paragraph 14(d) of the Resolution also excludes "[r]equests related to a particular matter or matters over which the Panel has already made its recommendation." However, requests previously acted upon by the panel may be entertained if this is "justified by new evidence or circumstances not known at the time of the prior request." This exclusion is also irrelevant to the Arun III Project at this stage.

Conclusion

By explaining in some detail the matters which the Inspection Panel is required by the Resolution to ascertain before making its recommendations to the Executive Directors on whether an investigation is warranted, this memorandum may have clarified the scope and limits of the Panel's role at this early stage of the inspection function. Two points should also be borne in mind. The first is clearly implied in the text of the Resolution and has been explicitly mentioned in the President's report to the Executive Directors on the inspection function.[6] The Panel is an investigative body. It may make recommendations on whether investigation is needed and, if the Executive Directors so decide, it may investigate the complaints found to be eligible for inspection and make its independent findings accordingly. The Panel does not, however, have the power of decision. And its function does not include making recommendations on the adequacy or suitability of existing policies and procedures.[7] To quote a judicial expression, such recommendations, if made, would be *obiter dictum*, i.e, "a saying by the way," not needed to reach the Panel's conclusion.

The second point is that, while the Panel is required to satisfy itself before recommending investigation that Management's response is not adequate to obviate the need for such investigation (pursuant to Paragraph 13 of the Resolution), it is neither required nor, in my view, advisable in this preliminary stage of assessing whether a complaint is eligible for inspection to declare that a failure of the Bank's observance of its policies and procedures has actually taken place. Not only would this make the subsequent inspection superfluous, it would cast doubt on the ability of the Panel to reach objective findings in the light of its subsequent in-depth investigation. At this early stage, the Panel's function is depicted in Paragraph 19 of the Resolution in the following clear words: "...the Panel shall determine whether the request meets the eligibility criteria set out in paragraphs 12 to 14 above and shall make a recommendation to the Executive Directors as to whether the matter should be investigated."

---

6. Operations Inspection Function: Objectives, Mandate and Operating Procedures for an Independent Inspection Panel, Memorandum from the President, R93–122/2, September 10, 1993. Although this memorandum was not specifically approved by the Executive Directors who focused their discussion on the draft resolution, the points addressed above were confirmed during Board discussion.

7. *Id.* at paragraph 8.

Annex I–5

July 4, 1997

Time-Limits on the Eligibility of Complaints Submitted to the Inspection Panel

Legal Opinion of the Senior Vice President and General Counsel

Introduction

On the one earlier occasion when the Executive Directors sought clarification from the General Counsel concerning the requirements of the Resolution establishing the Panel (the Resolution) in the early stage of the Panel's assessment of whether to recommend investigation of a specific complaint, I made it clear that I could only explain, as I did in some detail on that occasion, what the Resolution requires from the Panel in the abstract. I categorically stated that it would not be appropriate for me to pass any judgment on a specific recommendation by the Panel as "only the Board of Executive Directors is to pass judgment on the Panel's Report."[1] This position has been later confirmed by the Executive Directors' "Clarification of Certain Aspects of the Resolution," issued in 1996 which indicates that the Panel will apply the Resolution "as it understands it, subject to the Board's review." [2]

According to paragraph 19 of the Resolution, the Panel's role in this early stage is to *"determine whether the request meets the eligibility criteria set out in paragraphs 12 to 14"* (of the Resolution)

---

1. *See* the *Role of the Inspection Panel in the Preliminary Assessment of Whether to Recommend Inspection—A Memorandum of the Senior Vice President and General Counsel* (SecM95–11) January 3, 1995.
2. SecM96–60, Annex 1, October 24, 1996, at 2.

and to *"make a recommendation to the Executive Directors as to whether the matter should be investigated."* In the case at hand, the Panel has made a recommendation that the matter should be investigated, "subject to the guidance on eligibility requested from the Executive Directors" with respect to the scope of paragraph 14(c) of the Resolution as applied to the complaint.[3] The Panel's reasoning that the complaint was not time-barred under the Resolution has been questioned by an Executive Director on legal grounds.[4] The provision at issue in the Resolution is paragraph 14(c) which excludes *"requests filed after the Closing Date of the loan financing the project"* or *"after the loan financing the project has been substantially disbursed."*[5] The latter exclusion is explained in a note accompanying the text which defines it to exclude complaints filed *"when at least ninety-five percent of the loan proceeds has been substantially disbursed."*[6] These provisions set out the time limits on eligible complaints and thus determine the Panel's competence *ratione temporis.*[7]

Scope of the Time Exclusion

The above quoted text speaks of *"the loan financing the project"* and excludes from the Panel's competence complaints filed (i) after the closing date of such a loan; or (ii) after disbursement under such a loan has reached 95 percent of the loan amount. The "closing date" is defined in the General Conditions Applicable to Bank Loans to mean *"the date specified in the Loan Agreement after which the Bank may, by notice to the Borrower,*

---

3. *The Inspection Panel, Report and Recommendation on Request for Inspection—Brazil: Itaparica Resettlement and Irrigation project* (Loan 2883–1 BR), June 24, 1997, at para. 46.

4. EDS97–285, July 21, 1997.

5. *Resolution* 93–10 (SecM93–988), IDA93–6 (M93–313), para.14(c), September 23, 1993.

6. *Id.* at note 1.

7. For the distinction between competence *ratione personae* (concerning the standing of the complainant), *ratione materiae* (concerning the merits of the complaint, i.e., the alleged harm and violation) and *ratione temporis,* see the Legal Memorandum referred to in note 1, *supra.*

terminate the right of the borrower to withdraw funds from the loan account.[8] If such a date has been reached and has not been extended by the Bank, the borrower is notified that its right to withdraw funds from the loan is terminated and the loan becomes "closed." The time-limit on eligible complaints covers all loans which have been closed in this manner. In addition, it covers loans which have not yet been closed where disbursement under them reaches a certain advanced benchmark (95 percent of the total loan amount). The distinction between the phrase *"the loan financing the project"* which appears in this text and the term *"project"* which appears unqualified in other provisions related to eligibility of complaints under the Resolution should be noted.[9] While the substantive eligibility criterion speaks of the design, appraisal and/or implementation of *the project* as this term would be described in each loan agreement, the criterion of the time limitation specifically relates to the *loan financing the project,* which may be totally disbursed before the project concerned is completed.

The drafting history of paragraph 14(c) of the Resolution further explains the meaning of the time limit imposed in this text. In an earlier draft dated August 5, 1993, the time exclusion was drafted in a different fashion; it excluded *"complaints filed two years or more after the Closing Date of the loan financing the project with respect to which the complaint is filed."* Objections to this language were voiced by Executive Directors during the meeting of the Board's Committee of the Whole on August 26, 1993 on the ground that it would extend the Panel's review over matters

---

8. General Conditions, Article II, Section 2.01(20). *See also* OD13.30 Closing Dates (April 1989).

9. The substantive criterion for eligibility of complaints under the *Resolution* (para. 12) is that the rights or interests of the complainant "have been or are likely to be directly affected by an action or omission of the Bank as a result of a failure of the Bank to follow its operational policies and procedures with respect to the design, appraisal and/or implementation of a project financed by the Bank." According to the *Clarifications* issued by the Executive Directors in October 1996 (M96–60, Annex 1), the Panel is required at this stage to "establish whether the complaint is *prima facie* justified and warrants a full investigation because it is eligible under the Resolution."

falling within the purview of the Bank's Operations Evaluation Department (OED). A subsequent draft (dated September 9, 1993) simply excluded *"requests filed after the Closing Date."* The addition *"or after the loan financing the project has been substantially disbursed"* was inserted in the draft resolution during the Executive Directors' discussion in the Board meeting of September 21, 1993. It was originally suggested that a loan would be substantially disbursed if 75 percent of its proceeds were paid by the Bank. Other proposals were made for higher percentages, but below the 100 percent benchmark. Agreement was finally reached to provide for the 95 percent requirement in an explanatory note to paragraph 14(c) of the Resolution.[10]

Clearly, both the objective (ordinary meaning of the words in their context) and subjective (intended) meanings of this language disqualify a complaint with respect to a loan which has been at least 95 percent disbursed, regardless of whether the components of the project financed by the loan, or other components, if any, have been actually completed. However, for any loan where disbursement has not reached 95 percent of the total loan amount, the eligibility of the complaint would relate in substance to whether the alleged harm has resulted from the Bank's alleged serious violation of its policies and procedures in the design, appraisal and/or implementation of the project as described in the loan agreement. If two (or more) loans are made for the financing of the same, unchanged project (and a complaint is filed after disbursement of the first loan has reached 95 percent of the amount of this loan but before the subsequent loan has been similarly disbursed), the substantive criterion would clearly apply to the violation of Bank policies and procedures applicable to the *design* and/or *appraisal* of the project as a whole. Under this assumption, the project's design and appraisal are the same, both for the first and subsequent loan(s). *Implementation measures* are different, however, in the sense that complaints related to actions financed exclusively by proceeds of the first loan (whose disbursement has reached 95 percent of its

---

10. *See* Ibrahim F.I. Shihata, *The World Bank Inspection Panel* 50 (1994), at note 35.

amount) would be time-barred under the Resolution and the Panel's competence would be limited to actions (or omissions) taken under the subsequent loan to the extent that disbursement under it has not also reached 95 percent of its amount.

Complaints Related to Projects Receiving Supplemental Financing

Supplemental financing by the Bank of a certain project[11] may be introduced through a new, separate loan agreement or an amendment of the original loan agreement. The first approach is normally justified when the additional financing is accompanied by significant changes in the description of the project or the terms and conditions of the loan (including the repayment schedule). Introducing supplemental financing through an amending agreement is, however, the normal practice of the Bank,[12]—all the more so when the only change relates to the amount of the loan and consequently the repayment amount.[13] This drafting

---

11. For the purposes and conditions of such financing, *see* OP 13.20 (June, 1994). This OP replaced OPN 3.12 (February 1984) on the same subject, which was applicable to the Brazil Itaparica Resettlement and Irrigation Project.

12. *See* the descriptive statement in BP 13.20, para. 4 to the effect that "[t]he legal documentation for a supplemental loan usually consists of an amendment to the Loan Agreement, which normally incorporates the supplemental funds into the original amortization schedule." This BP, which was introduced in 1994, suggests that a separate amortization schedule may be considered when the supplemental financing is 25 percent or more of the original loan.

13. This is the case of the loan financing the Brazil Itaparica Resettlement and Irrigation Project which was first made by virtue of loan agreement 2883–BR (December 7, 1987) and then increased through an "Amending Agreement" 2883–1 (November 1, 1991) entered into between the Bank, the Borrower, the Project entity and the Guarantor (Brazil). The latter agreement simply increased the amount of the original loan, describing it as the "First Tranche," and added the supplemental financing as "Second Tranche." The first tranche is required to be repaid in installments from July 15, 1991 through January 15, 2003 (the schedule of the original loan) and the second tranche from July 15, 1993 through January 15, 2003. The total loan amount under the amending agreement (and under the amended guarantee agreement) consists of a single figure representing the aggregate of the two "tranches." The project description and the list of disbursement categories were not changed. The

approach allows the Bank and the borrower to treat the supplemental financing as merely an addition to the original loan and to continue referring to the increased loan as a single loan provided under one, amended loan agreement. While this is perfectly legitimate for certain purposes of the Bank and the borrower, it does not hide the fact that a supplemental loan was made resulting in an increase in the loan amount and, as disbursement continues, in the borrower's indebtedness. It would not therefore be unreasonable for purposes of determining the eligibility requirements provided for in paragraph 14(c) of the Resolution establishing the Panel to treat supplemental financing of an unchanged project as a "loan financing the project" even when it is introduced through an amendment of the original loan agreement and is treated for other purposes as part of a single loan. To conclude otherwise would ignore the reality of the situation (that a supplemental loan was made and has increased the amount of the original loan) simply in recognition of the drafting approach which introduced the supplemental loan by an amending agreement.

If the original loan has been fully disbursed but the disbursement under the supplemental loan stands short of 95 percent of its amount, a complaint concerning alleged harm under the second loan could not, in my view, be excluded on account of paragraph 14(c) of the Resolution. Once the eligibility of the complaint on account of its timing is established in this way, the complaint of a directly affected party may be considered by the Panel if the alleged harm is attributed to a serious violation by the Bank of its policies and procedures with respect to the design and/or appraisal of the project as a whole, as well as to the implementation of the project insofar as it is financed in whole or in part by the supplemental loan. Only complaints related to actions

---

closing date was extended by the amending agreement (and subsequently, by decisions of the Bank). The amending agreement also extended the Guarantor's obligations to the increased loan amount. At the time the complaint was filed, only about 2.5 percent of the aggregate amount was not disbursed as the first tranche was completely used (Loan 2883 BR was "closed" on December 31, 1994) and 94.14 percent of the second tranche was also disbursed.

exclusively financed by the original loan would in such a case be barred by paragraph 14(c) of the Resolution to the extent that they can be so identified.

Annex II

Bank Policies and Procedures Most Relevant to the Inspection Panel Function

ENVIRONMENTAL ASPECTS

Annex II–1–1

OP4.01 — January 1999

Environmental Assessment

1. The Bank[1] requires environmental assessment (EA) of projects proposed for Bank financing to help ensure that they are environmentally sound and sustainable, and thus to improve decision making.

2. EA is a process whose breadth, depth, and type of analysis depend on the nature, scale, and potential environmental impact of the proposed project. EA evaluates a project's potential

---

1. "Bank" includes IDA; "EA" refers to the entire process set out in OP/BP 4.01; "loans" includes credits; "borrower" includes, for guarantee operations, a private or public project sponsor receiving from another financial institution a loan guaranteed by the Bank; and "project" covers all operations financed by Bank loans or guarantees except structural adjustment loans (for which the environmental provisions are set out in OP/BP 8.60, *Adjustment Lending*, forthcoming) and debt and debt service operations, and also includes projects under adaptable lending program loans (APLs) and learning and innovation loans (LILs) and projects and components funded under the Global Environment Facility. The project is described in Schedule 2 to the Loan/Credit Agreement. This policy applies to all components of the project, regardless of the source of financing.

environmental risks and impacts in its area of influence;[2] examines project alternatives; identifies ways of improving project selection, siting, planning, design, and implementation by preventing, minimizing, mitigating, or compensating for adverse environmental impacts and enhancing positive impacts; and includes the process of mitigating and managing adverse environmental impacts throughout project implementation. The Bank favors preventive measures over mitigatory or compensatory measures, whenever feasible.

3. EA takes into account the natural environment (air, water, and land); human health and safety; social aspects (involuntary resettlement, indigenous peoples, and cultural property);[3] and transboundary and global environmental aspects.[4] EA considers natural and social aspects in an integrated way. It also takes into account the variations in project and country conditions; the findings of country environmental studies; national environmental action plans; the country's overall policy framework, national legislation, and institutional capabilities related to the environment and social aspects; and obligations of the country, pertaining to project activities, under relevant international environmental treaties and agreements. The Bank does not finance project activities that would contravene such country obligations, as identified during the EA. EA is initiated as early as possible in project processing and is integrated closely with the economic, financial, institutional, social, and technical analyses of a proposed project.

4. The borrower is responsible for carrying out the EA. For Category A projects,[5] the borrower retains independent EA

---

2. For definitions, *see* Annex A. The area of influence for any project is determined with the advice of environmental specialists and set out in the EA terms of reference.

3. See OP/BP/GP 4.12, *Involuntary Resettlement* (forthcoming); OD 4.20, *Indigenous Peoples*; and OP 4.11, *Safeguarding Cultural Property in Bank-Financed Projects* (forthcoming).

4. Global environmental issues include climate change, ozone-depleting substances, pollution of international waters, and adverse impacts on biodiversity.

5. For screening, *see* para. 8.

experts not affiliated with the project to carry out the EA.[6] For Category A projects that are highly risky or contentious or that involve serious and multidimensional environmental concerns, the borrower should normally also engage an advisory panel of independent, internationally recognized environmental specialists to advise on all aspects of the project relevant to the EA.[7] The role of the advisory panel depends on the degree to which project preparation has progressed, and on the extent and quality of any EA work completed, at the time the Bank begins to consider the project.

5. The Bank advises the borrower on the Bank's EA requirements. The Bank reviews the findings and recommendations of the EA to determine whether they provide an adequate basis for processing the project for Bank financing. When the borrower has completed or partially completed EA work prior to the Bank's involvement in a project, the Bank reviews the EA to ensure its consistency with this policy. The Bank may, if appropriate, require additional EA work, including public consultation and disclosure.

6. The *Pollution Prevention and Abatement Handbook* describes pollution prevention and abatement measures and emission levels that are normally acceptable to the Bank. However, taking into account borrower country legislation and local conditions, the EA may recommend alternative emission levels and approaches to pollution prevention and abatement for the project. The EA

---

6. EA is closely integrated with the project's economic, financial, institutional, social, and technical analyses to ensure that (a) environmental considerations are given adequate weight in project selection, siting, and design decisions; and (b) EA does not delay project processing. However, the borrower ensures that when individuals or entities are engaged to carry out EA activities, any conflict of interest is avoided. For example, when an independent EA is required, it is not carried out by the consultants hired to prepare the engineering design.

7. The panel (which is different from the dam safety panel required under OP/ BP 4.37, *Safety of Dams*) advises the borrower specifically on the following aspects: (a) the terms of reference for the EA, (b) key issues and methods for preparing the EA, (c) recommendations and findings of the EA, (d) implementation of the EA's recommendations, and (e) development of environmental management capacity.

report must provide full and detailed justification for the levels and approaches chosen for the particular project or site.

EA Instruments

7.   Depending on the project, a range of instruments can be used to satisfy the Bank's EA requirement: environmental impact assessment (EIA), regional or sectoral EA, environmental audit, hazard or risk assessment, and environmental management plan (EMP).[8] EA applies one or more of these instruments, or elements of them, as appropriate. When the project is likely to have sectoral or regional impacts, sectoral or regional EA is required.[9]

Environmental Screening

8.   The Bank undertakes environmental screening of each proposed project to determine the appropriate extent and type of EA. The Bank classifies the proposed project into one of four categories, depending on the type, location, sensitivity, and scale of the project and the nature and magnitude of its potential environmental impacts.

>   (a)   *Category A:* A proposed project is classified as Category A if it is likely to have significant adverse environmental impacts that are sensitive,[10] diverse, or unprecedented. These impacts may affect an area broader than the sites or facilities subject to physical works. EA for a Category A project examines the project's potential negative and positive environmental impacts, compares them with those of feasible alternatives (including the "without

---

8. These terms are defined in Annex A. Annexes B and C discuss the content of EA reports and EMPs.

9. Guidance on the use of sectoral and regional EA is available in EA Sourcebook Updates 4 and 15.

10. A potential impact is considered "sensitive" if it may be irreversible (e.g., lead to loss of a major natural habitat) or raise issues covered by OD 4.20, *Indigenous Peoples;* OP 4.04, *Natural Habitats;* OP 4.11, *Safeguarding Cultural Property in Bank-Financed Projects* (forthcoming); or OP 4.12, *Involuntary Resettlement* (forthcoming).

project" situation), and recommends any measures needed to prevent, minimize, mitigate, or compensate for adverse impacts and improve environmental performance. For a Category A project, the borrower is responsible for preparing a report, normally an EIA (or a suitably comprehensive regional or sectoral EA) that includes, as necessary, elements of the other instruments referred to in para. 7.

(b) *Category B:* A proposed project is classified as Category B if its potential adverse environmental impacts on human populations or environmentally important areas, including wetlands, forests, grasslands, and other natural habitats-are less adverse than those of Category A projects. These impacts are site specific; few if any of them are irreversible; and in most cases mitigatory measures can be designed more readily than for Category A projects. The scope of EA for a Category B project may vary from project to project, but it is narrower than that of Category A EA. Like Category A EA, it examines the project's potential negative and positive environmental impacts and recommends any measures needed to prevent, minimize, mitigate, or compensate for adverse impacts and improve environmental performance. The findings and results of Category B EA are described in the project documentation (Project Appraisal Document and Project Information Document).[11]

---

11. When the screening process determines, or national legislation requires, that any of the environmental issues identified warrant special attention, the findings and results of Category B EA may be set out in a separate report. Depending on the type of project and the nature and magnitude of the impacts, this report may include, for example, a limited environmental impact assessment, an environmental mitigation or management plan, an environmental audit, or a hazard assessment. For Category B projects that are not in environmentally sensitive areas and that present well-defined and well-understood issues of narrow scope, the Bank may accept alternative approaches for meeting EA requirements: for example, environmentally sound design criteria, siting criteria, or pollution standards for small-scale industrial plants or rural works; environmentally sound siting criteria, construction standards, or inspection

(c) *Category C:* A proposed project is classified as Category C if it is likely to have minimal or no adverse environmental impacts.

Beyond screening, no further EA action is required for a Category C project.

(d) *Category FI:* A proposed project is classified as Category FI if it involves investment of Bank funds through a financial intermediary, in subprojects that may result in adverse environmental impacts.

EA for Special Project Types

Sector Investment Lending

9. For sector investment loans (SILs),[12] during the preparation of each proposed subproject, the project coordinating entity or implementing institution carries out appropriate EA according to country requirements and the requirements of this policy.[13] The Bank appraises and, if necessary, includes in the SIL components to strengthen the capabilities of the coordinating entity or the implementing institution to (a) screen subprojects, (b) obtain the necessary expertise to carry out EA, (c) review all findings and results of EA for individual subprojects, (d) ensure implementation of mitigation measures (including, where applicable, an EMP), and (e) monitor environmental conditions during project implementation.[14] If the Bank is not satisfied that adequate

procedures for housing projects; or environmentally sound operating procedures for road rehabilitation projects.

12. SILs normally involve the preparation and implementation of annual investment plans or subprojects as time slice activities over the course of the project.

13. In addition, if there are sectorwide issues that cannot be addressed through individual subproject (and particularly if the SIL is likely to include Category A subprojects), the borrower may be required to carry out sectoral EA before the Bank appraises the SIL.

14. Where, pursuant to regulatory requirements or contractual arrangements acceptable to the Bank, any of these review functions are carried out by

capacity exists for carrying out EA, all Category A subprojects and, as appropriate, Category B subprojects—including any EA reports—are subject to prior review and approval by the Bank.

Sector Adjustment Lending

10. Sector adjustment loans (SECALs) are subject to the requirements of this policy. EA for a SECAL assesses the potential environmental impacts of planned policy, institutional, and regulatory actions under the loan.[15]

Financial Intermediary Lending

11. For a financial intermediary (FI) operation, the Bank requires that each FI screen proposed subprojects and ensure that subborrowers carry out appropriate EA for each subproject. Before approving a subproject, the FI verifies (through its own staff, outside experts, or existing environmental institutions) that the subproject meets the environmental requirements of appropriate national and local authorities and is consistent with this OP and other applicable environmental policies of the Bank.[16]

12. In appraising a proposed FI operation, the Bank reviews the adequacy of country environmental requirements relevant to the

---

an entity other than the coordinating entity or implementing institution, the Bank appraises such alternative arrangements; however, the borrower/coordinating entity/implementing institution remains ultimately responsible for ensuring that subprojects meet Bank requirements.

15. Actions that would require such assessment include, for example, privatization of environmentally sensitive enterprises, changes in land tenure in areas with important natural habitats, and relative price shifts in commodities such as pesticides, timber, and petroleum.

16. The requirements for FI operations are derived from the EA process and are consistent with the provisions of para. 6 of this OP. The EA process takes into account the type of finance being considered, the nature and scale of anticipated subprojects, and the environmental requirements of the jurisdiction in which subprojects will be located.

project and the proposed EA arrangements for subprojects, including the mechanisms and responsibilities for environmental screening and review of EA results. When necessary, the Bank ensures that the project includes components to strengthen such EA arrangements. For FI operations expected to have Category A subprojects, prior to the Bank's appraisal each identified participating FI provides to the Bank a written assessment of the institutional mechanisms (including, as necessary, identification of measures to strengthen capacity) for its subproject EA work.[17] If the Bank is not satisfied that adequate capacity exists for carrying out EA, all Category A subprojects and, as appropriate, Category B subprojects—including EA reports—are subject to prior review and approval by the Bank.[18]

Emergency Recovery Projects

13. The policy set out in OP 4.01 normally applies to emergency recovery projects processed under OP 8.50, *Emergency Recovery Assistance*. However, when compliance with any requirement of this policy would prevent the effective and timely achievement of the objectives of an emergency recovery project, the Bank may exempt the project from such a requirement. The justification for any such exemption is recorded in the loan documents. In all cases, however, the Bank requires at a minimum that (a) the extent to which the emergency was precipitated or exacerbated by inappropriate environmental practices be determined as part of the preparation of such projects, and (b) any necessary corrective measures be built into either the emergency project or a future lending operation.

---

17. Any FI included in the project after appraisal complies with the same requirement as a condition of its participation.

18. The criteria for prior review of Category B subprojects, which are based on such factors as type or size of the subproject and the EA capacity of the financial intermediary, are set out in the legal agreements for the project.

Institutional Capacity

14. When the borrower has inadequate legal or technical capacity to carry out key EA-related functions (such as review of EA, environmental monitoring, inspections, or management of mitigatory measures) for a proposed project, the project includes components to strengthen that capacity.

Public Consultation

15. For all Category A and B projects proposed for IBRD or IDA financing, during the EA process, the borrower consults project-affected groups and local nongovernmental organizations (NGOs) about the project's environmental aspects and takes their views into account.[19] The borrower initiates such consultations as early as possible. For Category A projects, the borrower consults these groups at least twice: (a) shortly after environmental screening and before the terms of reference for the EA are finalized; and (b) once a draft EA report is prepared. In addition, the borrower consults with such groups throughout project implementation as necessary to address EA-related issues that affect them.[20]

Disclosure

16. For meaningful consultations between the borrower and project-affected groups and local NGOs on all Category A and B projects proposed for IBRD or IDA financing, the borrower provides relevant material in a timely manner prior to consultation

---

19. For the Bank's approach to NGOs, see GP 14.70, *Involving Nongovernmental Organizations in Bank-Supported Activities*.

20. For projects with major social components, consultations are also required by other Bank policies, for example, OD 4.20, *Indigenous Peoples*, and OP/BP 4.12, *Involuntary Resettlement* (forthcoming).

and in a form and language that are understandable and accessible to the groups being consulted.

17. For a Category A project, the borrower provides for the initial consultation a summary of the proposed project's objectives, description, and potential impacts; for consultation after the draft EA report is prepared, the borrower provides a summary of the EA's conclusions. In addition, for a Category A project, the borrower makes the draft EA report available at a public place accessible to project-affected groups and local NGOs. For SILs and FI operations, the borrower/FI ensures that EA reports for Category A subprojects are made available in a public place accessible to affected groups and local NGOs.

18. Any separate Category B report for a project proposed for IDA financing is made available to project-affected groups and local NGOs. Public availability in the borrowing country and official receipt by the Bank of Category A reports for projects proposed for IBRD or IDA financing, and of any Category B EA report for projects proposed for IDA funding, are prerequisites to Bank appraisal of these projects.

19. Once the borrower officially transmits the Category A EA report to the Bank, the Bank distributes the summary (in English) to the executive directors (EDs) and makes the report available through its InfoShop. Once the borrower officially transmits any separate Category B EA report to the Bank, the Bank makes it available through its InfoShop.[21] If the borrower objects to the Bank's releasing an EA report through the World Bank InfoShop, Bank staff (a) do not continue processing an IDA project, or (b) for an IBRD project, submit the issue of further processing to the EDs.

---

21. For a further discussion of the Bank's disclosure procedures, *see The World Bank Policy on Disclosure of Information* (March 1994) and BP 17.50, *Disclosure of Operational Information.* Specific requirements for disclosure of resettlement plans and indigenous peoples development plans are set out in OP/BP 4.12, *Involuntary Resettlement* (forthcoming), and OP/BP 4.10, forthcoming revision of OD 4.20, *Indigenous Peoples.-*

Implementation

20. During project implementation, the borrower reports on (a) compliance with measures agreed with the Bank on the basis of the findings and results of the EA, including implementation of any EMP, as set out in the project documents; (b) the status of mitigatory measures; and (c) the findings of monitoring programs. The Bank bases supervision of the project's environmental aspects on the findings and recommendations of the EA, including measures set out in the legal agreements, any EMP, and other project documents.[22]

---

22. *See* OP/BP 13.05, *Project Supervision*, (forthcoming).

Annex II–1–2

BP 4.01—January 1999

Environmental Assessment

1. Environmental assessment (EA) for a proposed Bank-financed operation is the responsibility of the borrower. Bank[1] staff assist the borrower, as appropriate. The Region coordinates Bank review of EA in consultation with its Regional environment sector unit (RESU)[2] and, as necessary, with the support of the Environment Department (ENV).

Environmental Screening

2. In consultation with the RESU, the task team (TT) examines the type, location, sensitivity, and scale of the proposed project,[3]

---

1. "Bank" includes IDA; "EA" refers to the entire process set out in OP/BP 4.01; "project" covers all operations financed by Bank loans or guarantees except structural adjustment loans (for which the environmental provisions are set out in OP/BP 8.60, *Adjustment Lending*, forthcoming) and debt and debt service operations, and also includes projects under adaptable lending adaptable program loans (APLs) and learning and innovation loans (LILs) and projects and components funded under the Global Environment Facility; "loans" includes credits; "borrower" includes, for guarantee operations, a private or public project sponsor receiving from another financial institution a loan guaranteed by the Bank; "Project Concept Document" includes the Initiating Memorandum; and "Project Appraisal Document" includes the Report and Recommendation of the President (President's Report).

2. As of November 1998, the Regional environmental sector units are as follows: AFR Environment Group; EAP, SAR, and ECA Environment Sector Unit; MNA Rural Development, Water, and Environment Sector Unit; LCR Environmentally and Socially Sustainable Development Sector Unit.

3. "Location" refers to proximity to or encroachment on environmentally important areas, such as wetlands, forests, and other natural habitats. "Scale" is judged by Regional staff in the country context. "Sensitivity" refers to projects

as well as the nature and magnitude of its potential impacts. At the earliest stage of the project cycle, the TT, with the RESU's concurrence, assigns the proposed project to one of four categories (A, B, C, or FI; see OP 4.01, para. 8), reflecting the potential environmental risks associated with the project. Projects are categorized according to the component with the potentially most serious adverse effects; dual categories (e.g., A/C) are not used.

3. The TT records in the Project Concept Document (PCD) and the initial Project Information Document (PID) (a) the key environmental issues (including any resettlement, indigenous peoples, and cultural property concerns); (b) the project category and the type of EA and EA instruments needed; (c) proposed consultation with project-affected groups and local nongovernmental organizations (NGOs), including a preliminary schedule; and (d) a preliminary EA schedule.[4] The TT also reports the project's EA category in the *Monthly Operational Summary of Bank and IDA Proposed Projects* (MOS), and prepares (and updates as necessary) an Environmental Data Sheet (EDS)[5] for the project. For Category A projects, the EDS is included as a quarterly annex to the MOS.

4. If, during project preparation, the project is modified or new information becomes available, the TT, in consultation with the RESU, considers whether the project should be reclassified. The TT updates the PCD/PID and the EDS to reflect any new classification and record the rationale for the new classification. The new classification that appears in the MOS is followed by "(R)" to indicate a revision.

---

that may have irreversible impacts, affect vulnerable ethnic minorities, involve involuntary resettlement, or affect cultural heritage sites. For further discussion, see the *Environmental Assessment Sourcebook, Update No. 2: Environmental Screening* (available from the Environment Department).

   4. *See* OP/BP 10.00, *Investment Lending: Identification to Board Presentation,* for the loan processing context in which decisions on the environment category and the EA process are made.

   5. For the EDS, *see* Annex A.

5. Any exemption with respect to the application of this policy to any emergency recovery project processed under OP 8.50, *Emergency Recovery Assistance*,[6] is subject to approval by the Regional vice president (RVP), in consultation with the Chair, ENV, and the Legal Department (LEG).[7]

EA Preparation

6. During preparation of the PCD, the TT discusses with the borrower the scope of the EA[8] and the procedures, schedule, and outline for any EA report required. For Category A projects, a field visit by an environmental specialist for this purpose is normally necessary.[9] At the time of the Project Concept Review,[10] the RESU provides formal clearance of the environmental aspects of the PCD/PID. For Category B projects, the Concept Review decides whether an environmental management plan (EMP) will be required.

7. EA is an integral part of project preparation. As necessary, the TT assists the borrower in drafting the terms of reference (TOR) for any EA report.[11] The RESU reviews the coverage of the TOR, ensuring among other things that they provide for adequate interagency coordination and for consultation with affected groups and local NGOs. To support preparation of the TOR and the EA report, the TT gives the borrower the

---

6. *See* OP 4.01, para. 13.

7. LEG input is provided through the lawyer assigned to the project.

8. For sector investment and financial intermediary operations, Bank and borrower staff need to consider the potential for significant cumulative impacts from multiple subprojects.

9. Such a field visit by an environmental specialist may also be desirable for some Category B projects.

10. Or, for a sector adjustment loan (SECAL), the equivalent Regional review.

11. According to *Guidelines: Selection and Employment of Consultants by World Bank Borrowers* (Washington, D.C.: World Bank, January 1997, revised September 1997), the TT reviews the qualifications of and, if acceptable, gives a no-objection to any consultants retained by the borrower to prepare the EA report or to serve on a panel.

documents, *Content of an Environmental Assessment Report for a Category A Project and Environmental Management Plan.*[12] As applicable, Bank and borrower staff refer to the *Pollution Prevention and Abatement Handbook*, which contains pollution prevention and abatement measures and emission levels that are normally acceptable to the Bank.

8. For a Category A project, the TT advises the borrower that the EA report must be submitted to the Bank in English, French, or Spanish, and an executive summary in English.

9. For all Category A projects, and for Category B projects that are proposed for IDA funding and that will have a separate EA report, the TT advises the borrower in writing that (a) before the Bank proceeds to project appraisal, the EA report must be made available in a public place accessible to affected groups and local NGOs and must be officially submitted to the Bank; and (b) once the Bank officially receives the report, it will make the report available to the public through its InfoShop.[13]

10. During the design phase of a project, the TT advises the borrower on carrying out the EA in accordance with the requirements of OP 4.01. The TT and the lawyer identify any matters pertaining to the project's consistency with national legislation or international environmental treaties and agreements (referred to in OP 4.01, para. 3).

Review and Disclosure

11. When the borrower officially submits a Category A or Category B EA report to the Bank, the Region places a copy of the full report in the project file. It also sends the English-language executive summary of a Category A EA report to the Board Operations Division, Corporate Secretariat, under cover of a transmittal memorandum confirming that the executive

---

12. For these two documents, *see* OP 4.01, Annexes B and C.
13. *See* OP 4.01, para. 19, and BP 17.50, *Disclosure of Operational Information.*

summary and the full report (a) have been prepared by the borrower and have not been evaluated or endorsed by the Bank, and (b) are subject to change during appraisal. The results of a Category B EA, when there is no separate report, are summarized in the PID.

12. For Category A and B projects, the TT and the RESU review the results of the EA, ensuring that any EA report is consistent with the TOR agreed with the borrower. For Category A projects, and for Category B projects proposed for IDA funding that have a separate EA report, this review gives special attention to, among other things, the nature of the consultations with affected groups and local NGOs and the extent to which the views of such groups were considered; and the EMP with its measures for mitigating and monitoring environmental impacts and, as appropriate, strengthening institutional capacity. If not satisfied, the RESU may recommend to Regional management that (a) the appraisal mission be postponed, (b) the mission be considered a preappraisal mission, or (c) certain issues be reexamined during the appraisal mission. The RESU sends a copy of Category A reports to ENV.

13. For all Category A and B projects, the TT updates the status of the EA in the PCD/PID, describing how major environmental issues have been resolved or will be addressed and noting any proposed EA-related conditionalities. The TT sends the InfoShop a copy of all EA reports.

14. At the Project Decision stage,[14] the RESU provides formal clearance of the environmental aspects of the project, including their treatment in the draft legal documents prepared by LEG.

Project Appraisal

15. For Category A projects and for Category B projects proposed for IDA funding that have a separate report, the appraisal

---

14. Or, for SECALs, before departure of the appraisal mission.

mission normally departs only after the Bank has received the officially transmitted EA report and reviewed it (see paras. 11–13).[15] For Category A projects, the appraisal mission team includes one or more environmental specialists with relevant expertise.[16] The appraisal mission for any project (a) reviews both the procedural and substantive elements of the EA with the borrower, (b) resolves any issues, (c) assesses the adequacy of the institutions responsible for environmental management in light of the EA's findings, (d) ensures the adequacy of financing arrangements for the EMP, and (e) determines whether the EA's recommendations are properly addressed in project design and economic analysis. For Category A and B projects, the TT obtains the RESU's and LEG's concurrence with any change during appraisal and negotiations in any environment-related conditionality from that approved at the Project Decision stage.

Sector Investment and Financial Intermediary Lending

16. The appraisal mission develops clear arrangements with the borrower to ensure that the implementing institutions will be able to carry out or oversee EAs of proposed subprojects;[17] specifically, the mission confirms the sources of required expertise and the appropriate division of responsibilities among the ultimate borrower, the financial intermediary or sector agency, and

---

15. In exceptional cases, the RVP, with the prior concurrence of the Chair, ENV, may authorize the appraisal mission's departing before the Category A EA report is received. In such cases, the RESU's clearance of the project is conditional on the Bank's receiving, before appraisal ends and negotiations begin, an EA report that provides an adequate basis for continued project processing (GP 4.01 provides examples of such exceptional cases).

16. It may be desirable to include environmental specialists on the appraisal mission team for some Category B projects, as well.

17. The TT provides to the implementing institutions, for use (as appropriate) in the preparation and appraisal of subprojects, copies of *Content of an Environmental Assessment Report for a Category A Project* (OP 4.01, Annex B), *Environmental Management Plan* (OP 4.01, Annex C), and *Pollution Prevention and Abatement Handbook*.

the agencies responsible for environmental management and regulation. As appropriate, the TT reviews Category A and B subproject EA reports in accordance with OP 4.01, paras. 9 and 11–12.

Guarantee Operations

17. Environmental assessment of a guarantee operation is carried out in accordance with OP/BP 4.01. Any EA for an IBRD guarantee operation must be carried out in sufficient time for (a) the RESU to review the results of the EA, and (b) the TT to take the findings into account as part of appraisal. The TT ensures that a Category A EA report for such an IBRD guarantee operation is available at the InfoShop no later than 60 days before the expected date of Board presentation, and any required Category B EA report no later than 30 days before the expected date of Board presentation.

18. For the purposes of disclosure of EA reports, IDA guarantees are governed by the same policy framework as IDA credits. When a deviation from this policy framework is justified on operational grounds, the procedures for IBRD guarantees may be followed (see para. 17).

Documentation

19. The TT reviews the borrower's Project Implementation Plan to ensure that it incorporates EA findings and recommendations, including any EMP. In preparing the loan package for submission to the Board, the TT summarizes in the Project Appraisal Document (PAD) the reasons for the project classification; the findings and recommendations of the EA, including the justification for the recommended emission levels and approach to pollution prevention and abatement; and any issues related to the country's obligations under relevant international environmental treaties and agreements to which it is a party (see OP 4.01, para. 3). For a Category A project, the TT summarizes the

EA report in an annex to the PAD,[18] including such key elements as the procedures used to prepare the report; environmental baseline conditions; the alternatives considered; the predicted impacts of the chosen alternative; a summary of the EMP, covering the areas outlined in OP 4.01, Annex C; and the borrower's consultations with affected groups and local NGOs, including the issues raised and how they have been taken into account. The annex also describes negotiated environment-related loan conditionalities and covenants; when necessary, documentation of the government's intention to grant appropriate permits; and environmental supervision arrangements. For sector investment and financial intermediary loans, the documents include appropriate measures and conditions for subproject EA work. The TT and LEG ensure that loan conditions include an obligation to carry out the EMP and include as additional conditions specific measures under the EMP, as appropriate for facilitating effective supervision and monitoring of EMP implementation.

Supervision and Evaluation

20. During implementation, the TT supervises the project's environmental aspects on the basis of the environmental provisions and the borrower's reporting arrangements agreed in the legal documents and described in other project documentation.[19] The TT ensures that procurement arrangements are consistent with the environmental requirements set out in the project legal agreements. The TT also ensures that supervision missions contain adequate environmental expertise.

21. The TT ensures that environment-related covenants are included in the monitoring system. It also ensures that reports provided by the borrower on project progress adequately discuss the borrower's compliance with agreed environmental actions,

---

18. For a SECAL, a Category A EA report is summarized in a technical annex to the President's Report. This technical annex is made available to the public through the InfoShop.

19. *See* OP/BP 13.05, *Project Supervision* (forthcoming).

particularly the implementation of environmental mitigation, monitoring, and management measures. The TT, in consultation with the RESU and LEG, reviews this information and determines whether the borrower's compliance with environmental covenants is satisfactory. If compliance is not satisfactory, the TT discusses an appropriate course of action with the RESU and LEG. The TT discusses with the borrower actions necessary to correct the noncompliance, and it follows up on the implementation of such actions. The TT advises Regional management of the actions taken and recommends any further measures. During implementation, the TT obtains the RESU's concurrence with any change in enviro°nment-related aspects of the project, including environment-related conditions cleared by LEG.

22. The TT ensures that the borrower's operating plan for the project includes actions required to carry out the project's environment-related aspects, including provision for continued functioning of any environmental advisory panel as agreed with the Bank.

23. The Implementation Completion Report[20] evaluates (a) environmental impacts, noting whether they were anticipated in the EA report; and (b) the effectiveness of any mitigatory measures taken.

Role of the Environment Department

24. ENV supports the Regions throughout the EA process with advice, training, dissemination of good practice, and operational support. As appropriate, ENV provides to other Regions the EA reports, related materials, precedents, and experience that originate in any one Region or from external sources. ENV carries out project audits to help ensure compliance with the Bank's EA policy, and it conducts periodic reviews of the Bank's EA experience to identify and disseminate good practice and develop further guidance in this area.

---

20. *See* OP/BP/GP 13.55, *Implementation Completion Reporting.*

Financing EA

25. Project Preparation Facility advances[21] and trust funds may be available to potential borrowers that request Bank assistance in financing EA.

Specific Applications

26. Procedures for the environmental assessment of projects involving dams and reservoirs and pest management are set out in Annexes B and C, respectively.

---

21. *See* OP/BP 8.10, *Project Preparation Facility.*

Annex II-1-3

BP 4.01—Annex B

January 1999

Application of EA to Dam and Reservoir Projects

1. During project identification and before assigning an environmental category, the task team (TT) ensures that the borrower selects and engages independent, recognized experts or firms, whose qualifications and terms of reference (TOR) are acceptable to the Bank, to carry out environmental reconnaissance that includes

    (a) identifying the potential environmental impacts of the project;

    (b) ascertaining the scope of the environmental assessment (EA), including any resettlement and indigenous peoples concerns;

    (c) assessing the borrower's capacity to manage the EA process; and

    (d) advising on the need for an independent environmental advisory panel.[1]

The TT obtains from the borrower a copy of the results of the reconnaissance and ensures that they are taken into account in environmental screening and in the preparation of the EA TOR. For dam and reservoir projects that are in an advanced stage of preparation when proposed for financing to the Bank, the TT in consultation with the Regional environment sectoral unit

---

1. *See* OP 4.01, para. 4.

(RESU) determines whether any additional EA work is needed, and whether an independent environmental advisory panel is needed. A field visit for this purpose is normally required (see BP 4.01, para 6).

2. During project preparation, the TT assesses the environmental soundness of the country's macroeconomic and sector policies on matters that affect the project. If the TT identifies any issues, it discusses with the government measures to improve the policies.

3. If the borrower engages an environmental advisory panel, the TT reviews and indicates to the borrower the acceptability of the TOR and shortlists.

4. In reviewing the EA, the TT and the RESU ensure that the EA examines demand management opportunities. In appraising the project, they ensure that the project design adequately takes into account demand management as well as supply options (e.g., conservation of water and energy, efficiency improvements, system integration, cogeneration, and fuel substitution).

5. The TT ensures that the borrower establishes within the implementing ministry or agency an in-house environmental unit, with adequate budget and professional staffing strong in expertise relevant to the project, to manage the project's environmental aspects.

Annex II–1–4

BP 4.01—Annex C

January 1999

Application of EA to Projects Involving Pest Management

Sector Review

1. The task team (TT) ensures that any environmental assessment (EA) of the agriculture or health sector evaluates the country's capacity to manage the procurement, handling, application, and disposal of pest control products; to monitor the precision of pest control and the impact of pesticide use; and to develop and implement ecologically based pest management programs.

Project EA

2. During project identification, the TT assesses whether the proposed project may raise potential pest management issues. Projects that include the manufacture, use, or disposal of environmentally significant[1] quantities of pest control products are classified as Category A. Depending on the level of environmental risk, other projects involving pest management issues are classified as A, B, C, or FI.[2] When substantial quantities of highly toxic pesticide materials for use under the project are transported or stored, a hazard assessment may be appropriate.[3]

---

1. For the purposes of this statement, "environmental significance" takes into account the impacts (including benefits) on human health.

2. For environmental screening, *see* OP 4.01, para. 8.

3. For definitions, *see* OP 4.01, Annex A.

3. The TT records in the Project Concept Document (PCD) and the initial Project Information Document (PID) any pest management issues that the EA will address. For Category A projects, the TT reports in the *Monthly Operational Summary for Bank and IDA Proposed Projects* (MOS) whether the project (a) will finance procurement of pest control products directly or will provide credit that may be used to purchase pest control products (and whether any specific products are excluded from financing), (b) will finance goods or services that significantly change pesticide use patterns, or (c) includes components including support for development and implementation of integrated pest management (IPM) programs aimed at reducing environmental and health hazards associated with pest control and the use of pesticides.

4. The TT ensures that the EA covers potential issues related to pest management and considers appropriate alternative designs or mitigation measures. Depending on the issues identified, the environmental management plan[4] includes a pest management plan.

Pest Management Plan

5. A pest management plan is a comprehensive plan, developed when there are significant pest management issues such as (a) new land-use development or changed cultivation practices in an area, (b) significant expansion into new areas, (c) diversification into new crops in agriculture,[5] (d) intensification of existing low-technology systems, (e) proposed procurement of relatively hazardous pest control products or methods, or (f) specific environmental or health concerns (e.g., proximity of protected areas or important aquatic resources; worker safety). A pest management plan is also developed when proposed

---

4. *See* OP 4.01, Annex C.
5. Particularly such crops as cotton, vegetables, fruits, and rice, which are often associated with heavy use of pesticides.

financing of pest control products represents a large component of the project.[6]

6.   A pest management plan reflects the policies set out in OP 4.09, *Pest Management*. The plan is designed to minimize potential adverse impacts on human health and the environment and to advance ecologically based IPM.[7] The plan is based on on-site evaluations of local conditions conducted by appropriate technical specialists with experience in participatory IPM. The first phase of the plan involves an initial reconnaissance to identify the main pest problems and their contexts (ecological, agricultural, public health, economic, and institutional) and to define broad parameters and is carried out as part of project preparation and is evaluated at appraisal. The second phase includes the development of specific operational plans to address the pest problems identified and is often carried out as a component of the project itself.[8] As appropriate, the pest management plan specifies procedures for screening pest control products. In exceptional cases, the pest management plan may consist of pest control product screening only.

Screening of Pest Control Products

7.   Pest control product screening is required when a project finances pest control products. The screening establishes an authorized list of pest control products approved for financing, along with a mechanism to ensure that only the specified products will be procured with Bank funds. Screening without a pest management plan is appropriate only when all of the following conditions are met: (a) expected quantities of pest control products are not significant from a health or environment standpoint;

---

6. A pest management plan is not required for the procurement or use of impregnated bednets for malaria control, or of WHO Class III insecticides for intradomiciliary spraying for malaria control.

7. *See* GP 4.03, Part II, for information on IPM.

8. For the content of a pest management plan, *see* GP 4.03.

(b) no significant environmental or health concerns related to pest control need to be addressed; (c) the project will not introduce pesticide use or other nonindigenous biological control into an area, or significantly increase the level of pesticide use; and (d) no hazardous products[9] will be financed.[10]

Appraisal

8. Depending on the complexity of the issues involved and the degree of risk to human health or the environment, the appraisal mission includes appropriate technical specialists.

9. The TT records in the Project Appraisal Document (PAD) pest management concerns arising from the EA and any proposed project interventions pertinent to pest management, for example:

(a) a list of pest control products authorized for procurement, or an indication of when and how this list will be developed and agreed on;

(b) existing pest management practices; pesticide use; the policy, economic, institutional, and legal framework for regulating, procuring, and managing pesticides; and the extent to which all these are consistent with an IPM approach;

(c) proposed project activities (or ongoing parallel activities, including other projects supported by the Bank or other

---

9. Hazardous products include pesticides listed in Class Ia and Ib of the World Health Organization (WHO) *Classification of Pesticides by Hazard and Guidelines to Classification* (Geneva: WHO, 1994–95); materials listed in the UN *Consolidated List of Products Whose Consumption and/or Sale have been Banned, Withdrawn, Severely Restricted, or not Approved by Governments* (New York: UN, 1994); and other materials that are banned or severely restricted in the borrower country because of environmental or health hazards *(see* the country's national pesticide registration list, if it has one). Copies of the WHO classification and UN list, which are updated periodically, are available in the Bank's Sectoral Library. Staff may consult the Rural Development Department for further guidance.

10. GP 4.03, Part III, provides further information on pest control product screening.

donors) aimed at addressing (i) the shortcomings identified, and (ii) any constraints to adopting IPM;

(d) proposed mechanisms for financing, implementing,
monitoring, and supervising components relating to pest
management or pesticide use, including any role envisaged for local non-governmental organizations;

(e) the capacity of responsible institutions to carry out the
activities described; and

(f) the overall sectoral context and other issues that will not
be directly addressed under the project but that should
be addressed as long-term objectives.

10. The main elements of the pest management measures are
reflected in the legal agreements between the borrower and the
Bank.[11]

Supervision and Evaluation

11. Depending on the nature and complexity of the pest management and pesticide-related issues confirmed at appraisal,
supervision missions may need to include appropriate technical
specialists. This need is reflected in the supervision plan.

12. The Implementation Completion Report evaluates the environmental impact of pest management practices supported or
promoted by the project, as well as the borrower's institutional
oversight capacity. It also discusses whether the project has resulted in improved pest management practices according to the criteria that define the IPM approach.

---

11. Loan conditionality may be needed to ensure the effective implementation of project components; for example, (a) establishing or strengthening
pesticide regulatory and monitoring framework and capabilities, (b) properly
operating and/or constructing pesticide storage or disposal facilities, (c) agreeing on a time-bound program to phase out use of an undesirable pesticide and
properly dispose of any existing stocks, or (d) initiating research or extension
programs aimed at providing alternatives to undesirable pesticide use.

Annex II–2–1

OP 4.02—October 1994

Environmental Action Plans

1. The Bank[1] encourages and supports the efforts of borrowing governments to prepare and implement an appropriate Environmental Action Plan (EAP)[2] and to revise it periodically as necessary. Although the Bank may provide advice, responsibility for preparing and implementing the EAP rests with the government, and the EAP is the country's plan.

2. An EAP describes a country's major environmental concerns, identifies the principal causes of problems, and formulates policies and actions to deal with the problems.[3] In addition, when environmental information is lacking, the EAP identifies priority environmental information needs and indicates how essential data and related information systems will be developed. The EAP provides the preparation work for integrating environmental considerations into a country's overall economic and social development strategy. The EAP is a living document that is expected to contribute to the continuing process by which the government develops a comprehensive national environmental policy and programs to implement the policy. This process is expected to form an integral part of overall national development policy and decision making.

---

1. "Bank" includes IDA.

2. The term "EAP" may refer to a specific document formally designated as an EAP, or to a plan set forth in such comparable documents as a report of a task force, a conservation strategy, or an overall development strategy that treats environmental issues. National reports on the environment submitted by member countries for the United Nations Conference on Environment and Development (UNCED) (Rio de Janeiro, June 1992) are in principle similar to EAPs. If in scope and content a country's UNCED report is consistent with the requirements for an EAP, including those on broad public participation (see para. 4), the Bank may accept that report as an EAP.

3. For a description and contents of an EAP, *see* GP 4.02.

3. The Bank draws on the EAP for environmental information and analysis to plan its assistance with appropriate attention to environmental considerations. The Bank encourages each government to integrate its EAP into sectoral and national development plans. The Bank works with each government to ensure that information from the EAP (a) is integrated into Bank planning and country assistance documents, and (b) informs the development of program- and project-level details in a continuing process of environmental planning.

Participation

4. The Bank encourages the government to secure support for the EAP and to help ensure its effective implementation by (a) using multi-disciplinary teams from appropriate agencies within the government to assist with preparation, and (b) taking into account the views of interested parties (including local nongovernmental organizations [NGOs][4]), obtained through means that induce broad public participation.

Disclosure

5. While the EAP is being prepared, the Bank encourages the government to make drafts available to groups that will be affected by its implementation and to other interested groups, including NGOs. When the EAP is completed, the Bank encourages the government to issue it to aid agencies and the public. When the Bank has officially received an EAP and has obtained the government's consent, it makes the EAP available to interested parties through the Public Information Center.[5]

---

4. See GP 14.70, *Involving Nongovernmental Organizations in Bank-Supported Activities.*

5. See BP 17.50, *Disclosure of Operational Information, and The World Bank Policy on Disclosure of Information* (Washington, D.C.: World Bank, March 1994).

Annex II–2–2

BP 4.02—October 1994

Environmental Action Plans

Environmental Action Plans

1. The Bank's[1] role in preparing and implementing an Environmental Action Plan (EAP) is primarily to provide advice and help arrange technical assistance, if requested to do so by the government. The degree of Bank involvement depends on the capacity of the government to design and manage the process. Within the Bank, the responsibility for assisting in and monitoring the preparation of an EAP rests primarily with the concerned country department (CD), supported by the Regional environment division (RED). Additional support may be requested from other Bank units with particular expertise, such as the sectoral vice presidencies and the Environment and Legal Departments.

Bank Review

2. Bank staff review the draft EAP,[2] keeping in mind its usefulness in scope and content as a policy and investment planning document, and provide comments to the government. Bank staff also determine whether the EAP is supported and endorsed by the government agencies that need to approve it formally.

3. The country operations division (COD), the relevant sector operations divisions (SODs), and the RED review the completed

---

1. "Bank" includes IDA.
2. Bank staff review the document whether it is a single document or a compilation of several reports or working papers.

EAP and provide to the government comments on technical issues and the main environmental concerns.

EAP Monitoring

4. Bank staff periodically monitor and evaluate progress in implementing the EAP's action program, discuss their findings with the government, and identify and promote corrective actions. Bank staff encourage and support the government's efforts to periodically update the EAP in light of new information and changing priorities. If the government so requests, Bank staff assist in identifying financial resources and expertise to update the EAP.

Integration into Country Development Planning and Bank Work

5. As part of regular country assistance management, Bank staff identify potential gaps in country capability for EAP preparation, monitoring, and updating. The CD estimates when the entire EAP, or portions of it, will need to be monitored, reviewed, and updated for inclusion in the Bank's Country Assistance Strategy. The appropriate COD and SODs ensure that the Bank's country economic and sector work, Country Economic Memoranda, Country Assistance Strategy documents, and Policy Framework Papers integrate and properly reflect the findings of the EAP and identify areas in which environmental questions remain. Bank staff may also need to integrate EAP information into the Staff Appraisal Report and Memorandum and Recommendation of the President/President's Report for investment and adjustment lending operations.

6. The RED reviews the appropriate Bank documents to ensure that environmental actions identified and recommended in the EAP have been adequately taken into account.

7. Bank staff promote coordination among the efforts of the various aid agencies participating in the EAP process.

Status Reports and Release of the EAP

8.   The CD informs the executive directors of the status of EAP preparation and implementation through a section in the Country Brief and, for active IDA-eligible borrowers, through the IDA Annual Report to the Board. The CD reports the Bank's receipt of an EAP in the next issue of the Bank's *Report to the Executive Directors on Bank and IDA Operations*. When the government permits, the CD makes copies of the EAP available to the executive directors on request. Once the Bank has officially received the EAP and has obtained the government's consent, the CD sends a copy of the EAP to the Public Information Center, through which interested parties may obtain it.

Annex II–3–1

OP 4.04—September 1995

Natural Habitats

1. The conservation of natural habitats,[1] like other measures that protect and enhance the environment, is essential for long-term sustainable development. The Bank[2] therefore supports the protection, maintenance, and rehabilitation of natural habitats and their functions in its economic and sector work, project financing, and policy dialogue. The Bank supports, and expects borrowers to apply, a precautionary approach to natural resource management to ensure opportunities for environmentally sustainable development.

Economic and Sector Work

2. The Bank's economic and sector work includes identification of (a) natural habitat issues and special needs for natural habitat conservation, including the degree of threat to identified natural habitats (particularly critical natural habitats); and (b) measures for protecting such areas in the context of the country's development strategy. As appropriate, Country Assistance Strategies and projects incorporate findings from such economic and sector work.

---

1. *See* definitions in Annex A.
2. "Bank" includes IBRD and IDA, and "loans" includes credits, grants, and guarantees. This policy also covers GEF-funded projects. Adjustment loans are not covered by this policy but are subject to the general policies set out in OP 4.00, *Environmental Aspects of Bank Work* (forthcoming).

Project Design and Implementation

3. The Bank promotes and supports natural habitat conservation and improved land use by financing projects designed to integrate into national and regional development the conservation of natural habitats and the maintenance of ecological functions. Furthermore, the Bank promotes the rehabilitation of degraded natural habitats.

4. The Bank does not support projects that, in the Bank's opinion, involve the significant conversion or degradation[3] of critical natural habitats.

5. Wherever feasible, Bank-financed projects are sited on lands already converted (excluding any lands that in the Bank's opinion were converted in anticipation of the project). The Bank does not support projects involving the significant conversion of natural habitats unless there are no feasible alternatives for the project and its siting, and comprehensive analysis demonstrates that overall benefits from the project substantially outweigh the environmental costs. If the environmental assessment[4] indicates that a project would significantly convert or degrade natural habitats, the project includes mitigation measures acceptable to the Bank. Such mitigation measures include, as appropriate, minimizing habitat loss (e.g., strategic habitat retention and post-development restoration) and establishing and maintaining an ecologically similar protected area. The Bank accepts other forms of mitigation measures only when they are technically justified.

6. In deciding whether to support a project with potential adverse impacts on a natural habitat, the Bank takes into account the borrower's ability to implement the appropriate conservation and mitigation measures. If there are potential institutional capacity problems, the project includes components that develop the capacity of national and local institutions for effective

---

3. For definitions, *see* Annex A.
4. *See* OD 4.01, *Environmental Assessment,* to be reissued as OP/BP 4.01.
5. *See* OD 4.01, *Environmental Assessment,* to be reissued as OP/BP 4.01.

environmental planning and management. The mitigation measures specified for the project may be used to enhance the practical field capacity of national and local institutions.

7. In projects with natural habitat components, project preparation, appraisal, and supervision arrangements include appropriate environmental expertise to ensure adequate design and implementation of mitigation measures.

8. This policy applies to subprojects under sectoral loans or loans to financial intermediaries.[5] Regional Environment Divisions (REDs) oversee compliance with this requirement.

Policy Dialogue

9. The Bank encourages borrowers to incorporate into their development and environmental strategies analyses of any major natural habitat issues, including identification of important natural habitat sites, the ecological functions they perform, the degree of threat to the sites, priorities for conservation, and associated recurrent-funding and capacity-building needs.

10. The Bank expects the borrower to take into account the views, roles, and rights of groups, including local nongovernmental organizations and local communities,[6] affected by Bank-financed projects involving natural habitats, and to involve such people in planning, designing, implementing, monitoring, and evaluating such projects. Involvement may include identifying appropriate conservation measures, managing protected areas and other natural habitats, and monitoring and evaluating specific projects. The Bank encourages governments to provide such people with appropriate information and incentives to protect natural habitats.

---

6. *See* OD 4.20, *Indigenous Peoples,* when local communities include indigenous peoples.

Annex II–3–2

BP 4.04—September 1995

Natural Habitats

Project Processing

Project Preparation

1. Early in the preparation of a project proposed for Bank[1] financing, the project task manager (TM) consults with the Regional Environmental Division (RED) and, as necessary, with the Environment Department (ENV) and the Legal Department (LEG) to identify natural habitat issues likely to arise in the project.

2. If, as part of the environmental assessment process, environmental screening indicates the potential for significant conversion or degradation of critical or other natural habitats, the project is classified as Category A; projects otherwise involving natural habitats are classified as Category A or B, depending on the degree of their ecological impacts.[2]

3. Exceptions pursuant to OP 4.04, para. 5, are made only after consultation with the RED, ENV, and LEG and approval by the Regional vice president.

4. Natural habitat components of a project are linked as appropriate to the schedule of implementation for the project. The costs of conservation of any compensatory natural habitats are included in the project's financing. Mechanisms to ensure adequate recurrent cost financing are incorporated into project design.

---

1. "Bank" includes IBRD and IDA; and "loans" includes credits, grants, and guarantees.

2. *See* OD 4.01, *Environmental Assessment,* to be reissued as OP/BP 4.01.

Documentation

5. The TM identifies any natural habitat issues (including any significant conversion or degradation that would take place under the project, as well as any exceptions proposed under OP 4.04, para. 5) in the initial Project Information Document (PID) and in the early versions of the Environmental Data Sheet.[3] Updated PIDs reflect changes in the natural habitat issues. The Staff Appraisal Report and the Memorandum and Recommendation of the President indicate the types and estimated areas (in hectares) of affected natural habitats; the significance of the potential impacts; the project's consistency with national and regional land use and environmental planning initiatives, conservation strategies, and legislation; the mitigation measures planned; and any exceptions proposed under OP 4.04, para. 5.

6. The Implementation Completion Report[4] assesses the extent to which the project achieved its environmental objectives, including natural habitat conservation.

Regional and Sectoral EA Reports

7. Bank staff identify relevant natural habitat issues for regional and sectoral environmental assessment (EA) reports. Such reports indicate the present location of natural habitats in the region or sector involved, analyze the ecological functions and relative importance of such natural habitats, and describe the associated management issues. These analyses are used in subsequent project-specific environmental screening and other EA work.

Role of Bank Staff

8. REDs coordinate the preparation and use of any supplementary critical natural habitat lists and assist with project preparation

---

3. *See* OD 4.01, *Environmental Assessment,* to be reissued as OP/BP 4.01.
4. *See* OP / BP / GP 13.55, *Implementation Completion Reporting.*

(including EA) and supervision when requested. ENV guides TMs, country departments, and REDs in implementing OP 4.04 by disseminating best practices and providing training, reviews, advice, and operational support (including supervision).

Annex II–4

OP 4.09—December 1998

Pest Management

1.   In assisting borrowers to manage pests that affect either agriculture or public health, the Bank[1] supports a strategy that promotes the use of biological or environmental control methods and reduces reliance on synthetic chemical pesticides. In Bank-financed projects, the borrower addresses pest management issues in the context of the project's environmental assessment.[2]

2.   In appraising a project that will involve pest management, the Bank assesses the capacity of the country's regulatory framework and institutions to promote and support safe, effective, and environmentally sound pest management. As necessary, the Bank and the borrower incorporate in the project components to strengthen such capacity.

Agricultural Pest Management[3]

3.   The Bank uses various means to assess pest management in the country and support integrated pest management (IPM)[4]

---

1. "Bank" includes IDA, and "loans" includes credits.

2. *See* OP/BP 4.01, *Environmental Assessment.*

3. OP 4.09 applies to all Bank lending, whether or not the loan finances pesticides. Even if Bank lending for pesticides is not involved, an agricultural development project may lead to substantially increased pesticide use and subsequent environmental problems.

4. IPM refers to a mix of farmer-driven, ecologically based pest control practices that seeks to reduce reliance on synthetic chemical pesticides. It involves (a) managing pests (keeping them below economically damaging levels) rather than seeking to eradicate them; (b) relying, to the extent possible, on nonchemical measures to keep pest populations low; and (c) selecting and applying pesticides, when they have to be used, in a way that minimizes adverse effects on beneficial organisms, humans, and the environment.

and the safe use of agricultural pesticides: economic and sector work, sectoral or project-specific environmental assessments, participatory IPM assessments, and adjustment or investment projects and components aimed specifically at supporting the adoption and use of IPM.

4. In Bank-financed agriculture operations, pest populations are normally controlled through IPM approaches, such as biological control, cultural practices, and the development and use of crop varieties that are resistant or tolerant to the pest. The Bank may finance the purchase of pesticides when their use is justified under an IPM approach.

Pest Management in Public Health

5. In Bank-financed public health projects, the Bank supports controlling pests primarily through environmental methods. Where environmental methods alone are not effective, the Bank may finance the use of pesticides for control of disease vectors.

Criteria for Pesticide Selection and Use

6. The procurement of any pesticide in a Bank-financed project is contingent on an assessment of the nature and degree of associated risks, taking into account the proposed use and the intended users.[5] With respect to the classification of pesticides and their specific formulations, the Bank refers to the World Health Organization's *Recommended Classification of Pesticides by Hazard and Guidelines to Classification* (Geneva: WHO

---

5. This assessment is made in the context of the project's environmental assessment and is recorded in the project documents. The project documents also include (in the text or in an annex) a list of pesticide products authorized for procurement under the project, or an indication of when and how this list will be developed and agreed on. This authorized list is included by reference in legal documents relating to the project, with provisions for adding or deleting materials.

1994–95).[6] The following criteria apply to the selection and use of pesticides in Bank-financed projects:

(a) They must have negligible adverse human health effects.

(b) They must be shown to be effective against the target species.

(c) They must have minimal effect on nontarget species and the natural environment. The methods, timing, and frequency of pesticide application are aimed to minimize damage to natural enemies. Pesticides used in public health programs must be demonstrated to be safe for inhabitants and domestic animals in the treated areas, as well as for personnel applying them.

(d) Their use must take into account the need to prevent the development of resistance in pests.

7. The Bank requires that any pesticides it finances be manufactured, packaged, labeled, handled, stored, disposed of, and applied according to standards acceptable to the Bank.[7] The Bank does not finance formulated products that fall in WHO classes IA and IB, or formulations of products in Class II, if (a) the country lacks restrictions on their distribution and use; or (b) they are likely to be used by, or be accessible to, lay personnel, farmers, or others without training, equipment, and facilities to handle, store, and apply these products properly.

---

6. Copies of the classification, which is updated annually, are available in the Sectoral Library. A draft Standard Bidding Document for Procurement of Pesticides is available from OCSPR.

7. The FAO's *Guidelines for Packaging and Storage of Pesticides* (Rome, 1985), *Guidelines on Good Labeling Practice for Pesticides* (Rome, 1985), and *Guidelines for the Disposal of Waste Pesticide and Pesticide Containers on the Farm* (Rome, 1985) are used as minimum standards.

Annex II–5

OPN 11.03—September 1986

Management of Cultural Property in Bank-Financed Projects

Introduction

1. The United Nations term "cultural property" includes sites having archeological (prehistoric), paleontological, historical, religious, and unique natural values. Cultural property, therefore, encompasses both remains left by previous human inhabitants (for example, middens, shrines, and battlegrounds) and unique natural environmental features such as canyons and waterfalls. The rapid loss of cultural property in many countries is irreversible and often unnecessary. Detailed background information on all aspects of this note are contained in the technical paper of the same title, available from the Office of Environmental and Scientific Affairs, Projects Policy Department, which is ready to provide assistance on request.

Policy Guidance

2. The World Bank's[1] general policy regarding cultural properties is to assist in their preservation, and to seek to avoid their elimination. Specifically:

   a) The Bank normally declines to finance projects that will significantly damage non-replicable cultural property,

---

1. The World Bank includes the International Bank for Reconstruction and Development (IBRD), the International Development Association (IDA) and the International Finance Corporation (IFC).

and will assist only those projects that are sited or designed so as to prevent such damage.

b) The Bank will assist in the protection and enhancement of cultural properties encountered in Bank-financed projects, rather than leaving that protection to chance. In some cases, the project is best relocated in order that sites and structures can be preserved, studied, and restored intact *in situ*. In other cases, structures can be relocated, preserved, studied, and restored on alternate sites. Often, scientific study, selective salvage, and museum preservation before destruction is all that is necessary. Most such projects should include the training and strengthening of institutions entrusted with safeguarding a nation's cultural patrimony. Such activities should be directly included in the scope of the project, rather than being postponed for some possible future action, and the costs are to be internalized in computing overall project costs.

c) Deviations from this policy may be justified only where expected project benefits are great, and the loss of or damage to cultural property is judged by competent authorities to be unavoidable, minor, or otherwise acceptable. Specific details of the justification should be discussed in project documents.

d) This policy pertains to any project in which the Bank is involved, irrespective of whether the Bank is itself financing the part of the project that may affect cultural property.

Procedural Guidance

3. The management of cultural property of a country is the responsibility of the government. Before proceeding with a project, however, which *prima facie* entails the risk of damaging cultural property (e.g., any project that includes large scale

excavations, movement of earth, surficial environmental changes or demolition), Bank staff must: (1) determine what is known about the cultural property aspects of the proposed project site. The government's attention should be drawn specifically to that aspect and appropriate agencies, NGOs or university departments should be consulted; (2) If there is any question of cultural property in the area, a brief reconnaissance survey should be undertaken in the field by a specialist.[2] Procedures to be followed upon positive surveys are detailed in Chapter 6 of the technical paper.

---

2. A survey form is attached to the technical paper.

Annex II–6

OP 4.36—September 1993

Forestry

1. Bank[1] involvement in the forestry sector aims to reduce deforestation, enhance the environmental contribution of forested areas, promote afforestation, reduce poverty, and encourage economic development. In pursuit of these objectives, the Bank applies the following policies:

(a) The Bank does not finance commercial logging operations or the purchase of logging equipment for use in primary tropical moist forest.[2] In borrowing countries where logging is being done in such forests, the Bank seeks the government's commitment to move toward sustainable management of those forests, as described in para. 1(d) below, and to retain as much effective forest cover as possible. Where the government has made this commitment, the Bank may finance improvements in the planning, monitoring, and field control of forestry operations to maximize the capability of responsible agencies to carry out the sustainable management of the resource.

(b) The Bank uses a sectorwide approach to forestry and conservation work in order to address policy and institutional issues and to integrate forestry and forest conservation projects with initiatives in other sectors and with macroeconomic objectives.

(c) The Bank involves the private sector and local people in forestry and conservation management or in alternative

---

1. "Bank" includes IDA, and "loans" include credits.
2. Definitions are given in Annex A.

income-generating activities. The Bank requires borrowers to identify and consult the interest groups involved in a particular forest area.

(d) The Bank's lending operations in the forest sector are conditional on government commitment to undertake sustainable management and conservation-oriented forestry. Such a commitment (which may be reflected in specific conditionalities; see Good Practices 4.36 for examples) requires a client country to

(i) adopt policies and a legal and institutional framework to (a) ensure conservation and sustainable management of existing forests, and (b) promote active participation of local people and the private sector in the long-term sustainable management of natural forests (see paras. 19–20 of OD 4.01, *Environmental Assessment*);

(ii) adopt a comprehensive and environmentally sound forestry conservation and development plan that clearly defines the roles and rights of the government, the private sector, and local people (including forest dwellers) (see OD 4.20, *Indigenous Peoples*;

(iii) undertake social, economic, and environmental assessments of forests being considered for commercial use;

(iv) set aside adequate compensatory preservation forests to protect and conserve biological diversity and environmental services and to safeguard the interests of forest dwellers, specifically their rights of access to and use of designated forest areas; and

(v) establish institutional capacity to implement and enforce these commitments.

(e) The Bank distinguishes investment projects that are exclusively environmentally protective (e.g., management of protected areas or reforestation of degraded watersheds) or supportive of small farmers (e.g., farm

and community forestry) from all other forestry operations. Projects in this limited group may be appraised on
the basis of their own social, economic, and environmental merits. However, they may be pursued only
where broad sectoral reforms are in hand, or where
remaining forest cover in the client country is so limited
that preserving it in its entirety is the agreed course of
action.

(f)   In forest areas of high ecological value, the Bank finances
only preservation and light, nonextractive use of forest
resources. In areas where retaining the natural forest
cover and the associated soil, water, biological diversity,
and carbon sequestration values is the object, the Bank
may finance controlled sustained-yield forest management. The Bank finances plantations only on nonforest-
ed areas (including previously planted areas) or on
heavily degraded forestland.

2.   The Bank does not finance projects that contravene applicable international environmental agreements.

Annex II–7–1

OP 4.37—September 1996

Safety of Dams

1. For the life of any dam, the owner[1] has full responsibility for the safety of the dam, irrespective of its funding sources or construction status. Because there are serious consequences if a dam does not function properly or fails, the Bank[2] is concerned about the safety of new dams it finances and existing dams on which a Bank-financed project is directly dependent.

New Dams

2. When the Bank finances a project[3] that includes the construction of a new dam, it requires that the dam be designed and its construction supervised by experienced and competent professionals. It also requires that the borrower adopt and implement certain dam safety measures for the design, bid tendering, construction, operation, and maintenance of the dam and associated works.

3. For small dams (normally those less than 15 meters in height, such as farm ponds, local silt retention dams, and low-embankment tanks), generic dam safety measures designed by qualified engineers are usually adequate. For large dams—that is, dams that are 15 meters or more in height, or are between 10 and 15 meters

---

1. The owner of a dam may be a national or state government, a parastatal, a private company, or a consortium of entities.
2. "Bank" includes IDA, and "loans" includes credits.
3. For example, a hydropower, water supply, irrigation, flood control, or multipurpose project.

and present special design complexities (e.g., an unusually large flood-handling requirement, location in a zone of high seismicity, or foundations that are complex and difficult to prepare)[4]— the Bank requires

(a) reviews by an independent panel of experts throughout investigation, design, and construction of the dam and the start of operations;

(b) preparation and implementation of detailed plans: a plan for construction supervision and quality assurance, a plan for instrumentation, an operation and maintenance plan, and an emergency preparedness plan;[5]

(c) prequalification of bidders during procurement and bid tendering;[6] and

(d) periodic safety inspections of the dam after completion.

4. The independent review panel consists of three or more experts, appointed by the borrower and acceptable to the Bank, with expertise in the various technical fields relevant to the dam safety aspects of the particular dam.[7] The primary purpose of the panel is to review and advise the borrower on matters relative to dam safety and other critical aspects of the dam, its appurtenant structures, the catchment area, the area surrounding the reservoir, and downstream areas. However, the borrower normally extends the panel's composition and terms of reference beyond dam safety to cover such areas as project formulation; technical design; construction procedures; and associated works such as

---

4. For a full definition of "large dams," *see* the World Register of Dams, published by the International Commission on Large Dams and updated periodically.

5. BP 4.37, Annex A, sets out the content of these plans and the timetable for preparing and finalizing them.

6. *See* Guidelines: Procurement under IBRD Loans and IDA Credits (Washington, D.C.: World Bank, 1995).

7. The number, professional breadth, technical expertise, and experience of panel members are appropriate to the size, complexity, and hazard potential of the dam under consideration. For high-hazard dams, in particular, the panel experts should be internationally known experts in their field.

power facilities, river diversion during construction, shiplifts, and fish ladders.

5. The borrower contracts the services of the panel of experts and provides administrative support for the panel's activities. Beginning as early in project preparation as possible, the borrower arranges for periodic panel meetings and reviews, which continue through the investigation, design, construction, and initial filling and start-up phases of the dam. The borrower informs the Bank in advance of the panel meetings, and the Bank normally sends an observer. After each meeting, the panel provides the borrower a written report of its conclusions and recommendations, signed by each participating member; the borrower provides a copy of that report to the Bank. If there are no difficulties in the filling and start-up of the dam, the borrower may disband the panel of experts after that phase.

Existing Dams and Dams under Construction

6. The Bank frequently finances the following types of projects that do not include a new dam but will rely on the performance of an existing dam or a dam under construction (DUC): power stations or water supply systems that draw directly from a reservoir controlled by an existing dam or a DUC; diversion dams or hydraulic structures downstream from an existing dam or a DUC, where failure of the upstream dam could cause extensive damage to or failure of the new Bank-funded structure; and irrigation or water supply projects that will depend on the storage and operation of an existing dam or a DUC for their supply of water and could not function if the dam failed. For such projects, the Bank requires that the borrower arrange for one or more independent dam specialists to (a) inspect and evaluate the safety status of the existing dam or DUC, its appurtenances, and its performance history; (b) review and evaluate the owner's operation and maintenance procedures, and (c) provide a written report of findings and recommendations for any remedial work or safety-related measures necessary to upgrade the existing dam or DUC to an acceptable standard of safety.

7.   The Bank may accept previous assessments of dam safety or recommendations of improvements needed in the existing dam or DUC if (a) the dam or DUC is located in the same country as the subject project; (b) an effective dam safety program is already in operation there; and (c) full-level inspections and dam safety assessments of the existing dam or DUC have already been conducted and documented.

8.   Necessary additional dam safety measures or remedial work may be financed under the proposed project. When substantial remedial work is needed, the Bank requires that the borrower (a) employ competent professionals to design and supervise the work, and (b) prepare and implement the same reports and plans as for a new Bank-financed dam (see para. 3(b)). For high-hazard cases involving significant and complex remedial work, the Bank also requires that the borrower employ a panel of independent experts on the same basis as for a new Bank-financed dam (see paras. 3 (a) and 4).

9.   When the existing dam or DUC is owned and operated by an entity within the country other than the borrower, the Bank requires that the borrower cause the owner to perform the measures set out in paras. 6, 7, and 8.

Annex II–7–2

BP 4.37—September 1996

Safety of Dams

Project Processing

1. When the Bank[1] begins processing a project that includes a dam, the processing team includes individuals who have relevant experience in dam engineering and in preparation and supervision of previous Bank-funded projects that have included dams. If such individuals are not available within the country department (CD), project staff seek them from other CDs, Regional technical departments, or Environmentally Sustainable Development, or from outside the Bank.

2. Bank projects involving dams are processed according to the procedures set forth in BP 10.00, *Investment Lending: Identification to Board Presentation*.

3. As soon as a project involving a dam is identified, Bank staff discuss with the borrower the Bank's policy on dam safety (OP 4.37).

Preparation

4. Regional staff ensure that the borrower's terms of reference (TOR) for technical services to investigate the site and design the dam, supervise new or remedial construction, advise on initial reservoir filling and start-up operations, and perform inspections

---

1. "Bank" includes IDA, and "loans" includes credits.

and safety assessments, as well as the qualifications of the professionals (e.g., engineers, geologists, or hydrologists) to be employed by the borrower, are adequate to the complexity of the particular dam.

5. If an independent panel of experts is required, Regional staff advise borrower staff, as necessary, on the preparation of TOR. Regional staff review and clear the TOR and the panel members proposed by the borrower. Once the panel is in place, Regional staff normally attend panel meetings as observers.

6. Regional staff review all reports relating to dam safety prepared by the borrower, the panel, the independent specialists who assess an existing dam or a dam under construction (DUC), and the professionals hired by the borrower to design, construct, fill, and start up the dam.

7. Regional staff monitor the borrower's preparation of the plans for construction supervision and quality assurance, instrumentation, operation and maintenance, and emergency preparedness (see OP 4.37, para. 3(b), and BP 4.37, Annex A).

Appraisal

8. The appraisal team reviews all project information relevant to dam safety, including cost estimates; construction schedules; procurement procedures; technical assistance arrangements; environmental assessments; and the plans for construction supervision and quality assurance, instrumentation, operation and maintenance, and emergency preparedness. The team also reviews the project proposal, technical aspects, inspection reports, panel reports, and all other borrower action plans relating to dam safety. If a panel of experts has been required, the team verifies that the borrower has taken the panel's recommendations into consideration and, if necessary, assists the borrower in identifying sources for dam safety training or technical assistance.

9.   Regional staff and the assigned Bank lawyer ensure that the legal agreements between the Bank and the borrower require the borrower

(a)   if a panel has been required, to convene panel meetings periodically during project implementation and retain the panel through the start-up of a new dam;

(b)   to implement the required plans (see Annex A) and raise to the required standard any that have not been adequately developed; and

(c)   after filling and start-up of a new dam, to have periodic dam safety inspections performed by independent qualified professionals who have not been involved with the investigation, design, construction, or operation of the dam.

Supervision

10. During implementation, Regional staff monitor all activities relating to the dam safety provisions in the Loan Agreement, using technical staff and, as appropriate, consultants to assess the borrower's performance. If performance in regard to dam safety is found to be unsatisfactory, Regional staff promptly inform the borrower that the deficiencies must be remedied.

11. During the latter stages of project implementation, Regional staff discuss post-project operational procedures with the borrower, stressing the importance of ensuring that written instructions for flood operations and emergency preparedness are retained at the dam at all times. Regional staff also point out that the advent of new technology or new information (e.g., from floods, seismic events, or discovery of new regional or local geologic features) may in the future require the borrower to modify the technical criteria for evaluating dam safety; Regional staff urge the borrower to make such modifications and then apply the revised criteria to the project dam and, as necessary, to other dams under the borrower's jurisdiction.

12. To ensure that completed dams are inspected and maintained satisfactorily, Regional staff may carry out supervision beyond the closing date of the project, either during work on follow-up projects or during specially scheduled supervision missions.[2]

Policy Dialogue

13. As appropriate, Bank staff promote the adoption of institutional, legislative, and regulatory frameworks to upgrade dam safety programs in the country.

---

2.   *See* OD 13.05, *Project Supervision* (to be reissued as OP/BP 13.05).

Annex II–8

OD 4.20—September 1991

Indigenous Peoples

Introduction

1. This directive describes Bank[1] policies and processing procedures for projects that affect indigenous peoples. It sets out basic definitions, policy objectives, guidelines for the design and implementation of project provisions or components for indigenous peoples, and processing and documentation requirements.

2. The directive provides policy guidance to (a) ensure that indigenous people benefit from development projects, and (b) avoid or mitigate potentially adverse effects on indigenous people caused by Bank-assisted activities. Special action is required where Bank investments affect indigenous peoples, tribes, ethnic minorities, or other groups whose social and economic status restricts their capacity to assert their interests and rights in land and other productive resources.

Definitions

3. The terms "indigenous peoples," "indigenous ethnic minorities," "tribal groups," and "scheduled tribes" describe social groups with a social and cultural identity distinct from the

---

1. "Bank" includes IDA, and "loans" includes credits.

dominant society that makes them vulnerable to being disadvantaged in the development process. For the purposes of this directive, "indigenous peoples" is the term that will be used to refer to these groups.

4. Within their national constitutions, statutes, and relevant legislation, many of the Bank's borrower countries include specific definitional clauses and legal frameworks that provide a preliminary basis for identifying indigenous peoples.

5. Because of the varied and changing contexts in which indigenous peoples are found, no single definition can capture their diversity. Indigenous people are commonly among the poorest segments of a population. They engage in economic activities that range from shifting agriculture in or near forests to wage labor or even small-scale market-oriented activities. Indigenous peoples can be identified in particular geographical areas by the presence in varying degrees of the following characteristics:

(a) a close attachment to ancestral territories and to the natural resources in these areas;

(b) self-identification and identification by others as members of a distinct cultural group;

(c) an indigenous language, often different from the national language;

(d) presence of customary social and political institutions; and

(e) primarily subsistence-oriented production.

Task managers (TMs) must exercise judgment in determining the populations to which this directive applies and should make use of specialized anthropological and sociological experts throughout the project cycle.

Objective and Policy

6. The Bank's broad objective towards indigenous people, as for all the people in its member countries, is to ensure that the

development process fosters full respect for their dignity, human rights, and cultural uniqueness. More specifically, the objective at the center of this directive is to ensure that indigenous peoples do not suffer adverse effects during the development process, particularly from Bank-financed projects, and that they receive culturally compatible social and economic benefits.

7.   How to approach indigenous peoples affected by development projects is a controversial issue. Debate is often phrased as a choice between two opposed positions. One pole is to insulate indigenous populations whose cultural and economic practices make it difficult for them to deal with powerful outside groups. The advantages of this approach are the special protections that are provided and the preservation of cultural distinctiveness; the costs are the benefits foregone from development programs. The other pole argues that indigenous people must be acculturated to dominant society values and economic activities so that they can participate in national development. Here the benefits can include improved social and economic opportunities, but the cost is often the gradual loss of cultural differences.

8.   The Bank's policy is that the strategy for addressing the issues pertaining to indigenous peoples must be based on the *informed participation* of the indigenous people themselves. Thus, identifying local preferences through direct consultation, incorporation of indigenous knowledge into project approaches, and appropriate early use of experienced specialists are core activities for any project that affects indigenous peoples and their rights to natural and economic resources.

9.   Cases will occur, especially when dealing with the most isolated groups, where adverse impacts are unavoidable and adequate mitigation plans have not been developed. In such situations, the Bank will not appraise projects until suitable plans are developed by the borrower and reviewed by the Bank. In other cases, indigenous people may wish to be and can be incorporated into the development process. In sum, a full range of positive actions by the borrower must ensure that indigenous people benefit from development investments.

Bank Role

10. The Bank addresses issues on indigenous peoples through (a) country economic and sector work, (b) technical assistance, and (c) investment project components or provisions. Issues concerning indigenous peoples can arise in a variety of sectors that concern the Bank; those involving, for example, agriculture, road construction, forestry, hydropower, mining, tourism, education, and the environment should be carefully screened.[2] Issues related to indigenous peoples are commonly identified through the environmental assessment or social impact assessment processes, and appropriate measures should be taken under environmental mitigation actions (see OD 4.01, *Environmental Assessment*).

11. *Country Economic and Sector Work.* Country departments should maintain information on trends in government policies and institutions that deal with indigenous peoples. Issues concerning indigenous peoples should be addressed explicitly in sector and subsector work and brought into the Bank-country dialogue. National development policy frameworks and institutions for indigenous peoples often need to be strengthened in order to create a stronger basis for designing and processing projects with components dealing with indigenous peoples.

12. *Technical Assistance.* Technical assistance to develop the borrower's abilities to address issues on indigenous peoples can be provided by the Bank. Technical assistance is normally given within the context of project preparation, but technical assistance may also be needed to strengthen the relevant government institutions or to support development initiatives taken by indigenous people themselves.

13. *Investment Projects.* For an investment project that affects indigenous peoples, the borrower should prepare an indigenous

---

2. Displacement of indigenous people can be particularly damaging, and special efforts should be made to avoid it. *See* OD 4.30, *Involuntary Resettlement*, for additional policy guidance on resettlement issues involving indigenous people.

peoples development plan that is consistent with the Bank's policy. Any project that affects indigenous peoples is expected to include components or provisions that incorporate such a plan. When the bulk of the direct project beneficiaries are indigenous people, the Bank's concerns would be addressed by the project itself and the provisions of this OD would thus apply to the project in its entirety.

Indigenous Peoples Development Plan[3]

Prerequisites

14. Prerequisites of a successful development plan for indigenous peoples are as follows:

(a) The key step in project design is the preparation of a culturally appropriate development plan based on full consideration of the options preferred by the indigenous people affected by the project.

(b) Studies should make all efforts to *anticipate adverse trends* likely to be induced by the project and develop the means to avoid or mitigate harm.[4]

(c) The institutions responsible for government interaction with indigenous peoples should possess the social, technical, and legal skills needed for carrying out the proposed development activities. Implementation

---

3. Regionally specific technical guidelines for preparing indigenous peoples components, and case studies of best practices, are available from the Regional environment divisions (REDs).

4. For guidance on indigenous peoples and environmental assessment procedures, *see* OD 4.01, *Environmental Assessment*, and Chapter Seven of World Bank, *Environmental Assessment Sourcebook*, Technical Paper No. 139 (Washington, D.C., 1991).

arrangements should be kept simple. They should normally involve appropriate existing institutions, local organizations, and nongovernmental organizations (NGOs) with expertise in matters relating to indigenous peoples.

(d) Local patterns of social organization, religious beliefs, and resource use should be taken into account in the plan's design.

(e) Development activities should support production systems that are well adapted to the needs and environment of indigenous peoples, and should help production systems under stress to attain sustainable levels.

(f) The plan should avoid creating or aggravating the dependency of indigenous people on project entities. Planning should encourage early handover of project management to local people. As needed, the plan should include general education and training in management skills for indigenous people from the onset of the project.

(g) Successful planning for indigenous peoples frequently requires long lead times, as well as arrangements for extended follow-up. Remote or neglected areas where little previous experience is available often require additional research and pilot programs to fine-tune development proposals.

(h) Where effective programs are already functioning, Bank support can take the form of incremental funding to strengthen them rather than the development of entirely new programs.

Contents

15. The development plan should be prepared in tandem with the preparation of the main investment. In many cases, proper protection of the rights of indigenous people will require the implementation of special project components that may lie out-

side the primary project's objectives. These components can include activities related to health and nutrition, productive infrastructure, linguistic and cultural preservation, entitlement to natural resources, and education. The project component for indigenous peoples development should include the following elements, as needed:

(a) *Legal Framework.* The plan should contain an assessment of (i) the legal status of the groups covered by this OD, as reflected in the country's constitution, legislation, and subsidiary legislation (regulations, administrative orders, etc.); and (ii) the ability of such groups to obtain access to and effectively use the legal system to defend their rights. Particular attention should be given to the rights of indigenous peoples to use and develop the lands that they occupy, to be protected against illegal intruders, and to have access to natural resources (such as forests, wildlife, and water) vital to their subsistence and reproduction.

(b) *Baseline Data.* Baseline data should include (i) accurate, up-to-date maps and aerial photographs of the area of project influence and the areas inhabited by indigenous peoples; (ii) analysis of the social structure and income sources of the population; (iii) inventories of the resources that indigenous people use and technical data on their production systems; and (iv) the relationship of indigenous peoples to other local and national groups. It is particularly important that baseline studies capture the full range of production and marketing activities in which indigenous people are engaged. Site visits by qualified social and technical experts should verify and update secondary sources.

(c) *Land Tenure.* When local legislation needs strengthening, the Bank should offer to advise and assist the borrower in establishing legal recognition of the customary or traditional land tenure systems of indigenous peoples. Where the traditional lands of indigenous peoples have been brought by law into the domain of the state and where it is inappropriate to convert traditional rights into those of legal ownership, alternative arrangements should be implemented to grant long-term, renewable rights of custodianship and use to indigenous peoples. These steps should be taken before the initiation of other planning steps that may be contingent on recognized land titles.

(d) *Strategy for Local Participation.* Mechanisms should be devised and maintained for participation by indigenous people in decision making throughout project planning, implementation, and evaluation. Many of the larger groups of indigenous people have their own representative organizations that provide effective channels for communicating local preferences. Traditional leaders occupy pivotal positions for mobilizing people and should be brought into the planning process, with due concern for ensuring genuine representation of the indigenous population.[5] No foolproof methods exist, however, to guarantee full local-level participation. Sociological and technical advice provided through the Regional environment divisions (REDs) is often needed to develop mechanisms appropriate for the project area.

(e) *Technical Identification of Development or Mitigation Activities.* Technical proposals should proceed from on-site research by qualified professionals acceptable to the Bank. Detailed descriptions should be prepared and appraised for such proposed services as education, training, health, credit, and legal assistance. Technical descriptions should be included for the planned investments in productive infrastructure. Plans that draw upon indigenous knowledge are often more successful than

---

5. *See also* "Community Involvement and the Role of Nongovernmental Organizations in Environmental Assessment" in World Bank, *Environmental Sourcebook*, Technical Paper No. 139 (Washington, D.C., 1991).

those introducing entirely new principles and institutions. For example, the potential contribution of traditional health providers should be considered in planning delivery systems for health care.

(f) *Institutional Capacity.* The government institutions assigned responsibility for indigenous peoples are often weak. Assessing the track record, capabilities, and needs of those institutions is a fundamental requirement. Organizational issues that need to be addressed through Bank assistance are the (i) availability of funds for investments and field operations; (ii) adequacy of experienced professional staff; (iii) ability of indigenous peoples' own organizations, local administration authorities, and local NGOs to interact with specialized government institutions; (iv) ability of the executing agency to mobilize other agencies involved in the plan's implementation; and (v) adequacy of field presence.

(g) *Implementation Schedule.* Components should include an implementation schedule with benchmarks by which progress can be measured at appropriate intervals. Pilot programs are often needed to provide planning information for phasing the project component for indigenous peoples with the main investment. The plan should pursue the long-term sustainability of project activities subsequent to completion of disbursement.

(h) *Monitoring and Evaluation.*[6] Independent monitoring capacities are usually needed when the institutions responsible for indigenous populations have weak management histories. Monitoring by representatives of indigenous peoples' own organizations can be an efficient way for the project management to absorb the perspectives of indigenous beneficiaries and is encouraged by the Bank. Monitoring units should be staffed by experienced social science professionals, and reporting

---

6. *See* OD 10.70, *Project Monitoring and Evaluation.*

formats and schedules appropriate to the project's needs should be established. Monitoring and evaluation reports should be reviewed jointly by the senior management of the implementing agency and by the Bank. The evaluation reports should be made available to the public.

(i) *Cost Estimates and Financing Plan.* The plan should include detailed cost estimates for planned activities and investments. The estimates should be broken down into unit costs by project year and linked to a financing plan. Such programs as revolving credit funds that provide indigenous people with investment pools should indicate their accounting procedures and mechanisms for financial transfer and replenishment. It is usually helpful to have as high a share as possible of direct financial participation by the Bank in project components dealing with indigenous peoples.

Project Processing and Documentation

Identification

16. During project identification, the borrower should be informed of the Bank's policy for indigenous peoples. The approximate number of potentially affected people and their location should be determined and shown on maps of the project area. The legal status of any affected groups should also be discussed. TMs should ascertain the relevant government agencies, and their policies, procedures, programs, and plans for indigenous peoples affected by the proposed project (see paras. 11 and 15(a)). TMs should also initiate anthropological studies necessary to identify local needs and preferences (see para. 15(b)). TMs, in consultation with the REDs, should signal indigenous peoples issues and the overall project strategy in the Initial Executive Project Summary (IEPS).

Preparation

17. If it is agreed in the IEPS meeting that special action is needed, the indigenous peoples development plan or project component should be developed during project preparation. As necessary, the Bank should assist the borrower in preparing terms of reference and should provide specialized technical assistance (see para. 12). Early involvement of anthropologists and local NGOs with expertise in matters related to indigenous peoples is a useful way to identify mechanisms for effective participation and local development opportunities. In a project that involves the land rights of indigenous peoples, the Bank should work with the borrower to clarify the steps needed for putting land tenure on a regular footing as early as possible, since land disputes frequently lead to delays in executing measures that are contingent on proper land titles (see para. 15(c)).

Appraisal

18. The plan for the development component for indigenous peoples should be submitted to the Bank along with the project's overall feasibility report, prior to project appraisal. Appraisal should assess the adequacy of the plan, the suitability of policies and legal frameworks, the capabilities of the agencies charged with implementing the plan, and the adequacy of the allocated technical, financial, and social resources. Appraisal teams should be satisfied that indigenous people have participated meaningfully in the development of the plan as described in para. 14(a) (also see para. 15(d). It is particularly important to appraise proposals for regularizing land access and use.

Implementation and Supervision

19. Supervision planning should make provisions for including the appropriate anthropological, legal, and technical skills in Bank

supervision missions during project implementation (see paras. 15(g) and (h), and OD 13.05, *Project Supervision*). Site visits by TMs and specialists are essential. Midterm and final evaluations should assess progress and recommend corrective actions when necessary.

Documentation

20. The borrower's commitments for implementing the indigenous peoples development plan should be reflected in the loan documents; legal provisions should provide Bank staff with clear benchmarks that can be monitored during supervision. The Staff Appraisal Report and the Memorandum and Recommendation of the President should summarize the plan or project provisions.

Annex II–9

OD 4.30—June 1990

Involuntary Resettlement

Introduction

1. This directive describes Bank[1] policy and procedures on involuntary resettlement, as well as the conditions that borrowers are expected to meet in operations involving involuntary resettlement.[2] Planning and financing resettlement components or freestanding projects are an integral part of preparation for projects that cause involuntary displacement. Any operation that involves land acquisition or is screened as a Category A or B project for environmental assessment purposes[3] should be reviewed for potential resettlement requirements early in the project cycle (para. 20).

2. Development projects that displace people involuntarily[4] generally give rise to severe economic, social, and environmental problems: production systems are dismantled; productive assets and income sources are lost; people are relocated to environments where their productive skills may be less applicable and the competition for resources greater; community structures and social

---

1. "Bank" includes IDA, and "loans" includes credits.
2. *See also Involuntary Resettlement in Development Projects*, World Bank Technical Paper No. 80 (Washington, D.C.: The World Bank, 1988).
3. OD 4.00, Annex A, *Environmental Assessment*, para. 18.
4. Such projects may include construction or establishment of (a) dams, (b) new towns or ports, (c) housing and urban infrastructure, (d) mines, (e) large industrial plants, (f) railways or highways, (g) irrigation canals, and (h) national parks or protected areas. Refugees from natural disasters, war, or civil strife are also involuntary resettlers, but they are not discussed in this directive (see OP/BP/GP 8.50, *Emergency Recovery Assistance*).

networks are weakened; kin groups are dispersed; and cultural identity, traditional authority, and the potential for mutual help are diminished. Involuntary resettlement may cause severe long-term hardship, impoverishment, and environmental damage unless appropriate measures are carefully planned and carried out.[5]

Policy Objectives

3. The objective of the Bank's resettlement policy is to ensure that the population displaced by a project receives benefits from it. Involuntary resettlement is an integral part of project design and should be dealt with from the earliest stages of project preparation (para. 28), taking into account the following policy considerations:

(a) Involuntary resettlement should be avoided or minimized where feasible, exploring all viable alternative project designs. For example, realignment of roads or reductions in dam height may significantly reduce resettlement needs.

(b) Where displacement is unavoidable, resettlement plans should be developed. All involuntary resettlement should be conceived and executed as development programs, with resettlers provided with sufficient investment resources and opportunities to share in project benefits. Displaced persons should be (i) compensated for their losses at full replacement cost prior to the actual move; (ii) assisted with the move and supported during the transition period in the resettlement site; and (iii) assisted in their efforts to improve their former living standards, income earning capacity, and production levels, or at least to restore them. Particular attention should be paid to the needs of the poorest groups to be resettled.

---

5. OD 4.00, Annex A, *Environmental Assessment*, para. 2, and Annex A3.

(c) Community participation in planning and implementing resettlement should be encouraged. Appropriate patterns of social organization should be established, and existing social and cultural institutions of resettlers and their hosts[6] should be supported and used to the greatest extent possible.

(d) Resettlers should be integrated socially and economically into host communities so that adverse impacts on host communities are minimized. The best way of achieving this integration is for resettlement to be planned in areas benefiting from the project and through consultation with the future hosts.

(e) Land, housing, infrastructure, and other compensation should be provided to the adversely affected population, indigenous groups,[7] ethnic minorities, and pastoralists who may have usufruct or customary rights to the land or other resources taken for the project. The absence of legal title to land by such groups should not be a bar to compensation.

Resettlement Planning

4. Where large-scale[8] population displacement is unavoidable, a detailed resettlement plan, timetable, and budget are required. Resettlement plans should be built around a development strategy and package aimed at improving or at least restoring the economic base for those relocated. Experience indicates that cash compensation alone is normally inadequate. Voluntary settlement may form part of a resettlement plan, provided

---

6. Host communities are those receiving resettlers.

7. *See* OD 4.20, *Indigenous Peoples.*

8. Where only a few people (e.g., less than 100–200 individuals) are to be relocated, appropriate compensation for assets, logistical support for moving, and a relocation grant may be the only requirements. However, the principles on which compensation is to be based are the same as for larger groups.

measures to address the special circumstances of involuntary resettlers are included. Preference should be given to land-based resettlement strategies for people dislocated from agricultural settings. If suitable land is unavailable, nonland-based strategies built around opportunities for employment or self-employment may be used.

Plan Content

5. The content and level of detail of resettlement plans, which will vary with circumstances, especially the magnitude of resettlement, should normally include a statement of objectives and policies, an executive summary, and provision for the following:

(a) organizational responsibilities (para. 6);

(b) community participation and integration with host populations (paras. 7–10);

(c) socioeconomic survey (para. 11);

(d) legal framework (para. 12);

(e) alternative sites and selection (para. 13);

(f) valuation of and compensation for lost assets (paras. 14–16);

(g) land tenure, acquisition, and transfer (para. 17);

(h) access to training, employment, and credit (para. 18);

(i) shelter, infrastructure, and social services (para. 19);

(j) environmental protection and management (para. 20); and

(k) implementation schedule, monitoring, and evaluation (paras. 21–22).

Cost estimates should be prepared for these activities, and they should be budgeted and scheduled in coordination with the physical works of the main investment project.

Organizational Responsibilities

6. The responsibility for resettlement rests with the borrower. The organizational framework for managing resettlement must be developed during preparation and adequate resources provided to the responsible institutions. The organization responsible for resettlement should be strengthened when entities executing infrastructure or other sector-specific projects lack the experience and outlook needed to design and implement resettlement. One alternative is to create a special resettlement unit within the project entity: this can facilitate the involvement of other line agencies. Another alternative is to entrust resettlement to the regional or town administration that knows the population and area, can mobilize local expertise, speaks the resettlers' language, and will ultimately be responsible for the integration of resettlers into the host population and area. There also may be considerable scope for involving nongovernmental organizations (NGOs) in planning, implementing, and monitoring resettlement.[9]

Community Participation and Integration with Host Population

7. Most displaced people prefer to move as part of a preexisting community, neighborhood, or kinship group. The acceptability of a resettlement plan can be increased and the disruption caused by resettlement can be cushioned by moving people in groups, reducing dispersion, sustaining existing patterns of group organization, and retaining access to cultural property[10] (temples, pilgrimage centers, etc.), if necessary, through the relocation of the property.

---

9. *See* GP 14.70, *Involving Nongovernmental Organizations in Bank-Supported Activities.*

10. *See* OPN 11.03, *Management of Cultural Property in Bank-Financed Projects,* to be reissued as OP/BP 4.11, *Cultural Property.*

8. The involvement of involuntary resettlers and hosts in planning prior to the move is critical. Initial resistance to the idea of involuntary resettlement is to be expected. To obtain cooperation, participation, and feedback, the affected hosts and resettlers need to be systematically informed and consulted during preparation of the resettlement plan about their options and rights. They should also be able to choose from a number of acceptable resettlement alternatives. These steps can be taken directly or through formal and informal leaders and representatives. Experience has shown that local NGOs can often provide valuable assistance and ensure viable community participation. Moreover, institutionalized arrangements, such as regular meetings between project officials and communities, should be provided for resettlers and hosts to communicate their concerns about the resettlement program to project staff throughout planning and implementation.[11] Particular attention must be given to ensure that vulnerable groups such as indigenous people, ethnic minorities, the landless, and women are represented adequately in such arrangements.

9. The plan should address and mitigate resettlement's impact on host populations. Host communities and local governments should be informed and consulted. Any payment due the hosts for land or other assets provided to resettlers should be promptly rendered. Conflicts between hosts and resettlers may develop as increased demands are placed on land, water, forests, services, etc., or if the resettlers are provided services and housing superior to that of the hosts. Conditions and services in host communities should improve, or at least not deteriorate. Providing improved education, water, health, and production

---

11. Disputes of varying kinds may arise in the process of implementation of the agreed resettlement plan. These conflicts could take the form of appeals related to the compensation payable to affected persons, conflicts between the displaced persons and the host population, appeals to the agency charged with the implementation of the resettlement with regard to services promised, etc. It is therefore important to devise schemes for conflict resolution for all resettlement plans. Such schemes should, as far as possible, take into account existing procedures for settling disputes in the country or area concerned.

services to both groups fosters a better social climate for their integration. In the long run, the extra investment will help prevent conflicts and secure the project's aims.

10. Successful resettlement requires a timely transfer of responsibility from settlement agencies to the settlers themselves. Otherwise, a dependency relationship may arise, and agency resources may become tied up in a limited number of continually supervised schemes. Local leadership must be encouraged to assume responsibility for environmental management and infrastructure maintenance.

Socioeconomic Survey

11. Resettlement plans should be based on recent information about the scale and impact of resettlement on the displaced population. In addition to describing standard household characteristics, socioeconomic surveys should describe (a) the magnitude of displacement; (b) information on the full resource base of the affected population, including income derived from informal sector and nonfarm activities, and from common property; (c) the extent to which groups will experience total or partial loss of assets; (d) public infrastructure and social services that will be affected; (e) formal and informal institutions (such as community organizations, ritual groups, etc.) that can assist with designing and implementing the resettlement programs; and (f) attitudes on resettlement options. Socioeconomic surveys, recording the names of affected families, should be conducted as early as possible to prevent inflows of population ineligible for compensation.

Legal Framework

12. A clear understanding of the legal issues involved in resettlement is needed to design a feasible resettlement plan. An analysis should be made to determine the nature of the legal framework for the resettlement envisaged, including (a) the scope of the

power of eminent domain, the nature of compensation associated with it, both in terms of the valuation methodology and the timing of payment; (b) the legal and administrative procedures applicable, including the appeals process and the normal timeframe for such procedures; (c) land titling and registration procedures; and (d) laws and regulations relating to the agencies responsible for implementing resettlement and those related to land compensation, consolidation, land use, environment, water use, and social welfare.

Alternative Sites and Selection

13. The identification of several possible relocation sites and the demarcation of selected sites is a critical step for both rural and urban resettlement. For land-based resettlement, the new site's productive potential and locational advantages should be at least equivalent to those of the old site. The Bank encourages "land for land" approaches, providing replacement land at least equivalent to the lost land. For rural settlers, irrigation, land reclamation, tree crop development, intensification of production, and other innovations often can provide adequate production potential on limited amounts of land to resettle agriculturalists, even in countries with high population densities. In selecting sites, attention must be paid to the availability of sources of off-farm income (fishing, gathering forest products, seasonal wage employment) to complement farm income. For urban resettlers, the new site should ensure comparable access to employment, infrastructure, services, and production opportunities. For both rural and urban resettlement, the borrower needs to (a) develop institutional and technical arrangements for identifying and preparing relocation sites, e.g., pooling together small plots, wasteland reclamation, land leveling, and terracing; (b) draw up timetables and budgets for site preparation and transfer; (c) make legal arrangements for transferring titles to resettlers; and (d) consider, when necessary, a temporary freeze on land transactions within the relocation area to prevent land speculation. Though the Bank does not

normally disburse against land acquisition, it can finance land improvement to accommodate resettlers.

Valuation of and Compensation for Lost Assets

14. Valuation of lost assets should be made at their replacement cost. Compensation is facilitated by (a) paying special attention to the adequacy of the legal arrangements concerning land title, registration, and site occupation; (b) publicizing among people to be displaced the laws and regulations on valuation and compensation; (c) establishing criteria for determining the resettlement eligibility of affected households, e.g., households that have only partially lost their assets but are no longer economically viable should be entitled to full resettlement; and (d) developing mechanisms to prevent illegal encroachers and squatters, including an influx of nonresidents entering to take advantage of such benefits, from participating in the compensation arrangements, by an early recording of the numbers and names of affected populations entitled to compensation/rehabilitation.

15. Some types of loss, such as access to (a) public services; (b) customers and suppliers; and (c) fishing, grazing, or forest areas, cannot easily be evaluated or compensated for in monetary terms. Attempts must therefore be made to establish access to equivalent and culturally acceptable resources and earning opportunities.

16. Vulnerable groups at particular risk are indigenous people, the landless and semilandless, and households headed by females who, though displaced, may not be protected through national land compensation legislation. The resettlement plan must include land allocation or culturally acceptable alternative income-earning strategies to protect the livelihood of these people.

Land Tenure, Acquisition, and Transfer

17. Resettlement plans should review the main land tenure and transfer systems, including common property and nontitle-based

usufruct systems governed by locally recognized land allocation mechanisms. The objective is to treat customary and formal rights as equally as possible in devising compensation rules and procedures. The plan should address the issues raised by the different tenure systems found in a project area, including (a) the compensation eligibility of land-dependent populations; (b) the valuation procedures applicable to different tenure types; and (c) the grievance procedures available for disputes over land acquisition. Plans should contain provisions for conducting land surveys and regularizing land tenure in the earliest stages of project development. Planning should also anticipate the approximate time needed to acquire and transfer land.

Access to Training, Employment, and Credit

18. Normally, general economic growth cannot be relied upon to protect the welfare of the project-affected population. Thus, alternative employment strategies are needed for nonagricultural displaced people, or where the land that can be made available is not sufficient to accommodate all the displaced farmers. The resettlement plan should, where feasible, exploit new economic activities made possible by the main investment requiring the displacement. Vocational training, employment counseling, transportation to jobs, employment in the main investment project or in resettlement activities, establishment of industries, incentives for firms to locate in the area, credit and extension for small businesses or reservoir aquaculture, and preference in public sector employment should all be considered where appropriate.

Shelter, Infrastructure, and Social Services

19. To ensure the economic and social viability of the relocated communities, adequate resources should be allocated to provide shelter, infrastructure (e.g., water supply, feeder roads), and social

services (e.g., schools, health care centers).[12] Site development, engineering, and architectural designs should be prepared for shelter, infrastructure, and social services. Since community or self-built houses are often better accepted and more tailored to the resettlers' needs than contractor-built housing, provision of a building site with suitable infrastructure, model plans, building materials, technical assistance, and "construction allowances" (for income foregone while resettlers build their houses) is an option communities should be offered. Planning for shelter, infrastructure, and services should take into account population growth.

Environmental Protection and Management

20. The screening process for an environmental assessment (EA) normally classifies projects involving involuntary resettlement as Category A.[13] The EA of the main investment requiring the resettlement should thus cover the potential environmental impacts of the resettlement. The resettlement plan must be developed in coordination with the EA and define the boundaries of the relocation area, and calculate incremental population density per land unit. In agricultural projects (involving, for example, relocation to the catchment surrounding a reservoir, or to a downstream command area), if the incoming resettled population is large in relation to the host population, such environmental issues as deforestation, overgrazing, soil erosion, sanitation, and pollution are likely to become serious and plans should either include appropriate mitigating measures, including training of oustees, or else should allow for alternative sites to be selected.

---

12. Health care services, particularly for pregnant women, infants, and the elderly, may be important during and after relocation to prevent increases in morbidity and mortality due to malnutrition, the stress of being uprooted, and the usually increased risk of water-borne diseases.

13. *See* OD 4.00, Annex A, *Environmental Assessment*, and Annex B, *Environmental Policy for Dam and Reservoir Projects.* The environmental implications of involuntary resettlement will be further discussed under para 6.0, "Special Issues in Environmental Assessment," in *Environmental Assessment Sourcebook* (Washington, D.C.: The World Bank, to be issued).

Urban resettlement raises other density-related issues (e.g., transportation capacity, access to potable water, sanitation systems, health facilities, etc.). Constructive environmental management, provided through the EA's mitigation plan,[14] may provide good opportunities and benefits to resettlers and host populations alike (e.g., project-financed compensatory afforestation not only replaces the forests submerged by reservoirs but also offers gainful employment). If the likely consequences on the environment are unacceptable, alternative and/or additional relocation sites must be found.

Implementation Schedule, Monitoring, and Evaluation

21. The timing of resettlement should be coordinated with the implementation of the main investment component of the project requiring the resettlement. All resettlement plans should include an implementation schedule for each activity covering initial baseline and preparation, actual relocation, and post-relocation economic and social activities. The plan should include a target date when the expected benefits to resettlers and hosts would be achieved.

22. Arrangements for monitoring implementation of resettlement and evaluating its impact should be developed by the borrower during project preparation and used during supervision.[15] Monitoring provides both a warning system for project managers and a channel for the resettlers to make known their needs and their reactions to resettlement execution. Monitoring and evaluation units should be adequately funded and staffed by specialists in resettlement. In-house monitoring by the implementing agency may need to be supplemented by independent monitors to ensure complete and objective information. Annual and midterm reviews are desirable for large-scale resettlement. The

---

14. *See* Annex A1, para. 2, in OD 4.00, Annex A, *Environmental Assessment.*

15. *See* OD 10.70, *Project Monitoring and Evaluation.*

borrower should be required to continue impact evaluation for a reasonable period after all resettlement and related development activities have been completed. The borrower should also be required to inform the Bank about the findings.

Bank Role and Project Options

23. The Bank supports borrowers' efforts through (a) assistance in designing and assessing resettlement policy, strategies, laws, regulations, and specific plans; (b) financing technical assistance to strengthen the capacity of agencies responsible for resettlement; and (c) direct financing of the investment costs of resettlement. The Bank may sometimes finance resettlement even though it has not financed the main investment that made displacement and resettlement necessary (para. 26).

24. The task manager (TM) should inform the borrower of the Bank's resettlement policy. Starting early in the project cycle, the TM with the support of Bank operational, research, and legal staff should assess government policies, experiences, institutions, and the legal framework covering resettlement. In particular, the TM needs to ensure that involuntary resettlement is avoided or minimized, that laws and regulations concerning displaced people provide compensation sufficient to replace all lost assets, and that displaced persons are assisted to improve, or at least restore, their former living standards, income earning capacity, and production levels.

25. The adequacy of the resettlement plan should be reviewed by appropriate social, technical, and legal experts. Resettlement specialists should visit the possible resettlement sites and review their suitability. In the case of large-scale relocation, such experts should be included in independent technical or environmental review boards.[16]

---

16. *See* OD 4.00, Annex B, *Environmental Policy for Dam and Reservoir Projects.*

26. Bank financing of resettlement can be provided as follows: (a) As a component of the main investment project causing displacement and requiring resettlement. (b) If large enough, as a free-standing resettlement project with appropriate cross-conditionalities, processed and implemented in parallel with the investment project that causes the displacement. The latter approach may better focus country and Bank attention on the effective resolution of resettlement issues. (c) As a sector investment loan.[17] Where the specific resettlement needs of each subproject are not known in advance, the borrower would need to agree to resettlement policies, planning principles, institutional arrangements, and design criteria that meet Bank policy and requirements as a condition of the loan. An estimate should be provided of total population to be displaced and overall resettlement costs, as well as an evaluation of proposed resettlement sites. Subprojects in sector investment loans should be screened by the implementing agency to ensure consistency with this directive, and approved individually by the Bank. For countries with a series of operations requiring resettlement, efforts to improve the policy, institutional, and legal framework for resettlement should form part of the Bank's ongoing country and sector dialogue with the government. These efforts should be appropriately reflected in economic and sector work and in country strategy papers and briefs.

Processing and Documentation

27. The Regional Vice President (RVP) should be kept informed of major resettlement issues, and his guidance sought where necessary. The Regional Environment Division (RED), the Legal Department (LEG), and settlement specialists in Sector Policy and Research (PRS) should be consulted or included as necessary in peer reviews on involuntary resettlement issues throughout the project cycle.

---

17. *See* OP 1.00, *Bank Lending Instruments.*

Identification

28. The possibility of involuntary resettlement should be determined as early as possible and described in all project documents. The TM should (a) briefly summarize in the Initial Executive Project Summary (Initial EPS)[18] the magnitude, strategy, and timing of the resettlement; (b) inform borrowers of the Bank's resettlement policy; (c) review past borrower experience with similar operations; (d) invite agencies responsible for resettlement to discuss their policies, plans, and institutional, consultative, and legal arrangements for resettlement; and (e) where appropriate, ensure that technical assistance is provided early to borrowers. Such assistance should include the use of project preparation facility (PPF) resources[19] for planning resettlement and building institutional capacity.

Preparation

29. During project preparation, the feasibility of resettlement must be established, a strategy agreed upon, the resettlement plan drafted, and budget estimates prepared.[20] The full costs of resettlement should be identified and included in the total cost of the main investment project, regardless of financing source. The costs of resettlement should also be treated as a charge against the economic benefits of the investment project that causes the relocation. Any net benefits to resettlers (as compared to the "without project" circumstances) should be added to the benefit stream of the main investment. While the resettlement

---

18. *See* OP/BP 10.00, *Investment Lending: Identification to Board Presentation.*

19. *See* OP/BP 8.10, *Project Preparation Facility.*

20. Detailed guidelines for preparing and appraising resettlement plans are provided in *Involuntary Resettlement in Development Projects*, World Bank Technical Paper No. 80, Annex 1 (Washington, D.C.: The World Bank, 1988). Pro forma cost tables and guidelines for economic and financial analysis are provided in Annex 2.

component or free-standing project need not be economically viable on its own, it should be the least-cost approach consistent with the policies laid out above.

Appraisal and Negotiation

30. Submission to the Bank of a time-bound resettlement plan and budget that conforms to Bank policy is a condition of appraisal for projects involving resettlement, except for sector investment loans as discussed in para. 26. All final EPSs should confirm that this requirement has been met. The appraisal mission should ascertain (a) the extent that involuntary resettlement and human hardship will be minimized and whether borrowers can manage the process; (b) the adequacy of the plan, including the timetable and budget for resettlement and compensation; (c) the soundness of the economic and financial analysis; (d) the availability and adequacy of sites and funding for all resettlement activities; (e) the feasibility of the implementation arrangements; and (f) the extent of involvement of beneficiaries. At negotiations, the borrower and the Bank should agree on the resettlement plan. The resettlement plan and the borrower's obligation to carry it out should be reflected in the legal documents. Other necessary resettlement-related actions must be covenanted. The Staff Appraisal Report and the Memorandum and Recommendation of the President should summarize the plan and state that it meets Bank policy requirements.

Implementation and Supervision

31. Resettlement components should be supervised throughout implementation.[21] Supervision that is sporadic or left until late in implementation invariably jeopardizes the success of resettlement. Bank supervision missions should be staffed with the

---

21. *See* OD 13.05, *Project Supervision*, particularly paras. 44–47.

requisite social, economic, and technical expertise. Annual reviews of large-scale resettlement and in-depth Bank reviews of midterm progress are highly desirable. These reviews should be planned from the outset to allow the Bank and the borrower to make necessary adjustments in project implementation. Complete recovery from resettlement can be protracted and can often make it necessary to continue Bank supervision until well after populations have been relocated, sometimes even after a project has been closed.

Ex Post Evaluation

32. The project completion report[22] submitted to the Operations Evaluation Department should evaluate resettlement and its impact on the standards of living of the resettlers and the host population.

---

22. *See* OP/BP/GP 13.55, *Implementation Completion Reporting.*

INTERNATIONAL LAW ASPECTS

Annex II–10–1

OP/BP 7.50—October 1994

Projects on International Waterways

Applicability of Policy

1. The Bank's[1] operational policy covers the following types of international waterways:

   (a) any river, canal, lake, or similar body of water that forms a boundary between, or any river or body of surface water that flows through, two or more states, whether Bank members or not;

   (b) any tributary or other body of surface water that is a component of any waterway described in (a) above; and

   (c) any bay, gulf, strait, or channel bounded by two or more states or, if within one state, recognized as a necessary channel of communication between the open sea and other states—and any river flowing into such waters.

2. The policy applies to the following types of projects:

   (a) hydroelectric, irrigation, flood control, navigation, drainage, water and sewerage, industrial, and similar projects that involve the use or potential pollution of international waterways as described in para. 1 above; and

---

1. "Bank" includes IDA, and "loans" includes credits.

(b) detailed design and engineering studies of projects under
     para. 2(a) above, including those to be carried out by the
     Bank as executing agency or in any other capacity.

Agreements/Arrangements

3. Projects on international waterways may affect relations
between the Bank and its borrowers[2] and between states
(whether members of the Bank or not). The Bank recognizes that
the cooperation and goodwill of riparians is essential for the efficient utilization and protection of the waterway. Therefore, it
attaches great importance to riparians' making appropriate agreements or arrangements for these purposes for the entire waterway
or any part thereof. The Bank stands ready to assist riparians in
achieving this end. In cases where differences remain unresolved
between the state proposing the project (beneficiary state) and
the other riparians, prior to financing the project the Bank normally urges the beneficiary state to offer to negotiate in good
faith with the other riparians to reach appropriate agreements or
arrangements.

Notification

4. The Bank ensures that the international aspects of a project
on an international waterway are dealt with at the earliest possible opportunity. If such a project is proposed, the Bank requires
the beneficiary state, if it has not already done so, formally to
notify the other riparians of the proposed project and its Project
Details (see BP 7.50, para. 3). If the prospective borrower indicates to the Bank that it does not wish to give notification, normally the Bank itself does so. If the borrower also objects to the
Bank's doing so, the Bank discontinues processing of the project.
The executive directors concerned are informed of these developments and any further steps taken.

---

2.   "Borrower" refers to the member country in whose territory the project is carried out, whether the country is the borrower or the guarantor.

5. The Bank ascertains whether the riparians have entered into agreements or arrangements or have established any institutional framework for the waterway concerned. In the latter case, the Bank ascertains the scope of the institution's activities and functions and the status of its involvement in the proposed project, bearing in mind the possible need for notifying the institution.

6. Following notification, if the other riparians raise objections to the proposed project, the Bank in appropriate cases may appoint one or more independent experts to examine the issues in accordance with BP 7.50, paras. 8–12. Should the Bank decide to proceed with the project despite the objections of the other riparians, the Bank informs them of its decision.

Exceptions to Notification Requirement

7. The following exceptions are allowed to the Bank's requirement that the other riparian states be notified of the proposed project:

(a) For any ongoing schemes, projects involving additions or alterations that require rehabilitation, construction, or other changes that in the judgment of the Bank

    (i) will not adversely change the quality or quantity of water flows to the other riparians; and

    (ii) will not be adversely affected by the other riparians' possible water use.

    This exception applies only to minor additions or alterations to the ongoing scheme; it does not cover works and activities that would exceed the original scheme, change its nature, or so alter or expand its scope and extent as to make it appear a new or different scheme. In case of doubt regarding the extent to which a project meets the criteria of this exception, the executive directors representing the riparians concerned are informed and given at least two months to reply. Even if projects meet the criteria of this exception, the Bank tries to secure compliance with the requirements of any agreement or arrangement between the riparians.

(b) Water resource surveys and feasibility studies on or involving international waterways. However, the state proposing such activities includes in the terms of reference for the activities an examination of any potential riparian issues.

(c) Any project that relates to a tributary of an international waterway where the tributary runs exclusively in one state and the state is the lowest downstream riparian, unless there is concern that the project could cause appreciable harm to other states.

Presentation of Loans to the Executive Directors

8. For every project on an international waterway, the Staff Appraisal Report (SAR) and Memorandum and Recommendation of the President (MOP) deal with the international aspects of the project, and state that Bank staff have considered these aspects and are satisfied that

(a) the issues involved are covered by an appropriate agreement or arrangement between the beneficiary state and the other riparians; or

(b) the other riparians have given a positive response to the beneficiary state or Bank, in the form of consent, no objection, support to the project, or confirmation that the project will not harm their interests; or

(c) in all other cases, in the assessment of Bank staff, the project will not cause appreciable harm to the other riparians, and will not be appreciably harmed by the other riparians' possible water use. The MOP also contains in an annex the salient features of any objection and, where applicable, the report and conclusions of the independent experts.

Maps

9. Documentation for a project on an international waterway includes a map that clearly indicates the waterway and the location of the project's components. This requirement applies to the SAR, the MOP, the Project Information Document (PID), and any internal memoranda that deal with the riparian issues associated with the project. Maps are provided for projects on international waterways even when notification to riparians is not required by the provisions of OP 7.50. Maps are prepared and cleared in accordance with Administrative Manual Statement 7.10, *Cartographic Services*, and its annexes.

10. However, the inclusion of maps in the cited documents, except internal memoranda, is subject to any general instruction or decision of the Regional vice president, taken in consultation with the Senior Vice President and General Counsel, to omit maps of the beneficiary state in entirety or in part.

Annex II–10–2

BP 7.50—October 1994

Projects on International Waterways

1. A potential international water rights issue is assessed as early as possible in identification[1] and described in all project documents starting with the Project Information Document (PID). The cover memorandum for the preappraisal package including the PID is prepared in collaboration with the Legal Department (LEG) to convey all relevant information on international aspects of the project; the memorandum is addressed to the vice president of the Region processing the project (RVP) and copied to the Senior Vice President and General Counsel (LEGVP). Throughout the project cycle, the country department (CD) director, in consultation with LEG, keeps the managing director (MD), operations, concerned abreast of international aspects of the project and related events, through the RVP.

Notification

2. As early as possible during identification, the Bank[2] advises the state proposing the project on an international waterway (beneficiary state) that, if it has not already done so, it should formally notify the other riparians of the proposed project, including the Project Details (see para. 3). However, if the prospective borrower[3] indicates to the Bank that it does not wish to give notification, normally the Bank itself does so. If the beneficiary

---

1. *See* BP 10.00, *Investment Lending: Identification to Board Presentation*, step 1.
2. "Bank" includes IDA, and "loans" includes credits.
3. "Borrower" refers to the member country in whose territory the project is carried out, whether the country is the borrower or the guarantor.

state also objects to the Bank's doing so, the Bank discontinues processing of the project. The executive directors concerned (EDs) are informed of these developments and any further steps taken.

3.   The notification contains, to the extent available, sufficient technical specifications, information, and other data (Project Details) to enable the other riparians to determine as accurately as possible whether the proposed project has potential for causing appreciable harm through water deprivation or pollution or otherwise. Bank staff should be satisfied that the Project Details are adequate for making such a determination. If adequate Project Details are not available at the time of notification, they are made available to the other riparians as soon as possible after the notification. If, in exceptional circumstances, the Region proposes to go ahead with project appraisal before Project Details are available, the CD director, via a memorandum prepared in consultation with LEG and copied to the LEGVP, notifies the RVP of all relevant facts on international aspects and asks approval to proceed. In making this decision, the RVP seeks the advice of the MD concerned.

4.   The other riparians are allowed a reasonable period, normally not exceeding six months from the dispatch of the Project Details, to respond to the beneficiary state or Bank.

Responses/Objections

5.   After giving notice, if the beneficiary state or Bank receives a positive response from the other riparians (in the form of consent, no objection, support to the project, or confirmation that the project will not harm their interests), or if the other riparians have not responded within the stipulated time, the CD director, in consultation with LEG and other departments concerned, addresses a memorandum to the RVP. The memorandum reports all relevant facts, including staff assessment of whether the project would (a) cause appreciable harm to the interests of the other riparians, or (b) be appreciably harmed by the other riparians'

possible water use. The memorandum asks approval for further action. In making this decision, the RVP seeks the advice of the MD concerned.

6.   If the other riparians object to the proposed project, the CD director, in collaboration with LEG and other departments concerned, sends a memorandum on the objections to the RVP and copies it to the LEGVP. The memorandum addresses

(a) the nature of the riparian issues;

(b) the Bank staff's assessment of the objections raised, including the reasons for them and any available supporting data;

(c) the staff's assessment of whether the proposed project will cause appreciable harm to the interests of the other riparians, or be appreciably harmed by the other riparians' possible water use;

(d) the question of whether the circumstances of the case require that the Bank, before taking any further action, urge the parties to resolve the issues through amicable means such as consultations, negotiations, and good offices (which will normally be resorted to when the other riparians' objections are substantiated); and

(e) the question of whether the objections are of such a nature that it is advisable to obtain an additional opinion from independent experts in accordance with paras. 8–12.

7. The RVP seeks the advice of the MD concerned and the LEGVP, and decides whether and how to proceed. Based on these consultations, the RVP may recommend to the MD concerned that the Operations Committee consider the matter. The CD director then acts upon either the Operations Committee's instructions, which are issued by the chairman, or the RVP's instructions, and reports the outcome in a memorandum prepared in collaboration with LEG and other departments concerned. The memorandum, sent to the RVP and copied to the LEGVP, includes recommendations for processing the project further.

Seeking the Opinion of Independent Experts

8. If independent expert opinion is needed before further processing of the project (see OP 7.50, para. 6), the RVP requests the Vice President, Environmentally Sustainable Development (ESDVP) to initiate the process. The Office of the ESDVP maintains a record of such requests.

9. The ESDVP, in consultation with the RVP and LEG, selects one or more independent experts from a roster maintained by ESDVP (see para. 12). The experts selected may not be nationals of any of the riparians of the waterways in question, and also may not have any other conflicts of interest in the matter. The experts are engaged and their terms of reference prepared jointly by the offices of the ESDVP and the RVP. The latter finances the costs associated with engaging the experts. The experts are provided with the background information and assistance needed to complete their work efficiently.

10. The experts' terms of reference require that they examine the Project Details. If they deem it necessary to verify the Project Details or take any related action, the Bank makes its best efforts to assist. The experts meet on an ad hoc basis until they submit their report to the ESDVP and the RVP. The ESDVP or RVP may ask them to explain or clarify any aspect of their report.

11. The experts have no decision-making role in the project's processing. Their technical opinion is submitted for the Bank's purposes only, and does not in any way determine the rights and obligations of the riparians. Their conclusions are reviewed by the RVP and ESDVP, in consultation with the LEGVP.

12. The ESDVP maintains, in consultation with the RVPs and LEG, the roster of highly qualified independent experts, which consists of 10 names and is updated at the beginning of each fiscal year.

Annex II–11–1

OP 7.60—November 1994

Projects in Disputed Areas

1. Projects in disputed areas may raise a number of delicate problems affecting relations not only between the Bank[1] and its member countries, but also between the borrower[2] and one or more neighboring countries. In order not to prejudice the position of either the Bank or the countries concerned, any dispute over an area in which a proposed project is located is dealt with at the earliest possible stage.

2. The Bank may proceed with a project in a disputed area if the governments concerned agree that, pending the settlement of the dispute, the project proposed for country A should go forward without prejudice to the claims of country B.

Presentation of Loans to the Executive Directors

3. For every project in a disputed area, Bank staff consider the nature of the dispute. The Staff Appraisal Report (SAR) and Memorandum and Recommendation of the President (MOP) discuss the nature of the dispute and affirm that Bank staff have considered it and are satisfied that

   (a) the other claimants to the disputed area have no objection to the project, or

   (b) in all other instances, the special circumstances of the case support the Bank's financing the project

---

   1.   "Bank" includes IDA, and "loans" includes credits.

   2.   "Borrower" refers to the member country in whose territories the project is carried out, whether the country is the borrower or the guarantor.

notwithstanding any objection or lack of approval by the other claimants. Such special circumstances include the following: (i) that the project is not harmful to the interests of other claimants, or (ii) that a conflicting claim has not won international recognition or been actively pursued. For such cases, the MOP bears a disclaimer stating that, by supporting the project, the Bank does not intend to prejudice the final determination of the parties' claims. The relevant portions of the SAR and the MOP are prepared by the Legal Department.

Maps

4. For the delineation of boundaries on maps concerned, the applicable guidelines appear in Administrative Manual Statement 7.10, *Cartographic Services*, and its annexes. However, the inclusion of maps in the SAR and the MOP is subject to any general instruction or decision of the Regional vice president, taken in consultation with the Senior Vice President and General Counsel, to omit maps of the borrower in entirety or in part.

Annex II–11–2

BP 7.60—November 1994

Projects in Disputed Areas

1. The presence of any territorial dispute affecting a proposed Bank[1] project is ascertained as early as possible and described in all project documents starting with the initial Project Information Document (PID). The country department (CD) director, through the Regional vice president (RVP), promptly brings the dispute to the attention of the managing director (MD), operations, concerned and the Senior Vice President and General Counsel (LEGVP), and keeps them informed of the dispute throughout the project cycle.

2. For this purpose, the CD director prepares, in close collaboration with the Legal Department (LEG) and in consultation with other departments concerned, a memorandum to be submitted to the MD concerned through the RVP and copied to the LEGVP. The memorandum

   (a) conveys all pertinent information on the international aspects of the project, including information as to the procedure followed and the outcome of any earlier projects the Bank may have considered in the disputed area;

   (b) makes recommendations for dealing with the issue; and

   (c) seeks approval for taking the actions recommended and for proceeding with project processing.

3. Following project preparation, the full details of the dispute and the basis for the decision on whether to proceed to appraisal are included in the transmittal memorandum for the revised preappraisal package. This memorandum, addressed to the RVP and

---

1. "Bank" includes IDA, and "loans" includes credits.

copied to the LEGVP, is prepared in close collaboration with LEG and in consultation with other departments concerned. Based on the information in the memorandum, the RVP, on the advice of the MD concerned (who consults with the LEGVP), decides whether to proceed with appraisal.

4. The MD concerned may, in consultation with the LEGVP, decide at any stage of the project cycle to inform the executive directors concerned of the proposed project and the dispute.

BANK SUPERVISION OF PROJECT IMPLEMENTATION

Annex II–12

OD13.05—March 1989

Project Supervision

A. *Introduction*

1.   Project supervision is one of the Bank's most important activities.[1] Its main purposes are:

(a)   to ensure that the borrower implements the project with due diligence to achieve the agreed development objectives and in conformity with the loan agreement;[2]

(b)   to identify problems promptly as they arise during implementation and help the borrower resolve them, and to modify as necessary the project concept and design as the project evolves during implementation or as circumstances change (in this context, Bank supervision complements the borrower's implementation efforts and is one of the most effective ways in which the Bank provides technical assistance to its borrowers);

(c)   to take timely action to cancel a project if its continuation is no longer justified, particularly if it can no longer be expected to achieve the desired development objectives;

---

1.   "Bank" includes IDA, and "loans" includes credits; "project" includes all lending operations of the Bank.
2.   *Inter alia,* to ensure that Bank funds are used only for the agreed purposes of the loan.

(d) to disseminate significant lessons learned during supervision to Bank staff, management, and the Board, to enhance the standards of day-to-day Bank operations;

(e) to use the experience gained to improve the design of future projects, sector and country strategies, and policies; and

(f) to prepare Project Completion Reports (PCRs) to serve the purpose, among others, of fulfilling the Bank's statutory obligation to its shareholders to account for the management of its resources.

2. These activities are carried out through studying periodic reports and correspondence from project authorities, visits to borrowers and project sites, sector and country implementation reviews covering several or all projects in one country, and by other means, such as visits of senior Bank officials. The Staff Appraisal Report (SAR) is not part of the legal documents, but is an authoritative statement of the work to be carried out, the measures to be taken by the borrower and project entities, and the objectives to be achieved. Thus, it is an important guide for supervision. President's Reports serve the same purpose in the supervision of adjustment loans.[3] Other important reference documents are in the Project File.

3. This OD outlines the Bank's normal policies, procedures, and responsibilities for supervising projects it finances. The Regions are responsible for the day-to-day management of the supervision process, which should be consistent with the provisions of this OD.

B. Policy and Responsibilities

General

4. Since the Bank is committed to ensuring a level of supervision sufficient to meet the above requirements, supervision must

---

3. Adjustment loans refer to both structural adjustment loans (SALs) and sector adjustment loans (SECALs).

receive adequate priority in the allocation of Bank staff and other resources. The Regions should allocate these resources commensurate with the nature, complexity, and size of each project, with the problems experienced, and with the borrower's institutional capabilities and needs. This implies flexibility in the timing and frequency of supervision missions and in the frequency and content of borrowers' progress reports, and effective use of resident mission staff. To strengthen borrowers' institutional capabilities and increase the cost effectiveness of Bank supervision, country departments should (a) as much as possible integrate the Bank's progress reporting requirements with the borrowers' own monitoring and evaluation systems; (b) where necessary, assist in improving and/or developing such systems, and promoting their effective use; and (c) where appropriate, engage local agencies to help carry out supervision.

5. Where implementation problems are particularly severe, or where many projects face similar problems, project supervision may usefully be supplemented by country or sector implementation review meetings with the relevant country officials to review the loan portfolio, paying particular attention to problem and highly successful projects, sectoral, and cross-sectoral issues.

6. Efficient project execution and the resolution of implementation problems are the joint concern of the Bank and the borrower. Bank supervision staff are therefore encouraged to establish and maintain frank and close relationships with borrower staff, so that the latter will not hesitate to bring difficulties to the Bank's attention at the earliest opportunity. During supervision missions, Bank staff share their findings and recommendations with borrower staff, summarizing them in an aide memoire left with the borrower and implementing agencies at the end of each mission (para. 56).

Stages of Supervision

7. Supervision of an investment project normally has three phases, which may overlap: (a) the start-up phase, from loan

approval by the executive directors to effectiveness; (b) the investment phase following effectiveness; and (c) the operating phase, which often begins after physical completion, when the loan has been fully disbursed.

8. *The Start-up Phase.* Supervision concentrates initially on ensuring timely loan signing. Loan proceeds, however, cannot be drawn until after the borrower fulfills the conditions of effectiveness and the loan is declared effective.[4] To minimize delays in effectiveness, copies of the SAR or President's Report and conformed copies of loan documents (including supplemental letters and agreed minutes) setting out, among others, the conditions of effectiveness are sent as early as possible to all government and project staff responsible for project implementation. Thus, all concerned are fully informed of the project's development objectives, the commitments entered into, the assumptions underlying the project, actions to be taken, and the expected project benefits.

9. A number of actions are usually required to get the project off to a good start: (a) establishment of organizational arrangements for implementing the project; (b) appointment of key staff and consultants; (c) completion of local funding and on-lending arrangements; and (d) preparation of legal opinions before the Bank can declare the loan effective. To the extent possible, these actions are taken before presenting the project to the executive directors for approval. The primary task of supervision before effectiveness is to help the borrower complete remaining actions promptly, and to familiarize new borrowers and implementing agencies with Bank procedures, especially procurement, disbursement, reporting, and auditing. A supervision mission at this stage can help avoid delays in project execution.

10. Organizing a "project launch workshop" with government and project agency staff at this or an earlier stage has proved to

---

4. The Bank may, however, provide limited financing for project start-up activities by approving an advance under its Project Preparation Facility (OP/BP 8.10, *Project Preparation Facility*).

be especially effective. The workshop focuses on (a) clarifying project objectives and interagency coordination arrangements; (b) the implementation schedules, including the first year's work program; (c) funding requirements, including local budgetary resources; (d) monitoring and evaluation arrangements, including reporting to the Bank; and (e) Bank procurement, disbursement and other procedures and the immediate implementation actions required. The workshop may also be used to develop a Supervision Plan (paras. 44–47) if it was not prepared during appraisal.

11. *The Investment Phase.* Most supervision is carried out during the investment or project execution stage, when the borrower and the Bank need to be informed of (a) progress in all major aspects of the project, (b) any significant deviations from the original plans and the reasons for them, and (c) the steps necessary to get the project back on track or adapted to new circumstances. The Bank reviews all progress reports by the borrower on procurement, construction, costs, finance, auditing, staffing, training, and other project aspects. Bank staff also visit the borrower country and the project sites and facilities to review progress, provide advice, and obtain additional information. Monitoring and evaluation systems included in the project can play an important role in helping to improve the timeliness and quality of the information available on implementation and operation, thereby improving the planning and staffing of supervision missions.

12. For all projects, particularly those with important institutional development objectives, information is required about the performance of the implementing agency in effecting staff assignments, changes in organizational structure, improvements in efficiency, and pricing of services. Information on financial performance is necessary for projects implemented by revenue-earning entities, since any substantial deviation from the projected results may affect the financing plan and the achievement of development objectives.

13. Many projects, such as multipurpose hydroelectric or agricultural projects which proceed in stages, begin to generate benefits

before the investment stage is completed. In such cases, information is needed on the way benefits are materializing and being distributed during the early stages of operation, and on projected future benefits and their distribution. Such information sometimes leads to changes in the project during implementation.

14. *The Operating Phase.* Except for the preparation of ICRs (para. 65), there is usually little supervision after the loan account has been closed. However, supervision during the operating stage may be needed where (a) earlier difficulties have not been fully resolved; (b) important undertakings of the borrower continue in force; (c) operation poses special problems; (d) environmental concerns or long-term efforts at institution building need to be followed up; or (e) new circumstances arise which threaten the successful operation or sustainability of the project, or the distribution of its benefits. In the case of dam projects, the Bank wants to ensure that completed dams are inspected and maintained satisfactorily (see OP/BP 4.37 *Safety of Dams*). Supervision during the operating stage may also help ensure adequate assessment of the development impact after the completion of investment by providing information on project benefits. Operating projects are usually supervised during work on repeat or follow-up projects, but it may be necessary to schedule separate supervision missions in this stage.

Adjustment Operations

15. Structural and sector adjustment loans have become key elements in the Bank's adjustment-cum-growth strategy in many countries. The transfer of resources is important in these loans, but their success depends on the outcome of the adjustment process for a country's longer-term balance of payments prospects, creditworthiness, and ability to sustain satisfactory growth. It is, therefore, important that supervision closely monitors the implementation of adjustment programs along with a country's overall economic performance. Given the complexity and importance of such lending, specific aspects of the

supervision of adjustment loans are highlighted in Annexes A and A1 and in Circular Op 87/06, filed as OMS 2.01, *Guidelines for Preparing Adjustment Loans and Credits* (to be reissued as BP 8.60).

Supervision for and by Other Agencies and Institutions

16. Cofinanciers sometimes rely on the Bank for supervision. Their representatives may accompany Bank supervision missions. Formal arrangements for joint supervision are not always made, but in any case the role of each cofinancier and the arrangements for sharing the workload and supervision information should be specified at an early date. Occasionally, when the Bank cofinances a project with a regional bank or other donor, it may enter into an agreement for the cofinancier to carry out supervision on its behalf. In these cases, Bank supervision standards are applied, and the cofinancier keeps the Bank fully informed of project developments. When starting the supervision of cofinanced projects, task managers (TMs) should review with the office of the Vice President, Cofinancing, the need for follow-up on cofinancing aspects and integrate such requirements into the Supervision Plan (paras. 44–47).

17. The Bank (as executing agency) supervises a number of assistance projects financed by the United Nations Development Programme (UNDP), using the same standards as for Bank financed technical assistance projects. The Bank keeps UNDP informed of developments and the results of its supervision missions, and participates in periodic meetings with the recipient government and UNDP.

18. The Bank also supervises some projects financed by the International Fund for Agricultural Development (IFAD), using bank supervision procedures. The Bank informs IFAD of planned supervision missions so that IFAD staff may participate, and it promptly provides IFAD with copies of supervision reports. On policy problems, Bank staff advise IFAD, which then discusses suitable remedial action with the government

(OD 15.50, *Bank Staff Appraisal and Supervision of IFAD-Financed Projects*).

19. The Bank may furthermore under a trust fund (see OP/BP 14.40, *Trust Funds*) or other agreement undertake to supervise a project financed by another donor agency. In these instances, the Bank's supervision responsibilities including reporting to the other donor agency, and the procedures for recovering the Bank's administrative costs are specified in the agreement.

Responsibilities

20. The basic responsibility for project supervision rests with the Regions, but other parts of the Bank play important roles (para. 28). The Regions carry out project supervision through the country departments (CDs), in collaboration as required with the technical departments (TDs). Regions delegate decision-making authority to the lowest appropriate level, and establish clear supervision responsibility and accountability, especially of the task manager, the sector operations division (SOD) and country operations division chiefs, the CD director and the Regional vice president (RVP). The authority and responsibility for each project supervision stage are detailed in Annex B, and set out in the text below.

21. The TM has primary responsibility for monitoring and reporting on project progress and for the Bank's review and approval of implementation actions specified in the legal documents. This responsibility includes keeping the SOD or country operations division chief informed of the project's status and any issues that may arise. With the agreement of the SOD or the country operations division chief, the TM arranges the scheduling, staffing, and leadership of supervision missions, and agrees with project agencies and cofinanciers on actions required to resolve implementation issues. If necessary, the TM prepares proposals for modifying the project concept and design to meet changing circumstances, and in exceptional cases, for discontinuing the project or the Bank's association with it. For such

proposals and decisions, the TM obtains the necessary contributions, advice, endorsements, and approvals from other Bank units, as appropriate, and advises the SOD or country operations division chief on issues that require a decision by a higher level of management. The TM informs resident representatives of supervision missions and prepares the terms of reference (TOR) (para. 49).

22. The SOD *chief* and—for projects such as structural adjustment loans where task management resides in a country operations division—the country operations division chief, are responsible for allocating adequate resources for the supervision of the divisional project portfolio, organizing supervision activities, and selecting and guiding the TM.

23. The SOD/country operations division chief also approves (a) the declaration of effectiveness of loan agreements (with the concurrence of the Legal Department [LEG]); (b) changes in implementation schedules; (c) routine modifications of implementation targets or dates in the legal documents, such as the modification of the date for preparing a training program; (d) changes in the allocation of loan proceeds, if amendment of the project description is not required (para. 34); and (e) the extension of closing dates, unless approval by higher-level management is required (para. 33). The SOD/country operations division chief furthermore ensures that any proposed project changes are consistent with sector and country economic objectives.

24. Whenever possible, the SOD/country operations division chief should increase the cost effectiveness of supervision, for example, by using where appropriate, local consultants for data collection and technical inquiries, and by helping strengthen the implementation and monitoring capabilities of borrowers and local agencies to complement the Bank's supervision. Sector supervision missions covering all projects in a sector or subsector may be effective in a country with few Bank-financed projects in a given sector. When staff are supervising several projects during one field visit, or a supervision mission is combined with other operational activities, the SOD/country operations

division chief should ensure that this does not comprise supervision effectiveness.

25. The CD director is responsible for managing the department's project portfolio, and for reviewing it annually in the context of the Bank's Annual Review of Implementation and Supervision (ARIS) (see OP/BP/GP 13.16, *Country Portfolio Performance Reviews*). The CD director ensures that (a) supervision of all projects is carried out diligently and effectively; (b) the same supervision standards and procedures are used by all divisions; (c) the divisions deal with general portfolio issues consistently; (d) major changes in projects are consistent with the Bank's country strategy; and (e) the flow of information within the Bank on the status of the department's portfolio, on difficulties facing the operations, and on the actions recommended and taken, is accurate and prompt. The CD director is also responsible for ensuring that (a) divisional budgets and work programs are adequately staffed and funded, so that supervision can be carried out according to the needs of each project; and (b) SOD/country operations division chiefs makes effective use of supervision resources.

26. The CD director also decides if and when country implementation reviews should be held, and ensures that such reviews are organized with the support of the country and sector operations divisions and that issues-oriented briefs are prepared for the projects and the generic issues to be discussed.

27. The RVP has final responsibility for managing the Regional portfolio and ensuring that it is appropriately examined in the Annual Review of Implementation and Supervision (see OP/BP/GP 13.16, *Project Implementation and Supervision*). In particular, the RVP ensures that (a) sufficient resources are allocated to project supervision, (b) these resources are used effectively and efficiently, and (c) the Bank's supervision objectives are achieved. The RVP also ensures that implementation of each project and any significant changes from the initial concept and design are consistent with overall Bank policies and objectives, that the executive directors are properly advised of such changes,

and that their approval is sought where necessary (para. 34). The RVP furthermore recommends tranche releases under adjustment loans, after consultation with LEG. For proposed waivers of tranche release conditions, the RVP consults with the managing director, operations concerned. Major changes in the loan conditions for tranche releases require Board Approval (see para. 34 of main text).

28. Some *Bank departments outside the Regions* also play an important role in supervision, particularly in such areas as legal amendments, extensions of deadlines for loan effectiveness and closing dates, accounting, disbursements, suspensions and cancellations. They must be consulted on various supervision matters, and their endorsement or approval must be obtained on a number of actions (Annex B). LEG deals with all legal matters, the Loan and Trust Funds Department (LOA) with all disbursement matters, the Controller's Vice Presidency with the servicing of loans, and the Secretary's Department with the signing of loan documents and all matters requiring notification to or approval by the executive directors. The office of the Vice President, Cofinancing, assists the TM in planning the supervision of projects involving cofinancing. The Operations Policy Department (OPR), and the sector departments in Human Capital Development (HCD), Finance and Private Sector Development (FPD), and Environmentally Sustainable Development (ESD) (a) assist the Regions with advice on such matters as procurement, Bank policies, and technical issues; (b) promote the dissemination of information on Regional experience; (c) assist in the solution of procurement problems; (d) seek to improve policies and procedures; and (e) assist in bringing specific project and implementation difficulties to the attention of the senior management and the Board through the Bank-wide Annual Review of Implementation and Supervision and through the Annual Review of Development Effectiveness.

29. The technical departments exercise a quality assurance role in the supervision process for which detailed procedures and responsibilities are defined by each Region. Similarly, the super-

vision functions of resident missions, project advisers and senior operations advisers are matters for Regional decision.

Legal Aspects

30. *Compliance with Legal Covenants.* One of the major tasks of supervision is to monitor compliance with the legal agreements and, where conditions are not being fulfilled, to determine the causes and the best means for remedying the situation. Since supervision staff follow a project closely, they are in a position to recognize problem areas before they result in default. The extent to which the Bank will agree to modify or waive a particular project covenant depends upon its judgment of the relevance of the covenant to the prevailing circumstances and project development objectives. In case of a default, the Bank seeks to exhaust all methods of persuasion before exercising contractual remedies.

31. The legal remedies available to the Bank include (a) total or partial suspension of disbursements, and subsequent cancellation of the loan or part of the loan, if the suspension has been in effect for longer than a specified period (OP/BP 13.40, *Suspension of Disbursements*); (b) cancellation of a portion of the loan because of misprocurement (OD 11.00, *Procurement*); and (c) "acceleration of maturity." The events which can give rise to these remedies are stipulated in the General Conditions (Sections 6.02 and 7.01). Additional events may be specified in individual loan agreements.

32. *Modification of Legal Documents.* Legal documents may require modification due to changes in priorities, the circumstances surrounding the project, timing, organizational and managerial arrangements, or financial requirements. Substantial changes in the project description, procurement procedures, or the provision of supplemental financing, will usually require some reappraisal to confirm that the benefits and implementation arrangements are adequate. Thereafter, agreement with the borrower is reached, with or without formal negotiations.

Amendments are prepared by LEG on the advice of and in close collaboration with the TM and others concerned.

33. Changes in financial requirements are a frequent cause of revision. Where physical requirements or costs exceed appraisal estimates, the scope of the project and/or the original financing plan may need revision. Although the Bank does not normally provide supplemental financing in these circumstances, it may do so in special cases. Where project costs prove to have been over-estimated, the loan surplus is usually cancelled. However, in special cases the Bank may permit the savings to be used for additional project-related purposes. (For a discussion of these various issues, see OP/BP 13.20, *Supplemental Financing*, and OP/BP 13.25, *Use of Project Cost Savings*.) Delays in project completion frequently cause a borrower to request a change in the legal agreements. After reviewing the justification for continued Bank support, the Bank may extend the loan closing date. (See OP/BP/GP 13.30, *Closing Dates*.)

34. Except for routine modifications (para. 23), amendments to the legal agreements, including the waiver of conditions, require the approval of the CD director. If a proposed amendment is substantial, particularly if it involves a significant change in project scope and concept, or if the waiver of a condition is of major significance, it must be endorsed by the RVP and approved by the executive directors. The RVP in consultation with LEG, is responsible for deciding whether a proposed amendment to a Loan/Credit Agreement or a waiver is major and therefore needs to be submitted to the Board for approval on a no-objection basis. For amendment and waivers requiring Board approval, and for supplemental loans, the RVP may seek the guidance of the MD concerned.

35. The monthly *Report to the Executive Directors on Bank and IDA Operations*, prepared by the Secretary's Department in consultation with the Regions, informs the executive directors of minor changes in the project description and loan covenants. Substantial changes and supplemental loans are submitted by the appropriate RVP to the executive directors in the form of a

Memorandum and Recommendation of the President (MOP). Board approval is normally sought on a "no-objection" basis, but in special circumstances, for example, where the proposed change substantially alters the project concept or design, or where the supplemental loan is large, the MOP is considered at a Board meeting. The MOP focuses on the cause of the change or additional financing needs, the measures taken to deal with the situation, and any new arrangements for project execution. It is brief and provides the executive directors with background information and justification for continuing the project and, in the case of a supplemental loan, the need and justification for additional Bank financing. The MOP includes a newly esti-mated economic rate of return or other appropriate justifica-tions, supported by reference to changes in benefits and costs. The MOP concisely describes any changes required in the loan documents.

Procurement and Engagement of Consultants

36. The Bank must be assured that the borrower follows the Bank's policies and methods for procurement and for engaging consultants. Supervision staff help solve related implementation difficulties. The Bank's general requirements are set out in the *Guidelines for Procurement under World Bank Loans and IDA Credits* and in the *Guidelines: Use of Consultants by World Bank Borrowers and by the World Bank as Executing Agency*. The Bank's procurement policy is presented in OD 11.00, *Procurement*, and the policy for engaging consultants, and monitoring and evaluat-ing consulting services in OD 11.10, *Use of Consultants*. OPNs 4.07–4.08[5] and the Procurement Technical Notes discuss these aspects further.

37. Primary responsibility for monitoring the procurement process and the engagement and performance of consultants rests

---

5. OPN 4.07, *Guidelines for Engagement of Project Financing Advisers by Borrowers*.

with the TM, who refers decisions (including those on misprocurement) to senior levels of management, as required by OD 11.00, *Procurement*, and OD 11.10, *Use of Consultants*.

38. Procurement supervision by the Bank is continued throughout project implementation. Normally, borrowers are notified of the Bank's views on procurement documents within a week of their receipt (within ten working days in complicated cases). Exceptions should be made only when contract value thresholds established by each Region are exceeded and LEG needs to review the documents. Special efforts should be made early during supervision to (a) acquaint country officials with Bank procurement policies and procedures, and (b) where necessary, improve procurement procedures and arrangements for greater efficiency and effectiveness of implementation (e.g., through dissemination of the Bank's "Sample Bidding Documents").

39. Staff should ensure that borrowers comply with the Bank's policies and procedures as presented in OMS 2.50 when engaging Bank-financed consultants. In addition, Bank staff review and report on the consultants' performance, both during supervision missions and after completion of the consultants' assignments (details are in OD 11.10, *Use of Consultants*).

Disbursement

40. The Bank's disbursement policies and procedures are described in detail in OP/BP 12.00, *Disbursement*, the *Guidelines for Withdrawal of Proceeds of World Bank Loans* and *IDA Credits*, and the *Disbursement Handbook*. Disbursement is the responsibility of LOA. For certain disbursement issues, LOA staff will consult with and request endorsement from the TM concerned and, where necessary, from LEG. To ensure prompt disbursements, supervision staff must familiarize borrowers with the Bank's disbursement procedures. LOA staff provide intensive briefings for new borrowers and those encountering serious disbursement difficulties. The TM ensures that borrowers' documentation to support withdrawal applications on the basis of

Statements of Expenditure is appropriately reviewed during supervision missions. He should seek the advice and assistance of LOA staff, particularly when problems arise.

41. In cases where the borrower does not comply with project conditions, or where a country is in arrears in servicing its Bank loans, the Bank may suspend disbursement and, if necessary, subsequently cancel the loan or part of the loan. This is dealt with in detail in OP/BP 13.40, *Suspension of Disbursements*.

C. Supervision Planning

Effective and Efficient Use of Resources

42. Each SOD/country operations division chief is responsible for planning the division's supervision schedules. Supervision coefficients calculated by the Planning and Budgeting Department (annual staff-weeks per project, by sector and Region) can be used for estimating the overall work load, but should not be used for individual projects because they reflect averages for projects at different stages of implementation and with widely differing complexities. The appropriate level of supervision should therefore be programmed project by project.

43. Several measures should be considered for the effective and efficient use of supervision resources: (a) combining supervision missions on related projects, and combining supervision missions with missions dealing with other aspects of lending operations; (b) planning a mission soon after loan approval to expedite project start-up (para. 10); (c) distributing tasks between field offices and headquarters; (d) strengthening long-term divisional planning of supervision and making initial estimates of supervision requirements at appraisal (paras. 44–47); (e) ensuring staff continuity in the supervision of individual projects; and (f) matching the special skills and expertise of supervision mission members with the particular problems facing individual projects.

The Supervision Plan

44. A Supervision Plan (see Annex C) should be prepared and discussed for each project with the borrower during project appraisal.[6] The Plan should cover the entire supervision period and include (a) the schedule of key Bank supervision inputs and the skill mix required (e.g., for the project launch workshop or mid-term review, or to meet the needs of different implementation phases); (b) specialist staff input for tasks such as the review of work programs, procurement documents, progress reports, audited financial statements, and studies; (c) aspects of the project that require special Bank attention during supervision (e.g., environmental concerns, impact on the poor); and (d) the borrower's contribution to supervision, including (i) expected participation in supervision missions; (ii) monitoring efforts; (iii) measures for establishing or improving data collection systems; and (iv) data and reports, and the timing of their submission to the Bank.

45. Supervision requirements may change as each project evolves. Each supervision mission, therefore, examines whether changes in circumstances, unforeseen problems or other reasons require modification of the Plan. Proposed changes are discussed with the borrower and approved by the SOD/country operations division chief. The Plan thereby becomes a valuable tool in the Country Assistance Management (CAM) process and in the Bank's overall skills and staff resource planning. It also provides a basis for measuring supervision management performance for each project.

46. Supervision planning and the preparation and updating of the Plan must be based on the factors determining the requirements for each project, those related to the country and sector, the project, and the Bank. The country and sector factors are (a) the state of relations between the country and the Bank, and whether they are recent or long-standing; (b) the country's

---

6. OPN 4.08, *Procurement in Cofinanced Projects.*

overall economic and financial situation; (c) the commitment of the country and relevant agencies to project objectives throughout the implementation period; (d) the situation and issues in the sector; (e) the level of institutional strength, especially interagency coordination; and (f) changes in government policies or regulations that may affect project objectives or implementation.

47. Project factors include (a) technical, policy, and institutional complexity; (b) the level of innovation incorporated in the design; (c) the strength of project management and other agencies concerned with the project; (d) anticipated difficulties in procurement and disbursement; (e) whether the project is the first or a repeater for a particular agency, sector, or country; (f) the quality of project management reporting; (g) the extent and nature of cofinancing arrangements including export credit and quality of project preparation. Bank-related factors are (a) likely availability of qualified staff and consultants and (b) the Bank's administrative budget, which determines the total resources available for operational activities. Within these factors, the Supervision Plan must be prepared and the supervision effort to be devoted to each project must be decided.

Mission Planning

48. Projects under implementation should be visited at least once a year, up to three or four times a year for those with special problems, or where other factors demand a greater supervision effort. More intensive supervision may also be needed for adjustment operations, and emergency and innovative projects, particularly during the start-up phase. Indeed, supervision missions for adjustment operations should not be linked exclusively to the release of loan tranches.

49. Well before departure, the TM should prepare the TOR to ensure effective and well-focused supervision missions. In preparing the TOR, the TM should seek the advice of Regional staff and staff outside the Region, as appropriate. The TOR should (a) emphasize mission objectives and expected results; (b) link up

with the previous supervision mission, outline the problems to be addressed, and set out the recommended course of action; (c) ensure adequate attention to the project's role in achieving sector and macroeconomic objectives; and (d) specify the responsibilities of each mission member. In preparing the TOR, the TM should seek advice from appropriate Bank units. The TOR require the approval of the SOD chief or, for structural adjustment loans, the country operations division chief.

50. If the project is experiencing complex problems, the TM should normally prepare a premission issues paper. It should spell out the issues, examine alternative solutions, and recommend the positions the mission should take on the issues, keeping in view the sectoral and macroeconomic objectives of the borrower and the Bank. The TOR should reflect the Bank's position as agreed with the SOD/country operations division chief.

51. To reach a Bank position, particularly in cases where significant changes in project design or the loan documents are required, it may be necessary to hold a premission issues meeting involving staff from LEG and other organizational units such as the technical department, HCD, FPD, ESD, LOA, DPG, and OPR, as determined by the TM and the SOD/country operations division chief. An issues meeting should also normally precede missions conducting mid-term reviews, preparing tranche releases in adjustment operations and preparing the Implementation Completion Reporting (para. 65), to ensure that the Bank's position is clearly defined and endorsed by all departments concerned.

52. Well before the mission's departure (but preferably after the TOR have been agreed), a detailed message should be sent to the borrower stating the mission's objectives, the issues to be discussed, and the meetings and field visits scheduled. Requests for counterparts to participate in the mission, and for information, analyses, and reports should also be sent so that arrangements and documents will be ready upon mission arrival. Bank documents and reports that would assist in achieving the mission's objectives should be sent to the borrower in advance.

D. Monitoring and Reporting

Progress Reports

53. Project progress is monitored on the basis of the project implementation schedule in the SAR, or for adjustment loans on the basis of the policy matrix in the President's Report, and periodic progress reports by the borrower/project agencies. Progress reports are essential for planning supervision missions and reducing fact-finding during missions, so that the specialists can concentrate on problem-solving and technical assistance. The CD director should ensure that suitable systems and procedures for reviewing and responding to progress reports are established and being followed. Day-to-day responsibility for the review of progress reports and for follow-up with the borrower rests with the TM, under the supervision of the SOD/country operations division chief.

54. Progress reports summarize all important aspects of the project. When determining reporting requirements, Bank staff should take into consideration monitoring systems that may have been set up during the project design stage (OD 10.70, *Project Monitoring and Evaluation*). In all cases, the information required should be defined as early as possible, and the requirements simplified and adapted to the information available (including local reports) on each project. New or inexperienced borrowers may need technical assistance in designing the reporting system and preparing the first reports. For projects that are implemented by several agencies, one should be designated to collect and integrate the reports produced by all the others.

55. The TM is responsible for monitoring submission of progress reports, for which the Portfolio Management Module of the Management Information System (MIS) (para. 63) provides a system to record due dates. Reminders should be sent if the reports are not received on time. Upon submission, the reports should be reviewed thoroughly, and comments communicated promptly to project management. Important matters raised in the reports must be called to the attention of the

SOD/country operations division chief and higher management, as appropriate.

Mission Reporting[7]

56. *Aide Memoire and Mission Follow-up.* Upon completion of field work, each supervision mission prepares and leaves with the borrower and project management an aide memoire (Annex D4) summarizing the mission's findings, agreements reached, and actions to be taken. The aide memoire should be concise, concentrating mainly on implementation problems and actions required to overcome them. It should describe clearly what needs to be done, by whom, by what date, and what results are expected. It should also spell out unresolved issues and recommendations requiring Bank management approval such as tranche releases in adjustment operations, extension of closing dates and other matters having legal implications. The aide memoire is the Bank's main channel of communication with the borrower and project management on implementation matters, and represents the official view of the Bank unless modified by Bank management in the follow-up letter/telex/cable (Annex D4). The follow-up should be sent as soon as possible but normally not later than 15 working days after each supervision mission, with a copy of the aide memoire normally enclosed. As appropriate, it should underscore the issues and required actions presented in the aide memoire, and highlight decisions taken by Bank management and/or additional actions required by the borrower and implementing agencies.

57. The mission prepares a supervision report for each project which should normally be circulated within five and not later than ten working days of its return. It should not be delayed even

---

7. Where this is not possible, or for projects already approved, a Supervision Plan should be prepared during an early supervision mission. Guidelines for the preparation of supervision reports, including the Transmittal Memorandum, the Implementation Summary and mandatory annexes to the report, are presented in Annexes D, D1, D2, D3, D4, D5, and D6.

though mission follow-up letters and telexes may not have been finalized; rather, this should be noted in the Transmittal Memorandum (Annex D1). When the mission leader proceeds from one country to another, with unresolved matters that should not wait until the return of the mission, a summary of the main conclusions and recommendations should be sent to the Bank for action (or the aide memoire where this is feasible) as each country visit is concluded.

58. The mission findings and recommendations are discussed with the relevant SOD/country operations division chief, who approves the supervision report. If the findings are of broad significance beyond the project, particularly if the lessons learned may influence the design of new lending operations or sector and country strategies, the SOD/country operations division chief will arrange a debriefing meeting in which country officers, economists, and other staff participate, as appropriate. Such meetings are particularly important for projects with links to major policy issues. The SOD/country operations division chief, in consultation with the CD director, as appropriate, decides case-by-case who should chair the meeting.

59. *Implementation Summary (Form 590)*. The initial Form 590 must be completed by the TM as soon as a loan is approved by the Board. It is updated by each supervision mission, and also for the Annual Review of Portfolio Performance (ARPP), if during the preceding six months no supervision mission has been carried out. There may be further updates at each Region's discretion. The initial Form 590 and all updates should be sent electronically to the central files of the Bank's Management Information System (MIS), in line with the instructions in the *Portfolio Module User Guide*. The purpose of Form 590 is to inform the appropriate management of the current general status of each project under supervision, highlight implementation problems, recommend actions to be taken and, as far as possible, report on the project's progress in achieving its development objectives. Forms 590 also provide a basis for the review of general patterns in project implementation and supervision, and are processed

once a year for this purpose in conjunction with the ARPP. Furthermore, they assist in the preparation of studies by various parts of the Bank, and of project audits by the Operations Evaluation Department (OED). Guidelines for the preparation of Form 590 are in Annex D2.

60. An important component of Form 590 is the various ratings of project performance. An "Overall Status" rating alerts management to actual or potential implementation problems, and categorizes the project's implementation status as a means of identifying Bank-wide trends. The rating is based on the assessment of specific aspects of implementation progress and of likely progress in achieving development objectives as compared to expectations at the time of appraisal, or reappraisal, if the project has been restructured through a formal agreement with the borrower. Despite the great variety of projects, there are a number of basic indicators applicable to most; they are discussed in some detail in Annex D2. Some of these can be assessed quantitatively (e.g., closing date, project costs, and disbursements). Common benchmarks in these cases provide standardization in the ratings. The ratings of other aspects of performance have to be largely qualitative, e.g., achievement of the project development objectives, compliance with legal covenants, project management performance, availability of funds, procurement progress, training progress, technical assistance progress, studies progress, and environmental aspects. Each supervision mission should rate, in addition to the "Overall Status," the first four of these qualitative aspects, while some of the others may be left without a rating, if a definitive judgment could not be formed by the mission. The staff's judgment, in any case, is critical in evaluating performance in various areas to determine the project's "Overall Status" rating.

Audit Reports

61. The TM monitors timely submission of audited financial statements and audit reports in accordance with OP/BP 10.02, *Financial Management* and the Bank's Audit Reports

Compliance System (ARCS) (described in OD 13.10, *Borrower Compliance with Audit Covenants*), a subsystem of the Portfolio Management Module. The TM also ensures that the borrower and all project agencies appoint auditors acceptable to the Bank, and that they understand special audit requirements related to the Bank's disbursements against Statements of Expenditure and under Special Accounts arrangements. Audit reports are of crucial importance to supervision as they help to indicate whether the Bank's statutory requirements on proper accounting for the use of Bank funds have been satisfied, and whether financial and management controls are adequate.

The Project Implementation Index File

62. The detailed reports which record project implementation (such as progress reports, consultants' reports and other memoranda) are entered in the Project Implementation Index File and sent to the appropriate Regional Information Center (see Annexes E–E1). To ensure that a detailed history of the project is kept for ex-post evaluation, this File must be properly maintained. To achieve Bank-wide consistency, it is set out in a standard format. Instructions for establishing and maintaining this File are in Annex E1. The SOD/country operations division chief is responsible for ensuring that they are being followed.

The Portfolio Management Module of the Management Information System (MIS)

63. This module is intended to provide in easily accessible form basic information on project objectives, financing, withdrawal of loan proceeds, procurement, disbursement, loan covenants, borrower undertakings, etc., and reports to be made by the borrower on specific aspects of the project. Most of the information in the module is derived in the first instance during project appraisal and should be entered into the central files of the MIS as soon as the loan has been approved by the executive directors. The information is updated during supervision, particularly after

completion of supervision missions and whenever the Implementation Summary (Form 590) is updated during periodic portfolio reviews. The module is also the source for aggregate reports on the progress of the portfolio, for example, reports on disbursement, procurement, etc., Bank-wide, by sector, subsector, country, and Region in various sequences or combinations. For detailed instructions on the use of this module, consult the *Portfolio Module User Guide*.

Measurement of Quantity and Quality of Supervision

64. The effort expended on supervision is measured mainly by staff and consultant contributions. The staff-weeks spent and the skills devoted to each supervision mission are presented in Section 4 of the Implementation Summary (Form 590). The quality of supervision and its effectiveness are more difficult to determine, and are to some extent reflected by early and precise identification of implementation problems, clear definition of actions required to overcome them, and the ability to get appropriate actions taken. Sections 5–8 of Form 590 provide a record of this. Some other indicators that bear on the subject are (a) actual vs. recommended intervals between supervision missions, and (b) time elapsed between the return of a mission and the Bank management and/or the borrower taking the actions recommended by the mission. The supervision effort is compared periodically to the Supervision Plan (paras. 44–47) and to the work programs and travel schedules on which the annual budget was based. Overall trends in the Bank's supervision input and its adequacy are reviewed in the ARPP and during the CAM review.

Implementation Completion Reporting and Project Performance Audits

65. After the loan closing date a ICR is prepared, which reviews and records the lessons gained from that experience, and measures

the degree of success in meeting project objectives. Guidelines for the preparation of PCRs, including the time of their submission to the Operations Evaluation Department (OED) are set out in OP/BP/GP 13.55, *Implementation Completion Reporting*. OED reviews the PCR, and for selected projects carries out a full audit to determine (a) to what extent the original development objectives and expectations have been achieved, (b) the reasons for deviations, and (c) the lessons to be learned. General principles on audit and evaluation are presented in *Operations Evaluation, World Bank Standards and Procedures.*

DISCLOSURE OF INFORMATION

Annex II–13

March 1994

The World Bank Policy on Disclosure of Information

Foreword

The sharing of information is essential for effective and sustainable development: it stimulates debate and broadens understanding of development issues, and it facilitates coordination among the many parties involved in development. It serves to strengthen public support for efforts to improve the lives of people in developing countries. The World Bank's experience clearly indicates that the quality of many operations benefits when staff and government officials consult and share information with participants in development programs.

In 1993, the Bank undertook a major review of its disclosure policy to increase further the information made publicly available. Under the revised policy, the range of documents released is expanded significantly, and public access to those documents is made easier. The Bank has established a Public Information Center through which much of the material covered by the revised policy is available.

The expanded access to information will strengthen the Bank's links with all its partners in the development community—and make an important contribution to our joint efforts to reduce poverty and promote sustainable development.

Lewis T. Preston,
President
January 1994

Purpose

1. This statement sets out the policy of the World Bank[1] on disclosure of information held by it and describes the materials available to the public. It supersedes the Directive on Disclosure of Information dated July 1989. The policy is effective immediately. Individual provisions of the policy, respecting particular categories of documents, take effect on the dates indicated.[2]

2. The Bank's disclosure policy is set out in Part II of this statement. Part III describes the Bank's Public Information Center. Part IV indicates the categories of documents and data available to the public generally or to interested individuals or groups. Part V indicates the constraints that, while kept to a minimum, preclude external dissemination of some information.

Policy

3. The Bank recognizes and endorses the fundamental importance of accountability and transparency in the development process. Accordingly, it is the Bank's policy to be open about its activities and to welcome and seek out opportunities to explain its work to the widest possible audience.

 • As a development organization, the Bank wishes to stimulate debate and broaden understanding of development, to facilitate coordination with its partners—governments

---

1. In this policy statement, "World Bank" or "Bank" means the IBRD and IDA. The policy also applies to the disclosure of documents prepared for projects financed or co-financed from trust funds under the Global Environment Facility (GEF) and administered by the Bank, in particular the Global Environment Trust Fund. Except as the Bank and the Executive Committee of the Multilateral Fund for the Implementation of the Montreal Protocol may otherwise agree, this policy applies to operations financed through the Ozone Projects Trust Fund (OTF).

2. Requests for a document produced within the framework of earlier, more restrictive policy, or prior to the effective date of provisions related to particular categories of documents, will be addressed on a case-by-case basis in the context of the policy in effect when the document was prepared.

and other institutions—and to help create and nurture public support for activities which promote the economic and social progress of developing countries. To the same end, it makes the results of its research available to the development and academic communities and brings the lessons of its experience to policy makers and development practitioners. Dissemination of information to local groups affected by the projects supported by the Bank, including nongovernmental organizations, particularly as it will facilitate the participation of those groups in Bank-financed projects, is essential for the effective implementation and sustainability of the projects. Experience has demonstrated that consultation and sharing of information with co-financiers, partners, and groups and individuals with specialized knowledge of development issues help to enhance the quality of Bank-financed operations.

- As an organization owned by governments, the Bank is accountable for its stewardship of public moneys and has an obligation to be responsive to the questions and concerns of its shareholders.

- As a borrower, the Bank has established that disclosure of information concerning its financial condition and policies, additional to that which it is required to publish, helps to attract purchasers to its securities.

- As an employer, the Bank aims to ensure that staff receive the information they need to carry out their responsibilities, to contribute to policy formulation and decision making, and to understand the reasons underlying its policies.

4. It follows that there is a presumption in favor of disclosure. While in the past considerable information held by the Bank has been available without restriction through a variety of Bank publications and documents, the Bank has recently further broadened the scope of information about its activities that it makes publicly available. To facilitate the acquisition of this information, the Bank has established a Public Information Center (PIC) to serve as the central contact for persons seeking to

obtain Bank documents. The PIC, located at Bank headquarters, will service the public in member countries through the Internet and through Bank field offices.

The Public Information Center

5. Effective January 3, 1994, publicly available information about the Bank's activities is available at the Bank's Public Information Center (PIC), 1776 G Street, N.W., Washington D.C. 20433. Requests to the PIC may also be submitted through the Internet and the Bank's European (Paris and London) and Tokyo offices and through other Bank field offices, which are listed in the appendix.

6. The PIC offers, through the Internet network, a complete set of Project Information Documents (PIDs) (see paras. 10–12) and a catalog of Bank documents available to the public. Users of the Internet worldwide may select and request the documents they need. PIDs are provided free of charge, either in electronic form or in hard copy.

7. All documents available in Washington will also be available on request through the Bank's European and Tokyo offices and through other Bank field offices. There will be a standard charge for all hard-copy documents, other than PIDs, environmental data sheets (see para. 21), and OED Précis (see para. 25).[3]

8. Field offices other than the European and Tokyo offices will have available documents specific to the country in which the office is located, and policy papers; each office will meet requests from users in that country. Users in a country without a Bank field office may obtain documents on that country directly from the PIC. Documents on the user's country are provided free of charge; documents on other countries carry the standard charge.

---

3. As of January 3, 1994, the standard charge is US$15 or the equivalent for each document. The charge may be revised from time to time.

9. The PIC deals only with requests for specific documents, not blanket requests for information. Its staff will direct individuals to other sources of material available to the public.

Information Available from the Bank

A. *Operational Information*

Project Information Documents

10. The Project Information Document (PID), a new Bank document, is designed to make project information available to interested parties while a project is still under preparation. The PID provides a brief (initially two-page) factual summary of the main elements of the evolving project: objectives; expected or probable components; costs and financing; environmental and other issues as appropriate; procurement arrangements; studies to be undertaken; prospective implementing agency and relevant points of contact. It clearly indicates that its contents are subject to change and that the components described may not be included in the final project. For sector and structural adjustment operations, which do not finance physical investments, PIDs identify the areas being examined.

11. The PID is prepared when the first review of a proposed project is held by the Country Department (review of the Initial Executive Project Summary (IEPS))[4] and is updated and expanded periodically as project preparation proceeds. In all cases, it is revised before formal project appraisal; if changes are made after appraisal, a final revision of the PID is prepared. All PIDs are available through the PIC.

12. Should an interested party request more technical information about a project on which the Bank is working, the Country

---

4. For each new project that reaches the IEPS stage after October 1, 1993. For projects financed or co-financed from trust funds under the GEF and for projects financed through the OTF, a GEF-PID is produced for each project submitted to the GEF Implementation Committee after October 1, 1993.

Department Director responsible may release factual technical documents, or parts thereof, after consultation with the government concerned.

Staff Appraisal Reports

13. Once a project has been approved by the Executive Directors, the Staff Appraisal Report (SAR) is available to the public.[5] Summary documentation on any subsequent substantial change to a project approved by the Board is also made publicly available after Board approval, subject to the qualification in the following paragraph.

14. During negotiations the prospective borrowing government is asked to identify any text or data in the SAR that is confidential or sensitive or could adversely affect relations with the Bank. As appropriate, adjustments would be made to deal with matters of concern. If, in exceptional cases, extensive issues of confidentiality arise, the Country Director concerned may restrict release of the SAR. The cover of any such SAR will carry a note stating that release is restricted.

Country Economic and Sector Work

15. Following consultation with the government concerned, country economic and sector work (CESW) reports are publicly available once they are distributed to the Executive Directors.[6] These reports include country economic memoranda, country sector reports and country reports such as poverty assessments, private sector assessments, and public expenditure documents.

16. Prior to the final review of a draft CESW report with the government concerned, the government is asked to identify any confidential information in the report. These comments are taken into account in preparing the final report for distribution to the Executive Directors and the PIC. In exceptional cases, if

---

5. Effective with respect to SARs on projects for which the invitation to negotiate was issued after October 1, 1993.
6. Effective January 1, 1994.

extensive issues of confidentiality arise, exceptions to the policy of public release may be authorized, on a case-by-case basis, by the Country Director responsible. The cover of such a report carries a note indicating that release is restricted.

Sectoral Policy Papers

17. Sectoral policy papers are publicly available through the PIC following their approval by the Executive Directors.[7]

18. Prior to submission of sectoral policy papers to the Board, Bank staff may consult as appropriate with institutions and individuals outside the Bank with specialized knowledge of specific issues and may share drafts with them.

Other Documentation

19. Other publicly available sources of information about a country's economic situation and projects include the Bank's Annual Report, the Bank's International Business Opportunities Service, and the Monthly Operational Summary.

20. Reports prepared by the Bank and presented at consultative group meetings are, with the concurrence of the government concerned, publicly available after the meeting.

B.   Environment-Related Documents[8]

Environmental Data Sheets

21. The environmental data sheets[9] prepared and updated quarterly for each project in the Bank lending program are publicly available through the PIC.

---

7. Effective for all such papers approved by the Board after January 1, 1994.

8. For information on other Bank documents that contain environmental information, *see* also Section C, Evaluation Reports.

9. An environment data sheet briefly describes the major environmental issues identified or suspected in the project and issues of lesser scope. In addition, the environmental data sheet notes the actions proposed to mitigate adverse impact.

Environmental Assessments

22. Once the environmental assessment of a "Category A" project,[10] prepared by the borrower (and, accordingly, the borrower's property), has become publicly available in the borrowing country and has been officially received by the Bank, it will be made publicly available through the PIC.[11]

Environmental Analyses

23. The environmental analysis of a "Category B" project,[12] whether it is a separate document or is contained in a relevant section of the SAR, is attached as an annex to the PID and is publicly available through the PIC.[13]

Environmental Action Plans

24. Environmental action plans (EAPs) of borrower governments describe the major environmental concerns of a country, identify the principal causes of problems and formulate policies and concrete actions to deal with the problems. An EAP is

---

10. A project that is likely to have significant adverse impacts that may be sensitive, irreversible, or diverse. Public availability of the environmental assessment in the borrowing country and its submission to the Bank is a prerequisite to project appraisal. Environmental assessments and environmental analyses incorporate, wherever relevant, resettlement plans and indigenous peoples development plans.

11. Unless, in exceptional cases, the borrower objects. Effective January 1, 1994 for IBRD-financed "Category A" projects. Environmental assessments for IDA-financed "Category A" projects have been publicly available since July 1, 1993.

12. Compared with a "Category A" project, a "Category B" project is one in which the adverse environmental impacts are less significant: few, if any, are irreversible; they are not as sensitive, numerous, or diverse; remedial measures can be more easily designed.

13. Unless, in exceptional cases, the borrower objects to the release of an environmental analysis contained in a separate document of the borrower. Effective January 1, 1994. Environmental analyses of IDA-funded "Category B" projects have been publicly available since July 1,1993. Public availability in the borrowing country and official receipt by the Bank are prerequisites to appraisal of these projects.

publicly available through the PIC once the Bank has officially received it and has obtained the government's consent to release it.

C.   Other Project Data

Evaluation Reports

25. Publicly available reports include the "Annual Review of Evaluation Results" prepared by the Bank's Operations Evaluation Department; for selected projects, summaries of evaluation reports ("Précis"); and all Global Environment Facility (GEF) evaluation reports and the annual Project Implementation Performance Report on GEF projects.

Procurement Opportunities

26. Information on procurement opportunities is available through the PID, the Monthly Operational Summary, the Bank's International Business Opportunities Service, and the Technical Data Sheet issued after Board approval of a project, which describes in some detail the items to be financed under the project. A United Nations publication, Development Business, publishes for each Bank-financed project general procurement notices for goods and works to be procured through international competitive bidding as well as services.

Contract Awards

27. Information on major contract awards (a description of the contract, the name and nationality of the successful bidder, and the contract price) may be disclosed after the borrower has informed the Bank that the contract has been signed. Major contract award decisions are published in Development Business and in the International Business Opportunities Service.

D.   *Bank Financial Information*

28. Financial statements of the Bank are published quarterly. Audited financial statements as of the June 30 fiscal year-end appear in the Annual Report. Unaudited statements as of end December or the June 30 audited statements are included in the semi-annual update of the Bank's Information Statement (prospectus). The statements include a balance sheet; statements of income, changes in retained earnings and of cash flows; the amounts of paid in and callable capital; and for the December and June 30 financials, statements of changes in cumulative translation adjustment and of member subscriptions to capital stock and voting power, as well as tables showing data on currencies payable on loans outstanding, on the maturity structure of loans, and on borrowings (by maturity and currency). Notes to the financial statements include information on accounting and related financial policies and a summary description of the Staff Retirement Plan. The over-all borrowing plan is usually announced publicly at the beginning of the fiscal year (July 1).

29. Other financial data published in the Annual Report or the Information Statement include the average cost of borrowings, average interest rate on loans, return on liquid investments and on loans, aggregate information on consents by member states for release of local currency capital funds for lending, and aggregate information on private placements with member countries' monetary authorities. Other documents related to public offerings are released when the laws or regulations governing the market require that they be filed with a governmental agency.

30. Detailed statements of all loans and credits are published monthly and are available through the Loan Accounting and Borrower Services in the Loan Department.

31. Information on the finances of IDA is published in the IDA audited annual and unaudited quarterly financial statements. Replenishment terms and conditions are published in the Summary Proceedings of Annual Meetings. Information on

current replenishment negotiations is provided in press briefings at key stages of the process.

32. Estimates of future borrowings are made available to the Bank's underwriters.

E. Economics and Research

Economic and Social Data

33. Economic and social data on member countries are published in the Annual Report and in the World Development Report and its Annex. They include basic population and income data, data on consumption and investment, and data on flows of public external capital and debt and debt-service ratios. Regional and global aggregates of country economic data and primary commodity trade statistics and historical commodity price series are publicly available.

Economic Analysis and Reports

34. Economic analysis supporting a research project which is factual in nature and does not relate directly to the Bank's decision-making process may be made available to interested parties.

Research

35. The Annual Index of Publications and the bimonthly Publications Update, issued by the Office of the Publisher, list the Bank's published research output, which takes a variety of forms.

External Debt Data

36. Data processed by the Debt and International Finance Division are publicly available in the standard World Debt Tables (WDT) format following publication of the WDT. These tables consist of aggregate data on public and publicly guaranteed medium- and long-term debt and medium-term private nonguaranteed debt (when reported by the member country).

Data elements include outstanding debt, undisbursed amounts, commitments, disbursements, principal and interest repayments, and average terms by type of credit.

37. Aggregate estimates of private nonguaranteed debt (other than those reported by member countries), short-term loans, and future borrowing and debt-service streams are publicly available.

F. Administration

Board of Governors

38. The Annual Reports list members, Governors, and voting power. Summary Proceedings of Annual Meetings contain all speeches related to the Bank; decisions taken at the Meetings and by mail vote since the last Meetings; reports of the Executive Directors recommending decisions on such matters as capital increases and replenishments; and reports of committees, such as the Development Committee.

Executive Directors

39. The Annual Reports list Directors' names, the countries appointing or electing them, and their voting power. Rules for election are published in the Summary Proceedings.

Summary Proceedings

40. Most important decisions of the Executive Directors are announced through press releases or at press conferences of senior Bank officials. Approvals of individual lending operations are announced through issuance of press releases and fact sheets providing summary data on the project or program.

Management

41. Major decisions considered by management likely to be of interest outside the Bank are announced by press releases and other means.

42. Operational Policies and Bank Procedures are publicly available on request, as are those Operational Directives issued after March 1989 that have not been superseded by Operational Policies or Bank Procedures.[14] Operational Manual Statements issued before that date may be made available to the public, upon request, by decision of the Director, Operations Policy, in consultation with the Legal Department.

Staff

43. Organizational charts and descriptions of positions advertised for recruitment purposes are publicly available, as is the World Bank Group Directory, which contains organizational listings.

44. Basic employment data are included in the Annual Report. General information on the Bank's salary structure, the methodology employed in establishing salary levels, staff benefits, and similar information is publicly available. The Bank's broad objectives and strategy in recruiting, placing, redeploying, and retaining staff are available in brochures or other documents prepared specifically for publication.

Legal Information

45. The Articles of Agreement and By-Laws of the Bank and the Bank's agreements with the United Nations and with a number of United Nations entities are all public documents.

46. After loan and credit agreements are signed and declared effective, they are registered or filed with the United Nations and are public documents. Draft agreements prepared for negotiations may be made available to parties other than the prospective borrower where required, for example, for arranging cofinancing.

---

14. "Operational Policies" are short statements (usually one or two pages) of policy. "Bank Procedures" spell out the required documentation and common set of procedures needed to ensure operational consistency and quality. The Bank is in the process of replacing Operational Manual Statements and Operational Directives issued prior to 1992 with the above mentioned documents.

Agreements between other parties in relation to a Bank-financed project are released if the parties consider them public documents or have authorized release.

47. The Annual Report of the Appeals Committee is available on request. The proceedings of the Administrative Tribunal are held in public unless exceptional circumstances require otherwise. The Tribunal's decisions are published. Documents and proceedings related to external litigation to which the Bank is a party are generally public.

48. Legal opinions prepared for the Board by the Vice President and General Counsel may be made publicly available by decision of the Board on a case-by-case basis.

Constraints

49. While every effort is made to keep constraints to a minimum, the effective functioning of the Bank necessarily requires some derogation from complete openness.

50. Proceedings of the Board of Executive Directors and committees thereof are, under the Board's Rules of Procedure, confidential. Thus, unless disclosure is approved by the Board, documents prepared for the consideration or review and approval of the Executive Directors, such as President's Reports and Memoranda of the President for proposed loans and credits, and Operations Evaluation Reports, are not publicly available.

51. Some documents and information are provided to the Bank on the explicit or implied understanding that they will not be disclosed outside the Bank, or that they may not be disclosed without the consent of the source; or even, occasionally, that access within the Bank will be limited. The Bank must treat such information accordingly. A related consideration is the obligation to respect property rights over documents held by the Bank but owned by, or jointly with, other parties. The Bank, as a legal matter, does not publish such documents nor does it distribute them to the public without permission of the owner of such documents.

52. There is also a need to preserve the integrity of the delibera-tive process and to facilitate and safeguard the free and candid exchange of ideas between the Bank and its members. For this reason, documents that define the Bank's country strategy, analy-sis of country creditworthiness, supervision reports and project completion reports are not publicly available. The Bank also cooperates with various international organizations, bilateral aid agencies, and private commercial banks and institutions in the context of its operations in its member countries. In this context, documents exchanged with such entities on matters of common interest which are related to the decision-making processes of the Bank and such entities are not made available to the public.

53. The above-mentioned principle relating to the preservation of the integrity of the deliberative process also applies to the Bank's own decision-making processes. Thus, internal documents and memoranda written by staff to their colleagues, supervisors, or subordinates are considered confidential and not publicly available.

54. As an organization involved in dealings on the world's finan-cial markets, the Bank is required to maintain sound financial management practices, including the maintenance of utmost pru-dence in the disclosure of financial information related to its activities. For this reason, estimates of future borrowings (which are available to the Bank's underwriters), its financial forecasts, data on individual investment decisions, and credit assessments are not publicly available.

55. The Bank's Principles of Staff Employment require the Bank to maintain appropriate safeguards to respect the personal priva-cy of staff members and protect the confidentiality of personal information about them. Thus, individual staff records and per-sonal medical information, as well as proceedings of internal appeal mechanisms are not disclosed outside the Bank, except to the extent permitted by the Staff Rules.

56. Finally, external release of some information may be preclud-ed on an ad hoc basis when, because of its content, wording, or timing, disclosure would be detrimental to the interests of the

Bank, a member country, or Bank staff. Disclosure might, for example, adversely affect a Bank/country relationship because of the frankness of views expressed, or it might be premature. Information is not withheld solely because it is negative; the Bank, as an open, technically competent institution which learns from its mistakes, seeks to provide balanced information, reporting the failures or disappointments in its operations as well as the successes.

Annex II–14

BP 17.50—September 1993

Disclosure of Operational Information

1. This statement sets out the procedures for the implementation of policies specified in the Bank's[1] *Directive on Disclosure of Information* (Washington, D.C.: World Bank and International Finance Corporation, 1993, forthcoming)[2] (Disclosure Directive), with respect to Project Information Documents, Staff Appraisal Reports, gray cover country economic and sector work reports, sectoral policy papers, and environment-related documents.

2. The Bank's policy on disclosure of information applies also to the disclosure of documents prepared for projects financed or cofinanced from trust funds under the Global Environment Facility (GEF), including Montreal Protocol projects financed through the Ozone Projects Trust Fund. Specific procedures are set out in BP 17.50, Annex A.

Project Information Document

3. In tandem with the Initial Executive Project Summary (IEPS) for an investment operation or the Initiating Memorandum (IM) for an adjustment operation, Bank staff prepare the Project Information Document (PID), a brief (two-page) factual summary of the main elements of the evolving project. The PID

---

1. "Bank" includes IDA, and "loans" includes credits.
2. Also available as AMS 1.10, *Directive on Disclosure of Information* (forthcoming).

clearly indicates that its contents are subject to change and that the components described may not necessarily be included in the final project.[3] Once the PID is reviewed and approved at the country department level with the IEPS or draft IM,[4] a copy is sent to the Public Information Center (PIC), through which interested parties may obtain Bank documents.[5]

4.   As an investment project develops, Bank staff update the PID and send the update to the PIC, through which interested parties may obtain it. For all operations, the PID is updated before the Bank's formal project appraisal; for operations in which major changes are made after appraisal, a final revision of the PID is prepared following appraisal.

5.   If an interested party requests additional technical information about a project under preparation, the country department (CD) director releases factual technical documents, or portions of such documents, after consulting with the government to identify any sections that involve confidential material or that could compromise relations between the government and the Bank.

Staff Appraisal Reports

6.   Each Invitation to Negotiate includes a statement that it is the Bank's policy to release the Staff Appraisal Report (SAR) after the Board approves the project. The Invitation to Negotiate also requests that the prospective borrower's negotiating team be prepared to indicate, during negotiations, any section of the SAR that is confidential or sensitive, or that could adversely affect relations between the Bank and the government.[6] The Bank and the

---

3. *See* BP 10.00, Annex A, *Outline for Investment Project Information Document.*

4. For these procedures, *see* BP 10.00, *Investment Lending: Identification to Board Approval,* and Circular Op 87/06, *Guidelines for Preparing and Processing Adjustment Loans and Credits.*

5. The PIC deals only with requests for specific documents, not blanket requests for information. The PIC is described further in Annex B.

6. Annex C contains sample language.

prospective borrower discuss these sections during negotiations. Following negotiations, Bank staff take into account the government's comments in preparing the final SAR. They incorporate into the Memorandum and Recommendation of the President any information removed from the SAR that may be of interest to the Board in its decision-making process. In exceptional cases, if extensive issues of confidentiality arise, the option of restricting the release of an appraisal report may be justified on a project-specific basis by the CD director concerned; the Regional vice president (RVP) and the Operations Policy Department (OPR) are informed. The cover of such a report carries a note indicating that release is restricted.

7. After Board approval, a copy of the SAR is transmitted, as part of the normal distribution, to the PIC, through which interested parties may obtain it. If any substantial changes to a project that is being implemented are approved by the Board[7] Bank staff prepare and transmit to the PIC a summary document (typically two pages long) that explains the changes.

Gray Cover Country Economic and Sector Work Reports

8. Before Bank staff conduct the final review of each green cover country economic and sector work (CESW) report[8] with the government concerned, they advise the government that the Bank's policy is to make gray cover CESW reports available at the PIC, through which interested parties may obtain them. They also ask the government to identify all confidential information in the CESW report.[9] Bank staff then review the issues raised by the government and modify the report as appropriate. Any deletions or changes in information or analysis that may be of interest to the executive directors are presented in a covering note to the

---

7. *See* OD 13.05, *Project Supervision*, para. 34.

8. These reports include Country Economic Memoranda, country sector reports, country reports (such as poverty and private sector assessments), and public expenditure reports.

9. Annex C contains sample language.

gray cover report. In exceptional cases, if extensive issues of con-fidentiality arise, exceptions to the policy of releasing reports may be authorized on a case-by-case basis by the CD director respon-sible; the RVP and OPR are informed. The cover of such a report carries a note indicating that release is restricted.

9. A copy of the gray cover CESW report is transmitted, as part of the normal distribution, to the PIC, through which interested parties may obtain it.

Sectoral Policy Papers

10. In preparing sectoral policy papers, Bank staff may consult with, and make drafts available to, interested individuals and groups outside the Bank. When a Board seminar is scheduled to discuss a draft policy paper, the executive directors may make the draft available to outside interested parties for review and comment. However, the final paper submitted to the executive directors for approval may not be released.[10] Sectoral policy papers approved by the Board are transmitted by the originat-ing unit to the PIC, through which interested parties may obtain them.

Environment-Related Documents

Environmental Data Sheets

11. The environmental data sheets prepared as quarterly updates in the *Monthly Operational Summary* for all projects in the IBRD/IDA lending program are transmitted to the PIC, through which interested parties may obtain them.

---

10. "Rules of Procedure for the Meetings of Executive Directors," Section 7.

Environmental Assessments

12. For all Bank-funded Category A projects, the Bank advises the borrower in writing[11] that, in addition to other requirements set forth in OD 4.01,[12] (a) the borrower is responsible for the environmental assessment (EA); (b) before the Bank proceeds to appraisal, the EA must be made available in the borrowing country at some public place accessible to affected groups and local NGOs and must be submitted to the Bank; and (c) once the EA is released locally and officially received by the Bank, it will also be made available at the PIC. Once the EA has been released locally and officially submitted to the Bank, the CD sends a copy to the PIC, through which interested parties may obtain it. If, in an exceptional case, the government objects to broader release of the EA, staff should not continue with project processing.[13] For an IBRD project, the issue of further processing is submitted to the executive directors for consideration.

Environmental Analyses

13. For a Category B project, the environmental analysis[14] is summarized in an annex to the PID and documented in the SAR. If the environmental analysis for an IDA-funded Category B project results in a separate report, (a) before the Bank proceeds to appraisal, the separate report must be made available in the borrowing country at some public place accessible to affected groups and local NGOs and must be submitted to the Bank; and (b) once the separate report is released locally and officially received by the Bank, it is sent to the PIC, through which interested parties may obtain it.

---

11. Annex C contains sample language.

12. *See* OD 4.01, *Environmental Assessment*.

13. This provision for IDA projects reflects para. 21 of *Addition to IDA Resources: Tenth Replenishment*, approved by the Board on January 12, 1993, and adopted by the IDA Board of Governors (Resolution No. 174, March 31, 1993).

14. *See* OD 4.01, *Environmental Assessment*.

Environmental Action Plans

14. Bank staff encourage governments to make their environmental action plans (EAPs)[15] available to the public. Once the Bank has officially received the EAP and has obtained the government's consent, the country department transmits a copy of the EAP to the PIC, through which interested parties may obtain it.

Effectiveness

15. These procedures take effect on the dates shown in BP 17.50, Annex D.[16] Requests for SARs, CESW and environment-related reports, and sectoral policy papers produced before those dates are handled individually by the responsible director in consultation with the government concerned, under the policy in force at the time the documents were approved by the Bank or officially received from a government.

Other Documents

16. Procedures governing the release of any documents not referred to in this statement are provided for in the Disclosure Directive.

---

15. *See* OP/BP 4.02, *Environmental Action Plans.*
16. Annex D also sets out arrangements for handling requests before the PIC begins operation.

Annex III

Comparison between the Inspection Function at the World Bank, the IDB, and the ADB

	IBRD	**IDB**	**ADB**
General Approach	Mainly demand-driven (one or more EDs and board may also request investigation).	Mainly demand-driven (Board may also request investigation).	Mainly demand-driven (one or more EDs may also make a request for inspection to BIC after raising their concerns with management).
Objective of the Inspection Function	Enhance quality control in project preparation and supervision in implementation; improve accountability of IBRD for its own policies and procedures and transparency in its operations.	Idem.	Idem.

Substantive Requirements with Respect to Complaints

Scope of Panel's Mandate:

| • Institutional Coverage | IBRD/IDA, possibly Bank as trustee of GEF and other trust funds. Not IFC and MIGA. | IDB including private sector lending window and funds administered by IDB, but not IIC (Inter-American Investment Corporation) ["Bank-supported operations"]. | ADB ["Bank"]; but expressly excluding private sector loans. |

	IBRD	IDB	ADB
• Subject-matter of request	Rights and interests of complainant have or are likely to be directly affected by an "action or omission of the Bank" demonstrating a failure by the Bank "to follow its operational policies and procedures (OPs, BPs, ODs, not not Guidelines and Best Practices)."	"Bank has failed in design, analysis or implementation of proposed or ongoing operations to follow its own established operational policies, or norms formally adopted for the execution of those policies, when material adverse effects have or might reasonably be expected to occur as a result of such failure by the Bank."	"Bank has failed, in the formulation, processing and/or implementation of a proposed or ongoing project, to follow its operational policies or procedures (Operations Manual, but not Guidelines) [and] this failure had or is likely to have a direct and material adverse effect on the applicant group's rights and interests."
	Including failure in follow-up on the borrower's obligations under loan agreements.	Idem.	Resolution is silent on this point.
• Barred Complaints	Complaints with respect to action which are the responsibility of other parties, such as a borrower, or potential borrower and which do not involve any action or omission on the part of the Bank.	Idem.	Idem.

	IBRD	IDB	ADB
	Complaints against procurement decisions.	Idem.	Idem.
	Requests filed after the Closing Date of the loan financing the project has been substantially disbursed (95%).	Not specifically referred to.	Idem.
	Issue preclusion because issue has been dealt with before unless substantial new evidence is introduced.	Idem.	Idem.
Eligibility of the (non-ED) requester: • "affected party" = group of persons, not a single individual	a) "Affected party" is "not a single individual, i.e., a community of persons such as an organization, society or other grouping of individuals, in the territory of the Borrower."	"Community of persons such as an organization, association, society or other grouping of individuals in the territory of a borrower."	"Communities, organizations and other groups residing in the borrowing member country or country adjacent to such borrowing member country."

	IBRD	IDB	ADB
• Standing of local and foreign NGOs, the latter in exceptional cases acting as agents only	b) "Local representative of such party or by another representative in the exceptional cases where appropriate representation is not locally available."	Idem.	Idem.
• Exclusion of *actio popularis*	Affected party's "rights or interests" must be "directly" and "adversely" affected.	Idem. ("directly and materially affected")	Idem. ("directly, materially and adversely affected")
Eligible request (see also subject-matter of request)	Alleged "serious failure of the Bank to follow its operational policy and procedures."	Idem.	Idem.

Main Institutional Features of the Different Inspection Mechanisms

	IBRD	IDB	ADB
Type of body	Independent permanent body, the Inspection Panel.	Ad hoc composition of independent Investigation Mechanism from a Board-approved roster of investigators.	An ad hoc panel of outside experts from a Board-approved roster, selected by a new standing committee of Board of EDs, Board Inspection Committee (BIC).

	IBRD	IDB	ADB
Composition	3 members of different nationalities of member countries nominated by President, appointed by EDs.	Roster of 10 individuals of different nationalities of member countries nominated by President, appointed by EDs.	a) BIC: 6 members of the Board of EDs (4 regional and 2 non-regional members) appointed by President in consultation with EDs. b) Roster of at least 10 experts of different nationalities from member countries nominated by President, appointed by EDs.
Qualification of Panel/Roster Members	Ability, integrity, independence; exposure to developmental issues; knowledge and experience of Bank desirable.	Integrity and recognized competence in areas related to socio-economic development; broad range of technical expertise and skills.	Integrity and recognized competence in areas related to development; diverse backgrounds and disciplines.
Term of Appointment	Initially, 1 member for 3 years, 1 for 4 years and 1 for 5 years non-renewable term.	For 5 years non-renewable terms.	For 5 years non-renewable terms.
Service to institution:			
• Prior	2 years must have elapsed before serving on Panel.	2 years must have elapsed before becoming eligible.	2 years must have elapsed before becoming eligible.

	IBRD	IDB	ADB
• Subsequent	Prohibited.	2 years must elapse.	5 years must elapse.
• Compensation	When working on a full-time basis, remuneration at level determined by EDs upon recommendation of President plus benefits available to fixed-term Bank staff. Prior to that time, remuneration on a per diem basis (at levels of members of Adm. Tribunal) and reimbursement for expenses.	Compensation determined by EDs based on daily or monthly rates for actual service; reimbursement of expenses not to exceed levels for members of Adm. Tribunal.	Compensation determined by EDs for actual service.
Removal from office	By decision of the EDs, for cause.	Idem.	Idem.
Secretariat	Staff member assigned to act as Executive Secretary.	Secretariat of Bank.	Secretariat of Bank helping Panel; EDs budget covering BIC expenses
Review/evaluation	After 2 years.	Idem.	Idem.

Procedure before the Investigation Mechanisms

	IBRD	IDB	ADB
Filling of the complaint with	Inspection Panel, after grievance is raised with management to no avail.	President, after grievance is raised with management to no avail.	Board Inspection Committee (BIC), a newly created Standing Committee of the Board of Directors, after grievance is raised with management to no avail.
Management response as prerequisite of an investigation	After request has been filed with Panel, Panel gives management the opportunity to respond.	After request has been registered with the President, management is given the opportunity to respond.	After grievance has been raised with management to no avail, i.e. submission of initial complaint to President, a request may be filed with BIC which then asks the management for a response addressed to it.
Time for management response	21 days from notification.	30 days.	45 days for management's response to applicant; 30 days for management's response to BIC.
Addressee of management response	Inspection Panel.	President.	Applicant; BIC.

	IBRD	IDB	ADB
Preliminary assessment of request's admissibility and decision on investigation	By Board upon Panel's recommendation.	By Board in consideration of President's recommendation.	By Board in consideration of BIC's recommendation that inspection is not warranted, BIC must consult with a person on the roster.
Frivolous complaints	Complaints must relate to a serious violation.	President may without receiving a request for management's response send his negative recommendation to the Board.	BIC does not need to make sure that management has been addressed earlier but can directly recommend the Board not to investigate.
Time for recommendation on request's admissibility to Board	Panel recommends within 21 days from receipt of management response.	"Upon receipt of management response," i.e. without any delay.	Within 14 days after receiving management's response.
Time for Board to decide on investigation	Within normal distribution period.	Resolution is silent. Suggests normal course of business.	Within 21 days after circulation of recommendation to Board, BIC selects a panel of at least 3 individuals from roster to conduct investigation.
Activation of inspection mechanism	Inspection Panel goes immediately ahead with investigation upon Board's decision.	Board names a panel of at least 3 individuals from the roster in consultation with President.	BIC selects a panel of at least 3 individuals from roster to conduct investigation.

	IBRD	IDB	ADB
Access of Panel to information	Access to all Bank records and staff. In country, with country's consent.	Idem. Idem.	Idem. Idem.
Panel's activities subject to confidentiality/disclosure policy of Bank		Yes. (Express reference to IDB's policies on confidentiality.)	Yes. (Express reference to ADB's policies on confidentiality.)
The Panel's final Report	Panel submits its "findings" to Board.	Panel submits its "findings and recommendations" to President and Board.	Panel submits its "findings and recommendations" via BIC to Board.
Decisions within competence of Panel	By consensus; in the absence of consensus, the majority and minority views shall be stated.	By consensus; in the absence of consensus, each member view shall be stated.	By consensus; in the absence of consensus, each member view shall be stated.
Final decision making by	Board of Directors supposedly based on Panel's report and Management's comments.	Board of Directors based on Panel's report and a second view from management.	Board of Directors based on Panel's report, a report by BIC and a second view from management.
Content of Board decisions	Resolution is silent. Presumed remedial action if needed.	Preventive or corrective action, if any.	"Remedial steps," but not judicial type remedies such as injunctions or money damages.

Index